Battleground Africa

INTERNATIONAL HISTORY
PROJECT SERIES

James G. Hershberg
Series Editor

The Soviet Cuban Missile Crisis
Castro, Mikoyan, Kennedy, Khrushchev, and the Missiles of October
By Sergo Mikoyan. Edited by Svetlana Savranskaya

Divided Together
The United States and the Soviet Union in the United Nations, 1945–1965
By Ilya V. Gaiduk

Marigold
The Lost Chance for Peace in Vietnam
By James G. Hershberg

After Leaning to One Side
China and Its Allies in the Cold War
By Zhihua Shen and Danhui Li

The Cold War in East Asia 1945–1991
Edited by Tsuyoshi Hasegawa

Stalin and Togliatti
Italy and the Origins of the Cold War
By Elena Agarossi and Victor Zaslavsky

A Distant Front in the Cold War
The USSR in West Africa and the Congo, 1956–1964
By Sergey Mazov

Connecting Histories
Decolonization and the Cold War in Southeast Asia, 1945–1982
Edited by Christopher E. Goscha and Christian F. Ostermann

Rebellious Satellite: Poland 1956
By Paweł Machcewicz

Two Suns in the Heavens
The Sino-Soviet Struggle for Supremacy, 1962–1967
By Sergey Radchenko

The Soviet Union and the June 1967 Six-Day War
Edited by Yaacov Ro'i and Boris Morozov

Local Consequences of the Global Cold War
Edited by Jeffrey A. Engel

Behind the Bamboo Curtain
China, Vietnam, and the World beyond Asia
Edited by Priscilla Roberts

Failed Illusions
Moscow, Washington, Budapest, and the 1956 Hungarian Revolt
By Charles Gati

Kim Il Sung in the Khrushchev Era
Soviet-DPRK Relations and the Roots of North Korean Despotism, 1953–1964
By Balázs Szalontai

Confronting Vietnam
Soviet Policy toward the Indochina Conflict, 1954–1963
By Ilya V. Gaiduk

Economic Cold War
America's Embargo against China and the Sino-Soviet Alliance, 1949–1963
By Shu Guang Zhang

WOODROW WILSON CENTER PRESS
STANFORD UNIVERSITY PRESS

Battleground Africa
Cold War in the Congo, 1960–1965

Lise Namikas

Woodrow Wilson Center Press
Washington, D.C.

Stanford University Press
Stanford, California

EDITORIAL OFFICES
Woodrow Wilson Center Press
One Woodrow Wilson Plaza
1300 Pennsylvania Avenue, N.W.
Washington, D.C. 20004-3027
Telephone: 202-691-4029
www.wilsoncenter.org

ORDER FROM
Stanford University Press
Chicago Distribution Center
11030 South Langley Avenue
Chicago, Ill. 60628
Telephone: 1-800-621-2736

Library of Congress Cataloging-in-Publication Data

Namikas, Lise A.
  Battleground Africa : Cold War in the Congo, 1960–1965 / Lise Namikas.
    p. cm.
  Includes bibliographical references and index.
  1. Congo (Democratic Republic)—History—Civil War, 1960–1965. 2. Cold
War—Political aspects—Congo (Democratic Republic) 3. Congo (Democratic
Republic)—Foreign relations—United States. 4. United States—Foreign
relations—Congo (Democratic Republic) 5. Congo (Democratic Republic)—
Foreign relations—Soviet Union. 6. Soviet Union—Foreign relations—Congo
(Democratic Republic) I. Title.
  DT658.22.N36 2012
  967.51031—dc23

                                                              2012036962

ISBN 978-0-8047-8486-3 (cloth)
ISBN 978-0-8047-9680-4 (paperback)

The Wilson Center, chartered by Congress as the official memorial to President Woodrow Wilson, is the nation's key non-partisan policy forum for tackling global issues through independent research and open dialogue to inform actionable ideas for Congress, the Administration and the broader policy community.

Conclusions or opinions expressed in Center publications and programs are those of the authors and speakers and do not necessarily reflect the views of the Center staff, fellows, trustees, advisory groups, or any individuals or organizations that provide financial support to the Center.

The Center is the publisher of *The Wilson Quarterly* and home of Woodrow Wilson Center Press and *dialogue* television and radio. For more information about the Center's activities and publications, please visit us on the Web at www.wilsoncenter.org.

The Cold War International History Project

The Cold War International History Project was established by the Woodrow Wilson International Center for Scholars in 1991. The project supports the full and prompt release of historical materials by governments on all sides of the Cold War and seeks to disseminate new information and perspectives on Cold War history emerging from previously inaccessible sources on the "the other side"—the former Communist world—through publications, fellowships, and scholarly meetings and conferences. The project publishes the *Cold War International History Project Bulletin* and a working paper series and maintains a Web site at www.cwihp.org.

At the Woodrow Wilson Center, the project is part of the History and Public Policy Program, directed by Christian F. Ostermann. Previous directors include David Wolff (1997–98) and James G. Hershberg (1991–97). The project is overseen by an advisory committee chaired by William Taubman, Amherst College, and includes Michael Beschloss; James H. Billington, Librarian of Congress; Warren I. Cohen, University of Maryland Baltimore County; John Lewis Gaddis, Yale University; James G. Hershberg, George Washington University; Samuel F. Wells Jr., Woodrow Wilson Center; and Sharon Wolchik, George Washington University.

The Cold War International History Project has been supported by the Korea Foundation, Seoul; the Leon Levy Foundation, New York; the Henry Luce Foundation, New York; the John D. and Catherine T. MacArthur Foundation, Chicago; and the Smith Richardson Foundation, Westport, Conn.

Contents

Figures

Acknowledgments

Where there is no justice, there is no peace. A deep and growing respect for the people of the Congo kept this topic immediate and important over the years. At the University of Southern California, Roger Dingman, Michael Graham Fry, and Azade-Ayse Rorlich guided me as I formulated my first thoughts on the crisis and were always encouraging even across the miles. A number of reviewers, known and unknown, have helped me clarify and strengthen this work. A special thanks goes to James Hershberg, a reviewer and the Cold War International History Project (CWIHP) series editor. Additional special thanks to David Gibbs, Thomas Borstelmann, Andrew DeRoche, Stephen Weissman, Crawford Young, and the others who read all or part of the many versions of this manuscript over the years. The CWIHP Oral History Conference on the Congo Crisis renewed the meaningfulness of this project, and it was an honor to work with CWIHP director Christian Ostermann, the Russian historian Sergey Mazov, Herbert Weiss, and all the others involved. Thanks, too, to Joe Brinley, the director of the Woodrow Wilson Center Press, for seeing this project through its final stages, and to Alfred Imhoff, the project editor, for improving its clarity and readability. The team effort was truly professional.

Financial support made research a possibility. The David L. Boren National Security Education Fellowship program enabled travel to Russia, and the John F. Kennedy and Lyndon Baines Johnson presidential libraries funded trips to Boston and Austin. I would like to thank the many librarians and audiovisual specialists, especially at the Eisenhower, Kennedy, and Johnson presidential libraries; U.S. National Archives and Records Administration; the Library of Congress; and the Rossiiskii gosudarstvennyi arkhiv noveishei istorii and the Arkhiv vneshnei politiki Rossiskoi Federatsii. Special thanks to N. I. Gorlova, Mary Kennefick, M. Kirilov, N. I. Mozhukhina, S. V. Pavlov, Mikahil Iurevich

Prozymenshchikov, L. I. Semichastano, Galina Shulgina, Natal'ia Georgievna Tomilina, and John Wilson. Their knowledge of the archives was truly invaluable. Ruth Wallach at the University of Southern California also shared her time and expertise. A warm thanks to Luc Viaene for help from abroad. Thanks also to Nina Nikolaevna Belaeva and the entire Vizgini family for their support in Moscow and patience in teaching me the Russian language. My learning about the Congo was also made much easier with the friendship of Litofe Sloj Silika. Thank you.

This book is dedicated to Olivier B. Muloin (d. 1999). His passion for history inspired my own, while a mother's encouragement kept it going. My husband, Steven, offered support one day at a time. Though the book was begun long before they were born, my three children—Kalina, Benjamin, and Timothy—can now share in seeing this project in print.

Place Name Changes

Former name	Changed to
Albertville	Kalemie
Bakwanga	Mbuji-Mayi
Baudouinville	Moba
Coguilhatville	Mbandaka
Elizabethville	Lubumbashi
Jadotville	Lukasi
Katanga Province	Shaba
Leopoldville	Kinshasa
Luluabourg	Kananga
Paulis	Isiro
Port Francqui	Ilebo
Stanleyville	Kisangani
Thysville	Mbanza-Ngungu

Frequently Used Abbreviations

Abako	Alliance des Bakongo
ANC	Armée Nationale Congolaise (formerly Force Publique)
CC CPSU	Central Committee of the Communist Party of the Soviet Union
Cerea	Centre de Regroupment Africain
CIA	U.S. Central Intelligence Agency
CNL	Conseil National de Libération
Conakat	Confédération d'Associations Tribales du Katanga
CRISP	Centre de Recherche et d'Information Socio-Politiques, Brussels
FRUS	*Foreign Relations of the United States* (U.S. State Department publications)
KGB	Komitet Gosudarstvennoy Bezopastnosti (Committee for State Security), Soviet Union
MNC	Mouvement National Congolaise
NSC	National Security Council
OAU	Organization of African Unity
ONUC	Opération des Nations Unies au Congo (United Nations Operation in the Congo)
PSA	Parti Solidaire Africain
TASS	Telegrafnoye Agentstvo Sovetskogo Soyuza (Telegraph Agency of the Soviet Union)
UAR	United Arab Republic
UMHK	Union Minière du Haut Katanga
USUN	U.S. Mission to the United Nations

Battleground Africa

Introduction

On February 13, 1961, Godefroid Munongo—the interior minister for Katanga, the Congo's secessionist province, and a loyal supporter of its leader, Moise Tshombe—made an announcement that had been expected. Munongo had a reputation for being cold and calculating, and his words equaled it. With reporters listening around the world, he told how the former Congolese prime minister, Patrice Lumumba—now an accused communist sympathizer—had escaped from prison and been killed by the angry inhabitants of a village through which he fled. Munongo preempted denunciations of foul play: "If people accuse us of killing Lumumba, I will reply, 'Prove it!'" He then thanked the fictitious villager assassins by announcing a reward of $8,000 for ridding the Congo and the world of "a problem" that had "menaced the existence of humanity."[1]

What had actually happened to Lumumba was in fact even more gruesome than Munongo's story. On December 1, 1960, Lumumba fled across the Sankuru River on his way to Stanleyville, but he was overtaken by the forces of army chief Joseph Mobutu, who enjoyed "technical assistance" from the Belgian Sûreté (the former Belgian police force in the Congo, then operating out of Katanga) and the U.S. Central Intelligence Agency (CIA). On orders from Congolese president Joseph Kasavubu, backed up by advice from the CIA station chief, Lawrence Devlin, Lumumba was quickly captured and brought to Camp Hardy in Thysville, a military prison near the capital city of Leopoldville (figure I.1). Meanwhile, U.N. troops, as part of ONUC (Opération des Nations Unies au Congo, United Nations Operation in the Congo), stood by and refused to protect him. Despite the endless accusations that Lumumba was a communist puppet because he had accepted some aid from the Soviet Union and the Eastern Bloc, not one communist country came to his rescue.

Figure I.1. Lumumba Faces Mobutu after His Arrest, December 2, 1960

Source: Associated Press photograph, used with permission.

After pro-Lumumba riots erupted at Camp Hardy prison on the night of January 13, 1961, key Belgian officials in the Congo working for the government of Gaston Eyskens strongly urged Kasavubu to get rid of his infamous prisoner. Although Devlin himself expressed no objection, his silence in the context is indicative of tacit approval.[2]

In response, an apprehensive Kasavubu, along with Mobutu and Victor Nendaka, chief of the Sûreté Nationale (National Security Services), made an emergency trip to Thysville. Mobutu explained the daring trip to Devlin as an attempt to deal with the "all-or-nothing situation" there. The trio planned the transfer of Lumumba and two other prisoners—former minister of youth and sports Maurice Mpolo, and the former president of the Senate, Joseph Okito—to Bakwanga in Kasai Province. Nendaka was the one to shuffle the prisoners onto a small plane in the wee hours of January 17 and, en route, their destination was switched to Elizabethville, the capital of Katanga Province. All three were so badly beaten on the flight that the pilot, nauseated and disgusted, ordered the cockpit door shut. CIA agents in Elizabethville seemed unaware of what was going on, but wished otherwise. After the "package" had arrived, they thanked their superiors for sending Patrice, lamenting, "If we had known he was coming, we would have baked a snake."[3]

Katanga's leaders, including Tshombe and Munongo, presided over the assassination, while Belgian and Congolese military police—led by Captain Julien Gat and a police commissioner, Frans Verscheure—did the dirty work. Lumumba and his comrades, with only their dignity intact, were dragged off to the farmhouse of Lucien Brouwez where, amid drunken revelry, they were again beaten and abused. Lumumba watched the firing squad kill his friends and waited, trembling but quiet, until he was led to the big tree saved just for him. He crumpled as "a hail of bullets riddled" his body. In a bizarre sequel, the Belgian adviser to Katanga's police force, Gerard Soete, fearful of the consequences of the assassination, buried and exhumed Lumumba's remains several times over the next several days with the help of his brother and others. He and Verscheure, with blood on their hands, cut up Lumumba's body to make it "disappear" in vats of sulfuric acid, while the skull and teeth were apparently ground up and scattered to the winds.[4]

Lumumba was a clear victim of both nineteenth-century-style imperialism and the realities of the post-1945 Cold War. He had been born in a colonial stronghold, where little had changed in the last half century, and had matured during World War II and the early years of the U.S.–Soviet confrontation. He witnessed the promise of decolonization throughout Africa become engulfed in conflicts and challenges because of the Cold War. The United States and the Soviet Union each set out to prove the superiority of its ideology by attracting allies and expanding its sphere of influence in every part of the globe. Although both capitalism and communism promised a better future, the reality was disappointing: a world divided into East and West, whose leaders seemed only to care about themselves or narrowly defined national priorities (see figure I.2 for a map of the Congo; also see the appendix, which gives brief biographical data on the persons in this book).

There was a third way. Nationalists such as Egypt's Gamal Abdel Nasser, Ghana's Kwame Nkrumah, and Guinea's Sekou Touré did not wish to choose sides in a Cold War dispute that seemed to them artificial, being a power struggle and not a debate over human advancement. Instead, socialism promised more of what these new African leaders were looking for: a better life for their people and an alternative to the exploitative capitalist development brought by the imperialists. They joined together with leading Asian states to promote a new international economic framework that recognized the development needs of postcolonial states.[5] These new ideas became known as neutralism, and later nonalignment, and, along with pan-Africanism, appealed deeply to Lumumba, who harbored a great hope for justice and equality.

The goals of African socialists and neutralism fit neatly into the Soviet policy of expansion—to an extent. The 1917 Bolshevik Revolution was rooted in

Figure I.2. Map of the Congo, 1960

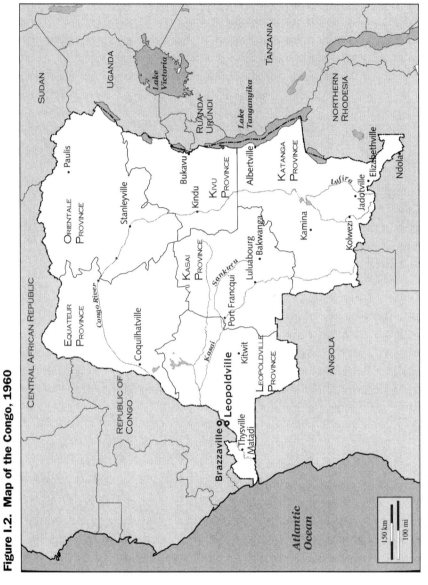

Sources: Author's data; base, d-map.com.

the promise of a worker-based egalitarian state, and the success of the Soviet Union depended on apparent progress toward this utopia. Soviet Communist Party general secretary Nikita Khrushchev was extraordinarily optimistic that Marxist-Leninist–based ideas of equality would flow freely into Africa. If, as Lenin had said, imperialism was the highest stage of capitalism, then Khrushchev had no trouble believing that the end of imperialism had to be its lowest. As if to confirm this optimism, Nkrumah and Touré not only talked about their socialist goals but eagerly established diplomatic relations with the Soviet Union as a way to declare their independence in the international arena. Given these sentiments, Soviet influence in Africa seemed poised and ready to grow.

Washington feared that if the Congo followed in the footsteps outlined by neutralism it would more easily succumb to Soviet-directed communism, and then neighboring or nearby countries would fall like a row of dominoes into the communist camp. Geographically speaking, the Congo was at the very center of Africa and pivotal to its stability. The country was surrounded by soon-to-be-independent French colonies to the north, the troubled Portuguese Angola to the west, the British colonies of Uganda to the east and Northern Rhodesia to the south, and the ethnically divided Sudan to the east as well. Just beyond its immediate border were nearby states such as Nigeria and Kenya, which were seen as critical for the future of the continent.

By the eve of the Congo's independence in June 1960, the administration of Dwight D. Eisenhower, following Belgium's lead, was coming to settle on a clear dislike of Lumumba. His insistence on a centralized government, not only anti-imperialist but in many respects also anticapitalist, appeared reckless and hostile to the West. His talk of pan-Africanism was met with outright scorn. Worse yet from the American perspective, Lumumba had sent a clear invitation to the Soviet Union to come to the Congo, and he had opened its doors without fully realizing the dangers. Keeping to its postwar policy of containment, Washington tried to warn the Congolese about the evil intentions of the Soviet Union and strongly suggested that they limit the Soviet presence. Containment policy, however, did not stop there. The Americans were very sensitive to smaller states, especially "inexperienced" ones like the Congo, playing the superpowers off against each other for their own gain. Lumumba, they feared, was on the verge of doing just that and was therefore endangering their goals in the Cold War.

Young and idealistic Congolese leaders like Lumumba saw no harm in establishing diplomatic relations with both superpowers nor in asking both powers for development aid. Lumumba and others truly believed in Western-inspired pledges to support self-determination and human rights such as the 1941 Atlantic Charter and the 1948 Universal Declaration of Human Rights.[6]

They soon found, however, that declarations and promises were pushed aside by the presumed needs of European reconstruction and the conflict with communism. Inevitably the Congolese were caught up in the Cold War, first by their link to Europe and then by their very independence. By 1960, the Congo's allegiance to either East or West had become the barometer for all Africa, and the way the entire continent would lean in the Cold War struggle.

Nothing about the Cold War was ever neatly bipolar. The United States often found itself awkwardly positioned between Europe on the one hand and the third world on the other. Its revolutionary language and bold liberal constitution, born in its own struggle for freedom two centuries earlier, proclaimed the rights of all humankind to liberate itself from oppression. The strengthening of independence movements in Africa in the late 1950s tugged at the strings of American "common sense" and the basic premise that all peoples deserved self-government. Often conflicting with this, the historic U.S. affinity to Europe, its commitment to fighting communist expansion, and its own capitalist goals comforted Americans with the fruits of imperialism. Now, in the days of post–World War II reconstruction, Washington easily justified its preference for Europe and did not challenge its allies' belief that raw materials and resources from Africa were necessary for their recovery. A stronger Europe would then be in a better position to help Africa.

Tiny but important Belgium was a clear beneficiary of this sentiment. In many ways Belgium had always treated the Congo as its private domain, and this had not changed. In the 1950s, King Baudouin, Leopold II's great grandnephew, stubbornly tied his own personal prestige to the continued presence of Belgium in the Congo. A product of formality and tradition, he was therefore reluctant to introduce any meaningful measures of self-government.[7] In June 1960, with the greatest investment in the Congo, and the most to lose, Belgium clumsily tried to deprive Lumumba of any leadership role. Its efforts failed, and Lumumba became the first democratically elected prime minister. Fast alienated in Leopoldville, Belgium backed the de facto independence of the mineral-rich province of Katanga in July 1960. Seeking to protect its substantial investments there, especially that of Société Générale and its affiliate, the mining giant Union Minière du Haut Katanga (UMHK), Brussels sent troops and other resources to Katanga. Belgium would quickly learn that its intervention was no longer an internal affair and it had serious international implications, which were themselves magnified by the Cold War.

For one of the few times during the Cold War, the United States and the Soviet Union agreed to establish a U.N. peacekeeping force in an area of crisis. There were many reasons to support a joint peacekeeping operation in the Congo. Eisenhower's main goal was to prevent the Soviet Union from directly intervening in the Congo without himself having to commit substantial resources to do so. He used the U.N. operation to promise the world that the superpowers would not expand the Cold War into Africa, at least not aggressively so. U.N. involvement also offered Eisenhower a way to distance himself from the Belgian intervention and, in effect, compel Belgium to cooperate with U.S.–U.N. goals. From Khrushchev's standpoint, the U.N. operation helped the Soviet Union expand its interests in what was, up to that point, a Western domain. The Soviet Union also used the operation to deflect some of the requests for greater bilateral economic aid by the Congo. Both superpowers therefore believed that an internationalization of the crisis would work in their favor.

Other states had incentives to support the peacekeeping operation. Britain and France retained some degree of influence as permanent members of the Security Council. Yet they were distinctly uneasy with the precedent-setting involvement in what, they argued, was a crisis of decolonization and therefore a matter for imperialists alone. The Congolese, who petitioned for the U.N. operation in the first place, wanted help in ending the Belgian-supported Katangan secession. The growing Afro-Asian bloc nations supported this goal but were more willing to give the United Nations greater freedom of action in getting to this end, and in the process strengthen its role in global decolonization.

If there was one truism about Congolese politics, it was that no Leopold-ville government could survive for long if Katanga remained in secession. The first goal of all leaders had to be reunification of the country. They had little choice. Without the wealth of Katanga, the country would be deprived of its principal resources for development and would suffer the continued insults imposed by imperialism. A divided Congo would easily attract the Cold War, which could then spread to all of Africa. The threat of division escalated in late August 1960 when Lumumba boldly accepted Soviet military aid to help end the Katangan secession. Although the amount of aid from the Soviet Union fell short of a full-scale commitment to the Congo, it spiked fears in the West that they were about to lose the continent. It was not long before both Belgium and the United States—for reasons both similar and different—sped up plans for Lumumba's assassination. Consumed by their fear and selfishness, both states seemed to forget that Lumumba's removal from power, however achieved, only eliminated one person, and solved nothing.

The "problem" of Katanga and its power struggle with Leopoldville was a thorny one, but one that history tells us should have come as no surprise. King Leopold had always treated Katanga differently. In 1900 Leopold established the separate administration of Katanga with the Comité Spécial du Katanga.

Even after the Belgian government took over the colony in 1908, colonial ministers worked to protect Katangan autonomy. State officials often had close connections with UMHK, the Belgian mining company that specialized in copper, cobalt, uranium, tin, and zinc.[8] Now, at the height of the Cold War, the Belgian government, still closely connected with UMHK, used its strong position in Katanga to argue that it could best represent and protect Western interests in the heart of Africa. Belgium cleverly couched its promises in Cold War language and adopted an anticommunist agenda that was particularly useful in its relations with the United States.

All hopes aside, Lumumba's assassination did not stop the Cold War from creeping forward in the Congo. The Eisenhower administration had plotted for the removal of Lumumba, but after his murder Washington still faced an escalating crisis with few concrete plans to resolve it. The Kremlin might have lost its closest ally in Africa south of the Sahara, but for political purposes Khrushchev wanted the world to know that he would not so easily lose interest in the Congo. Using the United Nations as their world stage, Soviet representatives cried foul play and tried to paint Moscow as the lone spokesperson of people's rights against Western greed-driven imperialism. They branded Secretary-General Hammarskjöld an "accomplice" to the murder and withdrew recognition of him as secretary-general.

The Afro-Asian bloc buried their highest hopes for the United Nations with Lumumba. Kwame Nkrumah publicly agreed that the United Nations had played a role in Lumumba's death, while Sekou Touré expressed the desire of many that newly inaugurated U.S. president John F. Kennedy take "concrete acts" to respond to the misdeeds in the Congo. The young American president, who had made Africa an important component of his election platform, expressed "great shock" at the turn of events. The news did not change Kennedy's public stand, and he solemnly stuck to the line of reaffirming U.S. support for the U.N. operation in the Congo.[9]

The longer Katanga held onto its secession, the more inevitable a permanent division seemed. Even after February 1961, when U.N. troops were given unprecedented latitude to use force if necessary to prevent a civil war in the Congo, the majority of U.N. members supported negotiations to peacefully reunify the country. This included the Kennedy administration. Still, negotiations stumbled along while Tshombe played games. Hoping to end the Belgian–Katangan standoff with the world and advance reunification, Hammarskjöld planned a rendezvous with Tshombe in the fall of 1961. En route, his plane crashed in Ndola, Rhodesia, and he tragically died with the rest of his crew.[10]

With or without Hammarskjöld, U.N.-sponsored talks proceeded slowly with no real pressure on Tshombe to cooperate. In late 1962, Kennedy finally firmed up his Congo policy. Soon thereafter, ONUC troops invaded Katanga for a third time and ousted the brash Katangan leader. Holding onto victory in the narrowest sense, the U.N. mission began its withdrawal in mid-1963 and Katanga was incorporated into the central government of the Congo. However, instability continued for the next two years. Even this late in the game, Khrushchev saw a chance in the Congo and temporarily increased Soviet aid to the pro-Lumumbist opposition in 1964. The rebels themselves made the fateful decision to take Western hostages and were decimated in a U.S.–Belgian-led "rescue." Communist aid was resuscitated by Cuban support for a few months in 1965, but subsequently dwindled away. In late 1965 the United States, along with Belgium, increased aid to Mobutu, who for the second time seized power and this time firmly brought the Congo into the Western camp.[11]

Sources and Historiography

No scholarly study has focused directly on the U.S.–Soviet confrontation in the Congo or the importance of the crisis in the larger Cold War.[12] Instead, scholars have offered separate histories of American and U.N. involvement in the crisis. As a result, the Cold War has been used to explain U.S. policy and ultimately its support of Mobutu, who would become a ruthless dictator for three decades before his overthrow in 1997. Other scholars have used the context of the Cold War to help understand one of the first and largest U.N. peacekeeping operations (after the U.N. Emergency Force for Egypt was created to help end the 1956 Suez war). The Cold War aspects of the Congo crisis were much more than this. The Congo crisis involved virtually every country (in some way or another) in what was seen at the time as a major crisis, one that would define the Cold War in Africa and the nature of decolonization to come. It is not an exaggeration then to suggest that the Congo crisis is one of the most overlooked crises of the Cold War, and particularly one of the most overlooked in Africa.

The opening of the Russian and Soviet Bloc archives has allowed scholars to improve their knowledge of the U.S.–Soviet confrontation and the global significance of events in the Congo. We can now get a much better picture of how the superpowers formulated their separate goals and policies in adversarial relation to each other during the crisis. In Moscow, the Rossiiskii gosudarstvennyi arkhiv noveishei istorii (RGANI; Russian Government Archive of Contemporary History, holding contemporary party materials from 1952 to 1991) and the Archiv vneshnei politiki Rossiskoi Federatsii (AVPRF; Archive of the Foreign Policy of the Russian Federation, which stores Foreign Ministry records) have released some important materials. A valuable collection of

Russian-language documents gathered by Apollon Basil Davidson and Sergey Mazov can be found in *Rossiia i Afrika: Dokumenty i materialy* (Moscow, 1999).[13] Still, many documents of the Communist Party and Foreign Ministry of the Soviet Union remain closed, as do all collections from the KGB (the Komitet Gosudarstvennoy Besopastnosti) and Defense Ministry. The archives of the former East Germany contribute new material on Soviet and Eastern Bloc policy, especially relating to events in early 1961 and 1964–65.[14] The same might eventually be said for the Chinese sources and information from other East European archives, such as those from the former Yugoslavia, which still remain closed and untapped.

The release of U.S. and other Western Bloc documents is perhaps less arbitrary, but here much remains closed as well. In the United States, the assassination of Lumumba naturally raised eyebrows and questions from the day it was announced. Almost fifteen years after the fact, in 1975, the Senate Select Committee chaired by Frank Church (D-Idaho) confirmed CIA plans for the assassination of Lumumba but cleared Washington from actual involvement in his death.[15] The lagging review process, however, has prompted the historians David Gibbs and Stephen Weissman separately to cite the *Foreign Relations of the United States* series (*FRUS*) as misrepresentative at best and misleading at worst, especially regarding the role of the CIA and the extent of U.S. clandestine activities.[16] Weissman, using both declassified and still classified documents connected with the Church Committee investigation, has definitively linked the CIA and Lawrence Devlin to the assassination of Lumumba.[17] The *FRUS* volume on the Congo for the Johnson years dealing with 1964, but which will also include a retrospective from 1960 onward, has remained held up in the declassification process since the late 1990s.[18]

National and presidential libraries in the United States have released some additional documents, such as transcripts of telephone conversations during the crisis and intelligence estimates, which are of importance. The work of organizations such as the National Security Archive directed by Thomas Blanton and the Cold War International History Project directed by Christian Ostermann, in obtaining documents from archives around the world and in sponsoring oral history conferences, including one on the Congo in 2004, has also advanced our understanding of the international Cold War.[19] Other Western sources have made a significant contribution to the study of the Congo crisis. The Belgian Parliamentary Commission report of 2001, spurred in part by the publication of Ludo de Witte's *The Assassination of Lumumba*, is the most notable. It has added to our understanding of events, especially Belgian relations with the Congo, even if underwhelming on the issue of responsibility for Lumumba's assassination and unenlightening on the questions about the extent of the CIA cooperation with Belgium.[20] Additionally, some new information is beginning to appear from the National Archives of the United Kingdom and the archives of the United Nations.[21]

Taken together, the new information we do have brings attention to the importance of the Congo crisis. The new evidence shows that the Soviet Union held a persistent interest in the Congo not accounted for in the previous literature. Russian scholars, especially Davidson and Mazov, among others, have shown a remarkable rise of Soviet ambitions in Africa in the early 1960s.[22] Sergey Mazov has uncovered information demonstrating much larger support of Lumumba's successor, Antoine Gizenga, than previously known.[23] None of this challenges the view that officials in Washington and in the field often exaggerated the immediate danger of the Soviet threat. But the fear that in the long term the Soviet Union could exploit radical nationalism becomes more tangible.[24] The new evidence also shows how the experimental managing of the crisis through the United Nations, and the role of Dag Hammarskjöld, changed the nature of superpower interaction, at least in this case, in light of nonalignment.

What becomes clear from the new evidence is that neither adversary ever adequately understood the other's goals or the degree to which they would (or would not) defend their position in the Congo. Ideologies that outlined larger-than-life pursuits further magnified the importance of the crisis. Both superpowers wanted to avert a major confrontation but they also wanted to avoid appearing too weak among newly independent states. Oddly, although Africa was held in a category of its own—not quite equal to Asia in the scheme of so-called third world states—neither the United States nor the Soviet Union wanted to "lose" Africa or become involved in a resource-draining battle for influence.[25] Contingencies constantly imposed themselves, and what Washington expected and feared was not always the case. Such fluidity and inherently conflicting ambitions resulted in a situation where the superpowers (especially the United States) often found themselves more involved in the crisis than they wished. It was here that mistakes, missteps, and bad policy choices frequently occurred and distinguished each presidential administration. As in many other cases in the Cold War, the web of allies, counterparts, clients, and neutral states could also exert enough pressure to demand superpower attention or even influence the superpower policymaking process.[26] Less measurable goals, such as decreasing the impact of neutralism, could be as important as upholding treaty rights or gaining access to specific bases.[27] The superpowers were not always able to control the course of events as much as they might have liked. For these reasons, the crisis became more dangerous than if it had been only between two states.

In the truest of senses, the Congo crisis was an international crisis. Scholar Michael Brecher has defined an "international crisis" as an event that disrupts relations between states, usually with a high probability of military hostilities, and challenges the existing structure of the international system.[28] Events in the Congo did both. Clearly, the pattern of interaction between the United States and the Soviet Union was not the same before and after the crisis. While some kind of accommodation on decolonization might have been found before the crisis, the crisis generated a Cold War competition in Africa that would not be reversed. And, while events in the Congo arguably do not explain entirely the new Soviet–American relationship in Africa, they played a major role in defining it. The new postcrisis competition in Africa that emerged had a sharper military edge to it, although it was never wholly militaristic.

The Congo crisis was moved along like most international crises by a combination of escalation and negotiation, top-level decisions, and bargaining table strategies. Again, crisis literature is helpful. What makes the outcome of a crisis so uncertain, according to Glenn Snyder and Paul Diesing, is the fact that it involves protagonists bargaining over "values, interests, and power relations that are inherent in the situation" but not fully known at the outset.[29] The decisionmaking process does not come from a black box, but from real leaders who are constantly making choices depending on time constraints, beliefs, available information, and their own experiences.[30] This outline of a crisis could not have been more true in the case of the Congo, where the superpowers began to see the crisis as a test case for the future of decolonization in Africa and even beyond. In Brecher's terms, the crisis became a challenge to the international system. What is most glaring in its absence is the lack of direct negotiation between the United States and the Soviet Union, and instead their mediation was typically carried out through the auspices of the United Nations, thereby complicating its management, while still protecting other states.

In the footsteps of John Lewis Gaddis, historians have worked hard to develop a new international view of the Cold War, one that accounts for the role of both ideology and realpolitik. Recent historical works have not always escaped the orthodox–revisionist debates, but have become much more situational in approach. Many historians, including Gaddis, still assign greater responsibility to the Soviet Union for perpetuating the Cold War, while the United States is seen as reacting to systemic insecurities, moderated by its democratic political process.[31] Conversely, and reinforcing this convention, Vladislav Zubok and Constantine Pleshakov developed the "revolutionary-imperial paradigm," referring to a combination of traditional Russian messianism and Marxist ideology to explain Soviet foreign policy behavior while also accounting for Russian national interests.[32]

Not everyone agrees. There is a growing group of scholars who are building on the work of earlier revisionists to argue that the United States was comparably ideological and culpable. Odd Arne Westad found in *The Global Cold War* (2005) that the United States followed its own "ideology of interventionism" in pursuit of what leaders perceived as their superior moral vision of the future.[33] Westad, with the support of other scholars such as Christopher Layne and Robert McMahon, argue that the United States and the West often adopted aggressive policies based on their misguided assumptions about the aggressiveness of Soviet foreign policy and the monolithic nature of the communist world.[34]

No scholar has done for U.S.–Belgian relations what historians Fredrik Logevall and Mark Atwood Lawrence and others are doing for our understanding of Cold War alliance politics, especially the British and French influence on U.S. policy.[35] Before the Congo crisis, the United States treated the Congo as an appendage of Belgium. Cold War goals demanded that, as NATO allies, the United States and Belgium present a united front to the communist world, although Washington would try to limit its association with the more blatant imperialist legacies of Leopold. Historians generally have emphasized the conservative Belgian influence on U.S. foreign policy. Armed with new evidence, especially from the Belgian Parliamentary Commission, we now see the U.S.–Belgian relationship was not as coordinated or as close as once believed. Although many records are still closed, it seems that U.S. officials knew much less about Belgian policy than even they previously assumed.

One way to realize more fully the international implications of the crisis is to broaden the chronology—its framework—to capture a greater part of colonialism and its legacy. The preindependence years of 1958 to 1960 show how the superpowers began to shape their still rudimentary policy on the Congo. Precedents set at this early stage often help explain the idiosyncrasies of superpower relations with the Congolese. This account also includes events through the end of 1965, which few historians of the crisis have done, most usually stopping in 1963, with the exception of Stephen Weissman. The unrest after the U.N. withdrawal clearly continued the crisis, and only Mobutu's second coup two years later ended this particular crisis cycle. As we will see within this framework, both superpowers were easily distracted and the crisis fluctuated in intensity over the years.

Scholarship on U.S. policy in the third world can be divided into three groups. "Middle of the roaders" argue, along with Thomas Noer, that U.S. policy followed an "ever-narrowing" but soft, grassy middle way between the radical nationalists of the decolonizing world and conservative European imperialists.[36] "Right-sider" revisionists argue that the United States found itself more naturally on the right side of the road and favored a more conservative, or proimperialist and anticommunist, policy usually to the detriment of basic liberal and democratic principles. From this view, Thomas Borstelmann has argued that "U.S. Cold War policies served primarily to slow down the process of ending white rule over people of color."[37] "Left-siders" point to the success of some administrations or officials in steering toward the colonies, and strengthening U.S. relations with the third world. They tend to point to the Kennedy administration, which clearly adopted a new rhetoric more favorable to nationalism.[38] Historians of all three "sides" generally agree that race unquestionably affected the foreign policy of the United States. Virtually all those in Washington, including the White House, the State Department, and the Central Intelligence Agency, saw Africa as needing "big brother" guidance away from socialism and if possible toward Western-style democracy. African leaders, in their view, were not prepared or savvy enough or simply did not have the resources to determine the best interests of their nations.

Interpretations of the Congo crisis fit into this "road-side" analogy. Providing the most comprehensive coverage of the Cold War in the Congo, "middle-of-the-roader" Madeleine Kalb described a test of wills between the "pragmatic" Eisenhower and Kennedy who protected American interests against the "idealistic" Khrushchev anxious for a quick communist victory in the Congo.[39] Stephen Weissman, a "right-sider," emphasized the fear in Washington of a move from "chaos to communism" in the third world and how this fear often translated into poorly devised responses to the crisis. Richard Mahoney, more typically a "left-sider," gave Kennedy a passing grade on the Congo test of credibility and concluded that his even-handed review of options brought an unexpected victory with the success of negotiations in 1963.

Bureaucratic differences played their part, particularly between the conservative Europeanists and the more liberal Africanists in the State Department, and the latter's differences with the Joint Chiefs of Staff and the CIA. Because of the nature of bureaucracy, compromises often had to be found, and there were plenty of them. Differences were "bureaucratic" but they also reflected a real debate over the best response to take, based on either diplomatic or military solutions. Perhaps ironically, it was the covert option that ultimately benefited, because the CIA saw increased funding and authorization for its programs. Each president of course had a great impact on managing these differences and shaping the U.S. response to the crisis.

The Soviet Union had its own dilemmas about what course to follow. While never enjoying the relative stability of the United States, the Soviet Union had some advantages. Born in a twentieth-century war against imperialism, it created an image of itself as strongly anticolonial, although of course it practiced its own kind of imperialism. Yet U.S. and Soviet responses to Africa had clear parallels. For the Soviet Union, the all-important question in its relations with Africa revolved around whether to support the struggling, radical leaders or the more conservative but often more popular nationalist leaders ("bourgeois nationalists" in Marxist terminology).[40]

The Russian scholar Sergey Mazov has recently challenged the dominant Western view that Khrushchev's Congo policy was driven by his adventurism and ideological goals. Mazov has argued that instead the Soviet role was "ambivalent," its political leverage on the Congo was "limited," and its involvement "paltry" compared with the United States.[41] This study agrees in principle when comparing Soviet and American policy. However, it emphasizes that from a global Cold War perspective, Soviet policy was cautiously ambitious. Khrushchev agreed to send economic and military aid first to Lumumba and then to Gizenga, all the while making sure that the crisis did not escalate into a direct confrontation with the United States. So he signed off on the U.N. operation, although his ambitions demanded that he did not follow all the rules. His policy often appeared (and was) uncertain because it was poorly divided between satisfying the socialist camp and moderating the crisis with the United States. While he made several major retreats, he never let go of the Congo entirely, keeping a small hope and a small stake in the country in case events would swing in favor of communist goals.

Khrushchev's decision to court African nationalists put him on a collision course with China, which had adopted a rigorously ideological stand.[42] The Sino–Soviet competition over Africa was not marginal, but central to their respective agendas. Although, as Sergey Radchenko has argued, the split would gain more ferocity after 1962, even by 1960 it helped shape their policies, in this case toward Africa.[43] Chairman Mao's prorevolutionary and anticapitalist talk appealed to radical nationalists who wanted to believe that home-grown resources could bring quick prosperity. Moscow needed to respond somehow, but the way it did was complicated and cumbersome. Khrushchev tried to retain his flexibility with the idea of a "noncapitalist path of development" and emphasized the benefits of Soviet experience and assistance.[44] Mostly, he wanted to build up the Soviet Union's image as a worldwide revolutionary leader.

The "noncapitalist path" was the Soviet answer not only to China but also to pan-Africanism. Soviet specialists warned that pan-Africanism exaggerated Africa's uniqueness and privately lamented that it impinged on Soviet expertise. So, just as Eisenhower had found for the United States, Africa did not fit neatly into standard Soviet security strategies. Much of Khrushchev's policy involved cutting ideological corners to make it fit. And while Africa was not at the center of strategy, policy toward the Congo was seen to reflect the Soviet Union's moral leadership and authenticity.

Many strong and vivid personalities dominated the crisis, arguably none more so than Nikita Khrushchev. Khrushchev was short and stout, had a penetrating glare, and was known for his rapid mood swings. He liked to surprise his rivals, but was not ready for surprises himself. He could be bold and optimistic, especially when it came to the third world. Khrushchev grandly promised that the Soviet Union "could be counted on to aid needy peoples the world over liberating themselves from colonial rule."[45] When something mattered to him, he could become intensely involved, as in the case of his appearance before the United Nations in September 1960.[46] Historians Alexandr Fursenko and Timothy Naftali describe Khrushchev's "diplomatic revolution," especially toward the third world, as a new, more realistic approach after Stalin's insular attitudes. Khrushchev's policies were often weakened by his emotionalism, as carefully illustrated by historian William Taubman. He could easily fly into a fit of rage, in public and also behind closed doors, and in the process alienate his friends and embitter his enemies. He was talkative to a fault, but at the same time could talk with anyone, and throughout it all held on to his basic sense of humanity.[47] Vladislav Zubok and Constantine Pleshakov tell of an impulsive and risky gambler. They believe that Khrushchev longed to improve the Soviet position in the Cold War, but often retreated to a more cautious policy once the dangers of open conflict became sufficiently obvious.[48]

Soviet interest in influencing events in the Congo continued even after Khrushchev was deposed in 1964, and therefore cannot be explained entirely as an aberration or a quirk of his personality. His successor Leonid Brezhnev continued to support Soviet interest throughout 1965, that is, before Joseph Mobutu realized his second coup at the end of that year. At this late stage Moscow kept its interest limited. As Piero Gleijeses has shown, Soviet military aid in 1964 and 1965 came in relatively small amounts and was often used ineffectively.[49] What is remarkable is the very fact that Moscow still approved aid for the Congo, and this suggested that it still had some aspirations in the region, whether in a concrete sense or at the international level.

Individual American presidents also left their very different marks on the crisis. World War II hero and president when the crisis began, Dwight D. Eisenhower initiated U.S. covert operations that were also used in some form by presidents Kennedy and Johnson. In a not-so-hidden-hand fashion, Eisenhower participated strongly in discussions about what to do in the Congo. He feared that given the troubled history of colonialism, the United States needed to reduce its reliance on European connections so as not to alienate newly independent African states. But in the end, he was much more comfortable in the halls of Europe, and his policy showed it. John F. Kennedy was young and optimistic, thoughtful and sensitive, and spoke as if he welcomed the new nationalism. While he wanted a fresh start, he, like his predecessor, quickly focused on the dangers of the Cold War at the expense of real political and economic development in the Congo. By contrast, President Lyndon B. Johnson had little time for Africa. As with anything, he could be strong and domineering, and he was when he had to turn his attention to the Congo. Faced with emergencies like the hostage crisis in Stanleyville in 1964, he preferred short-term responses to manage the problem and then expected it to be resolved. The different styles of crisis management become a key part of the crisis itself.

Economic motives cannot be considered separately from security issues, especially since the United States defined its security to include stability and prosperity. It was the pursuit of this security, beginning during World War II, that attracted the United States to the Congo in the first place. Proceeding from this basic premise, historian David Gibbs argued that U.S. business interests had a decisive influence on foreign policy. He divided business interests into pro-Katanga (or procolonial) and anti-Katanga (or anticolonial, anti-Belgian) factions. The pro-Katangan interests, such as Société Générale, UMHK, and American Metal Climax (AMAX), had favorable connections to the Eisenhower administration. Other more anticolonial business groups, including Maurice Tempelsman's diamond interests, preferred to see a limited Belgian role, and had greater influence during the Kennedy administration. LAMCO, with anti-Katangan interests, was led by Bo Gustav Hammarskjöld, brother of U.N. secretary-general Dag Hammarskjöld. As a result the secretary-general has been suspected of supporting pro-Swedish mining interests that sought to reduce Katangan copper output. Gibbs's argument, of course, is not as stiff as presented here, and he accounts for conflicting pressures on various individuals, such as Allen Dulles and C. Douglas Dillon. In the company of the new revisionists, Gibbs's account highlights dynamics between Washington and Brussels as the core of the crisis.[50]

Business connections do not necessarily translate into determinants and some of these influences are in fact hard to trace. In part, Washington wanted, and measured its success by, a favorable climate for business and investment in the Congo. A public individual could be associated with a particular company, but it is hard to ascertain the exact impact on policy amid a multitude of interests and investments. Of importance also is how the company's leadership might view the long-term prospects of their institution and defend that interest accordingly. Business and financial interests therefore often remain general and are broad in nature, and that truism is seen to work here.

Economic motives could also work in reverse. Ironically, Eisenhower's decision to reduce stockpiles of strategic minerals is suspected to have helped reduce the price of copper and could have thus triggered the defensiveness of the business community in the first place. Moreover, during his administration there was a pervasive sense of the need to control the costs of involvement in decolonization. Similarly, the economic wealth of the Congo certainly tantalized Soviet planners, but largely remained out of their reach. Instead, financial constraints probably had a greater impact on Soviet policy, since they had to start virtually from scratch in building a presence in Africa. Thus a political victory was important to the Soviet Union to justify the amount of money spent there.

Viewed from an international perspective, and in light of new evidence, foreign policy was defined more clearly by Cold War thinking and larger strategic goals. Economic interests played an important role, but must be considered as secondary. Most importantly, Washington feared that the fragmentation of the Congo would hatch a permanent base for communist and subversive activities in the heart of Africa. Secession might be tolerated in the short term until a "federal" solution emerged, but ultimately keeping the Congo united, and away from Soviet or communist influence, was the critical imperative. Western intervention was on a much larger scale than its Soviet counterpart, and this was because of the existing U.S.–Belgian cooperation and the importance that the two countries attached to maintaining their position in Africa. Yet their cooperation was often superficial and ill defined and their relationship was undergoing momentous change. What began as an uneasy partnership at the beginning of 1960 was remodeled into an American predominance of power by 1965.

The Congo crisis gave the United Nations one of its greatest challenges in history. In the words of Brian Urquhart, former undersecretary-general of the United Nations, and later a historian, it "nearly wrecked this organization."[51] ONUC was the largest peacekeeping force during the Cold War, numbering over 20,000 soldiers at its height. Numerous oral histories and memoirs have enriched our understanding of the U.N. operation. It is a common assertion that, although the United Nations is no more than the sum of its parts, the United States was the largest "part" and hence commanded the largest influence.[52] Many critics suggest that ONUC was subservient to U.S. interests, but that is not the whole story. Secretary-General Dag Hammarskjöld was basically pro-Western in his orientation and put the United Nations at the disposal of the United States at critical times, particularly during the events of September 1960 that resulted in Lumumba's dismissal, the days leading to his assassination, and during the Lovanium conference of mid-1961. However,

Hammarskjöld came under increasing pressure from African states to realign the organization and put it on a more neutral footing, and this was something new in the international arena. His successor, U Thant of Burma, was more comfortable in this role, and although less nuanced in his diplomacy, could be more forceful in his decisions, which ultimately helped bring the United Nations to a more independent position.[53]

Finally, it is important to remember that the Cold War crisis in the Congo evolved as it did because of the internal Congolese crisis. The crisis of decolonization involved questions of social reform and visions of nationalism that, being asked in the context of the Cold War, became international. As outlined by historian Georges Nzongola-Ntalaja, the internal crisis was a constitutional one, born with the Congo's rapid move toward independence and played out in rebellion. The life-and-death struggle among the Congolese is not too strong an adjective to describe their desire to eliminate Belgian influence and regain control over political and military power, economic resources, and nationalist expression. The superpowers, and particularly the United States, saw an opportunity to direct Congolese politics, although this does not mean that the Congolese always succumbed to superpower demands and exhortations. Coincidentally, the timing of the crisis, just as sixteen states were celebrating independence, reinforced its importance in redefining the Cold War in Africa. Did the Congolese help "design the architecture for U.S. interventions"[54] as one historian argued was the case elsewhere, or were Congolese interests trampled by superpower demands and Cold War priorities?[55] Applying the first version would assign too much agency to the Congolese, the second not enough. The Congolese depended on U.S. and Soviet anti-imperialism to help them define and defend their sovereignty against Belgium, but in doing so they lost a degree of freedom. In the process the Cold War became a part of the domestic crisis, and the domestic crisis a part of the Cold War.

Naturally, selectivity is required when dealing with a crisis as heterogeneous as the one in the Congo. Washington's handling of the crisis has traditionally received more attention than any other aspect, and while U.S. policy constitutes a central component of the crisis, this account is not solely about U.S. involvement in the Congo. Similarly it is not solely about covert action—much of the evidence concerning which is still classified—nor is it about the role of mercenaries in the Congo, a topic to which Piero Gleijeses and Frank Villafana have contributed significantly. This account is mindful that U.S. policy toward the Congo was shaped very much by the dominant "whiteness" of Washington and the tendency to treat Africans as uneducated, but certainly more could be said about racism in the case of the Congo.[56] Little has been written about Soviet racism, but it also existed and informs this analysis, although much more could be written about this topic. The Belgian role in the crisis and the domestic Congolese crisis for the years covered herein both easily deserve a new book of their own.

This book is about a crisis of state and international (over-)intervention. Because it began in 1960, it could not escape the twin forces of imperialism's decline and the U.S.–Soviet Cold War relationship. It is about the hubris of the United States, the Soviet Union, and even the United Nations in their crisis management and self-motivated interference. It is about the folly of Belgium and the fractured nature of Congolese politics. Although much has been written about the Congo, this story in all its comprehensive nature, remains to be told. To do this, *Battleground Africa* is as inclusive as possible in using new archival information, public sources, and a broad time frame. The image here is of a crisis that could have been avoided many times along the way, but whose escalation was never as bad as it could have been, and whose settlement in 1965 was anything but final.

Events moved quickly in Africa in the late 1950s and early 1960s. In response, both Washington and Moscow set about to reassess their future role and policy in what was now a "not-so-far" far-away continent. In many ways, this policy review showed how both superpowers were unprepared for the events that were to come. Yet their ideas for new directions in Africa, tentative and speculative at best, would have an important and lasting impact on their response when a relatively small mutiny of soldiers in the heart of Africa spiraled into an international crisis in July 1960.

1. Which Way Africa?

The United States and the Soviet Union had two things in common when it came to Africa.[1] The first was very little information about the political realities there, and the second was an even smaller presence. This is another way of saying that, viewed from their respective lenses of national security, Africa did not matter quite as much as the Middle East or Asia. The lack of sustained interest in Africa at this point was helped by the fact that the European imperialists, including Belgium, in theory at least, accepted the need to prepare their colonies for eventual independence while at the same time they kept a tight lid on their domains. Nothing seemed terribly out of place. As a result neither superpower spent much time thinking about Africa and they were not prepared for the magnitude of the crisis seen in 1960.

Alternatively, Africans looked to their Asian neighbors to support their transition to independence. The growing cooperation between Asia and Africa was reinforced at the first Afro-Asian conference of April 1955 in Bandung. Here, too, the United States and the Soviet Union had one more thing in common. Neither was invited as a full participant to the conference and both were indirectly censured at the meeting for their failure to support full independence in non-Western regions. In the beautiful Indonesian city of Bandung, graced by traditional and modern elements and surrounded by mountains, twenty-nine Asian and African leaders, including Indian prime minister Jawaharlal Nehru and Chinese premier Zhou Enlai, gathered with plans to form a third bloc.

At Bandung, China played an important, if muted, role. Zhou Enlai arrived triumphantly after surviving a CIA-led assassination attempt to blow up his plane.[2] Zhou toned down China's past revolutionary rhetoric and emphasized, in the words of Chen Jian, its "shared experiences" with Asian and African countries. To ease some suspicion of China's intentions, Zhou talked about friendship and cooperation, and respect for different ideologies and social systems.[3] At Bandung the participants reaffirmed their commitment to the principles of the U.N. Charter, denounced colonialism and imperialism, and promised to work toward greater economic independence.[4] They called themselves nonaligned and their hope was to take the global focus away from the debilitating issues of the Cold War between the East and the West.

Neither superpower wanted to see a third bloc, and each was privately scornful of Afro-Asian efforts to organize. The official response from both Washington and Moscow was guarded. In practice, Washington approached the conference and the new bloc with concern and caution, hoping it would just fade away. Eisenhower refused to send an observer to the conference, although invited to do so.[5] Moscow took a different approach and tried to woo the anti-imperialists by publicly welcoming their demands for independence and their attempts to distance themselves from the West. In reality, Moscow was no more enthusiastic about a new bloc than Washington. Of particular concern was the foothold it offered China in Asia and Africa. Moscow preferred to appear on the side of anti-imperialism and went along with the movement, expecting that it would be too diverse to really accomplish much. These different approaches to the Non-Aligned Movement reflect the earliest differences in U.S.–Soviet approaches to Africa, differences that were eventually mirrored in the Congo.

Bringing Containment to Africa

Africa was not a place that President Dwight D. Eisenhower devoted much attention to before his second term in 1957. Time and again, crises like the so-called Mau Mau insurrection in Kenya, growing apartheid in South Africa, and the war in Algeria were forcing their way into global discussion halls and onto White House agenda books. The British-French-Israeli attack on Egypt during the 1956 Suez crisis further highlighted the growing importance of the continent of Africa. After the attack on Egypt, Khrushchev cajoled Eisenhower to take a stronger stand against colonialism and offered to join forces with him in an anti-imperialist alliance. The president predictably scoffed at the offer and chose instead to distance the United States from the British and French. Eisenhower was just as cool toward Egypt's Gamal Abdul Nasser, whose form of radical nationalism seemed to be infecting the African continent. Of particular concern was the armed revolt in Algeria and the brutal methods used by the French in the Battle of Algiers that began in September 1956.

In many ways a lingering conservatism prevailed in Washington. In the words of historian Thomas Borstelmann, the administration's anticolonialism was a "thin veneer" at best and could not hide "marked disdain" for African and Asian leaders.[6] Officials in the administration never questioned their assumption that Africa was a backward continent, whose people were, in an often-repeated phrase, "barely out of the trees." Eisenhower's tough-minded, hard-working secretary of state John Foster Dulles remarked offhandedly, as late as the late 1950s, that none of the colonies were capable of governing themselves anytime soon.[7] The administration cautioned anxious Africans that "premature independence" would be exploited by Moscow.[8] Its preference for a slow-paced decolonization under heavy tutelage had firm support in academic circles. Experts such as Rupert Emerson, Walter Goldschmidt, and Vernon McKay emphasized the importance of Western efforts to nurture traditions and customs as valuable sources of stability for any society while at the same time carefully increasing technical assistance.[9]

Eisenhower always seemed more comfortable leaving Africa as a problem for the Europeans to handle. In light of the preparations being made for independence across the continent by the late 1950s, many in his administration recognized that they could no longer afford this approach. Nor could they ignore the fact that communism was quickly becoming an appealing alternative to the Western "model" of development, which was not really a model, of course, but in the African context, capitalism at its worst. Washington's fears were reinforced by the widely popular Kwame Nkrumah, Sekou Touré, Leopold Senghor of Senegal, and Julius Nyerere of Tanganyika, all of whom adopted socialist-inspired policies and were highly critical of the European colonialist legacy. Administration officials were concerned about the popularity of socialism and neutralism in Africa. Dulles vainly tried to convince third world leaders that neutralism worked to the Soviets' advantage. As he was often known to do, he leaned on moral principles, in this case calling neutralism "immoral" and "obsolete."[10] His strict demeanor won him few friends among those newly independent leaders tired of Western posturing.

Many critics saw the Eisenhower strategy as no more than arm-twisting. The anthropologist Melville Herskovits praised African attempts to combine old and new values in an effort to rejuvenate their societies after colonialism.[11] Liberal politicians picked up on some of these themes. The prominent Democratic Party activist Chester Bowles wrote about the right of self-government for all peoples, and wanted to see the United States move faster in support of Africa.[12] Senator John F. Kennedy (D-Massachusetts) called on Americans as early as 1956 to support the independence of colonial peoples to "win their hearts" and "hands" in "friendship." Later he would make self-determination a subject in his campaign for the presidency.[13]

A few voices within the Eisenhower administration began calling for a formal review of African policy. In fact, as early as 1955, Fred Hadsel, deputy director of the State Department's Office of African Affairs, urged Washington to develop a more "independent posture" and in effect create a policy "where none has ever existed." Hadsel made the whole idea of change sound too easy and glossed over the potential problems with Western European allies. Despite the report, Dulles remained skeptical of the need for change (and there is no evidence its message percolated any higher).[14] America's European friends were not likely to appreciate any overtures that Africans could interpret as support for independence. The allies—British, French, and Belgian—were always quick to point out that anything that would weaken their recovery would weaken the Western Bloc and the fight against communism.

It was not until April 1957, when Vice President Richard Nixon made a high-profile trip to Africa, that at least some top officials in the Eisenhower administration acknowledged the costs of failing to revise its policy.[15] Nixon toured Ghana, Liberia, and several other western and eastern African states. He returned home to warn that the United States could not afford to let its image spoil under attack from the communists. "We cannot talk equality to the peoples of Africa and Asia" he warned, "and practice inequality in the United States." He went on to urge that the United States needed to do a better job of highlighting the "real progress" that was being made at home in order to promote a "true picture" of American society abroad.[16] Despite Nixon's prompting, as biased as it was, there was no major change in U.S. policy. Eisenhower continued to show little interest in either Africa or racial matters and was "so uncomfortable" with the issue of civil rights, recorded Thomas Borstelmann, that he "simply avoided it."[17] Although the president would take some steps to improve race relations, such as supporting voting rights in the southern U.S. states and using federal troops to enforce desegregation at Little Rock Central High School in Arkansas, there was little real progress on ending segregation within U.S. boundaries, let alone applying enlightened principles to foreign policy in Africa.

Eisenhower and Dulles, however, did agree to a policy review, and the result was the first major position paper on Africa, NSC 5719/1, of July 1957. The historian George White has illustrated how this National Security Council (NSC) document incorporated the attitude of white superiority that guided the Eisenhower administration. The basic goal of U.S. foreign policy in Africa, as outlined in this policy statement, White argued, was to ensure an "orderly" development toward self-government "in cooperation with the European powers" that still controlled the continent at the expense of Africans themselves. The United States, as stated in the NSC 5719/1 paper, needed to do more to distance itself from "stagnant or repressive" colonial policies that could only fuel opposition movements. On the other hand, it also recommended joint economic plans with the colonial powers to emphasize that the United States was "not trying to supplant" its allies in Africa. The underlying fear was that a bungled imperialist retreat from the continent would hasten the arrival of communism. At the insistence of Nixon and with the backing of Dulles, the policy statement acknowledged that "communism" thus far "has not been a major problem in Africa South of the Sahara . . . but its potential influence is a matter of growing concern."[18] More foreboding than real, the statement was the first time the doctrine of containment was formally applied to Africa independent of European defense. It also testified to the fact that the administration was becoming more and more concerned that Africans did not understand the seriousness of Soviet subversive activities.

The authors of NSC 5719/1 credited Belgium with being in "the best position to continue the economic development of their dependent area, the Congo—a rich area in its own right."[19] So while Washington wanted a slice of the proverbial "magnificent cake" in the Congo, it would not press Belgium too hard to get it, at least for now. Ever since World War II, U.S. access to the Belgian Congo's strategic minerals, like uranium, industrial diamonds, cobalt, and copper found in the provinces of Katanga and Kasai, had been declared a national security priority. By the end of the 1950s, however, the importance of the Congo's resources was diminished by discoveries of uranium in Canada and South Africa, and Washington had even declined further purchases of uranium from the Congo. Likewise, depriving the Soviet Union of Congolese uranium became less critical after the Soviet Union found its own supplies in Central Asia.

Belgian authorities jealously kept the Congo as isolated as possible from both superpowers. They limited communist representation in the Congo to a single Czechoslovakian consulate, knowing this would help keep U.S. fears of communism at bay. Belgium also discouraged direct U.S. contacts with the Congolese. They were hypersensitive about any American outreach, fearing anything that would lead the Congolese to any interest in independence. The United States complied and kept its embassy small. Even as late as 1958, U.S. consul James Green had to meet furtively with leading Congolese representatives, including Joseph Kasavubu.[20] Good faith and the NATO alliance, however, eventually demanded that Belgium allow American corporate interests, primarily those of Rockefeller and Guggenheim, to make some direct financial and commercial investments in the Congo, without having to work through Belgian enterprises.[21]

Like U.S. economic interests, Washington's Cold War concerns crept into the region no matter how hard Belgium tried to keep them out. John Foster Dulles was soon lecturing Belgian foreign minister Pierre Wigny about the dangers of Belgian failure to introduce any measures of self-government and allowing its colony to become one of the "targets for international Communism." Belgium, Dulles warned, needed to better tailor its goals to coincide with Western Cold War interests. Wigny reassured him that Belgium would continue to foster good relations with the Congolese and keep the African "hinterland" in the Western camp.[22] Words aside, the tone of his message suggested that he meant Belgium could do this better than the leader of the Western camp itself.

The opening of the U.S. State Department's new Bureau of African Affairs in August 1958 signaled the growing importance of Africa. Still, the bureau lacked influence within the administration. The choice of a quiet career diplomat, Joseph C. Satterthwaite, to serve as the new assistant secretary of state for African affairs indicated its weak function in the administration's policymaking.[23] Ironically, given Africa's historic marginalization, the most important decisions about Africa continued to be made at the highest levels of the policymaking apparatus, the NSC. NSC members, however, were not generally familiar with the details of the Congo and this meant a gulf between the White House and the best and most recent information. Perhaps that is true in any case where the NSC is involved, but the problems were accentuated in the Congo, where the intricacies of its history and Belgian involvement were so little known and less understood.

It would take more than these initial steps to rescript U.S. policy. America was still closely associated with its European allies, and Eisenhower continued to mark time. He turned to Clarence Randall, head of the White House's Council of Foreign Economic Policy, for another look at Africa.[24] Randall was a lawyer and former president of the Inland Steel Company who openly criticized inefficiency and convention for convention's sake. He toured Africa in March and April 1958, and sided with Hadsel in his conclusions that the United States had not gone far enough in creating an independent policy. At an NSC meeting in May, Randall outlined the classic dilemma of being caught between the Scylla of NATO and the Charybdis of a free, noncommunist Africa. European imperialists, he said, "do not want the United States to provide any assistance to their African colonies" while "the newly independent states insist on knowing where the United States stands on the problem of colonialism."[25] Randall warned that a focus on economic development threatened to sideline the most pressing issues—which he clearly outlined as Cold War issues—of independence and self-determination. The United States, he recommended, must defend the principles of self-determination or lose Africa to the Soviet Union. Africans, after all, in his racist way of thinking, could hardly be expected to manage and defend their independence themselves.

Randall's message seemed to have some resonance, but as usual the president remained cautious to the point of neglect. At an NSC meeting in late 1958, Eisenhower again reiterated that the United States "must believe in the right of colonial peoples to achieve independence" but did not want to emphasize this too strongly and create a crisis in relations with Europe.[26] The president was gradually coming to see Africa with an independent role in the Cold War, but with a steady hand, he drew the line when it came to establishing a U.S. military presence there.[27] There would be no Dienbienphu for America—or direct intervention after a colonial failure—in Africa. When General Thomas White argued in favor of reestablishing a strategic presence in Africa, Eisenhower retorted that "our military installations are useless if the people don't want them. We must win Africa, but we can't win it by military activity. . . . We couldn't win wars unless we won the people."[28]

Yet "winning the people" seemed to be failing more and more. Despite all fears, Ghana's independence in 1958 had not damaged Western prestige to the extent that Washington had feared. Close on its heels, the abrupt French abandonment of Guinea left that already poor country financially ruined and showed all that was wrong with exploitative capitalism and jealous imperialism. Eisenhower expressed his concern that Guinea would now "be made a showcase for communism."[29] Could something similar happen in the Belgian Congo? That question lingered heavy in the air as events continued to unfold in the heart of Africa.

The New Soviet Course in Africa

In 1955 just as the Non-Aligned Movement itself was taking shape, Nikita Khrushchev was tightening his grip on power in Moscow. The new Soviet leader was a visionary who saw a great arc of opportunity in Africa.[30] Joseph Stalin had shown no particular interest in Africa and had generally paid little attention to the question of decolonization there, except briefly after World War II when the future of the former Italian colonies was up for debate. Stalin nevertheless had set important precedents by encouraging revolutionaries in Asia to rely on Soviet aid while also discouraging open and armed revolution for the time being. He backed opposition to the colonizer, with clear and limited goals, and not a broad-scale attack on imperialism.[31] Khrushchev turned the tables by offering revolutionaries a more peaceful and cooperative approach as a way to challenge colonialism. In this way he hoped to break down barriers still preventing a better Soviet footing in the third world.[32]

For Nikita Khrushchev, decolonization was a "deep personal concern," his son Sergei wrote years later. Nikita Khrushchev optimistically believed that the spread of communist ideas into the third world needed "only a small effort" or push, "to ensure that the imperialists did not stamp out" the new revolutionary movements that had a life and momentum of their own.[33] For the time being, with the proletariat in such small numbers in Africa, it made sense for him to build relations with nationalist leaders. Despite these new overtures, nationalists, even radical ones, would always remain suspect in communist eyes. They, in turn, were equally mistrustful of Soviet-directed communism and reinforced the uneasy relationship. To escape this conundrum Khrushchev looked for radical nationalists with socialist beliefs and then tried to cultivate the latter sentiments.

Despite his many mistakes and faux pas, Khrushchev used his congeniality to rejuvenate Soviet policy toward the decolonizing world. He toured India, Burma, and Afghanistan in 1955 and again in 1959. He also signaled his interest beyond Europe by approving the Czechoslovakian arms deal with Egypt in 1955, and later that year announced the Soviet Union would construct a steel mill in Bhilai, India.[34] Khrushchev's friendly position toward nationalists gradually helped to improve Soviet relations with third world leaders like the dynamic Indian president Jawaharlal Nehru and Egypt's Gamal Abdel Nasser. What his implacable enemy Vyacheslav Molotov called "adventurism," Khrushchev boasted helped break the Soviet Union out of its isolationism.[35]

The new Soviet policy did begin to chip away at the armor of the historically Western domain in Africa.[36] In 1956, Khrushchev made a special overture to Africa at the Twentieth Party Congress. "The awakening of the African peoples has begun," he declared, and called for the complete abolition of colonialism on that continent.[37] Africans, Khrushchev advised, needed to guard themselves against greedy Western capitalists by uniting to create a "zone of peace" with the socialist world. To soothe fears that communists advocated violence as the only way to "remake society," Khrushchev talked about a "parliamentary path" of development and pointed to rapid Soviet industrialization as a model of development. As Christopher Andrew has argued, he transferred his own optimism in the Soviet economy to Africa, and that optimism was welcomed in the context of liberation and planning for independence.[38] Khrushchev's new approach clearly suggested he would accept new ways—even to the point of tweaking the accepted Soviet ideology—to work against the imperialists.

The theme of unity among third world states could be very useful at times and played an important role in Soviet propaganda. Uniting against imperialists was good, but that was as far as Khrushchev wanted the initiative to go. The new presence of Africa on the global stage in fact helped shift some focus away from the strongly independent nationalists in the Arab world, such as Egypt's Gamal Abdel Nasser. As if to reinforce that new balance, the Soviet press paid much more attention to the smaller All-Africa People's Conference held in Accra than to the Afro-Asian Economic Conference held in Cairo in 1957.[39]

Khrushchev's new policy was not welcomed by all those in the communist world. China's formidable Mao Zedong may have "leaned" toward an alliance with the Soviet Union, despite some misgivings with Stalin's raw diplomacy. But his relations with Khrushchev were increasingly complicated by the Chinese leaders' growing confidence and sense of superiority, and a domestic program that did not match with Khrushchev's changes. Mao disliked Khrushchev's criticisms of Stalin's personality cult at the Twentieth Party Congress, believing he compromised revolutionary goals. Scornful of the Soviet emphasis on peaceful coexistence, Mao championed greater support for revolutionaries in Asia and Africa. For the time being, however, public relations seemed amicable. Differences between the two states were more likely to express themselves in non-European areas, especially India, although formally the alliance was still intact at the end of the 1950s.[40]

The Soviet Union would continue to take the lead over China for some time. Khrushchev typically used a very down-to-earth style of diplomacy that appealed to many African leaders tired of the pageantry of imperialism. Of peasant origin himself and with little formal training, he used his background to his benefit in the third world. In 1957 during the Youth Festival held in the Soviet Union, Khrushchev met with W. E. B. DuBois and the two agreed on the affinity between communist ideology and the goals of those nations about to be free from colonialism.[41] Soon thereafter Khrushchev agreed to establish the Soviet branch of the Afro-Asian Solidarity Organization. The Soviet committee was responsible for exchanging visits with African politicians, organizing conferences, and granting scholarships and other cultural exchanges.[42] His ideology helped control (or conceal) a traditional Russian racism but could not always supersede it. Like most Western leaders, however, Khrushchev thought of himself as a teacher—and an inherently superior one—and not a partner with African leaders.

The new Soviet approach to Africa began to have some real impact by early 1958. In March of that year, the Central Committee issued a top-secret decree outlining measures to improve social, cultural, and economic ties in Africa as a way to strengthen its ideological fight against capitalism. The Soviet Union would increase its criticism of imperialism, albeit for now at second-tier world gatherings such as the U.N. Trusteeship Council. Georgi A. Zhukov, a former *Pravda* editor, was to head up a new agency to manage cultural relations with the third world.[43] Zhukov had been one of the masterminds behind Khrushchev's vibrant public relations campaign abroad and it is significant that he now turned his attention to Africa. A sharp propagandist, Zhukov continued to expose the aggressive character of the imperialist powers but combined this message with a more positive one about building a socialist paradise in the not-too-distant future. He was aware that the Soviet Union would have a tough job selling its "paradise," particularly after the 1956 invasion of Hungary. Don't we "sometimes too easily" put the expression "free world" at the "disposal of the imperialists," he asked, and shouldn't we insist the Soviet Union is the genuinely free world? Glossing over troubles and inconsistencies in his messages did not particularly bother Zhukov (as it had not really bothered his counterpart, Richard Nixon).[44]

Money and profit were not initial concerns for the Soviet Union. Khrushchev was willing to accept that Soviet programs in Africa would cost more than they would return in the immediate future. In mid-1958 he acknowledged that "our economic and technical aid to the underdeveloped countries is unprofitable for us." That in itself was not enough to reconsider economic aid. Khrushchev justified Soviet expenditures by suggesting that with it, decolonized countries would not have to enter "any one-sided deal" with the colonizers or go "begging to them."[45] Obviously financial incentives could help build a larger Soviet sphere of influence. After France abruptly abandoned Guinea, the Soviet Union offered Sekou Touré a generous aid package, although one which emphasized showy projects over serious developmental programs. A loan to the generally pro-Western Ethiopia and the visit of its emperor Haile Selassie to the Soviet Union later showed even greater flexibility when it came to nurturing friends on the continent.[46] In general, Khrushchev balanced his message to Africa carefully, recommending that newly independent African states not cut all economic ties with the "metropole," but try to use for themselves what they can. This approach, however, apparently brought "stormy" debates in the Foreign Ministry and Central Committee meetings.[47]

Besides adding money, the Soviet Union clearly had to improve its knowledge about Africa. A few embarrassments, such as sending snow plows to Guinea, made it easy enough to convince anyone, including Khrushchev, of that need. Boris Ponomarev, a loyal member of the Central Committee's International Department, sent representatives to Africa to learn more about the continent's politics and to promote contact with pro-Soviet organizations. However, Ponomarev's strict views encouraged a cautious reporting that, as will be seen, did not always serve Soviet decisionmaking.[48] Khrushchev also used his trusted ally and deputy premier of the Soviet Union, Anastas Mikoyan, to prod scholars to do more. Mikoyan chastised members of the Institute of Oriental Studies of the Academy of Sciences for their lethargic approach to Africa. In response to Mikoyan's summons, academics scurried to found new institutes and rejuvenated editorial boards of major journals, like *Sovetskoe vostokovedenie* (Soviet Oriental Studies). Soon the number of books and articles about Africa doubled. Scholarly journals devoted special issues to the theme of Africa south of the Sahara. Books devoted to the Congo began to appear for the first time.[49]

A Soviet bureaucratic reorganization was soon under way. It naturally bred turf warfare and complicated information gathering about Africa. The Institute of Oriental Studies at the Academy of Sciences and its eminent Tajik director Bobodzhan G. Gafurov would have to surrender jurisdiction over Africa.[50] Instead in June 1959, the Central Committee approved the creation of the more specialized Africa Institute, and although not originally designed to come under the auspices of the Academy of Sciences, that is where it was placed. In addition to studying the historical and current political, economic, and social conditions in Africa, the Africa Institute had the responsibility of establishing contacts with African organizations. Ivan I. Potekhin, a member of the Bolshevik Party since the 1920s, became its first director and held that position until he became too sick to work in early 1960. Potekhin was one of the Soviet Union's few Africanists and had met with key personalities such as Nkrumah, Touré, and Lumumba. He often exaggerated the extent of local revolts and the strength of the African proletariat in the liberation movements. His views, which were colored by his long-standing devotion to Marxist ideology, struck a chord with Khrushchev.[51]

In January 1960, the Central Committee beefed up its new Soviet policy in Africa. The Kremlin would now begin to pay greater attention to local African communists. Another top-secret decree outlined more specific measures designed to "considerably increase" and strengthen Soviet influence in Africa south of the Sahara. Virtually all of these new measures dealt with strengthening cultural ties, for example increasing student exchanges and contacts with local councils, and continuing to improve propaganda. In order to accomplish its new goals, Moscow would have to downplay the many problems experienced by African students at the University of Moscow and at the People's Friendship University a few blocks away. African students were vocal in their opposition to censorship, such as the ban on the Black African Student Union, and reported a number of racist attacks, both violent and verbal.[52] So while policy was decreed from the top, local-level interaction still reflected the racism that was everywhere.

At the outset the superpowers had much in common in their approach to Africa. Both the United States and the Soviet Union wanted to carve out a new role for themselves in the Congo, but they wanted to keep it limited for the time being. The United States had the advantage of relying on its Belgian ally. The Soviet Union had the advantage of goodwill, growing anti-imperialism, and for a while the prosocialist sentiments of the Non-Aligned Movement. Both were heavily paternalistic and felt they had a lot to teach the Africans. The Bandung Conference had helped emphasize the need for policy reviews in Moscow and Washington, the Suez crisis highlighted the importance of the continent in general, and the continuing war in Algeria warned of pending problems. All that was needed was a crisis like the one in the Congo to bring all this together and truly raise Africa's importance in the Cold War.

2. A Cold War Nationalism

Virtually no event after 1945 was left untouched by the Cold War. Decolonization and nationalism in the Congo, like elsewhere, were profoundly affected by the ideological milieu. The Congolese looked to break out of their colonially enforced isolation by establishing relations with the United States and Soviet Union. As a result the bipolar Cold War paradigm tended to magnify any domestic discussion of social reform and force any visions of the future to be artificially labeled as either procapitalist or procommunist. The Congolese tried to moderate the tension of bipolarism by looking for allies in the third world and pledging their own neutralism. Other influences, including the deep roots of tradition, the legacy of the Belgian conquest, and demands for self-determination combined with the Cold War to shape the growing independence movement in the Congo. The problem for the Congolese was how to juggle all these multiple influences while keeping their goals of liberation in the forefront.

The "Magnificent Cake"?

Colonialism left the Congo exploited, underdeveloped, and poorly governed. The political and economic degradation of the last century meant that the lands around the Congo River had lost many resources and people. Education, agriculture, and infrastructure were woefully antiquated. Yet, there were bright spots amid the litany of problems. The Congo seemed ready to enter the global economy and had strong connections to Europe and through Europe to America. There was also the Asian experience with decolonization to build on and the new third world initiative to counterbalance the Cold War. An obvious lever for the Congo was its vast mineral wealth. In the 1950s, the Congo produced more than 85 percent of the cobalt in Africa, 65 percent of its industrial diamonds, and 35 percent of its copper. Famous mines such as those at Shinkolobwe were an important source of uranium, necessary in the production of nuclear weapons. This mineral advantage was growing relatively smaller, and by the late 1950s, the United States was reducing its reliance on the Congo. Still the mineral resources of the Congo were vital to the global economy and the key to its future, even if not quite in the same way as the preceding ten years.[1]

The Congolese used the term *bula matari* (breaker of bones) to refer to Henry Morton Stanley and later broadened it to mean "the state" and anyone who exercised power.[2] The term aptly captured the Belgian legacy in the Congo. In the 1870s, Belgian King Leopold II watched Henry Morton Stanley, the wayward journalist who had adopted the United States as his homeland, explore the African continent. Leopold convinced Stanley to return to the Congo with an expeditionary force to set up a confederation of "free" republics. The Belgian king so coveted an empire in Africa that he helped partition the continent at the Berlin Conference in 1885 by supporting the "effective occupation" clause and gaining international recognition for his rule of the Congo.[3] His rule was brutal and callous, the worst imperialism had to offer. Leopold treated the Congo's rubber and ivory as his own private property, mined only for his personal profit, and cared nothing for the well-being of workers. After humanitarian and activist E. D. Morel exposed his crimes and criminal treatment of plantation workers, Leopold decided to sell the Congo to the Belgian government for the handsome sum of roughly 220 million Belgian francs.[4]

In 1908, a rather apologetic Belgian parliament took over the colony and promised to civilize the land and eventually return it to the Congolese. Benign words did not hide the fact the "Belgian solution" was really a continuation of exploitation. The colony was now governed from Brussels by a minister of the Congo, whose policies were administered by a governor-general in Leopoldville. The Belgian government introduced *chefferies* (chiefdoms) into the Congo to reconstitute traditional kinship or clan groupings into larger formations. The chief became the agent of Belgium, and in return for a salary, was transformed into a civil servant. The *chefferie* system remained intact until 1957, when the first municipal elections were introduced.[5]

The first serious suggestion that Belgium consider an explicit time frame for Congolese independence came from Professor Antoine A. J. Van Bilsen in December 1955. Van Bilsen had traveled the Congo extensively and blamed his government for failing to prepare the Congolese for an eventual transfer of power. His pamphlet, *A Thirty-Year Plan for the Political Emancipation of Belgian Africa*, argued that if Belgium wanted to remain in control of the transfer of power to the Congo, and prevent it from slipping into the Soviet orbit, it needed to cooperate with other European imperialists to better prepare its colony for independence. Van Bilsen was artfully suggesting that Belgium use its European connections to circumscribe the growing Soviet—and of course American—interest in the Congo. Instead, most Belgians saw their colony in the Congo as a status symbol and argued that a strong Belgian presence was the best defense against any communist infiltration. Others bitterly condemned Van Bilsen and suggested that he be tried for treason.[6]

By the mid-1950s, as Van Bilsen's critique had implied, Belgian colonial policy seriously lagged behind that of the British and French, who had at least agreed to discuss demands for greater self-rule in Africa south of the Sahara. In 1957 Ghana (formerly the Gold Coast) became independent after Kwame Nkrumah and the Convention People's Party spent two decades building Ghanaian nationalism. Guinea soon followed in 1958 where Sekou Touré had worked for independence since the early 1950s through the Rassemblement Démocratique Africain. Although the independence of Ghana and Guinea put pressure on Belgium to begin thinking about a transfer of power, it also raised the question of whether the British and French plans for self-rule were appropriate for "Belgian Africa."[7]

When French president Charles De Gaulle visited Brazzaville in 1958 to offer independence to the French West and Equatorial African colonies, no one anticipated that just across the river young Congolese activists were also listening. Two days after De Gaulle's speech, a group of Congolese intellectuals, or *évolués*,[8] presented Governor-General Leon Petillon with a petition demanding that a date be set for independence.[9] The petition shocked everyone, including King Baudouin. Baudouin, Leopold II's great grandnephew, had visited the Congo in 1955 and played an active role in forming colonial policy.[10] Neither Baudouin nor the others were ready to consider independence. After all, there was no nationalist movement in the Congo nor even any single visionary modeled after Ghana or Guinea. Right up until the first days of 1960, most Belgians and many observers worldwide assumed that the Belgian Congo would become independent only twenty or thirty years after the British and French colonies in Africa had achieved that status.[11]

The real problem was that wealth bred greed. Those administering the Belgian colony were also heavily invested in its wealth. Despite the fact that Leopold had transferred administration of the colony to Belgium, the royal family remained very much connected to the mining companies and profits coming out of the Congo. In 1952, five holding companies controlled 70 percent of all Congolese investment; the government held a strong interest in all five, sometimes upwards of 50 percent. King Leopold had incorporated UMHK in 1906, which was controlled by the Société Générale holding company. UMHK produced over 60 percent of the world's cobalt (most of which was imported by the United States) and about 10 percent of the world's copper. It alone paid at least 20 percent of all Congolese taxes. Another important company created by Leopold was the Société Internationale Forestière et Minière du Congo, or Forminière, which dominated mining and agriculture in Kasai. In addition, numerous top government officials in the Belgian Congo received payments for "services rendered" from these companies, making any government oversight impossible for all practical purposes.[12]

Several American financial groups acquired interests in Belgian-dominated companies, including Thomas Ryan and Daniel Guggenheim (who invested in Forminière) and J.P. Morgan, who helped finance colonial development projects. Independent American interest in the Congo did not begin until the 1950s when the Rockefeller and Morgan firms began to float loans and invest directly in the Congo. Britain was the other major state to have substantial interest in Katanga. The British firm Tanganyika Concessions had a 15 percent share in UMHK, and the British owned the Benguela railway, which transported UMHK goods from Elizabethville to the port in Angola.[13]

By the 1950s Belgium was under greater international pressure to modernize its administration and to open up the Congo to more foreign investment. Belgian officials realized that they would have to do more to raise the standards of living for the Congolese or bear the criticism. Many Congolese still lived in squalor and destitution, and for those who could find work, it often meant travel far away from their families. In this spirit the Belgian parliament devised a Ten-Year Plan (1950 to 1959) to raise the standards of living while also recognizing that social progress "must be based upon a stable and prosperous economy." Critics charged, quite plausibly, that the reforms were at worst infrastructure investment to benefit business owners financed by Belgian taxpayers, or at best were designed to strengthen Belgian political control. The plan did little to advance higher education, which remained minimal among the Congolese. By 1960 Belgian analysts tracking the Congo counted only fifteen to eighteen university graduates, and a similar number with any kind of administrative or leadership experience.[14]

A New Nationalism in the Congo

By the late 1950s, Congolese *évolués* began to demand independence. Among the many new faces of the independence leaders, two stood out: Patrice Lumumba and Joseph Kasavubu. Both helped define the parameters of the

Figure 2.1. Ethnographic Map of the Congo

Sources: Author's data, which rely on the information and maps given by Young, *Politics in the Congo,* 233; and by Lemarchand, *Political Awakening in the Congo,* 11–17. The map base is from d-map.com.

independence movement, and ultimately, the future of the Congo. The two young Congolese quickly found themselves in competition with each other. In 1956, Lumumba and a handful of others associated with the Congolese journal *Conscience Africaine* signed a manifesto demanding "genuine responsibilities" for political, social, and economic development with the goal of "total emancipation." They formed the Mouvement National Congolais (MNC), which became the only nationwide political organization.[15] Immediately thereafter, Joseph Kasavubu, who led the Alliance des Bakongo (Abako), an ethnic organization in the Lower Congo (Leopoldville Province), called Lumumba's ideas too "complicated" and demanded political rights and all liberties for the Congolese without delay (figure 2.1).[16] However, at this early stage any disagreements between Lumumba and Kasavubu were not intractable, and when advantageous, they could still cooperate.

The stout and good-natured Kasavubu styled himself as a spokesperson for the Congolese. He was well experienced and in his late forties. In his younger days, Kasavubu had studied to become a priest but then chose to teach in Catholic schools. After his first political speeches had been called too radical, Kasavubu moderated his message and honed his diplomatic skills, although he would never become a strong public speaker. He became president of Abako, and then in 1957 became mayor of the Dendale district of the city of Leopoldville. Kasavubu guided Abako's support of a loose association of ministates for the Congo basin primarily in order to retain the identity of Leopoldville Province. Abako's blueprint was first referred to as "separatism" but then, as its views shifted toward greater unity for the Congo, its program was often called "federalist." Abako's focus on Leopoldville was often at odds with Kasavubu's aspirations as a national leader but the strength of the organization served him well at first.[17] By late 1958, Kasavubu was growing impatient and complained to the Americans that Belgium was interested only in "pillaging" the resources and cheap labor of the Congo and demanded immediate independence.[18]

Patrice Lumumba was Kasavubu's most prominent competitor. Lumumba was from the Batetela, a subgroup of the Mongo peoples, which made up for its smaller size by its pride of insurrection against Belgian rule. He was born in Onalua, Kasai and attended a Protestant mission school. He was always an avid reader and somewhere along the way he picked up an interest in the French Revolution. Lumumba became a clerk in the Stanleyville post office, where he worked for eleven years until accused of embezzling about $2,500. He was sentenced to two years in prison, although the sentence was suspended after the money was repaid by friends. Lumumba then moved to Leopoldville and became a sales manager for a local brewery. The job offered him a chance to socialize with the urban elite who frequented the pubs. He regularly wrote for Congolese journals and newspapers, and many of his earliest articles spoke out against the racial inequalities imposed by the colonial regime. The wrongs of racial and colonial injustice drove much of Lumumba's passion and he desperately wanted justice for all Congolese. As the independence movement gained momentum, Lumumba's views became increasingly radicalized. "Independence is never given," Lumumba often repeated, "it must be seized." It is not a "gift," he reminded the Belgians, but a "right."[19] Lumumba's ideas were predominantly anti-imperialist, but that did not mean anti-Western. He pleaded with peasants to understand the need to grow crops for export to Western countries despite their connection with imperialism.[20]

Lumumba also built on the harsh lessons of Batetela history by recommending cooperation as the best way to gain equality with white colonists.[21]

He was the first to develop a nationalist vision and appealed to people across the country using French, Swahili, and Lingala. Charismatic and perceptive, he crisscrossed the country making passionate speeches. Lumumba made a special effort to expand MNC membership, especially among youth groups and women. However, the traditional nature of Congolese politics demanded that he and the MNC develop regional support, for which Lumumba turned to the Mongo-speaking peoples of Equateur, the Bangala of Orientale, and the Batetela areas of Kasai and Kivu.[22]

Congolese politics was fractious by nature and a number of MNC leaders feared that Lumumba was becoming more of a demagogue than a leader. In July 1959, Albert Kalonji with help from Joseph Ileo formed a separate branch of the party known as the MNC-K (and party members who remained loyal to Lumumba eventually became the MNC-L). The MNC-K advocated a more conservative or moderate federalism. This faction was based in Kalonji's home province of Kasai. The MNC-K built its support on Kalonji's ethnic Baluba, while giving a cold shoulder to the province's pro-Lumumbist Lulua minority. Cyrille Adoula and Joseph Ngalula also defected to MNC-K and deprived Lumumba of considerable talent but also gave him more freedom to build up his own organization. The MNC-K would become an important challenge to Lumumba, one that he could never fully answer or overcome.[23]

Lumumba was eager to build foreign connections. He attended the All-Africa People's Conference in December 1958, where he met Tom Mboya of Kenya, Kwame Nkrumah, and author Frantz Fanon. He also accepted the services of an English translator, who was later discovered to be a CIA agent, and, as Thomas Kanza—Lumumba confidant and former ambassador to the United Nations—recalled, Lumumba "may well have told him more than was advisable."[24] After meeting so many illustrious African leaders and intellectuals, Lumumba fully embraced the pan-Africanism and positive neutralism they espoused. He agreed that Africans had the "same soul" and dreamed that united, they could defeat colonialism.[25]

As soon as Lumumba returned from the All-Africa People's Conference, he held a mass meeting in Leopoldville where he called for independence. Sensing a challenge to his own leadership ambitions, Kasavubu scheduled a rally for January 4, 1959. He still needed to obtain the proper permits, and having second thoughts, tried to delay the gathering. He was too late and that very day a crowd of 20,000 soccer fans were joined by others in Leopoldville. According to historian Georges Nzongola-Ntalaja, the result was a three-day revolt that radicalized the liberation movement.[26] Kasavubu now began to demand immediate independence. Abako sent a copy of his letter demanding independence to the Soviet Union and requested military aid on or before January 19, 1959, the day *before* the Soviet Foreign Ministry most likely received the request.[27] Still, the full extent of popular Congolese disaffection caught both Lumumba and Kasavubu by surprise. So, too, did it catch the Belgians off-guard.

Prime Minister Gaston Eyskens angrily blamed the January 1959 riots on Abako. He announced the dissolution of the organization and arrested Kasavubu and fourteen other Abako leaders. To calm the still explosive situation, King Baudouin responded on January 13 by promising the Congo eventual independence "without undue procrastination, but also without ill-considered haste." The very fact that the king responded showed the seriousness of the situation. His words might have sounded like a dramatic step for the Belgian royalty, but the slow pace of introducing any new forms of self-representation showed that again little had changed. Making matters worse, colonial authorities forced many newly radicalized Congolese to return to their rural homes, thus inadvertently spreading radical ideas.[28]

The Rise of Soviet Interest in the Congo

The January 1959 riots grabbed the attention of the Soviet Union. *Pravda* published six full-length articles on the riots and their aftermath that emphasized the unrest in the colonial world.[29] On January 30, the Soviet representative at the U.N. Trusteeship Council Ivan I. Lobanov charged that the riots were evidence of Belgian arrogance and refusal to introduce even the most basic steps toward self-determination.[30] In the first Russian-language book on the Congo published later in the year, Vladimir Martynov blamed the Belgian tactic of divide-and-rule for inciting the riots. He claimed that the riots were led by the proletariat, naming as one of its leaders Antoine Tshimanga, the twenty-five-year-old president of the leftist National Union of Congolese Workers and leader of the MNC's youth division.[31] Tshimanga had attracted the attention of not only the Soviets but also the Belgians. They deemed him one of the rebels to watch out for and the Belgian secret service followed him closely.[32]

The Soviet Embassy staff in Brussels tried to learn what they could about the riots from the Belgian newspapers. A sixteen-page embassy report stated that 50,000 unemployed Congolese workers (in reality, the 20,000 soccer fans) supplied the bulk of the protesters. The riots, according to the report, were spontaneous, and the leaders remained too divided to play a strong organizing role. The report accused Belgium of exploiting ethnic and tribal differences to prevent the Congolese from forming a united front. Moreover, Patrice Lumumba, the report continued, had "succumbed to the provocation of the Belgian colonizers" by refusing to cooperate with Abako and thus fed into Belgian machinations.[33] This initial Soviet coolness toward Lumumba would have long-lasting repercussions on their relationship and reinforced early doubts in Moscow about getting involved in the Congo.

Several meetings between Lumumba and Soviet officials in 1959 did little to improve the relationship. On April 18, 1959, Lumumba arrived at the Soviet Embassy in Conakry to meet with the Soviet ambassador to Guinea, Pavel I. Gerasimov, after attending a meeting of the standing committee of the All-African Peoples' movement. Lumumba promised that as soon as the Congolese won independence they would "immediately exchange diplomatic representatives with the USSR." Lumumba also told Gerasimov about his efforts to build a purely African trade union in the Congo. He requested aid to help him counteract the anti-Soviet slander spread by the Belgians. His enthusiasm could not change the slow-moving Soviet machine. Gerasimov mechanically reaffirmed that the Soviet people were the "true friends" of the national liberation movement in Africa but offered little else.[34] Khrushchev had built a general policy for Africa, but was not ready for individual petitions. In October that year, Lumumba requested Soviet help in organizing propaganda and preparing political cadres. Moscow was again noncommittal, and Lumumba, who was thrown in jail after the Stanleyville riots of that month, never received a response to any of his requests.[35]

Soviet contacts with other Congolese were not any easier. The October 1959 riots did much to embolden one of the most radical political parties, the Parti Solidaire Africain (PSA), led by Pierre Mulele and Antoine Gizenga. The PSA formed in Kwilu, the ethnically diverse eastern portion of Leopoldville Province, and temporarily joined with the larger Abako. Mulele and Gizenga promoted violence if negotiations with Belgium failed to produce any results.[36] They approached the Soviet Union on the basis of its strong anti-imperialist stance. In late December 1959, Mulele traveled to Guinea and met with Sekou Touré and the Soviet chargé d'affaires, Ivan I. Marchuk. He asked Marchuk for money, weapons, and the use of Radio Moscow in the fight for independence. Marchuk responded stiffly that the Soviet Union's support for the national liberation movement did not yet include support for the use of force. Such requests were out of line.[37] For now, the Soviet Union would continue to encourage small Marxist parties to ally with stronger nationalist movements for independence. The tone was set and Soviet relations with Mulele were also rough from the start. Mulele eventually turned to the Chinese for aid and in early 1960 would travel to China to learn about guerrilla tactics.

By the start of 1960, the Soviet Union became more open to establishing relations with emerging Congolese leaders. As the Russian historians Apollon Davidson and Sergey Mazov have shown, Moscow initially leaned toward

Antoine Gizenga, who was at least willing to openly call the communists his friends. Gizenga visited Prague and East Berlin, and was invited to the Soviet Union, although preparations for independence meant he never made the trip.[38] Always a difficult ally, Gizenga could be unpredictable and secretive. He had a hard time building up a base of support and in his early days was carelessly presumptive of his ability to rally the masses behind him. Nevertheless, Soviet interest was growing and for now Gizenga seemed to represent a reasonable promise of leadership.

There were certain clear themes that emerged in the first Soviet contacts with the Congolese. The Soviets were not interested in supporting an armed revolution or an independent radical leader, but preferred to see a united Marxist front of workers and peasants in which the goal was to work for social and agrarian reform and independence for the Congo. They were cautious toward the self-proclaimed leaders of independence and looked to other radicals with views friendlier to socialism as alternatives, but offered little more than expressions of support. The Soviet Union discouraged any long-term cooperation with colonizer nations and supported political and economic reform and socialist modernization to distinguish its approach from the more rigorous Chinese peasant model of development. The limited Soviet response to the growing independence movement showed that Khrushchev's optimism was clearly at odds with reality.

The U.S.–Belgian Knot

Early American impressions of the Congo seemed focused on fear of its fragmentation and reflected the influence of Belgian information. In June 1959, Secretary Satterthwaite traveled to Leopoldville and met with Kasavubu. By this time, Kasavubu had modified his talk of separatism and now explained to the U.S. official that Abako would support a federalist approach. Satterthwaite believed there to be little difference between the two forms and concluded that Kasavubu had "decided to press now for the establishment of a separate Bas-Congo political entity" and divide the country. If this were to happen, the subsequent chaos, he feared, would result in a balkanization of the Congo, bring chaos to the heart of Africa, and send an open invitation to the communists to meddle in Congolese affairs.[39]

Although events in the Congo were not a daily focus for the White House, concern with trends in Africa was on the rise. In October 1959, Eisenhower sent another trusted emissary to review the situation, asking the director of the Bureau of the Budget, Maurice Stans, to tour the continent. After a stopover in Leopoldville, Stans privately remarked that many Africans "still belonged in the trees" and warned that the communists could easily "prey on the superstitions of the people."[40] He predicted that there "would probably be a great deal of bloodshed in the Congo before the political problems of the area were settled."[41] At an NSC discussion three months later, another traveler, this time the undersecretary of state for political affairs, Livingston Merchant, reinforced this message and characterized the picture in the Congo as "confused, difficult and fragmented."[42]

In light of these forebodings, and its own disinterest in Africa in general, the Eisenhower administration kept its involvement at a minimum. But it was becoming increasingly hard to do so. In August 1959, the Belgian governor-general in the Congo, Henrik Cornélis, approached the U.S. embassy with a request for $40 million a year from the Development Loan Fund to promote development in the Congo. The U.S. consul in Leopoldville warned Cornélis that new aid appropriations would be contingent on Belgian promises to be "more candid" about its goals in the Congo than in the past. Belgium's search for new sources of American aid would dull some of their complaints about American activities in the Congo but accomplished little else.[43] For now, the Eisenhower administration tried to discourage Brussels' requests for aid.

Belgium was itself very much divided over the Congo. Prime Minister Eyskens led a weak coalition of Christian Socialist and Liberal parties that fought bitterly over the pace of decolonization. When the liberal minister of the Congo, Maurice Van Hemmelrijck, took steps to speed up granting measures of self-rule in the Congo, cabinet protests were backed by the king, and Van Hemmelrijck was forced to resign in September 1959. The new minister, August de Schryver, halted much of Van Hemmelrijck's legislation, and relations with the Congolese deteriorated.[44]

Problems in the Congo mounted. Upon learning of the reversals in reform, Lumumba demanded negotiations for immediate independence. Riots erupted in October in Stanleyville and Kasai Province and resulted in at least another twenty-six African deaths by the official toll. Belgian officials declared Lumumba responsible and threw him in jail. They began to paint him as a communist, not because they believed he was, but primarily to increase their latitude of action against him.[45] In November and December, the riots spread to Leopoldville. The marchers protested the fact that the upcoming December regional elections were not going to be held on the basis of universal suffrage, but would be indirect, with the voters selecting electors who would then designate members to parliament. This process seemed to the Congolese yet another way for the imperialists to continue their manipulation of affairs. Abako, MNC-L, the PSA, and other parties now showed their complete opposition to any further delay in self-government by boycotting the elections.[46]

Adding to the problems, Belgian business interests fretted over the growing seditiousness of the population. Under new direction (as of 1958), UMHK began to take baby steps to prepare for the Congo's eventual independence. It financed the Confédération d'Associations Tribales du Katanga (Conakat), led by Moise Tshombe and based among the Lunda peoples. Tshombe had a privileged upbringing as a member of the Lunda royal family. He was educated at an American mission school and later worked for Belgian financial interests. Under Tshombe, Conakat adopted a platform in favor of a loose alliance of provinces. This platform was favored by UMHK and other mining interests who feared that a strongly centralized government in Leopoldville would seize more in taxes to redistribute wealth around the Congo.[47] Tshombe's association with white interests also tended to marginalize him throughout the rest of the Congo and black Africa. His only friend seemed to be Roy Welensky, the white minority leader of Northern Rhodesia who invited Katanga to join the Central African Federation.[48]

Like the rest of the Congo, Katanga was ethnically and politically fragmented. The large Baluba population of northern Katanga formed an independent political party, the Balubakat, and challenged Tshombe's control of that province.[49] The Baluba of Katanga often looked to Leopoldville for protection, while Leopoldville saw them as a useful ally against Tshombe. The Baluba peoples were split geographically between Katanga and Kasai, but those in Kasai generally supported the MNC-Kalonji branch, putting them in opposition to Lumumba.

The Belgian claim to have built a "model" colony was always as flimsy as a house of cards and was only becoming flimsier. When the riots in the Congo continued into December 1959, the Belgian Socialist Party, the third largest political party in Belgium, withdrew its support of de Schryver. This act in effect threatened to bring down the government. The impact of the mounting political crisis on Belgian prestige and finances was enough to persuade Brussels of the need to reach a compromise with the Congolese. In December, de Schryver finally agreed to a "round table" conference to discuss the future of the Congo. After more hesitation and Congolese demands, de Schryver announced that the conference would discuss the granting of independence.[50] It was increasingly apparent that the conference would not be a last glorious moment for the colonizers; instead it became a rousing cheer for their exit and suddenly opened the Congo to U.S and Soviet influence.

The Round Table Conference

The beginning of the end for Belgian colonialism came not on the battlefield, as it had for France in Indochina and Algeria, or the Dutch in Indonesia, but on the political front at the Round Table Conference in early 1960.[51] The conference began on January 27, 1960, and lasted for almost one month. Its proceedings were held at the Palais de Congrès in Brussels where the sheer number of Congolese present attracted great attention. Much has already been written about the conference and its proceedings have been published. It was a lively affair from the outset. *Time* magazine called the conference a "three-week nightmare" for the "orderly" Belgians, filled with "a mad mélange of inflammatory speeches, door-slamming walkouts, rival press conferences and angry communiqués."[52] By the time the conference ended, the Congolese had achieved almost everything they wanted. The results were stunning and the Congolese euphoric. There was one major exception: economic questions were deferred to a subsequent conference. A peek into the future would have shown that that one little deferral would threaten to undermine all that was achieved at the Round Table.

Acting as if little had changed in fifty years, the Belgian ministers prepared for the conference still believing that they could create a centralized government without Lumumba.[53] The Congolese, however, quickly took the initiative. Even before the opening of the conference, Congolese delegates, including Kasavubu, insisted that Lumumba be released from prison and brought to Brussels to attend the conference. The Belgians relented so as not to appear like they had the conference scripted from the start. Lumumba arrived in Brussels several days later displaying his wrist bandages where handcuffs had been.[54] Henri Rolin, the Socialist Party representative, chaired the conference and took a leading role in the proceedings as a way to guarantee his party's support for its outcome. This too worked in favor of the Congolese, since Rolin himself supported Congolese independence. The Congolese, at least for now firmly united, demanded that the conference not just discuss, but result in independence for the Congo. Constitutionally, it was up to the Belgian parliament to accept the outcome, so de Schryver instead promised to resign as minister of the Congo if parliament rejected the results. Looking for a reason to safeguard his reputation should the conference fail, which was still a distinct possibility, Kasavubu rejected de Schryver's promise and walked out of the proceedings. The rest of the Congolese delegates agreed to the promise and then demanded that a date be set for independence. Again, the Belgians could not come up with any other compromise and conceded. Independence was set for June 30, 1960, less than six months away.

The hemorrhaging did not stop there. The Belgians still planned to keep final control of defense, finance, and foreign affairs, and expected the Congolese to agree to some form of continued guardianship. Not surprisingly, all the major Congolese participants, except Tshombe, objected. So did Rolin. After

Rolin threatened to walk out, the Eyskens government agreed to grant the Congolese full political powers.[55] Still, the Belgians believed that they could keep control, even if informally. That last expectation, however, was in stark contrast to reality.

The conference then moved on to the formal business of outlining the future form of the Congolese government. It created a government based on a federal model, with a legislature composed of a Chamber of Representatives and a Senate. National elections to the legislature were scheduled for May 1960. The two houses would then draw up a constitution (loosely known as the Loi Fondamentale, or Basic Law) and decide on a chief of state.[56] Another round table conference was planned for April to address all economic issues. Last, and fatefully as it would turn out, Belgian and Congolese leaders pledged to sign a treaty of friendship.[57] The proceedings of the conference and the nature of discussions made it apparent that the Belgians and the Congolese were finding it almost impossible to cooperate.

The conference also accentuated the growing separation between the policy of the Belgian government and that of the king. Given his past position on the Congo, the king could not have liked the results of the conference. Two days before the end of the Round Table, the king approved the establishment of a Crown Council, which he would call together at critical moments during the crisis. Little is known about the Crown Council, and what is known comes from oral testimony rather than documents. What we now know, however, is that King Baudouin played a greater role in managing Congo affairs than previously understood.[58]

By 1960, Belgium could no longer keep the Congo isolated. With independence at hand, the Congolese leaders increasingly turned to both the United States and the Soviet Union for moral and financial support. Excited by their new international freedoms, the Congolese yet remained wary of the negative effects of the Cold War. The Cold War did not cause the division of the country, which had obviously slipped down that slope long before independence, but it certainly raised domestic and international tensions and encouraged the secession that did come about. Given the superpowers' policy revisions and growing interest in the Congo, it is not surprising that they were soon on a collision course there.

3. Collision Course: The Superpowers in the Congo

In early 1960, both Washington and Moscow decided to review their African foreign policies. The timing was not coincidental. The year 1960 had been designated the "Year of Africa," with seventeen countries preparing for independence. Events in the Congo emphasized that it would not be an easy year. With Africa now opening up, the question arose of precisely how the Cold War would move into the continent. In its rawest form, both superpowers wanted as many allies as possible in the Cold War, and would compete strongly for the allegiance of any newly independent African state. This set them on a collision course. Yet as always with Africa, there was a reluctance to go too far. The problems left by imperialism were just too deep, the continent too uncertain, and the potential advantages too unknown. Superimposed onto the North–South history, the Cold War paradigm was always an awkward fit.

Moscow's New Course

In January 1960, just as the Round Table Conference was convening in Brussels, the Kremlin agreed to "considerably expand" its relations with African peoples to help them in their struggle for national liberation. This expansion took place along familiar lines and would include academic and political exchanges, the signing of cultural treaties with Ethiopia, Ghana, Liberia, and Sudan, and improved radio broadcasts across the continent.[1] Along with the new emphasis on cultural connections came a new systematic reporting devoted to events in Africa. The Congo was an early beneficiary of this new approach.

The Kremlin gave public notice to its new course by publishing an article in the major scholarly journal, *Mirovaia ekonomika i mezhdunarodnie otnosheniia* (The world economy and international relations), written by a leading member of the Belgian Communist Party (BCP), Albert de Coninck. De Coninck summarized how the BCP had helped spread communist ideas and literature among the Congolese, which had in turn helped to advance its national liberation movement. He specifically applauded the efforts of Gaston Moulin, the only Communist Party deputy in the Belgian parliament, to demand an end to political repression in the Congo, including restrictions on trade union activity. De Coninck ended his article by calling on his readers to help the Congo fight for democracy and socialism in the heart of Africa.[2]

The Soviet Union relied heavily on the BCP for information on the Congo. The BCP was the only party in Brussels to support the colony's independence, and as early as 1951 began to establish a presence there. The BCP's support of Congolese independence increased its prestige among the Congolese and served it well as the linchpin with Moscow. Still, its work was difficult. The BCP had been lobbying the Soviet Union for years to increase its aid to the Congo, but with little success. Seeking to boost the Kremlin's interest in the Congo, BCP secretary Ernest Burnelle attended the Twenty-First Party Congress in 1959. Burnelle persuaded Khrushchev to allow a handful of Congolese students to study in the Soviet Union, but that is all.[3]

At last by 1960 the level of interaction was increasing. Key personalities in the BCP, such as Albert de Coninck and lawyer Jean Terfve, now regularly facilitated Soviet contacts with the Congolese. De Coninck and Terfve advised the Soviet Embassy secretary in Belgium, B. A. Savinov, who reported directly to the Central Committee on events in the Congo. De Coninck strongly encouraged Savinov to meet with the Congolese who were in Brussels for the Round Table Conference and also arranged for most of those meetings. Terfve's role as an adviser to Anicet Kashamura, a leading Congolese activist from Kivu Province and president of the leftist political party Centre de Regroupement Africain (Cerea), was the only way the small BCP would have access to the Round Table Conference, but it was an important opening for the communists.

Savinov listened carefully to BCP recommendations, but he naturally reformulated them for the Kremlin. He certainly overemphasized the importance of the workers in the context of Congolese politics. His reports on the growing interest in the Marxist-Leninist movement were more realistic than those of his sources but were still exaggerated.[4] Despite these positive developments, Savinov found that the Kremlin had some communist competition. He discovered that China had already established relations with the Congolese perhaps as much as a year earlier. Worse, the Chinese were filling Congolese ears with messages about their own experience with communism in a peasant society. China, he reported, had already invited the leaders of Abako to visit the

People's Republic of China. In response, the Soviet Union quickly matched the invitation.[5]

The Chinese were nimbly trying to establish themselves as better suited to transforming peasant societies than their counterparts in Moscow. Alphonse Nguvulu, president of the Parti du Peuple, told Savinov that the Congolese leftists were "very much interested in the experience of building socialism in the USSR and . . . other countries of the socialist camp, especially China." Nguvulu believed the Congo "had much in common with China and the experience of the CCP would help them very much in the building of socialism."[6] With these words, the damage was done, and Nguvulu would never be well received by the Soviet Union.

Reports from Savinov returned often to the growing interest in Marxist-Leninist organizations among the Congolese. The reports were well founded but cautious. On February 11, de Coninck invited Savinov to meet with BCP deputy Gaston Moulin, Henri Kasongo of the Fédération Générale du Congo, and two other representatives from the Parti du Peuple. The group assembled in Moulin's apartment and discussed the prospects for communism in the Congo. Kasongo talked about his proposed new united party based on the fundamentals of Marxism. He told Savinov that the Fédération Générale, Cerea, and the PSA had agreed to join his new party. De Coninck and Moulin seconded his requests for material aid from the Soviet Union.[7] At first Savinov thought Kasongo "created the impression of a mature political official of leftist democratic tendencies."[8] Within days Savinov learned that Cerea and the Fédération Générale were making plans to join the expanded Abako cartel, and since the latter was distrusted by the Soviet Union, this was hardly a step forward in Savinov's eyes.[9] The disappointment of this development would be repeated, but the Soviet Union did little itself to push forward this most recent formation of a Marxist-Leninist party.

Nguvulu tried hard to appeal to the Soviet Union, despite his gaffe on China. His Parti du Peuple called for the socialization of big business, and he himself talked about establishing a Marxist party in the Congo that would support the nationalization of property. The Congolese, Nguvulu claimed, are "close in spirit to the Soviet Union" and socialism is "the moving force of future progress in Africa."[10] Savinov, however, criticized Nguvulu for lacking a certain consistency and sent mixed reviews about him to Moscow. On the plus side, Savinov wrote, "he [Nguvulu] openly curses socialists and appears to hold a Marxist, communist ideology" and "he eagerly supports communications with our Belgian [communist] contacts." On the minus side, Savinov feared Nguvulu had fallen under the influences of social democracy. Nguvulu "does not have a clear understanding of the communist movement," he warned.[11]

Nguvulu was not alone. Many of the Congolese, Savinov told his superiors, seemed to be swept away with "social-democratic ideology."[12] Nguvulu's and others' poor understanding of Marxism probably did not surprise Savinov or the Kremlin. What is notable is the persistence of Savinov's reporting on this topic and the importance that Moscow placed on a united, socialist-leaning or Marxist party.

Despite its flirtations with the Congolese to date, the Kremlin held back when it came to another meeting with Lumumba. Terfve urged Savinov that the Soviet Union really should meet openly with Congolese leaders, including Lumumba and others. He suggested a cocktail party at the Soviet Embassy in Brussels for all the Congolese leaders who had gathered for the Round Table Conference. Savinov used Terfve's arguments to suggest to his superiors in Moscow that this would "emphasize our general sympathy with the Congolese people" and distract attention away from any one specific meeting. The winds of caution prevailed. Savinov was authorized to set up a meeting with Lumumba, but not in a public venue. He explained to Terfve that the Soviet Union "did not want to complicate the position of the Congolese representatives and give the reactionary press a reason for all sorts of slanderous attacks both against us and against the Congolese" if there were to be a public assembly.[13]

Savinov's tête-à-tête with Lumumba took place four days later, on February 15. The Soviet representative anticipated the importance of the meeting and opened with a flattering reception for Lumumba.[14] Lumumba himself came prepared with an eloquent plea for Soviet aid. The need for funds was "acute and urgent," he emphasized. Lumumba alluded to the "convention nationale," a group of smaller parties that had agreed to form a united party on the basis of Marxist doctrine. By now the promise sounded all too familiar to Savinov. He asked for proof of the widespread interest in Lumumba's new united party. Lumumba told him that Anicet Kashamura would lead the party's propaganda department. Kashamura enjoyed great prestige among Soviet officials and was making plans to study in the Soviet Union. "If this is true," wrote Savinov in a report to Moscow about Kashamura's involvement, "then it makes sense to regard such a combination [i.e., the convention nationale] as a positive development since the MNC, led by Lumumba, is the largest political movement in the Congo. Lumumba enjoys enormous popularity and the possibility is not excluded that he will be one of the main contenders for the post of premier or president of the Congolese state."[15] Talk about the united Marxist party in part masked the larger issue of whom to support. The MNC, Savinov seemed to be saying, could be supported because of its popularity and the involvement of a few pro-Soviet members, but this was no guarantee that Lumumba would be a pliable ally.

Savinov in fact had doubts that Lumumba would ever establish a Marxist party. Perhaps the hidden reasons for Savinov's view were more than just a general ambivalence toward the Congo, but originated with de Coninck's own suspicion that Lumumba had taken aid from the Americans. De Coninck revealed this news to Savinov just days before his meeting with Lumumba.[16] Savinov continued to find evidence that Lumumba might return to the Congo to collaborate with the proimperialist nationalists. When he had a chance to guarantee himself a position of power and support a provisional government, Savinov complained, Lumumba did not. Lumumba told Savinov that the Abako leader was seeking contact with him. Savinov wrote that according to Lumumba, "the fact that Kasavubu needs an alliance with him [Lumumba], . . . means that he [Kasavubu] needs to leave the confines of ethnic groupings . . . and break onto the national scene."[17] The Soviet Union was not likely to be impressed by an alliance with Kasavubu, whom by now they fully distrusted. Savinov's ambivalence toward Lumumba could only contribute to the general ambivalence already prevalent in the Kremlin. Lumumba after all was still straddling both sides of the Cold War divide, and any commitment to him might risk precious resources and even more precious prestige in Africa, were any alliance or association to miscarry.

The Economic Round Table: A Silent Bombshell

The Economic Round Table Conference in April reinforced the Kremlin's caution. As the Congolese rushed home after the first Round Table Conference to prepare for the election campaign, they directed young Congolese university graduates in Belgium to fill in as temporary representatives at the economic conference.[18] Economic problems ran deep and ranged from the need to stop the outflow of capital to stabilizing the state's growing debt. These, however, were not the focus of the conference. The real discussions went on among the Belgians themselves, guided by the members of the National Bank of Belgium, who devised a series of sophisticated bookkeeping techniques to protect investors. On June 23, Belgium dissolved the Comité Spécial du Katanga, a parent company of UMHK, and gave one-third of its assets to a new shareholder (the Compagnie du Katanga). The other two-thirds were to be transferred to the Congo Portfolio and eventually to be controlled by the Congolese government. The Portfolio, however, was saddled with debt and deprived the Congo government of a controlling interest in UMHK. UMHK now became a Belgian-registered company and could avoid disadvantageous Congolese laws.[19] Although the Economic Round Table has long been overlooked, Belgian backroom dealing during the conference represented a sharp attack on Congolese independence and well-being. This outcome shows that Belgian intentions were nothing less than to retain profits even if this meant fully undermining Congolese sovereignty.

The Soviet Embassy followed the economic conference closely. It was well known that the Congolese did not wish to adopt any formal resolutions, but Belgium's precise activities were unknown. Savinov's discussions with Terfve and de Coninck reinforced the Soviet suspicion that the Economic Round Table Conference was a smokescreen designed to mask what were in fact traditional imperialist ambitions.[20] The brothers and political activists Philippe and Thomas Kanza also told Soviet Embassy officials that all conference decisions would be reviewed by the Congolese leaders, but they were nonetheless braced for negative results. Their Soviet counterparts agreed and recognized that "sharp" discussions about economic questions, including the future of Belgian capital in the Congo, would continue long after the meeting.[21]

For many reasons, Washington also should have been alarmed by the conference or at least the obvious Belgian maneuvering, but apparently U.S. officials were not. American policymakers seemed to ignore the conference and did not concern itself with Belgian economic restructuring activities in the Congo. They, like the Congolese, were waiting for independence to sort things out. Perhaps they believed that independence would mean a fresh start, although the historical record showed that this was rare. The United States long wanted greater access to the Congo, including more economic freedom, and its failure to pay more attention to the conference or its related activities was a clear oversight.

Steering to the (American) Right

Just as was the case for the Soviet Union, the United States found itself with few direct contacts in the Congo in the months before its independence. The U.S. ambassador in Brussels, William Burden, was instrumental in recommending that the United States take a more active role in encouraging the political and economic stability of the Congo.[22] Burden was a wealthy New Yorker and former Wall Street executive who maintained interests in American Metal Climax (AMAX), which invested in Rhodesian copper (in Gibbs's terminology, a pro-Katangan, pro-Belgian stance). His basic friendliness toward Belgium certainly would have made his recommendations easier to accept.

Neither the State Department nor the White House was ready for Burden's initiative or subsequent steps to increase contacts with the Congolese. Undersecretary of State Douglas Dillon approved Burden's request to seek Belgian approval of several meetings with the Congolese while the latter were in Brussels for the Round Table Conference.[23] Dillon cautioned Burden, however, that cooperation with Belgium was the "best, if not only, means of influencing [the] future independent Congo." Dillon worried about European resentment of the United States. Nor did he want to be faced with an impossible "shopping list" request for aid from soon-to-be-independent colonies like the Congo.[24] He nevertheless agreed that Burden should expand his contacts and the U.S. ambassador was finally able to set up a meeting with Lumumba for February 25. Curiously the meeting was delayed by Lumumba, who claimed a hectic conference schedule.

Burden painted a complex picture of Lumumba. The ambassador wrote that Lumumba maintained a "fundamental friendliness toward Belgium." He (Lumumba) "talked a very good game indeed" about the "very bad" influences of communism, but at the same time Burden also suspected that Lumumba had accepted financial support from communist sources. Burden welcomed Lumumba's pledge to protect foreign investment in the Congo, although he was somewhat disappointed that Lumumba did not mention guarantees for specific investment projects, a stand that was seen as necessary for a better U.S. economic footing in the Congo. Nevertheless, Burden left the meeting with the impression that Lumumba had a "highly articulate, sophisticated, subtle and unprincipled intelligence." Lumumba was "not quite as naive as might be expected," Burden concluded, and "would probably go far in spite of the fact that almost nobody trusts him; who is certainly for sale, but only on his own terms."[25] Burden's characterization of Lumumba, although not effuse with praise, gives the impression of shrewdness and one who would certainly play one superpower off against the other to get what he wanted. Despite this, Burden recommended that Lumumba be invited to the United States that coming March.

The ambiguity toward Lumumba, however, did not last long. Intelligence gathering from the U.S. Embassy in Brussels concentrated on Lumumba's communist connections. Lawrence Devlin, a CIA officer attached to the embassy, met separately with Albert Kalonji and Victor Nendaka after the Round Table Conference. Nendaka claimed to have resigned from the MNC-L because he learned that Lumumba was accepting substantial aid from the communists, including the Soviet Union and the Belgian Communist Party. He declined to show any hard evidence in support of his charges.[26] Criticisms of Lumumba would percolate with Devlin and others not because they believed Lumumba was a communist at heart, but because they showed his corruption tendencies. Americans were also meeting with other Congolese who could have offered compromising information about Lumumba. At a reception given by Burden for the Congolese, Devlin claims to have met Mobutu, very briefly, for the first and only time before independence. Mobutu had begun his career in the Force Publique, rising to sergeant major, the highest level open to an African. He left in 1956 to work as a reporter for *L'Avenir* and later *Actualités Africaines*. It has long been suspected, however, that Mobutu was already a Belgian informant.[27]

After the Round Table, Ambassador Burden wanted a firsthand look at the Congo and traveled there at the end of March. In his report, Burden immediately recommended that the United States increase aid to the Congo. Belgian businessmen had been returning home in large numbers, taking their capital investments and leaving the Congo in dire straits. Eyskens had recognized the problem and had petitioned the United States for more aid, but not surprisingly had found little enthusiasm in Washington. The ambassador now emphasized the impact that the Belgian withdrawal would have on the Cold War. The Congo was on the brink of economic disaster, Burden said, with the "real possibility" that it would "start its life as an independent nation with a completely empty till and heavy debts." He recommended that the United States have an ambassador in the Congo promptly on July 1, since the Soviet Union would have its ambassador on site by that date. He also suggested that $5 million from the president's Contingency Fund be set aside for the Congo to help subsidize such projects as scholarships, training programs, communications, and radio broadcasts.[28]

With independence looming, the State Department was also increasing its contacts with the Congolese. In March, Joseph Ngalula visited the United States as the first Congolese participant in the State Department's International Education Exchange Service. Ngalula was a member of the MNC, an original signatory of the *Conscience Africaine* manifesto, and editor of the weekly *Présence Congolaise*.[29] These contacts, although little is known about them, seem to have done little to calm the concerns of U.S. officials about growing Congolese radicalism.[30] A number of Congolese anxiously came to the United States only to see the deep racial problems there and subsequently gravitated toward more radical beliefs. It was not long before Washington saw these travels as "counterproductive" in the words of a former diplomat and expert on the Congo, and began to discourage them altogether.[31]

By May, on the eve of the national elections in the Congo, the State Department remained concerned about radicalization in the Congo. Satterthwaite proposed using moderate nationalism as a tool against its radical variant. In April 1960, he instructed the U.S. ambassador to Ghana, Wilson Flake, to "encourage Nkrumah" to increase "[his] influence on Congolese even though this may mean expansion of Nkrumah-type extreme anticolonialism and Pan-Africanism" as a less evil alternative.[32] The U.S. Embassy in Brussels was appalled at this startling recommendation. Opinion there also had been hardening, but the focus was more clearly against Lumumba, paralleling Belgian fears of Lumumba's growing popularity during the election campaign. An embassy telegram to Washington warned that only Lumumba would benefit from this course and possibly emerge more strongly in the upcoming elections.[33]

Despite the urging of many in his administration that Eisenhower take more interest in the Congo and devote more money to its economic development, the president turned a deaf ear. His fiscal conservatism prevailed and instead he thought the colonizers should be the ones to adopt a more enlightened policy. He continued with his new get-tough policy outlined in March 1960, and instructed administration officials to convince the European imperialists "as hard as possible to give as much assistance as they could" to their colonies with the idea that then "we would take up the slack." Along with the secretary of the Treasury, Robert B. Anderson, Bureau of the Budget director Maurice Stans, NSC secretaries Marion Boggs and James S. Lay, and special assistant Gordon Gray, Eisenhower preferred to limit U.S. economic aid. For now this would discourage the Europeans from coming hat in hand to request more money in support of their colonies. Anderson argued that "it was more important to the Free World for the United States to maintain a sound position as the world's reserve banker than it was for the [United States] to give a billion or so more in assistance."[34]

Not everyone agreed. Vice President Nixon, the new secretary of state, Christian Herter (after Dulles had resigned due to illness in April 1959), Undersecretary Dillon, and Chief of Naval Operations Admiral Arleigh Burke wanted to retain, and possibly increase, the current levels of aid. Joseph Satterthwaite argued that economic influence translated into political influence and he also wanted to see more economic aid. But even a memorandum from Dillon on the subject chided Satterthwaite to tone down his views on economic aid to Africa and bring them more in line with the White House.[35] For the time being, supplying funds for economic development was not a priority in Africa, even among many of its proponents.

Just as the administration was deciding to become tougher with its allies, Belgium renewed a six-month-old request for U.S. cooperation in a joint economic assistance program for the Congo. The White House briskly rejected the request and privately became more disdainful of the Belgian commitment and ability to keep the Congo in the Western camp and keep their toes to the Cold War line.[36] Officials were tiring of the short Belgian leash on Americans in the Congo and were unenthusiastic about a joint economic assistance program that was more designed to keep a watch on their activity than contribute to development or protect Cold War interests.

All this new thinking came at a time when American economic interests in the Congo were not large. The American share of the Congo market had dropped from 1957 to 1959 to roughly 15 percent of total imports, down from the 20 percent or more of the market since 1950.[37] By 1960, *Time* magazine reported that the biggest single U.S. investment was the Ryan and Guggenheim groups' 25 percent share in Forminière, and the Rockefeller share of roughly $3 million in Congolese mining and textile production. That left the total U.S. share of all Congo investment somewhere between 1 and 2 percent.[38]

The uncertainty of any investment or development aid after the results of the Round Table Conference only confounded matters. Eisenhower logically did not want to pour money into a region where private American interest was so small. And with no clear picture of who would be controlling the economy after independence, he was reluctant to commit resources to the region. At this stage, Eisenhower even wondered about the very future of the Congo itself since, he said, it had no seaports (forgetting about the narrow outlet provided by the port of Matadi).[39] Although more a reflective statement rather than a policy directive, it nevertheless gave an indication of his ambivalence.

A Contentious Election

After the Round Table Conference, the Congolese participants returned home to prepare for elections. They were optimistic about their future despite the warning signs of difficult relations with Belgium and the growing ideological differences among themselves. They were also optimistic about their ability to attract superpower aid and support for their independence. Their optimism was reinforced by foreign contacts that often filled their pockets with cash and their minds with promises of more support.

The election campaign itself reflected the weak organization of political parties. Despite the flurry of activity, it is fair to say that most people, especially the majority in the smaller villages, did not understand the importance of the elections or even of political independence itself.[40] Where a party's support was already strong, like the Abako in Lower Congo, the campaign was relatively easy and not very active. Only the MNC campaigned on a truly national level and worked to build alliances with other political parties or traditional leaders. MNC leaders traveled from province to province, their message blaring out of car speakers all along the way. To get their message out farther, the MNC held a series of lively meetings around the country. Lumumba showed his charisma and ability to talk to crowds. According to the foreign correspondent D'Lynn Waldron, who was in the Congo at the time, Lumumba often expressed an admiration for America, but his words rarely made it into print.[41]

The Congo attracted foreign revolutionaries like Andrée Blouin, daughter of a French explorer and a Banziri woman in Ubangi-Shari, now in the Central African Republic. Blouin arrived in Congo in January 1960 at the request of the PSA, and while on the campaign trail boasted of enrolling 45,000 women in the Feminine Movement for African Solidarity (Mouvement Feminin de la Solidarité Africaine) in Kwilu, Kwango, and Kasai. She also supported registration efforts to ensure that all Congolese had the chance to vote. Blouin was often too revolutionary and did not follow the PSA party line when talking to women (whom she saw as caught between tradition and the failures of education). But Blouin spoke French; the wife of Cleophas Kamitatu translated her message, and while "pretending to translate her words" she "was in fact reproducing the PSA's agenda."[42]

The high pitch of election politics gave voice to many rivalries. Relations between the Eyskens government and Lumumba again sharply deteriorated in the months before the May elections. To guard against the rise in tension, Brussels sent reinforcements to the bases at Kamina and Kitona. Lumumba accused Belgium of intimidation and trying to sabotage the elections. He called for new elections to be organized by a provisional government. Several small-scale riots in Stanleyville accompanied the mounting tensions.[43] Tshombe and other pro-Belgian Congolese portrayed Lumumba, Gizenga, and their allies as communists, in an effort to damage their reputation as nationalists and scare wealthy Westerners. Ethnic differences also played their role, particularly between the Baluba and Lulua. Clashes between the two groups erupted on and off in Kasai during the campaign. Kalonji in this instance charged "white elements" with fanning the flames of unrest in his province. Efforts by police to stop the violence were met with distrust. Episodes such as these showed that racial tensions were never far from the surface in any of these clashes.[44]

During the election campaign, talk of socialism in the Congo actually receded. After returning from Brussels, Nguvulu, to give an example, no longer talked about a "socialist economy" but made reference to "Bantu solidarism" and Africanization.[45] Others tried to balance their statements to have it both ways. Gizenga became more openly socialist, but at the same time said that "traditional African structures" were the foundation for the PSA.[46] Part of the problem, Philippe and Thomas Kanza frankly told Soviet Embassy officials, was that the Soviet Union was "insufficiently active" in aiding the national liberation movement and conducted its propaganda campaign in Congo poorly, while the pro-Belgian Parti National du Progrès (PNP) and other collaborationist groups benefited from Western activism.[47]

Overall, Savinov portrayed the Congolese election campaign as a missed opportunity, but missed by design. The failure of the Congolese to create a Marxist party continued to disappoint Savinov, at least as reflected in his messages to the Kremlin. The ambassador traced the slow development of a Marxist party and advised his superiors to wait for the campaign to produce stronger political unions and key political platforms before making any determinations on the future role in the Congo.[48] At the beginning of May, de Coninck told Savinov that Union leader Antoine Tshimanga planned to wait until after the national elections and greater freedom from Belgian influence to launch a Marxist party.[49] Savinov was probably not surprised, nor enamored at the delay.

After the Kanzas' warning that the Soviet Union was being cut out by Western largesse, it seems probable that the Kremlin gave at least some financial aid to the Congolese. Perhaps not coincidentally, in April 1960, the Soviet Union and China openly clashed over the idea that without the Cold War more funds would be available for development. This suggested that Moscow believed more aid would mean more influence, while Beijing did not think in such zero-sum terms.[50] The MNC, PSA, and Cerea reportedly received subsidies from Moscow and Prague, as well as Accra, Conakry, and Cairo. Given the close relationship between the MNC and the Belgian communists, who did have monies donated by Moscow, at least some indirect financial support would have been forthcoming.[51] According to historian Fritz Schatten, Lumumba's deputies made an agreement with Chou Tzu-chi of the Peking Afro-Asian Solidarity Committee to provide the MNC with campaign funds.[52] Chinese aid was still more symbolic than substantial, not surprising given China's concurrent Great Leap Forward campaign to jumpstart development and the resultant famines and food crises that would continue into 1961.

How much did foreign aid really matter? All political parties spent more than they could have raised independently, so whether traceable or not, monies were coming from somewhere. However, most outside observers at the time and since have considered the elections a fairly accurate reflection of the Congolese political cross-section, given the circumstances, Belgian pressure, and untested voting procedures.[53] For the Belgians, the extent of anti-imperialist feelings in the election was unexpected. Growing nationalism and the force of Lumumba's personality at the grassroots now made their impact clear. In the lower chamber, the MNC won 31 out of 137 seats, the most of any party, and had 10 close allies that they could count on. The PSA won 13 seats, Abako only 12 seats, and Conakat 8 seats (a slim majority from Katanga).[54]

In Katanga's provincial elections, no single party won an absolute majority. Conakat scraped out a bare plurality with twenty-five out of sixty seats, the Balubakat took a close second with twenty-three seats. To protest the inherent inequality of the party-slate system, Tshombe's rival Jason Sendwe and the

Balubakat of north Katanga decided not to attend the parliament session to elect a president and thus denied the two-thirds needed for a quorum. The vice governor-general of the Congo, André Schoeller, recommended changing the quorum rule to a simple majority (to circumvent the Baluba boycott). On June 15, a simple majority amendment was rushed through the Belgian parliament on the basis of the argument that if it was not, Katanga would be without a legal government. The amendment ensured that Tshombe would preside over Katanga. Conakat threatened to declare the independence of Katanga, citing its concern that the Baluba would ally with the MNC-Lumumba and deepen the danger of a "Lumumba-Communism" takeover.[55]

Major problems also plagued the formation of the central government. The king of Belgium was supposed to select a *formateur* who would then appoint a cabinet that needed legislative approval. The only real contender able to get a cabinet approved by parliament was Patrice Lumumba. Still thinking this might be avoidable, the Belgian minister without portfolio in charge of African affairs, Hans Ganshof van der Meersch, offered the position to Kasavubu. Belgium could do little with the numbers, and Kasavubu was unable to form a government. Lumumba swung into action, gaining the support of both Kasavubu and the parliament for the position of prime minister.[56] As agreed beforehand, Lumumba then asked Kasavubu to accept the role of president in his new government.

Lumumba announced his new government five days later. He called it a "morning in the heart of Africa" and the sun was indeed rising in the east.[57] Fourteen out of twenty-four ministers were clearly of leftist sympathy, including Antoine Gizenga, who became vice prime minister; Pierre Mulele, minister of education; and Christophe Gbenye, minister of the interior. The president of Cerea, Anicet Kashamura, became the minister of information, while Marcel Bisukiro became minister of foreign trade. Lumumba paid a price for his choices by barely being able to win parliamentary approval; only 74 votes out of a total of 137 voted for his government.[58] One of Lumumba's appointments should be mentioned, as it stood out against the rest—Joseph Mobutu as secretary of state. The marginal positions awarded to Conakat were much more marginal than Tshombe could bear and probably sealed his decision to secede from the Congo.

Reactions from Afar

The election campaign brought a government that the Soviet Union could count on as favorable, and Khrushchev could feel that time and events were once again on his side. By June, the Soviet Union was hopefully watching

Congolese politics, albeit somewhat wary of its direction. Further Belgian missteps and estrangement with the Congolese seemed likely and U.S. reluctance to criticize its ally hurt its prestige. Soviet analysts began to suspect that the United States might be caught off-guard by developments in the Congo, distracted by its jealous Belgian ally. A Soviet Embassy officer predicted increased tension in the U.S.–Belgian relationship after the Congo became independent as a result of continued Belgian attempts to restrict U.S. trade with the Congo.[59] Now seemed a perfect time for the Soviet Union to strengthen its own standing in the Congo. Newspapers in Britain reported that the Soviet Union offered economic and technical aid to the Congo to counter the U.N. aid package then under study.[60] Although there was little mention of this offer elsewhere, it showed that the Soviet Union was definitely paying close attention to what was going on in the Congo and seemed ready to act on its independence.

On June 25, the Soviet government published a statement warning that the Belgians were plotting to remove Lumumba. In defense of Lumumba, *Pravda* supported his three demands as he formed his government: full independence, preservation of the unity of the country, and the immediate withdrawal of Belgian troops still scattered in bases around the country.[61] It was their clearest public defense of Lumumba to date, and it paid off. Lumumba lived up to his promise to immediately accept Soviet representatives in the Congo. There would be no long, drawn-out negotiations as in Ghana regarding diplomatic representation, and a Soviet ambassador would attend the independence day celebrations. Soviet support of Lumumba was finally beginning to firm up, but no one knew how far it would go.

While Moscow saw advantage in Lumumba's government, Washington seemed unprepared and unsure how to respond. The Eisenhower administration watched as Belgium clumsily transferred power to the one Congolese leader, Lumumba, who seemed the most willing to welcome the communists and limit Western influence. During the election campaign the U.S. Embassy in Brussels warned of growing Soviet interest, finding that "it is inevitable Communists envisage the Congo as a fertile field of activity." The embassy recommended that the best chance to keep order in the Congo was to strengthen the Force Publique, still under Belgian command.[62] The origins of this recommendation of course could be traced directly to the Belgians, whose authorities were at that time sending 1,200 reinforcements to the 2,500 soldiers already stationed at the Kamina and Kitona bases.[63] So while Washington increasingly disliked being publicly associated with Belgian actions, and was not happy with the sloppy transfer of power, it still had no plans of its own to improve the situation.

Eisenhower was apprehensive about where the Cold War was headed in Asia and Africa. He gave what sounded like a melancholy speech during a National Security Council meeting on June 30, the very day of the Congolese independence celebrations and six months before the end of his presidency. Deputy director of intelligence General Charles Cabell had just explained that Lumumba's new government would have a leftist tinge and was recognized by Communist China and the Soviet Union. Eisenshower seemed troubled. "In the last six months or so," he said, "there has been a rash of revolutions which have overthrown governments—in Cuba, Turkey and almost in Japan." The president noted that the United States had worked hard to achieve stability, but instead has been faced with "unrest and unhappiness." Was the United States, asked the president, "stupidly pushing ahead, carrying out programs without taking into account the effects these programs might be having? . . . Perhaps . . . we could only stand by and watch" the wave of revolutions. Even he did not believe his own words. The president had recently approved a destabilization campaign against Fidel Castro and began to plan an invasion of the island led by Cuban exiles.[64] Nor could he—and he did not—stand aside when crisis exploded in the Congo. The course for collision, as incomplete as it was, was set.

4. A "Stopgap Arrangement": ONUC

On the surface, the story of the Congo at its independence is a familiar one: buoyant Congolese independence day celebrations and more violence, followed by Katanga's declaration of independence and the approval of the U.N. operation for the Congo. What makes a review of these events so interesting is the incorporation of Congolese agency and the firmness of Belgian plans to act, and act fast. In response, the international community ignored their differences and in the Security Council of the United Nations produced a precedent-setting resolution to resolve the problems tearing at the Congo's independence. Along with the various interests in the Congo, the prevalence of Cold War dynamics makes a striking impression.

Trials of Independence

On June 30, 1960, diplomats from around the world arrived at the national palace in Leopoldville to witness the transfer of power from the Belgian government to the Congolese. Former undersecretary of state Robert Murphy and ambassador-to-be Clare Timberlake represented the United States. Murphy, a longtime career diplomat, and Timberlake, a counselor at the U.S. Embassy in Bonn, were seasoned Cold Warriors. Not far away stood the Soviet delegation headed by another seasoned figure, Mirzo R. Rakhmatov, vice president of the Presidium of the Supreme Soviet. Also attending was U.N. undersecretary Ralph Bunche, an esteemed African American intellectual, diplomat, and 1950 Nobel Peace Prize winner (for his efforts in mediating an armistice between Israel and its Arab neighbors). The relatively senior level of those present was evidence of the significance that the United States and the Soviet Union attached to Congolese independence and Africa's growing role in the Cold War.

King Baudouin got the ceremonies off to a bad start with an ill-advised speech claiming to have delivered the Congo from Arab slavery while putting it on the path of modern civilization. As pompous as the speech was, referring to Leopold as a *civilisateur*, it was modified from its original reference to him as a *libérateur*. The king asked his former Congolese subjects not to let inexperience and the attraction to foreign powers—alluding to both the Soviet Union and the United States—undermine the progressive path Belgium had laid out for its colony over the last eighty years.[1]

As if he had not even heard the speech or its provocations, President Kasavubu expressed Congolese goodwill and promised to continue working with the Belgians. Prime Minister Lumumba boldly approached the lectern. He had not been scheduled to speak, but his speech made evident the layers of tension between the Belgians and Congolese during the past year. The independence of the Congo, a charismatic Lumumba reminded his audience, came as the result of a long struggle to put an end to "the humiliating slavery that had been forced upon us."[2] Lumumba's speech so offended King Baudouin that the king had to be persuaded not to walk out of the ceremonies. Robert Murphy remembered how "the veins on his [King Baudouin's] forehead stood out as indication of the violence of his feelings."[3]

Reflecting on the day's events, Ralph Bunche jotted down some notes after retiring to his room in the Stanley Hotel. He observed a rare but eerie calm, and sensed that among the Congolese there was a lack of jubilation over independence and what it meant for their future.[4] The sentiment was not a surprise to his boss, U.N. secretary-general Dag Hammarskjöld, who like many other informed observers sincerely believed that the Congolese had not been adequately prepared for independence. U.S. ambassador Murphy sent an analogous message to Washington, reporting that "if we are not here soon with enough aid the Communists will be."[5]

Almost immediately there were reports that Soviet personnel were arriving in disproportionate numbers. In an estimate based on a count of each white person disembarking from a Russian plane, there were soon two to three hundred Soviet citizens, many of them assumed to be agents of the Soviet Union's Komitet Gosudarstvennoy Bezopastnosti (KGB; Committee for State Security) in the Congo. The figure was generally accepted by U.S. officials as possible based on the number of planes, crew sizes, and support needed. The planes were carrying boxes marked by a Red Cross symbol, and later evidence confirmed suspicions that the supplies included rifles, machine guns, and ammunition. While some Soviet aid stayed in Leopoldville, some found its way to Stanleyville where Rakhmatov and others were visiting and stirring suspicions.[6]

The CIA began immediately to strengthen its own presence and intelligence network. Lawrence Devlin had been reassigned from Brussels to Leopoldville and on his way stopped in France for a short vacation when the crisis erupted. He arrived a few days after independence. Although officially an embassy secretary, it was an open secret that Devlin worked for the CIA. Devlin remembered a good working relationship with the U.S. ambassador, Clare Timberlake, or "Tim" as he knew him. His main job was to keep watch on the Soviets and to report back to CIA headquarters, independent of the embassy. Both he and Frank Carlucci, the second secretary at the embassy, were the two Americans who had the most interaction with Patrice Lumumba. They also set up a series of contacts with other Congolese friendly to the West, soon to be known as the Binza group, after a suburb in Leopoldville, a group that would provide serious opposition to Lumumba.[7]

Only forty-eight hours after independence, the optimism of the Congolese met the harsh realities of postcolonial life. The Belgians remained insensitive to the needs of the new state and continued to act as if their colonial privileges had not changed. The infamous comment scribbled on the blackboard by army chief General Émile Janssens, that "before independence = after independence," reinforced the Congolese soldiers' resentment toward their Belgian officers.[8] On July 5, the Congolese soldiers at the Thysville barracks, ninety miles south of the capital, mutinied. Lumumba tried to calm the soldiers by announcing promotions and the Africanization of the army, renamed the Armée Nationale Congolaise (ANC). At this time he also named Mobutu as army chief of staff. Lumumba's efforts made little difference, and the general disappointment continued to spread as people realized that independence ceremonies changed few of their daily realities. In a show of support for the soldiers, workers began to strike, threatening generalized chaos.[9] Even women, feeling marginalized in the independence process, began to organize, and were led, surprisingly, by Pauline Opango, Lumumba's wife. Her involvement is indicative of the fact that the protests were directed against the Belgians more than the new government itself.[10]

Despite the long and troubled years preceding the Congo's independence, a Belgian parliamentary commission in 2001 concluded that the unrest was a "surprise." Yet everyone had seemed fully aware that trouble was inevitable. King Baudouin rushed home from a vacation and asked Prime Minister Eyskens to form a government of national unity to deal with the crisis and better formulate a response. This was not the first time he made the suggestion, and as previously, it was rejected. According to the commission, the

Belgian government split in response to the crisis, not along party lines, but along bureaucratic ones, more specifically over the advantages of a diplomatic versus a military response. Foreign Minister Pierre Wigny fought for a political solution with the support of his minister for the Congo, August de Schryver, and Raymond Scheyven, minister without portfolio in charge of economic and financial affairs in the Congo and Ruanda-Urundi. The minister of defense, Arthur Gilson, with the support of Harold d'Aspremont Lynden (who would take over de Schryver's position as minister for African affairs in September), advocated a firm approach backed by military power if necessary.[11] Thus, not unlike American bureaucratic divisions, the Belgians were divided over the best form of action in the Congo, making any response difficult and controversial.

On July 9, Lumumba and Kasavubu received word that Belgium was sending reinforcements to the Congo under the pretext of restoring order and protecting its citizens.[12] After a confusing day, Lumumba and Kasavubu agreed to the help but then, without the proper guarantees forthcoming from Brussels, they became fearful of infringements on Congolese sovereignty and demanded that Belgium withdraw its forces.[13] Eyskens, Gilson, and Wigny ignored the demand and went ahead with the intervention that night. While the position of King Baudouin is not known precisely, he had long assumed that intervention would be necessary, so his support seems a foregone conclusion.[14]

The next day, July 10, Lumumba and Kasavubu realized they needed immediate help to stop Belgian intervention. Under Timberlake's advice, they sent a verbal request to Ralph Bunche asking for food aid and U.N. "technical assistance" to improve the country's security administration. Most importantly, a request for technical assistance would keep the operation within the competence of the secretary-general and away from a Security Council vote where a veto could possibly derail it.[15] But what they really wanted was immediate help responding to Belgian aggression. Timberlake himself believed it better to bring the growing number of Belgian troops under a U.N. umbrella, ward off chaos in case of a Belgian withdrawal, and "keep the [Russian] bears out of the Congo caviar" for which, Timberlake concluded, "most Americans have not yet developed a great taste."[16] His efforts were imbued with a sense of urgency, and for good reason.

The crisis escalated quickly. On July 11, Tshombe declared the independence of Katanga from the Congo. He publicly asked Belgium "to continue its technical, financial, and military support" to Katanga,[17] and privately asked for official Belgian recognition of his secession, and therefore of Katanga's independence. Brussels rejected his request for formal recognition, knowing that Katanga's independence would be opposed by the international community.[18]

Although there is no evidence that the king or the government encouraged secession, once it was a reality, they both supported it. The Belgian government told Tshombe that it wanted to help "create the conditions" for genuine independence. It recommended writing a new constitution and devising a new bank and security apparatus. Belgian troops stationed all across the Congo hastily withdrew to Katanga. The retreat was in some ways reminiscent of the French withdrawal from Guinea several years earlier. Poorly trained Belgian soldiers wrecked the police stations, destroyed communications, and damaged infrastructure.[19]

There is little doubt that the Belgian government was pushed by Société Générale and UMHK to support Katanga. UMHK supplied 80 percent of Katanga's revenues. White Belgian colonists, most of whom were tied to UMHK, supported Conakat and the secession.[20] Even the chairman of Société Générale, Paul Gillet, asked the king that the government of Belgium "not interfere" in Katanga and warned Wigny of the communist threat. Although always elusive and secretive, Gillet had earlier broken his silence to speak out against independence, saying that the Congo was "not ripe" for it.[21] UMHK claimed that it had no choice but to continue to pay Tshombe or face a shutdown of its mining operations.[22] In fact, UMHK did more than just pay Tshombe. With virtually a free hand, it organized the new state and represented it in Brussels, while recruiting Belgian scholar René Clemens to draft its new constitution. It set up the new bank and helped issue the new currency. In the months before independence, Herman Robiliart, UMHK's top executive, expressed his concern with Lumumba and received backing by d'Aspremont Lynden.[23] In the long term, however, UMHK's short-sightedness in refusing to negotiate with the central government, or playing by accepted international rules, would forever impair its ability to work with the elected or accepted leaders of the country, and would help seal its long-term fate in the Congo.

Belgium was a small country, and what everyone else thought mattered. Brussels therefore tried to defend its actions in a larger Cold War sense by claiming that Tshombe represented Western interests against the growing communist presence in the rest of the Congo. Tshombe accused the central government of "communistic intentions" and justified his opposition to Lumumba by suggesting that he used the "tactic of disruption and subversion" similar to that of the communists in establishing dictatorships in Eastern Europe and around the world.[24] Instead, Belgian officials, particularly Pierre Wigny, referred to Tshombe's goal of a "confederal Congo," or loose alliance of free states, as a solution to what they insisted was a constitutional crisis, and not one of decolonization. From this (biased) perspective, Belgian aid did not seek to shatter, but to repair.[25]

Trying to reexert sovereignty over Katanga, Kasavubu and Lumumba attempted to fly to Elizabethville to confront Tshombe, but their plane was denied landing rights.[26] On July 12, ostensibly without Lumumba's knowledge, the foreign minister, Justin Bomboko, and the vice prime minister, Antoine Gizenga, petitioned U.S. ambassador Timberlake about the possibility of sending American troops to the Congo to help keep peace and order. Timberlake replied that an approach to the United Nations would probably be more successful.[27] Kasavubu and Lumumba then sent Hammarskjöld (via Bunche) a second urgent appeal for aid—this time with a major reinterpretation of events. They accused Belgium of launching an aggressive and hostile intervention and requested military aid "to protect the national territory of the Congo against the present external aggression which is a threat to international peace."[28]

The superpowers were sending signals that they would work through the United Nations, or at least would not oppose U.N. involvement. At a press conference on July 12, Eisenhower summarily ruled out the formal use of U.S. troops in the Congo, even as part of a U.N. contingent. This came despite private requests from Ambassador Timberlake that a "token force of two companies" might be necessary to stabilize the situation.[29] In a carefully measured statement from Newport, Rhode Island, the president insisted that the crisis was a problem for the United Nations, not the United States.[30] The Soviets had been quick to build their presence after independence and any direct U.S. role would, Secretary of State Herter warned, further raise the risks of confrontation, and was something the United States wanted to avoid.[31] The public statements combined to challenge the Soviet Union to work through the United Nations.

Khrushchev was in Austria at the time and made no public comments about the brewing crisis. *Izvestia* and *Pravda*, the two main Soviet newspapers, waited a full week, until July 12, to report on the mutiny or the Belgian invasion. The belated show of support for Lumumba made it seem like Khrushchev was caught off guard, as he had been during the Suez crisis and the revolution in Cuba that brought Fidel Castro to power. Nor did Soviet policy appear to have any firm direction. *Pravda*'s correspondent, Oleg Orestov, blamed the imperialists for all the problems. Nikolai Khokhlov reported for *Izvestia* that the interparty struggle in the Congo might even change the Soviet position, and by implication Moscow's declaration of support for Lumumba.[32] To add to these criticisms, a separate Soviet statement lambasted Tshombe and called his secession "unlawful" and driven by the "selfish ends" of a small circle of capitalists.[33]

Wanting to underline the emergency and the need for the United Nations to act quickly, Kasavubu and Lumumba clarified their request twenty-four hours later. "The purpose of the aid requested," they reaffirmed, "is not to restore the internal situation in Congo but rather to protect the national territory against acts of aggression committed by Belgian metropolitan troops." If aid was not received, they would "be obliged to appeal to the Bandung Treaty powers" referring particularly to Communist China.[34] The wording suggested that they wanted to convince the world that imperialist aggression, not tribal division, was at the root of the problems in the Congo and that aggression had to be stopped as quickly as possible.

On July 13, the Belgians occupied the airport at Leopoldville, and temporarily as it turned out, extended their control beyond Katanga. Kasavubu and Lumumba on their return to Leopoldville (after being shut out of Katanga) were asked to inspect a Belgian honor guard. Lumumba exploded at the ludicrousness of the situation and refused. The pair would try to get to Stanleyville later that day, only to have to retreat again this time with the help of Larry Devlin, who commandeered a car to get them out of the airport. That seemed to be all the help the United States was offering for the moment. Frustrated with their treatment, the president and prime minister publicly appealed to Khrushchev to "follow hour-by-hour" the developments in the Congo and warned the world that they might be forced to "ask for the intervention of the Soviet Union" if the West did not stop its aggression. Their brief request ended with the claim that their lives were in danger.[35] Despite the dual signatures, Lumumba has been universally cited as the instigator who held Kasavubu hostage to his intentions.

Khrushchev responded with a press conference and public letter of his own. Now that the Soviet chairman had learned about the second Congolese request specifically referring to Belgian aggression, it became much easier to support Lumumba and U.N. involvement. Khrushchev had a prime opportunity to challenge colonialism head on and demanded that the United Nations "take immediate steps to end the aggression and restore sovereign rights" in the Congo. At a press conference on July 14, he doubted that the "fair claim" of the Congolese would receive unbiased treatment. His official statement of July 15 went even further. The government of the Congo, he said, can "be assured" that the Soviet government would render "the assistance necessary that may be required for the victory of your rightful cause." If the aggression continued, the Soviet Union would insist on "more resolute measures" both "in the United Nations and in cooperation with other peace-loving states" in support of the Congo. *Izvestia* punctuated the whole exchange by publishing it under the title "Hands Off the Congo" one day later.[36]

The international escalation of the conflict was matched by growing internal opposition to Lumumba. The Baluba in Kasai via the MNC-K, the

Bakongo in Leopoldville, the Bangala in Equateur, trade unionists (syndicalists), Abako's youth movement, and Puna, a strong civilian group of English speakers and other smaller groups now all spoke out against Lumumba.[37] The MNC-K and its leader Albert Kalonji represented the most serious threat. Two days after Lumumba's appeal to the Soviet Union, Kalonji's representative in Brussels reportedly made contact with the chief of staff of the Belgian king, although Kalonji, years later, denied this contact.[38] Kalonji blamed Lumumba for the Lulua massacre of the Baluba that happened in the wake of independence.[39] His hatred for Lumumba now ran deep and he spoke out bitterly against him from this time forward. While few of his opponents believed that Lumumba's appeal to the Soviet Union made him a communist, it allowed them a clear issue on which to center their opposition to his government and indeed all its problems.

The Stopgap Arrangement

Perhaps no one, including Dag Hammarskjöld, was ready for the crisis in the Congo as it played out. Hammarskjöld, son of a former prime minister of Sweden, had always shown savvy intelligence when it came to diplomacy. He was by all accounts athletic, artistic, aloof, and academic. He enjoyed a meteoric career in the Swedish Foreign Office, where he quickly rose to the top position. In taking over from U.N. secretary-general Trygve Lie after the latter's estrangement with Moscow and resignation in 1952, Hammarskjöld was keenly aware of the negative impacts of the Cold War.[40] Despite some serious challenges of his own with Moscow, Hammarskjöld defended the Secretariat and the diplomatic strength of its office.

In light of the soldiers' mutiny, Hammarskjöld was not quick to support U.N. involvement in the Congo.[41] Sensing that his original conception of a technical mission was now outdated by events, he would have to wait for a greater international common ground to emerge. Hammarskjöld had learned firsthand about the troubles brewing in the Congo during a visit he made to the colony in January 1960. On his return he had asked Ralph Bunche and his longtime friend Sture Linnér to travel to the Congo to find out how the United Nations might provide "technical assistance" to the newly independent state.[42] His former aide Brian Urquhart remembered Hammarskjöld's optimism in the ability of the United Nations to "be the bridge over which the former colonial powers and the United States would be able, in a completely un-colonial way, to help in the development of the independent African countries."[43] While trying to remain neutral, yet with pro-Western ideals at heart, Hammarskjöld clung to his perception that the United Nations could serve as a way to facilitate decolonization and prevent or limit a Cold War battle in the Congo (figure 4.1). The operation that eventually came about was clearly not the one he—or the Congolese—initially envisioned, but some remnants of these initial plans are evident.

Hammarskjöld's tactical pause meant that Washington had to appear to convince him to take a leading role in shaping an operation for the Congo. Eisenhower generally preferred to make his policy independent of the United Nations, as was the case in Indochina, Cuba, Lebanon, and Guatemala. In this case and for the moment, a U.N. operation served U.S. interests and avoided an independent or unilateral U.S. action.[44] Coming after successful U.N. peacekeeping at Suez, there was a new attitude in the State Department to "let Dag do it."[45] The Suez crisis had shown that U.N. peacekeeping could help keep the Cold War at bay, something for Africa that Eisenhower believed in the best interests of the United States at the time.

Security could not be left to chance. With the tone and tenor of the U.N. operation still to be decided, Eisenhower reluctantly made preparations to intervene in the Congo if necessary. The Defense Department put two companies of the 24th Infantry Division in West Germany on alert and sent the aircraft carrier U.S.S. *Wasp* to the Congo in case evacuations were necessary. Marines were aboard the carrier, but Herter told Hammarskjöld that this fact was kept "very secret" and that he "had a strong feeling" that the Congo was not the place for "white troops not speaking French."[46] With anti-imperialist sentiment at fever pitch, it was obviously prudent not to get mixed up in the wrong battle, and one brewing along racial lines at that. From this perspective, a U.N. operation also had some internal domestic benefits by minimizing the risk of putting U.S. soldiers into a situation where "the question of language and color" was potentially more explosive than it had been in Korea or now was in Vietnam and might even reverberate at home.[47]

The Belgian occupation of Katanga and the posting of U.N. troops created a thorny issue for the United States. Belgium was a close NATO ally and a strong ally in Africa. Eisenhower was aware that if Belgium perceived the United States as pushing it aside, then Brussels just might accuse Washington of its own greed and dump the problem on the United States, as had the French in Vietnam in 1954. Far from this, and unknown to Washington at the time, the Belgian cabinet concluded that the United States and its other allies should be informed that any outside intervention into Katanga would be considered a casus belli. Yet the cabinet also went on to emphasize that it would try all means to convince U.N. troops not to enter Katanga, but if they did, in the end Belgian troops would not forcefully oppose them.[48] The level of belligerence in Brussels was certainly not recognized by Washington. U.S.

Figure 4.1. Dag Saves the World (Cartoon), July 24, 1960

Source: Bill Mauldin, *St. Louis Post-Dispatch;* used with permission.

ambassador William Burden expressed exasperation in his report that Brussels was unable to give any reassuring arguments for its actions in Katanga.[49] The Cold War often muted U.S.–Belgian differences, as serious as they were. In this case, the U.N. operation would have the added benefit of tracking the Belgian intervention and put international, not just U.S., pressure on its NATO ally to cooperate.[50]

Given the fluidity of the situation, working through the United Nations had advantages for Khrushchev as well. He used the term "useful" to refer to the institution several times in his memoirs.[51] Khrushchev had an interest in strengthening the Soviet position at the United Nations, but he remained suspicious of its Western and U.S. bias. There was a safety valve in working through the Security Council, where the Soviet Union had a veto. Moreover, a political loss could be buried in the endless debates of the General Assembly if the crisis came to that. Thus, to internationalize the crisis gave the Soviet Union stature, and while it might somewhat restrict Moscow's freedom of movement, the Soviets were also protected from too much involvement and responsibility.

In supporting a U.N. operation, Khrushchev precluded a major role for China, which had been shut out of that organization in 1949. Soviet relations with China were deteriorating faster than anyone suspected. On July 14, the first deputy premier, Frol Kozlov, privately accused the Chinese of undermining the international communist movement for their own gain.[52] By the end of the month, Khrushchev recalled all Soviet experts from the People's Republic of China. The growing dispute between the two communist giants quickly reflected itself in the Congo crisis. Mao angrily let Khrushchev know that he was ready to use his position outside the United Nations to pressure the Soviet Union to offer support for the Congolese. In an official Chinese statement, Mao accused the United States of using any means available to impose its own form of imperialism, either "under the mask of a hypocrite" (that is, the United Nations) or "without any disguise" whatsoever. Mao's statement boldly linked Soviet support of the U.N. operation with American imperialism.[53] Khrushchev would counter Mao's criticism by setting the Soviet Union apart from the imperialists in the United Nations (as we will see).

A Safety Valve, Cold War Style

Despite the initial U.S. and Soviet indications that they would approve a U.N. operation in the Congo, there was still a long way to go to make this a reality. Hammarskjöld knew he would need unanimous Security Council approval for any operation to move ahead.[54] This meant a broad resolution that all permanent members of the Security Council could accept.[55] Hammarskjöld discouraged debate over the Belgian action and outlined the U.N. mission in neutral terms that avoided the Congolese request for protection against external aggression.[56] On July 14, Tunisia introduced a resolution that called on Belgium "to withdraw its troops," and authorized the secretary-general "to take the necessary steps" in consultation with the government of the Congo to provide it with military and technical assistance "until the national security forces may be able . . . to meet fully their tasks."[57] By papering over international differences, the resolution passed with eight in favor and three abstaining (Republic of China, France, and the United Kingdom). Thus was born the United Nations operation in the Congo, or ONUC. Hammarskjöld called the operation "a stop-gap arrangement" designed to forestall a larger crisis.[58] ONUC, arguably, eventually did accomplish this objective, but for the moment the crisis continued to escalate.

After some intense negotiations, the Eyskens government agreed with Hammarskjöld to "welcome" the U.N. forces in an effort to rescue some of its seriously damaged international prestige. The welcome was for appearances only, and Belgium continued to send more armed forces into Katanga. Eyskens also sent diplomat André Wendelen and a secret agent by the name of Athos to destabilize the political situation in Leopoldville. Kasavubu and Lumumba were so angry at the Belgian provocations that they broke relations with their former colonizer. The situation deteriorated to such an extent that Belgian leaders anticipated a declaration of war, but decided not to reciprocate if that happened. Belgium had already secretly agreed to support the de facto independence of Katanga with military and financial aid. Brussels argued that Katanga could serve as a base from which to reunite the Congo under an anticommunist, pro-Western government.[59] Belgian actions came dangerously close to supporting the permanent partition that Washington wanted to avoid.

Two key NATO allies, Britain and France, cringed at any precedent-setting international intervention in what they deemed a private matter of decolonization. British prime minister Harold Macmillan publicly supported the U.N. operation, but not the use of force against Katanga or any precedents that might be set for the Rhodesians.[60] In contrast, France strictly opposed ONUC as interference in colonial affairs. Nevertheless, De Gaulle suppressed his reservations. Since Belgium had agreed to accept the resolution, the British and the French abstained from the Security Council vote, thereby acceding to ONUC.[61] Canada (and the other rotating members of the Security Council) supported the intervention in the hopes that the United Nations could help avoid a Cold War battle in Africa.[62]

The Soviet Union voted for the resolution, but quickly established independence from it. Soviet representatives were anxious to point out that the resolution was disappointing in not mandating a Belgian troop withdrawal or putting a time frame on that withdrawal. On July 14, Soviet foreign minister Andrei Gromyko delivered a note to the U.S. and Belgian representatives protesting the Belgian violation of the territorial integrity and political independence of the Congo.[63] At the United Nations, Arkady Sobolev demanded the "immediate" withdrawal of Belgian troops and a formal condemnation of Belgian "armed aggression." He also suggested limiting the U.N. troops to those from African states.[64] Since there were few independent African states able to commit forces, this would have skewed contributions by the neutral, or nonaligned, states. The U.S. representative to the United Nations, Henry Cabot Lodge, responded to the Soviet demands by insisting that Belgian troop withdrawal was necessary only after the restoration of order.[65] American excuses for Belgium seemed outside the spirit of the resolution and show that in this respect Washington was not ready to diverge too far from its ally.

The Kremlin was convinced at this point that the United States fully intended to support the independence of Katanga as the only way to reserve for itself the minerals of that province.[66] Khrushchev believed that U.S. support of Katanga was greater than it actually was, and this constrained his own decisions. He made no mention of any specific actions to support the Leopoldville government, but left the door open for greater cooperation, if only other African and Asian states would take a stronger stand against imperialism. For now the Soviet Union continued to shield itself behind the United Nations.[67]

With the U.N. forces rapidly preparing to arrive in the Congo, the Eisenhower administration remained confident that the crisis was under control (figure 4.2). Khrushchev, after all, had spoken out against the West, but had not really done anything, and the chance that he would seemed small.[68] During preliminary National Security Council discussions, CIA director Allen Dulles described Lumumba as "especially anti-Western" but did not indicate any need for immediate action.[69] Later that day Herter met with Belgian ambassador Louis Scheyven and tried to find out if there was any real way the Soviets could intervene. Scheyven tried, but could not convince him that the Soviets could move in by air. Herter knew that the U.S.S. *Wasp* would be at Matadi before the Soviets could get there anyway. The secretary did, however, agree with Scheyven that Lumumba had moved demonstrably closer to the Soviet Union.[70]

Meanwhile, Lumumba was still not satisfied that enough was being done. On July 17, Lumumba, again nominally with Kasavubu, handed Bunche an ultimatum stating that if "the United Nations is unable to discharge the mission which we have entrusted to it" (i.e., to get the Belgian troops out of the Congo) then they "may be obliged to call upon the Soviet Union to intervene." He now attached a seventy-two-hour time frame with which to complete the withdrawal.[71] In a radio address to the country, Lumumba tried to guard against criticism of his appeal to the Soviet Union. "We want nothing to do with imported doctrines," he asserted, being interested only in building a strong Congo "so as to liberate the rest of Africa."[72]

The ultimatum raised hackles in Washington. Herter rushed to Rhode Island to consult with the president, where the two studied possible U.S. options to expedite the ONUC deployment. A potential scenario involved U.S. protection of Belgian civilians before handing the situation over to the United Nations. In reviewing the implications of this activity, Eisenhower worried about whether the United Nations "was getting into something that it could not bring to a conclusion."[73] For now, the immediate concern was to limit

Figure 4.2. United Nations Forces in the Congo, July 27, 1960

Source: United Nations photograph.

Soviet involvement without extending the U.S. commitment much further. The two also began thinking about the need to get rid of Lumumba and had clearly hardened their attitude against him.

U.N. leaders were equally indignant at the ultimatum. In Leopoldville, Ralph Bunche told the "stunned" Congolese foreign minister Justin Bomboko and Thomas Kanza, minister delegate to the United Nations, that his organization did not accept ultimatums.[74] Bunche then wrote Hammarskjöld that he could "sit on" Lumumba for a short time and try to persuade him to give ONUC more time to restore order in the Congo. Hammarskjöld knew he would have to get U.N. troops into the Congo quickly if he was to have any chance at controlling the situation.[75] Careful to appear neutral, he asked Britain, the United States, and the Soviet Union to provide aircraft to transport ONUC troops to the Congo. The United States was the only one in a position to help, and it did without much fanfare.[76] Foreign Minister Gromyko mildly protested the U.S. logistical support to highlight the Western dependence on the United Nations but privately had not opposed the U.S. airlift.[77]

Khrushchev tried to make the best of the weaker state of the Soviet position. He remained reluctant to support Lumumba and the MNC outright, which still seemed "extremely unstable" according to Soviet observers.[78] Khrushchev chose instead to announce an increase in economic and humanitarian aid in contrast to the U.S. military contribution to ONUC. Hammarskjöld publicly expressed his appreciation for the aid but privately he sensed Khrushchev was trying to sabotage the U.N.'s own program.[79] Although the aid was supposed to be delivered through U.N. channels, the small amount actually sent was done so independently.[80] On July 16, the Soviet Union pledged 2.5 million rubles in economic aid and also agreed to send 10,000 tons of food to the Congo. One of the ships full of wheat later docked at Matadi, but had to be reloaded and a place found for it to be milled elsewhere since the Congo did not have a mill of its own.[81] The entire affair showed the Soviets still had a lot to learn.

Khrushchev kept the pressure on the United Nations by requesting a second Security Council session for July 20. He then sent the Soviet deputy foreign minister and representative at the United Nations, Vasili Kuznetsov, and Anatoly Dobrynin, a rising star in the Ministry of Foreign Affairs, to tell Hammarskjöld that the Soviet Union intended to back Lumumba's demand for an immediate Belgian withdrawal.[82] The new resolution on the Congo, adopted on July 22, did not go as far as the Soviets pushed for, but called on the Belgian government to "speedily" withdraw its troops and authorized the secretary-general to "take all necessary action to this effect." It included a clause asking all states to refrain from independent intervention.[83] Kuznetsov excused the Soviet Union from adhering to this clause, saying that any aid that helped the central government restore law and order could not be considered an impediment.[84] *Izvestia* toughened the message by adding that Hammarskjöld's failure to act against the Belgian troops would be contrary to the intent of the resolution.[85]

Ambassador Lodge responded right away to these intimidations. He forcefully warned the Soviet Union against unilateral intervention. "We will do whatever may be necessary to prevent the intrusion of any military forces not requested by the United Nations." Such forces, he said, "would be in defiance of the United Nations."[86] Lodge did not name names, but the message was clear to all who heard. But his statement, phrased so generally, also raised uncomfortable questions about Belgium's position.

For the time being, Belgium continued to act unilaterally and unopposed in Katanga and contrary to the U.N. operation. After a trip to Katanga, Eyskens' deputy, Harold d'Aspremont Lynden, proposed a technical mission to the province, which would become known as Mistebel. D'Aspremont Lynden became head of Mistebel, which was created on July 20 to "coordinate Belgian action in Katanga." The decision for d'Aspremont Lynden was made "in the absence and against the wishes of" Foreign Minister Wigny, who was then in New York, and was probably done at the urging of the king. It deepened the division between those supporting a diplomatic versus a military option. In protest, Wigny presented his resignation, but Eyskens refused it. The July 22 resolution and what to do about Katanga also further divided the government from the king, who was now convinced that Katanga was somehow his "last card" to save the Congo.[87] Exactly how much Washington knew about the seriousness of these divisions or the intentions to support Katanga is unclear, and its failure to probe further to find out is indicative that it was still leaving Belgium to find a solution.

Up until this point, the United Nations option seemed to be working at least to all appearances. ONUC troops had arrived in the Congo just two days after the first resolution was adopted, thanks in large part to the U.S. airlift. U.N. troops in the Congo numbered an amazing 11,000 by the end of July. By mid-August, the number would surpass 14,500. The troops were primarily from African states, the largest contingents from Morocco, Ghana, and Tunisia, with more than 2,000 each, and Ethiopia sent 1,800 troops. Ireland and Sweden also sent troops (about 600 each).[88] Still, ONUC operated without a formal agreement with the Congolese government. Belgian actions continued to undermine true cooperation or even communication between Elizabethville and Leopoldville. The United States and the Soviet Union were at odds over interpretation of the resolution, and their differences at least threatened to bring about a direct intervention. If ONUC can be viewed as a safety valve, its sheer size can be considered proportional to the seriousness of the crisis and the danger it brought to the world. The real question was whether it was enough to contain the crisis.

5. A "Castro or Worse": Lumumba in Charge

Lumumba was a man in a hurry. He had no reason to be complacent about the continued Belgian presence in the Congo. He distrusted the Belgians, and the latter's close alliance with the United States was troubling. His ultimatums had only exacerbated relations with the Eisenhower administration. As a result, Lumumba found himself pushed further and further into the arms of the Soviet Union, a useful friend, but one that had not come through with much aid or support. Still believing, naively, that he could balance U.S. and Soviet interests to his advantage, Lumumba struck upon another bold plan: He would go to the United States himself and convince Washington that all he wanted for the Congo was its independence and some small help to make this a reality.

Opposing Lumumba

As far as Washington was concerned, Lumumba was not just another African revolutionary who mixed nationalism and socialism. His actions, especially the July 17 ultimatum, symbolized the aggressive influence of communism and the willingness of the Soviet Union to exploit African inexperience. Even more foreboding for Washington, Lumumba had promised to help spread independence to all of Africa. Chaos in Africa now struck at the core of the U.S. postwar alliance with the European imperial regimes. The whole idea of gradual decolonization was to guide Africa toward peaceful independence; without that, there was little justification for close cooperation with the imperialists. Underlying U.S. policy was the assumption that if the imperialists could not get it right, then America would have to step in to make sure that the communists were kept out of Africa.

In Washington on July 21, the National Security Council met and confirmed growing fears about Lumumba. The key participants at the meeting—including NSC special assistant Gordon Gray; CIA director Allen Dulles; the secretary of state, Christian Herter; and the secretary of defense, Thomas Gates—all agreed there could be no reconciliation with Lumumba. Allen Dulles began the deliberations by characterizing Lumumba as a "Castro or worse." Dulles outlined his conclusions about Lumumba. "It is safe to go on the assumption that Lumumba has been bought by the Communists," but even if he had not, Dulles said, such an alliance "fits with his own orientation."[1] So the precise nature of Lumumba's relations with the communists really did not matter all that much. The comparison with Castro was crafted in such a way that it played on Eisenhower's fear of another revolutionary leader. Earlier that year, the administration had approved a covert action to overthrow Castro. Castro himself became increasingly anti-American and with his brother Raul Castro and Che Guevara, the Argentine soldier of communism, successfully appealed to Khrushchev to send greater Soviet military aid to Cuba.[2]

Intelligence reports reflect the growing sense of vulnerability that Dulles and others felt in the third world. "The Soviet Union," a top report summarized, "has asserted its willingness in recent weeks to give military support to any regime which seems to serve Soviet purposes," and is a "reflection of the Soviet belief in its present military power." Such has been the case with Cuba, and "in more generalized terms" with the Congo. The threats were "part of the current war of nerves designed . . . to weaken the prestige and leadership of the United States, to separate it from its allies, and in particular to pose as champion of all colonial or former colonial peoples in the world."[3] Clearly, tensions were on the rise.

It was not only Lumumba's willingness to turn to the Soviet Union for aid, but his unpredictability that concerned Washington. Something needed to be done about the leadership in Leopoldville, but until that was secure, at least the province of Katanga needed to remain in the Western sphere of influence. "At [the] very least," a State Department circular explained, "denial of Katanga assets to Soviet influence through communist-oriented central government" was "extremely important." The best option was a United Nations–sponsored economic recovery plan without Lumumba to prevent the "definitive independence [of] Katanga."[4] But how, "without Lumumba"? Although the Cold War costs of a division might have been only too apparent, given the events in Korea and the growing troubles in Vietnam, the administration seemed on the verge of going down the same road. The State Department's analysis avoided the real questions about what to do and how to solve the crisis in a way best for those affected most, the Congolese.

Figure 5.1. Lumumba Talks with Andrew Cordier, July 1960

Source: New York World-Telegram & Sun photograph (public domain), Library of Congress Collection.

Lumumba was determined to reexert sovereignty over Katanga as soon as he could. It was with this goal in mind that he made his bold trip across the Atlantic. At the end of July, Lumumba flew to New York and met with Hammarskjöld and his advisers (figure 5.1). He urged the secretary-general to authorize the United Nations' entry into Katanga. Hammarskjöld refused, knowing that would mean a showdown between U.N. and Belgian troops in Katanga. King Baudouin had also formally asked him not to intervene in Katanga in order to give Belgium a chance to set things straight and he had agreed to honor that request.[5] Despite the brewing personality conflict, Hammarskjöld reported to the Eisenhower administration that he saw Lumumba's demands as clear-sighted, not "irrational."[6] Yet whatever happened during that meeting convinced both that their goals were different, and their relationship would degenerate thereafter (figure 5.2).

Hammarskjöld's pro-Western policies were reinforced by his "Congo Club" of advisers, which, according to Conor Cruise O'Brien, included three influential Americans—Ralph Bunche, Heinz Wieschhoff, and Andrew Cordier—along with other junior members. Shortly after the independence day celebrations,

Figure 5.2. Lumumba and Bomboko at a Press Conference in New York, July 25, 1960

Source: United Nations photograph.

Bunche reportedly requested a transfer out of Congo, in large part because he had never truly established a connection with the Congolese people, or Lumumba, who he thought was "crazy." Despite some of his misgivings, his voice remained a moderate one while he argued for a firm interpretation of U.N. neutrality in the Congo. His views tended to isolate him from his American and Congolese counterparts, both of whom preferred to see the United Nations take stronger action. Wieschhoff was an anthropologist and Hammarskjöld's expert on Africa. According to O'Brien, he tended to dislike the new nationalism and "was apt to urge . . . strong action" in the Congo. Cordier, a legal specialist, had been present at the creation of the United Nations, and thereafter served as an undersecretary and special representative for the secretary-general. During the Congo Club discussions, Cordier often remained silent, leaving his views for the secretary-general to hear alone.[7] He had open access to the State Department and was the primary conduit through which the Eisenhower administration, at least unofficially, coordinated U.S.–U.N. policy. Cordier was on the verge of retirement, which might explain his risk-taking nature and singularly clear opposition to the Soviet Union and to

Lumumba. But it is still fair to say that Hammarskjöld made his own decisions and relied on various members of his team when expedient.

After a disappointing visit in New York, Lumumba traveled to Washington to meet with Secretary Herter on July 28. As he had when Castro visited the city in 1959, Eisenhower left the nation's capital to avoid any official sanction of the visit. Whereas Castro had been silent on the subject of aid,[8] Lumumba expressly asked for economic support, transport planes, and political help to persuade the Belgians to leave.[9] Herter rebuffed each of Lumumba's requests, repeating that all U.S. aid would be channeled through the United Nations.[10] After reconsidering the negative implications of Lumumba's empty-handed departure, Herter later announced at a press conference that a package of technical and economic aid was under consideration for the Congo but that no details had been worked out.[11] Belgium quickly protested that U.S. policy had "swung too far toward the Congo"[12] and actually served the interests of the communists.[13] The United States thus felt the pinch of being caught between colony and colonizer.

The failure of Lumumba's meetings and his trip in general left him little choice but to turn to the Soviet Union for help getting the Belgians out of Katanga. Leaving Herter's office, Lumumba learned that soldiers friendly to the central government had skirmished with pro-Belgian forces at Kolwezi.[14] He told a group of reporters that "the Soviet Union has been the only great power which supported the Congolese people in their struggle from the beginning. I express the deepest gratitude . . . to Nikita Khrushchev for the moral support . . . when we needed it most against the imperialists and the colonialists."[15] American journalists judged Lumumba's outburst on U.S. soil as another example of his volatile temperament. Viewed from a different light, it represented his deep frustration with his trip to the United States and the refusal of the American government to acknowledge the Belgian aggression against his country.

Historian Thomas Borstelmann has argued that while some members of the State Department characterized Lumumba positively, including Ambassador Lodge, most of the administration now openly disliked him. They and others viewed Lumumba just as he was portrayed in the press—irrational, emotional, and childlike, all terms usually used by white Americans for blacks in general. Lumumba furthermore was rumored to be a dope addict, and his licentious behavior in requesting a blonde companion for the night he stayed in Blair House only reinforced the idea that he was "head of a nation of black rapists."[16] By coming to America, Lumumba in a sense forfeited his stature as a foreign leader and found himself lost in a sea of racism for which he was not prepared.

On July 31, the National Security Council met again, this time with Ambassador Clare Timberlake present. At this critical moment both he and Devlin were summoned to Washington for discussions. Timberlake was a thirty-year veteran of the Foreign Service and had served as chief of the Africa Division for several years after World War II before spending time in Latin America and Germany. Thrown into the whirlwind of Congolese politics, he immediately took a negative view of Lumumba.[17] At the NSC meeting, Timberlake warned that "Lumumba is not anxious to see the [United Nations] succeed in the Congo." He brought the message that the Soviet Union was dangerously throwing its weight around as well. Eisenhower agreed, saying that if the Soviet Union intervened, "we would all be in the fight."[18] Later that day Herter would inform the U.S. ambassador in Brussels that given Lumumba's unclear intentions, the United States would "continue to search for more trustworthy elements."[19] Shortly after this meeting, the administration established a $100 million Contingency Fund for Africa, although the bulk of the funds were intended to meet potential needs and emergencies in the Congo.[20]

Hammarskjöld Confronts Katanga

With Lumumba becoming more desperate, Hammarskjöld knew he would have to do something dramatic to avoid a Cold War showdown, potentially one that could bring about the failure of ONUC. With his perception as sharp as ever, he went right to the core of the problem: Katanga. His chance to act boldly came just a few days later, on August 2. After intense negotiations with Belgium, the Eyskens government finally accepted that the U.N. resolution did apply to Katanga. Hammarskjöld understood this to mean that Belgium would agree to allow U.N. troops into Katanga. In return Hammarskjöld guaranteed that, at least from U.N. quarters, no harm would come to the Tshombe government. Belgium interpreted this as support for a confederation-style government.[21] Only hours after forging this quid pro quo, Hammarskjöld announced that U.N. forces would enter Katanga on August 6. He sent Bunche to begin negotiations with Tshombe to pave the way for ONUC troops.

As one might expect, Lumumba was incensed at Hammarskjöld's initiative and opposed Bunche's visit to Katanga. He angrily told Hammarskjöld that the Congolese government "is resolved to assume its own responsibilities" in Katanga "if it does not receive immediate satisfaction" on the withdrawal of Belgian troops.[22] His talk was bravado and Lumumba's own power was eroding daily. By early August, there were demonstrations in Leopoldville (where Abako had withdrawn its support for him), in Kasai (which had proclaimed its independence), and in both Kivu and Orientale provinces.[23] Lumumba desperately wanted to reassert his control over the Congo. On August 8, he declared a state of emergency and arrested a number of his enemies. A Sûreté report dated four days later speculated that Lumumba was following the advice of Albert de Coninck, whom, it was suspected, he had met with while in London on his way back to the Congo from New York.[24]

Tshombe continued to stonewall everyone. He threatened to attack any U.N. forces that entered Katanga. His audaciousness was fed in part by support from the Belgian king, who kept in close touch with the Katangans.[25] In these circumstances, Bunche's meeting with Tshombe was so difficult that he recommended to Hammarskjöld delaying entry of U.N. troops into Katanga.[26] Hammarskjöld agreed, despite the fact that Lumumba resented the move and could theoretically call for the United Nations to withdraw.[27]

A third U.N. Security Council meeting on the Congo crisis changed little. Hammarskjöld called the meeting for August 8 but preempted its discussion by declaring that the Council must either "change the character of the Force" or "resort to other methods" (by which he apparently meant negotiation) to fulfill the July 22 resolution. Changing the character of the force, he suggested, was out of the question. Hammarskjöld argued that the withdrawal of Belgian forces was an "international" issue, while Lumumba's differences with Tshombe reflected an internal constitutional debate over how much power to give the central government. The secretary-general now stated that an armed entry into Katanga would make the U.N. forces a political instrument of the central government and would thus constitute interference in the internal affairs of the Congo.[28]

Khrushchev was outraged at what he saw as the growing U.N. bias and stepped up his criticism of Hammarskjöld. He demanded that the Security Council approve an invasion of Katanga, even if by force, as the only way to restore the unity of the Congo. His demands were couched in terms that supported Congolese unity, but they also were designed to question ONUC methods. Khrushchev alleged that U.N. forces were illegally disarming and "even coming into armed collision" with the Congolese national army as that army was struggling against Belgian interference.[29] His criticisms were not too far from the truth. Instead of appearing enlightened or consistent, however, Khrushchev appeared even more contradictory in his support for the United Nations.

Desperation made strange bedfellows, and pro-Western Congolese now found themselves making the same arguments as the Soviet Union. The Congo's U.N. representative Justin Bomboko made a last-ditch effort to convince the Security Council that the crisis would not be resolved unless U.N. forces entered Katanga. Bomboko rejected Hammarskjöld's argument that the dispute with Tshombe was an internal one. Tshombe's reliance on Belgian force, he insisted, automatically made any dispute an international one.[30] He reiterated Lumumba's charge that Belgian troops "systematically looted our garrisons" while ONUC had forced the ANC to lay down its weapons. A united Congo, he emphasized, would strengthen the central government, and implicitly suggested this did not necessarily equate with strengthening Lumumba.[31] His entire speech pointed to the fact that the United Nations could not expect to be welcomed in the Congo, even by one of its most pro-Western spokesmen, if it did not respect Congolese unity or if it left the Congolese defenseless against the Belgians.

On August 9, a third U.N. resolution again successfully avoided Security Council vetoes. The resolution called on Belgium to "withdraw immediately" from the Congo "under speedy modalities determined by the secretary-general." It declared the entry of U.N. forces into Katanga as "necessary for the full implementation of this resolution," but also reaffirmed the principle of nonintervention in the internal affairs of the Congo. Washington went along but without much enthusiasm for the newest provisions in support of the use of force. Moscow introduced a draft resolution authorizing the use of force to enter Katanga. The Soviet Union did not insist on a vote on its own resolution, but the charade again emphasized the weakness of the resolution that was adopted.[32] Kuznetsov credited African solidarity and the firm Soviet position for the strength of the resolution that was passed.[33]

A Cold Embrace

The aftermath of Lumumba's trip to New York and Washington surprised Khrushchev. He did not understand, from a Cold War zero-sum perspective, why Eisenhower refused to consider Lumumba's request for "weapons and support." Speech writer Oleg Grinevsky remembered his reaction. As he banged his fist on the table, an incredulous Khrushchev asked his advisers about the American rebuff of Lumumba, "Why? Explain to me why. . . . Really, are the Americans that stupid?" His advisers gave a hodgepodge of responses, which taken together suggested that Khrushchev had to balance competing interests. Alexandr Shelepin, head of the KGB, seized the opportunity to request permission to establish an intelligence operation and investigate the American role in the Congo. Gromyko, in academic style, addressed the ambiguous character of the national liberation movement that evoked American wariness. Central Committee secretary Boris Ponomarov added a dose of ideological medicine. American imperialism, he explained, is already so decrepit that it is unable to discern the subtleties of political development in the third world, and is beginning to show its decay.[34]

All of Khrushchev's advisers recognized that the American rebuff would turn Lumumba toward the Soviet Union. After his failed meeting with Herter, Lumumba returned to New York to meet twice with Kuznetsov, and then went to Ottawa and met with the Soviet ambassador to Canada, Suren Arutyunyan. After this visit Moscow beefed up its technical aid, but still kept within the confines of the U.N. operation. The Kremlin justified the aid by citing the deplorable domestic situation created by the imperialist aggressors who were "organizing hunger" and disrupting the economic life of the country. Soviet aircraft now would help lift more U.N. troops and equipment to the Congo, and supply a hundred trucks, spare parts, and instructors. In addition, doctors and medical supplies were on their way to the Congo.[35] This new interest gave international notice that the Soviet Union was paying attention to the Congo.

KGB director Shelepin now received permission to set up an intelligence operation in the Congo. He directed Vadim Kirpichenko to help him. According to Kirpichenko, at least three top intelligence officers worked in the Congo: Leonid Podgornov and Oleg Nazhestkin, who both worked under diplomatic cover, and Georgii Fediashin, who worked for TASS.[36] On August 13, Shelepin, who was rumored to have visited the Congo, informed the Central Committee of a request by Vice President Antoine Gizenga, provided via the Czechoslovakian representative Joseph Virius, for greater Soviet military aid. Gizenga wanted more airplanes in order to improve "communication with the provinces" and also asked the Soviet Union to speed the arrival of doctors and medical supplies.[37] The Politburo would continue to weigh the requests for more aid. Meanwhile, the next day, the Soviet ambassador to the Congo, former foreign minister of the Russian republic Mikhail Yakovlev, presented his credentials to Kasavubu and Lumumba. Lumumba announced that Yakovlev brought with him a gift, an Ilyushin-14, symbolic as the long-sought-after personal plane for the president and prime minister to travel around the country, freeing them from the whims of the Western powers.[38]

Despite improvements to its position in the Congo, the Soviet Union still felt overshadowed by the West. In a memorandum to the Central Committee, Shelepin warned that the cultural contacts and activity of the United States and its allies in the Congo were far greater than had been expected. The United States, he said, has already "taken over" the system of education, and Western advisers were active all over the Congo.[39] Soviet plans for closer cultural ties were pressed forward. Cultural attaché Georgi A. Zhukov arrived in Leopoldville at the end of August to sign a treaty of friendship with the Congolese government. He had just come from Accra where he signed a similar agreement.[40] Some help came from the Belgian Communist Party, which continued to play an important behind-the-scenes role in the Congo. In August 1960, Jan

Terfve and Albert de Coninck received visas for travel to the Congo, and they almost certainly became involved in the Soviet aid program, whether this help was prearranged or not.[41]

As in the case of sending arms to Egypt in the 1950s, the Soviet Union enlisted a bloc ally, in this case East Germany, to test the waters and send additional aid to the Congo. East German representative [F.] Thun was redirected from Moscow to represent East Germany in Leopoldville.[42] Meanwhile, the East German Politburo, acting on instructions from Moscow, approved a plan to send economic advisers and international trade and legal consultants to the Congo. The East Germans had few contacts with the Congolese, and had to ask the Belgian Communist Party to have Lumumba send them a formal request for the aid.[43] These documents are evidence of Khrushchev's broad commitment to support Lumumba's government, although not in a front-line position.

Lumumba tried to get friendly African states to send their aid directly to him. He toured Africa after his visit to North America to make his case. But Lumumba found that not even the radical African states were ready to give up on the United Nations. Only Nasser, Nkrumah, and Touré agreed to redirect their armed forces to the Congo to help oust the Belgians, but only after a clear U.N. failure. Nkrumah was clearly concerned by Lumumba's growing dispute with Hammarskjöld. In fact, at this time Nkrumah wrote Hammarskjöld that Ghana would stand by the United Nations for the foreseeable future.[44] Other moderate African states generally still followed his lead.

Breaking with Hammarskjöld

With Soviet aid trickling in and Lumumba's growing hostility to the United Nations, Hammarskjöld had little chance left to find a diplomatic end to the crisis. He now ignored Lumumba, gambling that if he could find a solution, Lumumba would have no choice but to go along.[45] Hammarskjöld took a "daring and unprecedented" step and arranged a personal meeting with Tshombe.[46] Where Bunche had failed, he hoped he could convince Tshombe to let U.N. troops enter Katanga peacefully and begin the reunification process. The secretary-general flew to Katanga on August 12 accompanied by a U.N. contingent of Swedish troops (figure 5.3). True to his ways and his Belgian benefactors, Tshombe refused to budge. Hammarskjöld left with nothing.

Lumumba now poured out his fury at Hammarskjöld. In a letter to the secretary-general on August 14, he blasted Hammarskjöld's decision to deal directly with Tshombe. Again he gave the secretary-general a thinly veiled ultimatum to modify his interpretation of the resolution's phrase to take "all necessary steps" to end the secession or face the expulsion of ONUC from the

Figure 5.3. Hammarskjöld Arrives in Elizabethville for Talks, August 14, 1960

Source: United Nations photograph.

Congo. Hammarskjöld decided not to reply this newest provocation and very undiplomatic letter.[47] Lumumba responded that the people of the Congo "have lost their faith in the secretary-general" and charged that the United Nations was no longer a positive force in the Congo.[48]

Lumumba's next step was to break relations with Hammarskjöld. He did not insist on the withdrawal of all ONUC forces, but called for the withdrawal of all non-African troops. On August 17, several white U.N. security personnel were mistreated when they tried to deliver a letter to Lumumba. Sporadic attacks continued the next day against a group of Canadian soldiers, and ten days later American crew members of a supply plane were attacked.[49] Hammarskjöld threatened that he would withdraw the entire U.N. force if Lumumba persisted with what were obviously racial attacks.[50]

Dismay rang out in Washington when the administration learned of Hammarskjöld's threat. The last thing that Eisenhower wanted was a withdrawal of the U.N. troops, a step that would surely catalyze the crisis between the United States and the Soviet Union. Undersecretary Dillon wrote to Lodge that a U.N. withdrawal would be nothing but "calamitous" and told Lodge to relay this concern to Hammarskjöld as soon as possible.[51] It was also becoming increasingly obvious in Washington that relations with the United Nations were becoming more distant and more difficult. The administration began to take a more independent approach and came to rely more heavily on covert action to help solve its problems in the Congo.

Hammarskjöld's own growing impatience contributed to the tense atmosphere. Lumumba must be "broken," he told Washington, and only then will the Katanga problem "solve itself."[52] Hammarskjöld now saw that ONUC was a handy excuse that the Soviet Union used to explain away its supposed nonintervention while saving its prestige.[53] Hammarskjöld concluded that the United Nations should do nothing less but take over control of the Congo. The Congo, he said, had to be run as "a trusteeship," but "without calling it that."[54] It was an astonishing statement, coming from the highest office of the United Nations. With the situation deteriorating, and in light of the break with Lumumba, Hammarskjöld called a fourth Security Council meeting on August 21 to consider the future of ONUC. It was not just another effort to clarify the existing resolutions. At the meeting, Hammarskjöld dramatically announced that he had convinced Belgium to withdraw all its troops from the Congo in eight days. He also proposed plans for a civilian component to ONUC to create a "balanced" political, economic, and social life in the Congo."[55] The civilian operation, to be directed by Hammarskjöld's old friend Sture Linnér, was to have "advisory" powers over education, trade, finance, industry, and foreign affairs.[56]

Both the Congolese and the Kremlin soundly rejected Hammarskjöld's civilian operation as blatant interference in the internal affairs of the Congo. Kuznetsov protested that the secretary-general was acting "contrary to the clear instructions of the Security Council" and had become a "traitor" to the Congolese people.[57] Antoine Gizenga, who had replaced the more moderate Bomboko as the Congolese delegate at the United Nations, clearly at his wits' end, denounced the plan as illegal. Gizenga suggested, although probably without much hope, that there was still room for cooperation between the United Nations and the Congolese if only Hammarskjöld would ally with the nonaligned states and rely on their advice instead of Washington's.[58]

Halting a "Classic Communist" Takeover

Amid the rising violence in the Congo, including the attacks on white U.N. personnel and the troubles at the United Nations, Lawrence Devlin sent an urgent cable to CIA headquarters in Washington.[59] Devlin called the situation desperate and summed up the problems: "Embassy and station believe Congo experiencing classic communist effort take-over government. Many forces at work here: Soviets, Communist Party, etc. . . . Decisive period not far off. Whether or not Lumumba actually Commie or just play Commie game to assist his solidifying power, anti-Western forces rapidly increasing power [in] Congo and there may be little time left in which take action to avoid another Cuba."[60] Years later, Devlin explained the general fear that the Congo would break down into numerous small, ethnic-based states, and "some would have been puppet states of the East Germans, others puppet states of the Czechs, the Soviets, the Americans—whatever. And it would have been a disaster." This too, he said, added to the urgency of the situation at the time.[61]

Devlin proposed an operation with the objective of "replacing Lumumba with [a] pro-Western group." Devlin was perhaps taking a page from Timberlake. The ambassador had also recommended replacing Lumumba, although he warned that any successor would not have the current prime minister's stature. His most likely replacement would be Joseph Ileo, a senator strongly opposed to Lumumba. Devlin's proposal went to Bronson Tweedy, chief of the CIA's Africa Division, who agreed that Lumumba must be removed "if possible." Tweedy had served as chief of station in Vienna and London and now took an active interest in saving Africa from communism. Tweedy told Devlin he would seek State Department approval. The operation was quickly authorized.[62]

On August 18, the National Security Council met again to discuss the problem of Lumumba, or "Stinky" by his code name.[63] Dillon warned Eisenhower that Hammarskjöld and Lodge did not think that keeping ONUC in the Congo would be possible in the face of Congolese opposition. Eisenhower snapped back that Lodge was wrong and that one man, Lumumba, backed by the Soviets, was "forcing us out of the Congo," and added that there was no indication that the rest of the Congolese "did not want U.N. support." He insisted that ONUC would stay in the Congo even if the only way to do this was with European troops and "a fight" with the Soviet Union. Dulles then reiterated the need to preserve Katanga as "a separate viable asset" for the time being, to which the president concurred and suggested that "the UN might recognize Katanga."[64] Just as he had with Fidel Castro, Eisenhower had personalized problems with Lumumba, isolated the solution, and failed to grasp the larger problems of decolonization in the Congo.

The NSC discussion gravitated quickly toward the idea of getting rid of Lumumba. The discussion apparently avoided explicit references to the highly charged issue of assassination, perhaps in an effort to maintain "plausible denial" of presidential involvement. Robert Johnson, a member of the NSC staff since 1951 and note taker at the meeting, remembered the president saying something that came across like an assassination order. Dillon agreed that this was possible. Richard Bissell, the CIA's deputy director for planning, believed that Eisenhower wanted to get rid of Lumumba first without killing him, but that if killing him was the only way, then he would accept that. Bissell had been in charge of developing the highly successful U-2 spy plane and now had turned his attention to this most recent "black operation" of removing a foreign leader from power. He cabled Devlin to "proceed with operation."[65]

A week later, on August 25, the NSC Special Group responsible for covert operations held a meeting. Gordon Gray, Eisenhower's top security adviser and a close confidant, emphasized that Eisenhower had "extremely strong feelings on the necessity for very straightforward action in this situation and he wondered whether the plans as outlined were sufficient to accomplish this." The Special Group agreed that planning for the Congo "would not rule out consideration of any particular kind of activity which might contribute to getting rid of Lumumba."[66] With this series of words and innuendos, the swift removal of Lumumba had been made a top priority.

Dulles followed up the next day (August 26) with a cable to the station officer: "In high quarters here it is the clear-cut conclusion that if [Lumumba] continues to hold high office the inevitable result will at best be chaos and at worse pave the way to communist takeover of the Congo with disastrous consequences for the prestige of the United Nations and for the interests of the free world generally. Consequently we conclude that his removal must be an urgent and prime objective and that under existing conditions this should be a high priority of our covert action."[67] The ball that Devlin himself had set rolling was not about to stop now.

Dulles further instructed Devlin to broaden his scope of activity. Dulles informed Devlin that he was being given "wider authority" to replace Lumumba, "including even more aggressive action if it can remain covert." While usual procedures would have demanded approval of any action taken, these were not usual times or usual instructions. Dulles continued that "we realize that targets of opportunity may present themselves to you" and therefore Devlin was authorized to spend up to $100,000 "to carry out any crash programs on which you do not have the opportunity to consult [headquarters]." Furthermore, he could—but need not—consult the ambassador, depending on his own and the latter's preferences. Dulles assured Devlin that his authority for this new action had been approved at a "competent level."[68]

The alarm in Washington was matched by near panic in the upper echelons of the Belgian government. The Belgian government began taking emergency measures to prepare for an increased commitment to the Congo, and in early August Prime Minister Eyskens cut Belgian contributions to NATO.[69] Belgium had held onto considerable power in Katanga and could lose it all. According to an October 1960 intelligence report, "Virtually all key civilian and security posts are either held directly by officials of Belgian nationality or controlled by advisers to recently appointed and often inexperienced Congolese officials." Belgium was also quietly building its influence in Leopoldville again and had advisers at the Ministry of Information and at the Ministry of National Defense, as well as others working with Mobutu.[70] Lumumba was vilified not only for his intent to recapture Katanga, but for wanting to spread communism and seize all Belgian assets and privileges for good.

Belgian assassination plans almost certainly were initiated before they were in Washington. In mid-August, the Belgian state security service, the Sûreté de l'État, proposed "Operation L," a covert operation to poison Lumumba. Still another plan for Lumumba's assassination, Operation Barracuda, formed in September 1960, and as outlined by Ludo de Witte in his ground-breaking book, was directed by the highest levels of government. The Belgian Parliamentary Commission established that a September 15 memorandum referring to this operation was read by Major Loos, an aide to Harold d'Aspremont Lynden, who had recently been made the minister of African affairs. Lynden had served as head of Mistebel in support of Tshombe, and his desire to see Lumumba gone was no secret. He must have been astonished to learn when he took over his new job that as minister he now had access to the tidy sum of 50 million Belgian francs ($1 million) earmarked for the sole purpose of getting rid of Lumumba.[71] Still another plan for an attack or possibly the assassination of Lumumba was Action 58316, which involved supplying aid to Mobutu and others. Belgians were also known to facilitate other plans originating in Brazzaville and elsewhere to assassinate Lumumba. King Baudouin knew by late October that at least at one point Lumumba's life was in danger, and did nothing.[72] Given the hatred that Lumumba generated among Belgians, it is not surprising that they were so heavily engaged in their own plans for assassination.

Arming Lumumba

The Soviet Union was up against a lot. The Kremlin was certainly aware of increased Western activity in the Congo, although it gave no indication that it knew of any specific assassination plans. Khrushchev seemed stuck on trying to get greater African support for a larger Soviet role in the Congo. He was not having much luck, and used African refusal to deflect criticisms that the Soviet Union was not doing enough for Lumumba. When thirteen independent African states met in Leopoldville from August 25 to 30 to reevaluate their support for ONUC, Khrushchev had another chance to point out the need for unity, a call in effect to back the Soviet stand.[73] He sent a greeting to the conference warning that imperialist aggression against the Congo was an "aggression against all African nations" and intended to "strike a blow at the other African states."[74] He renewed an invitation to the African states to help create a united front against imperialism. Khrushchev's statements clearly implied that the Soviet Union could not be expected to offer significant aid while the rest of Africa stood by and watched.

The African representatives in Leopoldville remained noncommittal to Lumumba's pleas for aid. They urged Lumumba to cooperate with the United Nations and refused to abandon hopes that the United Nations could bring stability to Africa and the Congo. During the conference, Ghana's representative to the United Nations, Alex Quaison-Sackey, announced that Ghana's troops were committed to ONUC and would not support Lumumba's independent attack on Katanga. Even the other more radical states, including Egypt, Guinea, and Mali, agreed with Ghana's position. Lumumba abruptly left the conference on August 27, and began preparations for his military campaign against Tshombe. Frustrated and still suspicious of ONUC, Lumumba announced that U.N. troops must leave as soon as the Belgians withdrew.[75]

Isolated, Lumumba's reliance on the Soviet Union now deepened. Khrushchev decided, despite the weak African response, to step up its commitment to the Congo. But how much, according to Sergey Mazov, "remains debatable." A memorandum of the last days of August listed ten Ilyushin-14s and five Antonov-12s that would be approved for the Congo. The Ilyushins left Moscow on August 28 loaded with foodstuffs, landed in Stanleyville on September 2, and then made their way to Leopoldville. The Soviet Union also lent ten smaller Antonov-2 biplanes used for transport and five helicopters for one year. These planes, to be shipped by boat, had yet to leave for the Congo. Khrushchev designated a total of twenty-six planes and five helicopters for the Congo, five for Ghana (Ilyushin-18s), and two for Guinea (Ilyushin-14s).[76] Additional weapons were also delivered to Ghana around this time to help with the crisis in the Congo, if the need arose.[77] The nature of the memorandum and the outline of the aid suggested it was made on an ad hoc basis, outside the United Nations, but without any larger strategic goals in mind. Whether there was ever a formal agreement with the Congolese government is unclear.[78]

Soviet military assistance did not mean that Moscow had become a major military supplier to the Congo, but it did represent a greater commitment to Lumumba. The aid helped get Lumumba's attack on Katanga off the ground, which escalated the Cold War crisis. It also boosted the physical presence of the Soviet Union in the Congo denied it by the United Nations. The very fact of Soviet aid also embarrassed other African states, which remained reluctant to take a stand against imperialist aggression. If, however, the Kremlin was trying to buy influence in Africa, this backfired with the use of military aid, since most African states continued to oppose a Soviet military presence. Soviet representatives in Africa had already warned the Ministry of Foreign Affairs about African ambivalence toward increased Soviet military aid in Africa. A young member of the embassy in Ghana reported that Nkrumah did not want to see the strengthening of Soviet influence in the Congo, and in fact feared the strengthening of the Soviet Union in Africa as much as he feared the imperialists.[79]

Lumumba was not ready to make these distinctions. Any progress on Katanga in his mind was urgent and any aid in support of his effort a huge relief. Lumumba had first talked over his plans with Ambassador Yakovlev.[80] Lumumba's strategy against Katanga consisted of a two-pronged attack. First his troops, with the help of Soviet planes, prepared to attack Kasai, where Albert Kalonji had declared his own secession, and then from there launch an attack on Katanga. It was an ambitious strategy. His troops were soon bogged down in a battle with the Baluba and an inadvertent clash with U.N. troops. The U.N. troops were, for the first time in the Congo, forced to fire in self-defense. The second prong, initially delayed, began on September 6 when Soviet planes flew in an additional 450 troops to attack Katanga from Kivu.[81]

Lumumba's two-pronged campaign made a surprisingly good start. He benefited from the fact that Belgium, under great pressure from Hammarskjöld, was supposed to be withdrawing its troops from Katanga by August 29.[82] Even though many Belgians remained in Katanga unofficially, Tshombe's defenses were in a state of confusion. Moreover, if Lumumba's attack revealed that the Belgians still maintained a considerable presence in the Congo, he might be able to stir the growing Afro-Asian disenchantment with the United Nations despite the recent failure of their meeting in Leopoldville.

By the last days of August, the Eisenhower administration was carefully measuring Soviet aid.[83] U.S. intelligence was tracking the trip of five Ilyushins on their way to the Congo via Nasser's United Arab Republic (UAR). It was also tracking several ships with unknown cargo (probably carrying the smaller transport planes designated for the Congo) on their way to Port Matadi. U.S. monitors could not determine whether the cargo of these ships or planes included arms and weapons, but they did not want to take chances, and recommended that Washington assume they were loaded with military aid.[84]

With the situation unraveling before their eyes, the U.S. administration was woefully unprepared for any kind of action in the Congo. On September 2, a joint State–Defense Department working group met to study contingency plans in the case of unilateral Soviet intervention. The working group recommended sustaining U.N. economic and technical assistance as the best course of action. Only if the United Nations was forced out of the Congo did the report suggest U.S. military assistance to the provinces, including Katanga.[85] The chief of naval operations, Admiral Arleigh Burke, endorsed the recommendation and reinforced U.S. cooperation with the United Nations.[86] Known for his preparedness, Burke had once argued for strong action against another radical nationalist, Fidel Castro, in Cuba.[87] It was noteworthy, therefore, that even he did not have the stomach for action in the Congo. Clearly the Pentagon remained unenthusiastic about any independent U.S. operation in the Congo. However, right on the heels of this discussion on September 3, Herter pressed Hammarskjöld that it would be "highly desirable" to bring the Congo's airports under U.N. control as soon as possible to forestall Soviet aircraft shipments to Lumumba.[88]

Momentum was gathering against Lumumba in Leopoldville. At this time Prime Minister Eyskens told Jef van Bilsen, a Belgian adviser on the Congo, that "Kasavubu must dismiss Lumumba from his duties." Van Bilsen then let Kasavubu "understand" that he should "kick Lumumba out." Two days prior to Lumumba's dismissal, two Belgian agents in Brazzaville contacted the Ministry of Foreign Affairs there to discuss the imminent "overthrow of the government according to our wishes."[89] How much Washington knew about these proposed actions is unknown. It is difficult to believe that Devlin, Washington's most prominent figure in the Congo, and with numerous connections in Leopoldville, would not have somehow known of this Belgian advice.

The Americans also encouraged the dismissal of Lumumba. According to historian Stephen Weissman, the NSC Special Group for the Congo authorized Project Wizard on September 1. An unreleased study on covert action in the Congo cited Project Wizard as involving a "provision of funds to President Kasavubu in connection with anti-Lumumba program."[90] If, or how, this plan was put into effect remains unknown. Lawrence Devlin confirmed that Timberlake met with Kasavubu in August and warned him that Lumumba was "a dangerous man," implying that he should be removed. Timberlake apparently felt that he had been ignored.[91] Kasavubu later approached Andrew Cordier with plans to dismiss Lumumba. For the space of about ten days, Cordier was Hammarskjöld's temporary special representative before the arrival of his permanent representative, Rajeshwar Dayal of India. Cordier had little respect or use for Lumumba. It was during one of their four meetings that Kasavubu requested that Cordier close the radio station and the Ndjili airport.[92]

Altogether, these discussions were a harbinger of things to come. Given the forces gathering against Lumumba, it is a testament to his charisma and cunning that he lasted for as long as he did. It also had a lot to do with plain old-fashioned luck. The imminent arrival of Dayal was indicative that time was running out. Hammarskjöld's intent was to appeal to the "five big neutralist" states of Egypt, Ghana, India, Indonesia, and Morocco, which supported Lumumba. Dayal was a polished diplomat, Oxford educated, and had more than twenty-five years of experience in the civil service. He could be a bit haughty and dismissive of criticism at times, but was strongly independent. He had worked well with Hammarskjöld in Lebanon and was liked in the Afro-Asian states. Hammarskjöld hoped that Dayal's appointment might temper some of the growing criticisms of ONUC.[93] But in the meantime, drastic action was set to take place.

6. Coups d'État and Troikas

Nothing in the Congo in 1960 was permanent—including the Constitution, a document hastily written in the days before independence. On Monday, September 5, Kasavubu spent a long and nervous day thinking about his plans that would inevitably challenge the new state's fundamental law. It was his intention to dismiss the prime minister, but his presidential prerogative was not clearly established. As the workday came to a close, Kasavubu walked into the offices of the state radio station, took the microphone, and announced the dismissal of Lumumba and six other ministers.[1] The six ministers were all close to Lumumba, and most were leftist in orientation.[2] Kasavubu instructed the national army, the ANC, to lay down its arms and accept a period of training conducted by the United Nations. He then designated Joseph Ileo, the president of the Senate, to set up a new government.[3]

Kasavubu's speech "fell like a bomb," recalled Thomas Kanza, then the Congolese representative at the United Nations.[4] Lumumba rushed to the radio station where U.N. troops from Ghana let him into the building. Lumumba offered a moderate compromise, typically using his carrot-and-stick approach. When Kasavubu did not respond to his message, Lumumba angrily announced that all nationalist parties would "withdraw their trust in him [Kasavubu]. He is no longer the chief of state." Lumumba called the Council of Ministers into session, which met later that night. The Council endorsed Lumumba's counterdismissal of Kasavubu.[5]

On Wednesday, Lumumba continued his rally, addressing the Chamber of Representatives. He charged Kasavubu, probably correctly, with exceeding his powers in the Loi Fondamentale. He told the Chamber that he stood for the rights of all Africa. "In Africa," he said bitterly, "anyone who is for the people and against the imperialists is a communist, an agent of Moscow! But anyone who approves of the imperialists . . . is an exemplary man," and the imperialists "will praise him and bless him."[6] His speech achieved its desired effects. The Chamber revoked the dismissals of both Lumumba and Kasavubu by a vote of 60 to 19. The Senate also passed a vote of confidence favoring Lumumba 41 to 2 with 6 abstentions. A few days later, a joint session of the Chamber and Senate voted 88 to 1 with 3 abstentions to restore Lumumba as prime minister and grant him "full powers" under the supervision of a parliamentary commission.[7]

The CIA had spent the last several weeks trying to influence the parliament and was disappointed by the vote. It determined that "a better solution" was needed.[8] Ironically, the parliament did not have the power to enforce its decisions either lawfully or militarily, thus providing the CIA with their answer. Lumumba was never able to resume his responsibilities. It was also clear that any government formed by Ileo would not have a constitutional cover in the present circumstances. Over the next few months, Lumumba tried to hold on to his political power. In a characteristic pattern, Lumumba would regain strength, only to face another setback. A key to Lumumba's tenacity lay in the fact that most Congolese believed there could be no solution to their political troubles without including the very leader who had provided the Congo with its unifying nationalist vision and who had been in the forefront of its independence.

In light of the ongoing uncertainty, Andrew Cordier was ready to take action. Cordier came to the Congo with unprecedented authority from Hammarskjöld to act on his own initiative if circumstances warranted.[9] Now as the U.N. temporary representative, Cordier ordered the closing of the airport and radio station in Leopoldville with the stated intention of "safeguarding law and order" after Lumumba's radio response.[10] The radio closing did not adversely affect Kasavubu too much since he had prearranged access to the radio station in Congo-Brazzaville where his friend Abbé Fulbert Youlou held power. ONUC commander General Carl von Horn held control of the station in Leopoldville even after the Egyptian commander refused to obey his orders. The airport closing helped prevent General Lundula, who was responsible for Lumumba's offensive in Kasai, from landing his Ilyushin in Leopoldville. The United Nations continued to use the airport and permitted Kasavubu to send supporters by plane into the provinces to rally the people against Lumumba. This time the U.N. command ordered its troops, in this case Ghanaian, to prevent Lumumba from retaking the radio station.[11]

The significance of these events took time to be appreciated. Newspaper reports on September 7 indicated that Lumumba had resumed his role as prime minister and was continuing his offensive against Katanga and Kasai.[12]

It is likely that Gizenga was working hard to firm up Soviet aid and support.[13] Continuing their mission inside the Congo, the Soviet Ilyushins used other internal airfields to transport troops to Kasai. Soviet planes on their way to the Congo now traveled via Cairo and not the previously negotiated Athens route. Support from Egypt at this point was critical. President Nasser had announced that he was withdrawing his troops from ONUC, whom he felt had been misused in the airport-closing incident (although he would ultimately relent, on Hammarskjöld's request). These developments were particularly troubling to Washington, for if Khrushchev could collaborate with Nasser, then the combination of Soviet-Egyptian aid might be enough to challenge the U.S.–U.N. role in the Congo.[14] Along with this, CIA intelligence found that the Egyptian leader was providing large sums of money to Lumumba and pressuring African states to support pro-Lumumba policies.[15]

Troubling as well was the growing interest of China. Lumumba had reportedly approached the Chinese ambassador to Cairo, who was then in Leopoldville, for aid. The ambassador and his associates seemed naively optimistic.[16] Chinese interest had been on the rise, and in August China sent Ch'en Chiak'ang to Leopoldville to learn more about the crisis.[17] The Chinese strongly condemned Lumumba's dismissal as prime minister.[18] Gizenga fueled the fear that China might easily gain a greater role by requesting personnel, arms, financial aid, and foodstuffs from Beijing. The Chinese ambassador would ultimately respond that aid was impossible, perhaps because of economic dislocation at home in the midst of the Great Leap Forward.[19] The real question regarding the Chinese, however, was not immediate aid, but the extent to which they might increase aid to the Congolese radicals in the future.

Eisenhower believed that Hammarskjöld could—and should—have taken stronger measures to prevent Lumumba from returning to power. The president now clearly took the position that the United States would never have a secure place in the Congo so long as Lumumba was active. To get this message to Hammarskjöld, the U.S. representative in New York complained to the secretary-general that ONUC had only "gone half-way against Lumumba."[20] Hammarskjöld's deputy Heinz Wieschhoff defended ONUC. The United Nations, he warned, could not risk "too clearly" intervening in Congolese internal affairs without jeopardizing its very presence.

There were additional signs that all was not well with African support of ONUC (especially after the airport and radio station closing) and this probably explains Hammarskjöld's tactical retreat. The secretary of the All-Africa's People's Conference urged African nations to demand that the United Nations return the airport and radio station to the control of the Congolese government. Ghana added that the United Nations should not recognize Joseph Ileo as prime minister.[21] Hammarskjöld was feeling the fire. He had staked his prestige on settling the crisis in the Congo, and now he risked losing support from the African states on which he depended, especially for troops to serve in the Congo.

The U.S. Response

The Eisenhower administration immediately looked to portray Kasavubu as a popular leader. Publicly, U.S. officials defended Kasavubu's dismissal of Lumumba as perfectly within his constitutional rights, but privately they referred to his action as a coup.[22] Timberlake tried to convince Kasavubu that he needed to polish his public appearances and make more of them to reassure the people about his decision to dismiss Lumumba.[23] He also pressured Kasavubu to have Ileo propose a new cabinet as soon as possible. Both Washington and Brussels were anxious to see Ileo as prime minister, believing that he would be easy to work with.[24]

Still relatively new on the job, the soft-spoken secretary of state Christian Herter presumed that, with its newest resolution, ONUC could secure the Congo from outside (that is, Soviet) interference.[25] Hammarskjöld explained crisply that he could not act against the Soviet Union after having learned that 650 Belgian paratroopers remained in the Congo—this despite Belgian assurances that all paratroopers had been evacuated. Otherwise he would be forced to act against them too. Belgian "lies," Hammarskjöld regretted, had significantly weakened his position.[26] His refusal to do any more to stop Soviet aid from arriving in turn pressured the United States to get its imperial ally to behave in accordance with its promises.

The turn of events put the Congo at the forefront of the Cold War. The NSC was very concerned about the amount of aid and equipment that was being sent by the Soviet Union to Lumumba. With Hammarskjöld saying he could not stop that aid, Eisenhower made a bold statement on the Congo at a press conference on September 7. The president rarely spoke out about events in the Congo, making his press conference more than somewhat unusual. Just as unusual, he directly answered questions about the U.N. operation rather than deferring to New York.[27] Eisenhower denounced "the unilateral action of the Soviet Union in supplying aircraft and other equipment for military purposes to the Congo," which was "aggravating an already serious situation," and urged the Soviet Union to "desist" in its actions. He hinted that he did not have sufficient evidence to prove whether Soviet aid went beyond the boundaries of the U.N. mandate. Even if he had such evidence, he might not have wanted to admit it. "If these planes [the Ilyushins] are flown by Soviet military personnel this would be contrary to the principles so far applied . . . [by] the larger powers." Had he known conclusively, or admitted he knew, that the planes were flown by Soviet military personnel in civilian clothes, his words suggested he would have to take tougher action.[28]

Despite the series of recent events, ambiguity still dominated the discussions of the State–Defense Department working group, although there was a new sense that some better preparation was needed. At a meeting on September 9, Admiral Burke immediately raised the question on everyone's mind: if Lumumba returned to power, "does this mean we would move in?" "Yes," answered the undersecretary of state for political affairs, Livingston Merchant. The rest of the discussion exposed the woeful lack of planning for such a move. General Nathan Twinning, chairman of the Joint Chiefs of Staff, reported that the chiefs "were puzzled" over whether the commander for Europe or the Atlantic should supervise the planning or whether it was to be done in Washington.[29] A basic starting point had not even been reached.

Misunderstandings: New York in September

Khrushchev was about to leave for New York to appear before the U.N. General Assembly when he learned about the airport closings at Leopoldville. He reacted furiously to the latest news of ONUC's violation of neutrality, criticizing it as more proof of the United Nations' pro-Western bias. Coincidentally, Sekou Touré was visiting the Soviet Union at the time of Lumumba's dismissal. At the end of his visit, Touré and Khrushchev issued a very bland joint communiqué devoid of the familiar Soviet denunciations of ONUC.[30] Former Khrushchev speech writer, adviser, and biographer Fedor Burlatsky recalled Khrushchev's growing frustration with African states. He linked their general reluctance to support the Soviet Union to the Soviet inability to change ONUC policy or force the withdrawal of Belgian troops from the Congo.[31]

Khrushchev's condemnations of ONUC were matched, and even surpassed, by the Chinese. Chinese government statements repeatedly condemned the "acts of aggression and intervention" in the Congo "carried out under the flag of the United Nations by imperialism headed by the United States."[32] Chairman Mao now began to support greater contact with the Congolese and had the China Peace Committee send Lumumba a telegram expressing the Chinese people's support for his struggle against imperialist interference. Three weeks later Antoine Mandungo, vice president of the Congo-China association, would travel to China and be received by the vice premier and foreign minister, Chen Yi. China again paraded its advancements as an alternative to the Soviet model of development, paying particular attention to how the

101

communes improved rural village life.[33] These were all small, but sharp, jabs at the Soviet Union.

Khrushchev grew even angrier when he learned about the démarche Hammarskjöld gave to Kuznetsov on September 7 demanding a clarification on the status of Soviet individuals and equipment in the Congo. Kuznetsov called Hammarskjöld's complaint about Soviet aid "unfounded." He defended Soviet supplies of airplanes and other vehicles, which he claimed were not military detachments, but civilian equipment. *Pravda* published his text under the title "We shall continue to help the Congo in the future."[34] A Soviet statement several days later attacked Hammarskjöld and called for the United Nations to restore the airport and radio station to full Congolese sovereignty. The statement also warned the African states that had contributed troops to ONUC—specifically citing Tunisia, Morocco, Ethiopia, and Ghana—that they were being duped into supporting the policy of the colonialists.[35]

On September 9, Khrushchev boarded the *Baltika* ocean liner headed for New York and prepared to keep abreast of the crisis as he traveled. Perhaps the voyage would allow his diplomats some time to make their case to the African states in advance of his arrival in "the apple city." Khrushchev's incommunicado status also offered a convenient excuse for inaction on the Congo crisis, especially if the African states refused to jump on the bandwagon. He used his time crossing the Atlantic to prepare for the U.N. session and clarify his attack on colonialism.[36] Khrushchev was under pressure to aid national liberation movements and to counter Chinese criticism, while at the same time defend his growing pace of activity. He wanted his appearance to shine all around. But Khrushchev had a difficult task ahead of him, and as his speeches would show, he was sometimes cornered, rather than always blinded, by ideology.

As Khrushchev boarded his ship, the Security Council sat down to meet from September 9 to 16 to discuss the situation in the Congo for the fifth time. The representatives from the United States and the Soviet Union in New York were ready for a showdown. Neither state wanted an armed clash with the other in Africa, but both had adopted a course of action that made conflict escalation hard to avoid. The United States had reached the limit of its accord with the United Nations and was now faced with the question of how far to go in its own direction. The Soviet Union was at a turning point and could either continue its attack from within ONUC or work against the U.N. operation in its entirety. It ultimately chose the latter, on a smaller scale, but only after further provocations from Hammarskjöld.

As usual Hammarskjöld took the lead in focusing the Security Council meeting. He firmly defended ONUC's actions in the Congo.[37] Then he made what can only be interpreted as another bold and stunning statement. He carefully made the observation that Lumumba's troops broke away from their command on August 30, and then took actions in Bakwanga that "involve a flagrant violation of elementary human rights" and "have the characteristics of the crime of genocide."[38] His evidence involved reports from the World Health Organization and the Red Cross that cited hundreds of Baluba civilians had been killed by ANC troops. Hammarskjöld's accusation was uncharacteristically unfair, but it allowed him to dramatize the considerable dangers of escalation and prepare the international community for the need to take more action.[39]

Hammarskjöld also believed that the credibility of the United Nations was at stake and distanced ONUC from the United States. He told U.S. representatives in New York that in order to "explode" what Soviets are doing, the United Nations needed to be "absolutely clean"—in other words, to reestablish his neutrality, which had been lost under the weight of Lumumba's dismissal.[40] What the secretary-general had in mind was of no comfort to Washington. Hammarskjöld asked the Security Council to adopt a new resolution that would "take a clear line" supporting "all assistance to the Congo" via the United Nations and condemn direct aid, including that from the Soviet Union and Belgium. He recommended a renewed focus on technical aid to solve more of the Congo's domestic problems and asked for any voluntary aid to be channeled through the United Nations. Luckily for Washington, Hammarskjöld's plan gave the United States a built-in response: simply let the Soviets defeat it.

The Soviet response to Hammarskjöld's proposal was angry. The new Soviet representative, the dogmatic and vitriolic Valerian Zorin, charged that Hammarskjöld's proposals were an "abuse of power" and "failed to display the minimum of impartiality required of him." Zorin submitted a draft resolution that called for the United Nations to cease its interference in the internal affairs of the Congo, and to remove ONUC commander General von Horn for his failure to implement the U.N. mandate.[41] The appeal to remove von Horn was the first of what was to be many Soviet attempts to alter the character of ONUC.

The Soviet attack on Hammarskjöld backfired in the sense that it drove the United States to support the secretary-general at a time when the U.S. administration's relationship with him was the most fragile. At the time, James J. Wadsworth, the U.S. representative, was also new, but, unlike his Soviet counterpart, was considered rather affable. He warned that if the Soviet Union forced ONUC out of the Congo, "there will be no alternative to unilateral action."[42] Wadsworth, who a few years earlier had patiently led the nuclear test ban talks with the Soviets, now proposed a resolution expressing confidence in the secretary-general and asking other states to "refrain from any action which might tend to impede the restoration of law and order." Such a clause would have allowed (or maybe forced) Hammarskjöld to act against the Soviet Union, while circumventing the inclusion of Belgium.[43] The U.S. resolution, like the Soviet one, had little chance of success. It was the first time that U.S. and Soviet representatives had themselves introduced resolutions, neither of which had much chance of passing.

The Soviet attack on Hammarskjöld also backfired in that it convinced the Afro-Asian states to rally to the support of the secretary-general. On September 16, Ceylon and Tunisia introduced a third draft resolution close to the American one in its support for the secretary-general. Ghana, Guinea, Morocco, and the UAR agreed to go along with this new resolution.[44] Zorin eased his attack on the secretary-general, but refused to support the Afro-Asian draft. For the moment Zorin was isolated. Even if ONUC itself was a violation of sovereignty, no one wanted to listen to his argument. His veto had sealed the deadlock in the Security Council and left ONUC without clear instructions. The veto also meant that Hammarskjöld would not get his resolution to prevent bilateral aid to the Congo, even if it did include Belgium. Chances are the United States did not want such a resolution on the books anyway.

The Soviets had done Washington's dirty work, but at considerable cost. The Kremlin did not realize the extent to which its attack alienated the Afro-Asian world. No Afro-Asian state wanted the United Nations to fail, not because it supported its actions in the Congo, but because the United Nations still served as a positive venue that could help safeguard newly won independence. Nor did Khrushchev realize the extent to which his policy also helped realign U.S.–U.N. goals. Ironically, while he was making his case against Western bias he also helped to solidify that bias.

Mobutu's First Coup

The deadlock at the United Nations paralleled the deadlock in the Congo between Kasavubu and Lumumba. Dramatic events there, however, brought an end to the deadlock. On September 14, Joseph Mobutu announced that he was "neutralizing" both Kasavubu and Lumumba and relieving them of their official responsibilities. He immediately expelled Soviet, Czech, and other Communist Bloc personnel and withdrew his earlier support of Lumumba's attack on Katanga.[45] Like the rest of the country, the ANC chief claimed only to be tired of the political turmoil of the past two months.

Why Mobutu and why now? Mobutu was, as the saying goes, in the right place at the right time. Both Lumumba and Kasavubu had been competing for his support, and they both failed to recognize that Mobutu had ambitions of his own. During the colonial era, Mobutu had served in the Force Publique after being expelled from school. It was here that he learned to read and write, and developed a strong sense of discipline. He habitually read the Bible, newspapers, and the works of famous leaders, especially Charles de Gaulle and Winston Churchill. Indicative of the future, the Bible would soon be traded for Nicolò Machiavelli. And he did learn the cunning of a fox, holding close to a pledge, as a member of the armed forces, not to express political opinions. He had a sharp memory and could be "all things to all men" and when necessary roar like a lion to scare the wolves.[46]

Mobutu's coup was a surprise to many, but not to Lawrence Devlin. The CIA station chief vividly remembered his third encounter with Mobutu even decades after the event. Mobutu appeared in Devlin's doorway in full military dress flanked by soldiers the night before his coup. The meeting, according to Devlin, was full of suspense. Mobutu told Devlin that if the United States could guarantee recognition of his planned new government, a coup would go forward that night. Devlin demurred, knowing that even if he could get a message to Washington in a matter of hours, he would not get a response soon enough. Mobutu emphatically demanded to know the U.S. position and Devlin took a great professional risk and guaranteed U.S. support, political and financial.[47] The coup proceeded.

Devlin, according to Weissman, told the Church Committee that when Kasavubu proved ineffective, the CIA station "arranged and supported and indeed, managed" Mobutu's coup. What exactly Devlin might have meant, that is, the precise nature of the CIA's participation in the coup, is not clear. By this point the CIA station in the Congo was building a much deeper relationship with its preferred Congolese leaders. The still classified Church Committee report apparently referred to their "daily intimate working relationship," which Weissman explained began with the Congolese who would "take decisions, and then call in their CIA advisers who would have a chance to react effectively."[48] Decisions thus were never really permanent unless approved by foreign benefactors. The strategy, of course, had a number of advantages for all involved.

If Mobutu's coup were to fail, and both Timberlake and Dulles thought it might, the entire U.S.–U.N. position in the Congo could be jeopardized. Two weeks after the coup Timberlake reported that Mobutu "may be yielding to pressure" to accept the return of Lumumba.[49] The ambassador had done his fair share to raise concerns about "Lumumbavitch" and preferred his removal from power but also wanted to see a parliamentary solution.[50] Even Dulles was unsure about Mobutu's intentions in the crucial weeks after the coup. Dulles characterized Mobutu as "ill and discouraged" but swung behind him and argued that the United States should nonetheless increase its support for him.[51] Devlin was doing just that in the Congo, at one time even dramatically saving Mobutu's life by jumping on a gunman assassin connected to Pierre Mulele. At the moment, Dulles argued that Mobutu was the "strong man" in the Congo and no matter how weak he really was, at least for now he was advancing U.S. interests.[52] Eisenhower and Herter agreed.[53]

Mobutu had yet to make his coup effective. He gave the practical tasks of government to a College of Commissioners and promised a conference for all Congolese political leaders.[54] According to Weissman, the College was dominated by the pro-Western Justin Bomboko, Albert Ndele, and Victor Nendaka, and was perhaps even financed with the help of the NSC-authorized Project Wizard.[55] At the same time, Washington took some of the wind out of the sails of Mobutu's coup by insisting on the deneutralization of Kasavubu. The idea was to associate Kasavubu with the new government by having him swear in the College of Commissioners. Since he was the only one with any credibility as an elected leader, this would give the government a fig leaf of legitimacy. Mobutu made some mild protests, but did not prevent Kasavubu's endorsement of the College. Eventually he agreed that the College would transfer power to a government led by Kasavubu and Ileo, which seemed to satisfy Washington.[56]

Mobutu's closing of the Soviet Embassy and eviction of Communist Bloc personnel took care of one major problem. He had clearly aligned himself with the West and thus in a sense eliminated larger Cold War pressures. Sergey Mazov described the Soviet evacuation as a rather solemn affair, not accompanied by much protest. Documents were burned all night long. Soviet supplies and matériel were left for humanitarian reasons, returned to Moscow via Cairo, or seized by the Mobutu regime and used against the people it was sent to help.[57]

Mobutu's two most urgent remaining problems were Lumumba and the ANC. To deal with the first problem, Mobutu immediately issued a warrant for Lumumba's arrest. Dayal rejected the arrest warrant as illegal, meaning that ONUC would shield Lumumba for the time being. In fact, Lumumba was arrested on September 24, but released two days later by Mobutu under pressure from Dayal and a U.N. general, Ben Hammon Kettani. More help was forthcoming from Cordier to deal with the problem of the ANC. Concerned about the unrest in the ANC, Cordier asked Hammarskjöld to release $1 million to pay the soldiers and win their loyalty to Mobutu. Although not clearly within his authority to do so, Hammarskjöld agreed.[58] Belgium decided for the moment to cooperate with the United Nations and designated 20 million Belgian francs (roughly $400,000) to help Mobutu, a large portion of which went to pay his troops.[59] Mobutu now claimed to have control of 90 percent of the ANC, but Mobutu's bravado gave Timberlake the impression of a "man whistling in the dark."[60] Still, the payments bought Mobutu valuable time after his coup to bring order to the Congo.

With the controversial coup behind him, Hammarskjöld now tried to shift the United Nations into a more neutral position. Hammarskjöld "firmly" upheld Dayal's refusal to accept Mobutu's arrest warrant for Lumumba. He promised Dayal that he would "try to put Western eager beavers straight on where we stand" and put a brake on the speed of events in the Congo.[61] The secretary-general offered Lumumba the "protection" of U.N. troops from Mobutu's arrest and stationed a ring of troops around his residence. A side effect, of course, was to isolate Lumumba until a constitutional government was revived. An angry Mobutu stationed his own troops around the U.N. guard.[62] Hammarskjöld in part feared the arrest of Lumumba might force the African states to withdraw from, or worse, call for an end to, ONUC altogether.[63] He demonstrated that with enough pressure he could get Lumumba released and protect him.

Khrushchev's Retreat and Attack

Khrushchev learned about Mobutu's coup and the expulsion of Soviet diplomats while crossing the Atlantic Ocean on board the *Baltika*. It looked like Soviet foreign policy was not going to win anything too easily in the Congo. The fact that Khrushchev was on a ship in the middle of the Atlantic and without the usual means of communication made it unlikely that he would take any drastic action in the Congo. Khrushchev in fact accepted Mobutu's expulsion of Soviet diplomats without much protest.[64] About 450 Soviet personnel left the Congo, making their way to Accra, Cairo, and Conakry. The Ilyushins too would eventually be withdrawn. Soviet news correspondents left by the end of September.[65]

While Khrushchev retreated on the Congo front, he stepped up the Soviet attack against ONUC and Hammarskjöld in New York. According to his speech writer Oleg Grinevsky, Khrushchev closely followed events in the Congo while he sailed across the Atlantic. He labored intensively over policy with his foreign minister, Andrei Gromyko, the ambassador to Britain, Alexandr Soldatov, and N. I. Moliakov, the secretary of the U.N. delegation.[66] Two speech writers remembered Khrushchev's disappointment with the turn of events and his obsession with finding a way to reduce the Western bias of the United Nations. Oleg Grinevsky recorded the reactions of his boss. "I spit on the U.N.," Khrushchev cried in anger. "It is not our organization." Most of his invective was reserved for Hammarskjöld. "Ham," Khrushchev stormed, using his nickname for the secretary-general (a Russian word meaning "boor"), "sat behind the scenes" and watched "the final act of the Congolese tragedy play itself out."[67] In words very close to Grinevsky, another young speech writer named Arkady Shevchenko, who would defect from the Soviet Union in 1978, remembered Khrushchev's concern that the Congo "is slipping through our fingers." He recalled Khrushchev's words in anticipation of the upcoming General Assembly meeting. "Ham is sticking his nose in important affairs which are none of his business. . . . He has seized authority that doesn't belong to him. He must pay for that. We have to get rid of him by any means. We'll really make it hot for him."[68]

Khrushchev's idea to "get rid" of Hammarskjöld was his "troika" proposal, a three-person triumvirate designed to replace the secretary-generalship with representatives from each bloc (Western, socialist, neutral). He worked on the details of this plan during the voyage and would not listen to any words of caution from his advisers. Andrei Gromyko tried to talk him out of the troika proposal with the argument that it contradicted the standing Soviet line to oppose U.N. Charter revisions.[69] Years later Khrushchev, undaunted, continued to defend his proposal.[70] On the morning the Soviet ship reached New York, Khrushchev was ready to deal with the "imperialist sharks." He disembarked onto a dilapidated pier in the New York harbor assigned to the Soviet ship, a setting appropriate to his irascible mood.[71]

Events at the United Nations did not wait for Khrushchev. The United States had used the "uniting for peace" resolution to open a special session of the General Assembly to discuss what was happening in the Congo before Khrushchev arrived.[72] Although African support for ONUC had held in the Security Council, there were no guarantees that it would do so in the General Assembly. Ceylon and Tunisia had introduced a resolution, similar to the one they had introduced in the Security Council earlier, expressing support for Hammarskjöld and asking states to refrain from providing military aid or support to the Congo outside U.N. channels. But it was clear from the overall tenor of the discussion that the African states were becoming more critical of Hammarskjöld in general. In his speech in support of this resolution, Nkrumah called for the creation of a unified African command under U.N. auspices, and in the meantime demanded that the United Nations support the legitimate government of Lumumba.[73] To address some of these concerns, the Ceylon-Tunisian resolution included a recommendation for the creation of an advisory committee of states contributing forces to ONUC as a way to oversee Hammarskjöld's activity.[74]

The White House decided to support the resolution, believing that anything which the Afro-Asians could support would be very difficult for Soviet Union to veto. The General Assembly resolution was adopted 70 to 0 with 11 abstentions (France and the Soviet Bloc). France abstained as always because it opposed U.N. intervention. The abstention of the Soviet Union was in fact a decision not to veto the resolution because, as Zorin explained, even though it did not sanction the use of force against Katanga, it was still consistent with previous mandates.[75] The special session thus managed to maintain the fiction of superpower agreement before Khrushchev arrived.

The regular General Assembly session opened on September 20. Thirty-two heads of state from around the world attended. The idea for such a grandiloquent meeting had originated with Khrushchev, who had proposed that world leaders come to New York to discuss disarmament after the failed summit of May 1960.[76] And grandiloquent it became when many world leaders obliged, browbeating Eisenhower into attending. By opening day, the star-studded list of attendees included Khrushchev, Eisenhower, Macmillan, Yugoslavia's ruler Joseph Broz Tito, Castro, Nkrumah, Nehru, Indonesia's leader Achmed Sukarno, Nasser, and Touré. Lumumba, who had wanted to go, watched jealously from Leopoldville because Mobutu threatened to arrest him if he attempted to leave the country. He, and the rest of the world, saw Khrushchev triumphantly lead a procession of third world leaders through the crowded streets of New York City toward the U.N. buildings. The Soviet leader would remain in the New York area for almost a month, from September 19 to October 13, spending some time at the Soviet U.N. mission house in Glen Cove, Long Island.[77]

The American and Soviet appearances at the General Assembly were in stark contrast to each other. Eisenhower rather lifelessly defended U.S. foreign policy in the third world and its support of the United Nations in the Congo. The president read from his speech papers that "nowhere is the challenge to the international community and to peace and orderly progress more evident than in Africa." He offered a five-point program to improve relations, including a pledge of noninterference and support for security and development.[78] The program was so vague as to be virtually meaningless. Two days later, to give some substance to Eisenhower's speech, Secretary Herter announced a $5 million grant to help pay for ONUC.[79]

Khrushchev's performance at the U.N. meetings, in the words of historian William Taubman, "was not just extravagant and erratic; it was bizarre" (figure 6.1). Khrushchev himself remembers that "our presentation made an impact" and he seemed to relish the commotion he caused in a parliamentary body on capitalist soil. Khrushchev's first speech on September 23 was characteristically flamboyant. He denounced colonial greed, which, he said, was forcing the world to slide "headlong towards a precipice" and suggested the troika proposal to guarantee stricter neutrality for the United Nations. He strongly

Figure 6.1. Nikita Khrushchev at the United Nations, October 11, 1960

Source: United Nations photograph.

criticized Hammarskjöld for abusing his position in support of Western colonialist goals.[80] Throughout the meetings, Khrushchev continued to attract attention when he began banging his fists on his desk and shouting disapproval of the United Nations' Congo policy in response to a speech by British prime minister Harold Macmillan as he was defending Hammarskjöld. The lack of decorum was considered shocking to some, but not to seasoned Soviet specialists who saw the tactic used numerous times in the past. A few days later, on October 3, in a much more measured appearance, the Soviet leader reaffirmed his troika proposal, which included a call for Hammarskjöld's resignation. "If he himself [i.e., Hammarskjöld] cannot muster the courage to resign in, let us say, a chivalrous way, we shall draw the inevitable conclusions," Khrushchev fumed, implying that Hammarskjöld should be replaced. He also hinted that if his demands were not met, he would bypass the United Nations, implying again direct intervention in the Congo, albeit his hints and demands were made obsolete by Mobutu's coup.[81]

A couple of hours later, Hammarskjöld responded with one of the most eloquent and passionate speeches of his career. He would not, he said, "throw the Organization to the winds" since he had a "responsibility to all those Member

States for which the Organization is of decisive importance." It "is not the Soviet Union, or indeed any other Big Power who need the United Nations for their protection: it is all the others. . . . I shall remain in my post during the term of my office . . . as long as they wish me to do so."[82] Let the majority replace me if they want, he retorted. Privately, he concluded that Khrushchev's words were so violent because the Soviet Union was "making the Congo a major element of their African designs" and wondered facetiously if they had been "involved in [the] initial mutiny" of the ANC after all.[83] His own anger is indicative of the fact that he too now found the Soviet Union at the root of his problems in the Congo.

Hammarskjöld knew that he would have to prove his neutrality to the Afro-Asian states if he wanted ONUC to continue to operate. He asked Washington to tone down its public support for him, since in the face of the Soviet attack, strong backing from the United States only made it more difficult to prove his neutrality.[84] Hammarskjöld also approached Nasser directly in New York. Nasser cut right to the point and told Hammarskjöld that "we trust you, yet we cannot approve of what you are doing. You are asking for a mandate from us, and we are going to back you against the troika idea, [but] nevertheless we feel that you are undertaking something you cannot control and we can blame nobody but you."[85] Nasser made clear that the Afro-Asian states did not like the U.N.'s dependence on the United States and wanted Hammarskjöld to focus more solidly on finding an end to the Belgian aggression. That events were moving toward a climax seemed clear to everyone. Just how much more the United States and Soviet Union would become involved was not so obvious.

7. Murder and Malice

Eisenhower and Khrushchev took home with them unexpected messages from the General Assembly meeting in New York. President Eisenhower became demonstrably more concerned that the crisis was not stabilized. During a meeting with British foreign secretary Lord Home, Eisenhower wistfully commented that he could think of nothing better than if Lumumba would "fall into a river full of crocodiles."[1] In the event that was unlikely to happen, or happen soon, Eisenhower was convinced that he had to do more to prevent Soviet or other aid, including Egyptian or Chinese, from reaching Lumumba. He suggested that ONUC should seal off the Congo's borders to prevent any outside aid from entering, knowing that was not really possible. To his chagrin, Hammarskjöld seemed more willing than ever to compromise with the neutral states although the latter seemed more suspicious than ever.[2] For his part, Nikita Khrushchev returned home and met with the Politburo. After his outburst a month earlier, he now asserted that events in the Congo were in "our favor" and would "discredit imperialism" and "discredit the United Nations." His comments were very much obsolete and effectively reflected the lack of interest he faced in the Soviet Union. Khrushchev followed up with little of any real substance.

"PROPrietary" Action

Many in Washington feared that Lumumba, even under house arrest, could be just as dangerous as he was as prime minister. His assassination or "elimination" remained a high priority, and Devlin was still actively seeking ways to "dispose of" Lumumba. Most likely around this time, mid-September,

Washington established the ultrasecret "PROP" channel of cable communications for the specific purpose of advancing the assassination operation. The code word "PROP" restricted the distribution of the cables to Dulles, Bissell, Tweedy, Tweedy's deputy, and in the Congo to Devlin only.[3]

On September 19, Devlin received stunning news in a PROP cable from Richard Bissell. Someone whom he would recognize and who would identify himself as "Joe from Paris" would approach him about the problem of Lumumba. To follow up, on September 24, Allen Dulles ordered Devlin to "give every possible support in eliminating Lumumba from any possibility [of] resuming [a] governmental position" or of "setting himself [up] in Stanleyville or elsewhere."[4] The stakes were high and the message was clear. Devlin would learn that "Joe" was actually Sidney Gottleib, a longtime acquaintance. Gottleib was the CIA's chemist who won the accolade of "Black Sorcerer" for his expertise in poisons and masterminding the testing of LSD and other drugs in the early 1950s under Project MKULTRA. Gottleib had been instructed by Bissell to prepare materials to "either kill" or "incapacitate" Lumumba, and he told Devlin that he believed the program had approval at the highest level.[5] Gottleib brought with him a vial of poison, rubber gloves, a syringe, and a mask. The poison had to go on toothpaste or food or somehow actually get into Lumumba's mouth. First, the CIA had to get past the ring of U.N. troops that surrounded Lumumba and then find Lumumba's living quarters and eventually his personal accoutrements.

Devlin vividly recalled Gottleib's message: "It's your responsibility to carry out the operation, you alone." Devlin's response, he said years later, was "fall-to-the-floor shock."[6] As many scholars have made clear, including Stephen Weissman, Devlin had left the impression in the cable traffic that he was actively seeking to implement the goals of PROP and find a way to assassinate Lumumba. Devlin claims that he did not want to be directly involved in the killing. He was a relatively young station officer who wanted to do his job, but clearly did not want to end his career if he was linked to the assassination. He was playing two sides and playing them carefully. Devlin immediately began to look for ways to gain access to Lumumba. He asked headquarters to authorize "exploratory conversations" with his agent who was trying to get the poison into Lumumba's food. The agent was unable to gain sufficient access, however, and other avenues had to be explored.[7]

Even at this early stage, Devlin was becoming increasingly hopeful that others, maybe the Congolese, would "permanently" take care of Lumumba. According to Weissman, evidence clearly suggests that "a leading Congolese Senator," possibly Joseph Ileo, suggested to Devlin that he might be able to orchestrate a plan to "physically eliminate Lumumba" and asked for small arms for that purpose. Besides the Congolese there were also Belgian assassination operations under way. Andre LeHaye (a Belgian intelligence operator and adviser to Nendaka) has stated that he and Colonel Louis Marlière (a Belgian adviser to Mobutu) were "in 'regular contact' with Devlin" during the autumn of 1960. The connection suggests, as Stephen Weissman has pointed out, that Devlin was aware of more of the Belgian plans than he has revealed.[8]

Assassination plans were shuffled along. On October 15, Dulles sent a cable through standard CIA channels, not PROP, stating that the "only direct action we can now stand behind is to support immobilizing or arresting [Lumumba], desirable as more definitive action might be. Any action taken would have to be entirely Congolese." The cable also mentioned supplying Congolese leaders with funds and military aid.[9] Dulles sent a message later that same day, this time through the PROP channels and for Devlin's "eyes only." The latter cable reaffirmed that PROP "remains for specific purpose you discussed with colleague and also remains highest priority." Tweedy later clarified that this "purpose" was the assassination of Lumumba.[10]

The more general cables seemed to be an effort to distance the United States from any plans of assassination. Timing might be a clue to this nuance. The administration wanted to reduce the risk of any (overt) U.S. connection to an assassination for two reasons. First, such a serious blow to ONUC (which was still guarding Lumumba) if it were implicated in any assassination would probably force the United Nations to leave and raise the question of U.S. intervention. Second, there was a presidential election campaign under way, and further chaos in the Congo would only highlight the unsolved problems of U.S. foreign policy. Such a two-track policy might have been disingenuous, but it does show the additional pressures on the United States.

Belgian assassination plans were also undergoing some important revisions. Operation Barracuda was slow to start, but by October was moving along. On October 6, the Belgian minister of African affairs, Harold d'Aspremont Lynden, telegrammed Robert Rothschild at Mistebel that Lumumba's "élimination définitive" was "the main aim to pursue." On that day Brussels also instructed Mistebel to send someone to meet Major Loos in Congo-Brazzaville. Loos, who was part of the Barracuda plans, had contact with Colonel Marlière, and therefore Mobutu in Leopoldville. Belgium would soon also know that Mobutu met with Tshombe on October 16, and agreed to the "complete neutralization (physically if possible)" of Lumumba.[11] However, by mid to late October, Marlière wrote to Loos that "Lumumba's arrest is going badly." Devlin would not have been surprised to hear this, since he himself had urged Mobutu not to carry out a risky plan to break through the U.N. cordon around Lumumba. By late October, Mistebel would be reincarnated as the Bureau Conseil, representing the Belgians' hope to make their influence more effective.[12]

By mid-October, Tweedy asked Devlin if he could use a senior CIA officer to "concentrate entirely on this aspect" of the mission, referring to the assassination. Devlin agreed. He did tell the Church Committee that he believed the dispatch of a senior officer was a signal that headquarters was "dissatisfied with my handling of" the mission. Bissell and Tweedy apparently had a hard time finding help for the operation. Bissell approached Justin O'Donnell with the request. O'Donnell had served as CIA station chief at The Hague, perhaps a reflection of his greater desire for a cover of legality and morality.[13] He "reacted negatively" to Bissell's request, stating that assassination was "an inappropriate action" and he was "morally opposed" to killing Lumumba. He did agree, however, to go on a general mission to the Congo to "neutralize" Lumumba "as a political factor."[14]

The search for alternatives produced few tangible results. O'Donnell arrived in the Congo on November 3, 1960. He immediately began to look for ways to lure Lumumba out of U.N. custody and turn him over to Congolese authorities. At least that way Lumumba would have been judged by his peers, claimed O'Donnell, even though he recognized that capital punishment, not a trial, was a "very, very high probability." Morality, it seems, only went so far. O'Donnell was responsible for guiding CIA agent QJ/WIN, who knew he had been recruited for a highly sensitive mission involving considerable personal risk. QJ/WIN was a shady foreign national with a criminal background recruited in Europe. He was asked by another CIA agent, WI/ROGUE, to join an execution squad. WI/ROGUE himself was a stateless soldier of fortune whom Devlin described as having an "unsavory reputation" and "who would try anything once, at least." The CIA paid the two assassins $7,200 plus expenses, and it has been suggested that Devlin gave the vial of poison to the assassins, but Devlin himself makes no mention of this.[15]

Neither Brussels nor Washington seemed to be able to write the script entirely as they would have liked it. Many Congolese legislators still refused to abandon Lumumba as the rightful prime minister. Adding to the problems for Washington, Hammarskjöld continued to refuse to support Mobutu's coup. The secretary-general let it be known to top U.S. officials that Lumumba had a greater claim to be prime minister than anyone else, especially after the Congolese parliament refused to confirm Joseph Ileo.[16] More bad news came from Timberlake, who sent messages to Washington raising doubts about the desirability of sticking with Ileo. Instead, he suggested that the relatively unknown Cyrille Adoula might be the better choice. Adoula had diverse experience as the first African employee of the Central Bank in the Congo and then served in the Algemeen Belgisch Vakverbond / Fédération Générale du Travail de Belgique (General Labor Federation of Belgium) in the Congo, gaining important experience as a labor advocate in the late 1950s. He had helped Lumumba found the MNC but broke with him in 1959. After independence, Adoula became known as a moderate and "strong anticommunist" who was outspoken against Lumumba.[17]

The Eisenhower administration's search for a strong leader kept on returning to Mobutu, behind the facade of a Kasavubu presidency. According to Stephen Weissman, on October 27, the NSC Special Group put $250,000 at the CIA's discretion to use in their efforts to win parliamentary support for a pro-Mobutu government. Much of the money, if it went anywhere, was used for petty bribes that accomplished little.[18] Mobutu was young, however, and still played by some of the rules of international decorum in trying to find a legally acceptable government.

Credentials versus Credibility

Two further developments at the United Nations did not help Washington. On November 2, Hammarskjöld's representative in the Congo, Rajeshwar Dayal, submitted a report to the secretary-general filled with complaints about Mobutu. In the report Dayal questioned Hammarskjöld's own accusations that Lumumba was inciting civil war or had engaged in genocide in the Congo. He opposed U.N. recognition of Mobutu's College of Commissioners because the institution had no legal basis, and supported the reconvening of parliament as the best way to settle the crisis.[19] While Washington steamed over Dayal, another ominous development took place in New York. The General Assembly recommended the formation of a U.N. Conciliation Commission for the Congo "with a view to the speedy restoration of parliamentary institutions."[20] The fifteen non-European states that contributed troops to ONUC were ex officio members of the commission, giving it a pro-Lumumba majority.[21] With this gesture, Washington could have easily concluded that international support was tilting toward a pro-Lumumba government.

The Eisenhower administration was now convinced, correctly as it soon turned out, that Dayal was "preventing" the arrest of Lumumba and was even "supporting [the] necessity" of keeping him as prime minister.[22] But the White House did not suspect that Hammarskjöld himself might agree, and was shocked when the secretary-general accepted the conclusions of Dayal's report. Herter did his best to muffle U.S. discontent.[23] But, he told Wadsworth, if Lumumba escaped his Leopoldville guard and made it to Stanleyville, his opposition movement would be a "major threat to peace and [the] future of

[the] Congo." If the Lumumbists received aid from the Soviet Union, Soviet satellites, or friendly African support, it "would bring about [a] critical world security situation" that the very presence of the United Nations had been designed to avoid."[24] One way to prevent this would have included strengthening the U.N. presence in Orientale Province, a move that would have worked against Lumumba, but Hammarskjöld refused.[25]

Uncertainty in the Congo precipitated another international debate, this time around the issue of credibility and which government to seat at the United Nations. On November 2, Guinea made a motion to seat the Lumumba government. Its motion did not result in a rally for support of Lumumba, but instead brought the issue of credibility into the realm of public discussion. Up to this point most states, including the United States, had preferred to wait until the situation in the Congo stabilized before approving its representatives. Belgium, however, took the bold stand to suggest that Kasavubu in person should petition the world to seat his government. After some consideration, Washington adopted the Belgian proposal as a way to finally strike a blow at Lumumba and strengthen Kasavubu's position at home. Not all Western and pro-Western states, or even U.S. representatives, believed that Kasavubu could get enough support. Timberlake, as usual out of sync with his superiors, warned that it was still premature to seek a vote in favor of Kasavubu.

Ghana spoke for the majority and called for postponing the credentials debate. On November 9, its proposal was supported by a majority of member states, including the Soviet Bloc, African and Asian states, and Latin America. As Madeleine Kalb originally outlined, the U.S. delegation swung into action and tightened the screws on its allies, friends, and acquaintances. It forced the matter through the credentials committee; then it had to reverse Ghana's vote on postponement. Britain complained that the Americans were rushing a decision without giving other views a chance to be aired. Dayal was predictably upset, and even Hammarskjöld, he said, was "appalled." Nigeria complained that the United States was excessively interfering. Kasavubu, whose presence ruffled as many feathers as it smoothed, caused more problems when he rebuffed the French African states, especially Dahomey, whose support was crucial. Finally, on November 22, the General Assembly voted 53 to 24 with 19 abstentions to seat the Kasavubu delegation.[26] The vote, and international opinion, although close, had swung to the West again.

The next critical question was the transfer of power from the College of Commissioners to a government that could win parliamentary approval. Timberlake had placed his bets on Adoula, but the State Department now believed that Bomboko was their man. There were clues that Egypt had already disbursed large amounts of cash to pro-Lumumba supporters in the hopes of reviving Lumumba's legal claim to the office of prime minister. The White House of course had a lot of clout, and it hedged its bets by taking further steps to strengthen Mobutu so that he could better handle a shift in power. On November 20, according to Stephen Weissman, the NSC Special Group authorized the CIA to provide arms, ammunition, and advisers to Mobutu's ANC to prepare for action against Lumumba's forces.[27]

Although a lame duck president at this point, Eisenhower seemed determined to prove that he could bring the crisis to an end and get America back on track in Africa. Despite his apparent ambivalence toward Nixon's run for the presidency, he was stung by criticism from Democratic nominee John F. Kennedy, who blamed the administration for failing to stop the "giant communist offensive" in Africa or failing "to take effective counteraction" in the Congo before events "reached the crisis stage."[28] The U.S. presidential election was much more about directions in domestic policy and the Cold War in general than about Africa per se. Yet events in the Congo seemed to bolster Kennedy's contention that history was "running the wrong way" while Americans recklessly left the advantage to the Soviet Union.[29]

Captured!

Everyone sensed that time was running out. Lumumba's arrest and assassination, while still murky in parts, is a familiar story. On the night of November 27, in heavy rain Lumumba slipped past U.N. and ANC guards guarding his residence in Leopoldville while hidden in a black Chevrolet and headed directly for Stanleyville. Why Lumumba left at that moment is uncertain. He himself gave the reason that his young daughter was about to buried in Stanleyville. Since his official status had not been honored for a long time and U.N. recognition was now given to Kasavubu, Lumumba perhaps justifiably feared that Hammarskjöld would withdraw ONUC troops from their ring around his residence, leaving him at the mercy of Mobutu's forces.[30] Or perhaps he learned about the scheme of CIA agent QJ/WIN to abduct him. On November 26, QJ/WIN had asked Mobutu for help and the latter promised four U.N. vehicles and six soldiers ready to impersonate U.N. guards.[31] Whatever the reason, it was no secret that Lumumba long wanted to get to "Stan." Five other MNC ministers (including Gizenga, Kashamura, and interior minister Christophe Gbenye) were already in or had left for the capital of Orientale.

The CIA and Belgian intelligence were waiting for an escape. The CIA was aware that Lumumba's followers expected his "decision on breakout" soon.[32] Along the route to Stanleyville, Lumumba was greeted by local authorities and crowds threw flowers and cheered for him. Lumumba's own boldness in speaking publicly was symptomatic of his failure to be low-key when necessary. The Sûreté tracked Lumumba rather easily. Despite the long history of antipathy toward Lumumba, the Belgians sought an American stamp of approval for their action and used the Cold War as a cover for it. Belgian officials justified their pursuit of Lumumba and the need to stop him from reaching Stanleyville by citing evidence that the CIA believed it "certain" that Soviet aid to him had been funneled through Cairo. Robert Rothschild, working with Mistebel / Bureau Conseil, believed that Timberlake "seemed very firm and had decided to react with force" to stop Lumumba, leaving the obvious impression that Belgian policy mimicked that of the Americans at this point.[33]

On learning of Lumumba's escape, the CIA station informed headquarters that it was working with the Congolese government "to get roads blocked and troops alerted." Lumumba crossed the Sankuru River once with members of his entourage, but went back for his wife and son. That is where Mobutu's troops arrested him. Pierre Mulele, who was with Lumumba at that time, managed to escape. Two other MNC leaders—Maurice Mpolo, former minister of youth and sports, and Joseph Okito, once president of the Senate—were also arrested on their way to Stanleyville. Gbenye and Kashamura made it to their destination. Ludo De Witte and others have argued that ONUC forces (Ghanaians) were in a place to stop the arrest, but that they, under orders from Hammarskjöld (and conveyed through Dayal), refused to provide protection to Lumumba. A British lieutenant watched as Lumumba was taken off a lorry and, hands tied behind his back, was pushed into a small red Opel automobile.[34]

After his arrest, Lumumba was kept at the Camp Hardy prison in Thysville. Kasavubu claimed to have plans to bring Lumumba to trial, but no charges were ever brought forth and no trial proceedings ever begun.[35] Newspaper photos told of the brutality of the arrest, with pictures of Lumumba seriously beaten and with hands cuffed behind him. A number of countries expressed their concern to the secretary-general that due process of the law would not be followed under such obviously brutal circumstances.[36]

News of Lumumba's arrest brought the Security Council into session for the sixth time on December 7, 1960. Hammarskjöld defended the right of Congolese authorities to arrest Lumumba and insisted that the principle of noninterference in internal affairs meant that he could do little.[37] It was arguably one of the greatest abdications of responsibility of his career. In a sense, the earlier Soviet attack on him personally gave Hammarskjöld the political freedom to acquiesce in an arrest, since Moscow now opposed anything he did. Nasser was the first to give Hammarskjöld notice that the Africans could no longer tolerate his bias. Soon after Lumumba's arrest, Egypt announced that it was withdrawing its troops from the U.N. command. Other pro-Lumumba states soon followed his announcement.[38]

Khrushchev accused the West of plotting to assassinate Lumumba in an effort to "snuff out" the Congo's independence. His loud accusations spoke to his search for a scapegoat to explain away Soviet inaction. He lashed out not only at the West but also at the failure of African and Asian states to support greater independence for the Congolese. Had Asian and African governments "maintained the unity and determination which, for instance, they showed, together with the socialist countries at the time of the Suez crisis," he said, "the criminal schemes of the imperialists in the Congo could not possibly have been carried out."[39]

A superpower standoff at the United Nations seemed almost inevitable. Competing U.S. and Soviet resolutions at the United Nations put mainstream Afro-Asian support of ONUC to the test. Zorin proposed a draft resolution in the Security Council that called for the release of Lumumba and the disarming of Mobutu. Only Ceylon voted with the Soviet Union. The United States put forward its own resolution expressing the "hope" that the Red Cross would be allowed to examine those in detention. Few Afro-Asian states could support such a weak resolution. Instead the majority sided with Indian representative Krishna Menon's appeal to "rethink" the U.N. operation, claiming that they needed more time to consider the rapidly changing conditions.[40] The Security Council remained deadlocked and similar resolutions in the General Assembly made no headway there.[41]

Unable to exert much influence on the Congo operation, Khrushchev tried to paralyze the United Nations by withholding Soviet assessments to pay for ONUC. It was a strategy that Khrushchev had used after the Suez crisis in opposition to the United Nations Emergency Force in Egypt. This time around, it threatened to be more effective because ONUC did not have outside backing, as the United States had provided for the United Nations Emergency Force. Khrushchev's nonpayment policy immediately caused a storm of protest. Lodge complained that Khrushchev was trying to "bust up" the United Nations.[42] The charge was not far-fetched.

The cost of the military operation in the Congo was huge. In 1960 the bills for the operation had reached $50 million, many still unpaid. Hammarskjöld warned that U.N. solvency was in peril as a result of ONUC's growing debts and hinted that U.N. troops might have to be withdrawn for purely financial reasons. At the end of November, the Soviet representative, A. A. Roshchin, demanded that Hammarskjöld make plans to end the U.N. operation to avoid a financial collapse of the United Nations. To help alleviate the financial difficulties, the General Assembly on December 20 established a special budget for ONUC to which member states would be obliged to pay their share. The Soviet Union, South Africa, and France continued to refuse to pay their assessments. In response to the debt crisis, the United States gave the United Nations $20 million in advance for its 1961 payments.[43] Although financial difficulties were pasted over in the short run, ultimately Soviet nonpayment would raise the question of the role of peacekeeping in the United Nations and in the Cold War.

Moscow's Second (Low-Risk) Gamble

In Stanleyville, Lumumba's supporters struggled to build their opposition movement. Gizenga led the opposition after Lumumba's arrest and declared himself acting prime minister. Christophe Gbenye took the title of minister of the interior, Marcel Bisukiro minister of foreign commerce, and Pierre Mulele minister of defense, education, and fine arts.[44] The Soviet Union, China, Egypt, Yugoslavia, Ghana, Guinea, and Mali all sent envoys to Stanleyville, and by December, envoys from Morocco, Iraq, and Indonesia joined them.

With the United Nations deadlocked and the pro-Lumumba states looking as if they might reconsider their support of ONUC, Gizenga made a broad appeal for greater direct support. First, he sent Khrushchev an urgent request for aid on December 15.[45] The next day, perhaps prompted, Gizenga forwarded his request for aid to the German Democratic Republic. The East German leader Walter Ulbricht was ready as always to serve Moscow, especially when he could paint himself as an opponent of imperialism and racism. Characteristically terse, Ulbricht responded with a telegram asking Gizenga for a concrete list of desired measures of support.[46] Gizenga sent another request to Moscow, on December 22, this time asking to set up a Congolese embassy in the Soviet Union.[47]

Other feelers for aid were put out across Africa. Thomas Kanza had fled to Guinea with members of the Belgian Communist Party. He appealed directly to Touré, Nkrumah, and Mali's president Mobido Keita in his search for aid.[48] Kanza later joined Mulele in Cairo, where he found that Mulele was "well dug in at the African department of the Egyptian presidency." Mulele had met with Nasser on several occasions, and reportedly had open access to Nasser's private secretary Mohammed Fayek.[49] In an interview with S. Kondrashov, *Izvestia*'s correspondent in Cairo, Mulele claimed that the Stanleyville opposition had full control over Orientale Province and sufficient force to ward off an attack by Mobutu.[50] On December 19, Gizenga's representatives in Cairo, desperate, sent a plea directly to Moscow. Dropping diplomatic decorum, they admonished the Soviet Union for its passivity and called for immediate intervention. The statement pointed out that while the Belgian and American colonizers will stop at nothing, the Soviet Union does not even help the legitimate and democratic government.[51]

Khrushchev had long made greater aid for the Congo contingent on greater African support, and he stuck to this. By mid-December, African countries were talking about creating a joint command, based on the General Assembly proposal by Kwame Nkrumah in September. The idea took on new life after Lumumba's arrest. On December 13, the Egyptian ambassador in Moscow approached the deputy secretary for foreign affairs, V. S. Semenov, about the Soviet position on the African proposal. Semenov said that while the Kremlin's evaluation was ongoing, he thought the idea of a joint command was "useful" and asked if there was anything more to it. The Egyptian ambassador admitted that at this stage the command did not have material resources or a direct channel to Lumumba. But, he said, Egypt could do "nothing in the Congo alone and without the support the USSR and its other friends."[52] He seemed to be turning the tables on Khrushchev.

Khrushchev's own decision over whether to aid Gizenga seemed to weigh on the Soviet leader, considering that he did not dismiss the Congolese telegrams. Khrushchev sent Gizenga's requests for aid to the upper echelon of the Central Committee and the Foreign Ministry. Although it was unlikely that he sought a new debate, he just might have generated one.[53] It did not take long to come to a decision. Ten days after Gizenga's original request, Khrushchev promised "every possible aid and support to the Congolese people," but offered no concrete plans. On December 24, *Pravda* published the exchange of telegrams between Gizenga and Khrushchev, thus letting the world know of the alternate path available to the Soviet Union.[54]

It was not as if the Lumumbists were ineffective; in fact they were still a force to be reckoned with. In late December, Lumumbist soldiers captured Kivu and made Anicet Kashamura president of that easternmost province. The move was a bold one, in defiance of Belgian troops who were then massing on the Ruanda-Urundi border.[55] On January 1, Lumumbists again clashed with Mobutu's ANC in the provincial capital of Bukavu.[56] Several days later, 900 troops from Stanleyville invaded northern Katanga, and in support the local Balubas declared independence from the rest of the province. Desperate not to lose any more ground, Mobutu looked for ways to firm up Leopoldville's blockade against Stanleyville and starve it into submission. Hammarskjöld doubted that Mobutu had enough strength or control over the ANC to mount a successful attack, and threatened to pull U.N. forces out of the Congo if he moved against Stanleyville.[57]

On January 4, Gizenga, full of confidence after his increasingly success-ful attacks against northern Katanga, again asked for "direct and immediate" Soviet military intervention. Again Khrushchev sent officials in the Central Committee and Foreign Ministry a circular informing them of the request for aid.[58] Khrushchev was at a crossroads. Military aid raised all sorts of questions about intervention and the potential international reaction. On the one hand, it would be a last opportunity to get aid under way before Kennedy assumed the presidency and perhaps beefed up U.S. expansion into Africa. On the other hand, it might be better to wait for the inexperienced new president to take over and see where events led.

At this crucial moment, the pro-Lumumba Afro-Asian states gathered for the Casablanca conference on January 7. The heads of state of Morocco, the UAR, Ghana, Guinea, Mali, and the provisional government of Algeria, plus representatives from Ceylon and Libya, all attended. The majority wanted to see more support for Gizenga. They called for military aid to Stanleyville and for the transfer of Casablanca troops in ONUC to Gizenga. Kwame Nkrumah once again served as a brake on the radical momentum. Instead, the confer-ence issued a moderate statement, which reaffirmed support for "the legally constituted" government of the Congo in Stanleyville, called for the release of all political prisoners, the disarming of Mobutu, and the withdrawal of Bel-gian troops. The conference did agree to continue the discussion of aid to Giz-enga by setting up the International Committee for Aid to the Congo, which held its first meeting on January 24. The committee was immediately taken over by the more radical states and appealed to Afro-Asians participating in ONUC to transfer their troops to Stanleyville.[59]

The question of how to actually get any aid into Stanleyville now became a harsh reality. In response to the Casablanca declaration, the Soviet Union urged even "quicker" and "more energetic" moral and material support for the Lumumbists' legitimate government.[60] What Khrushchev seemed to be suggesting was that if anyone could figure out how to do this, he still held a favorable attitude toward aid to Gizenga. But he would not forge ahead by himself. He would soon learn that even the African states did not want to leave their troops stranded in Stanleyville. Egypt, Guinea, Morocco, and Indonesia announced the withdrawal of their troops from ONUC by February 1, 1961. Egypt agreed to leave its rather moderate arsenal of supplies for Gizenga, which included small arms and ammunition, seven tons of Soviet-made weap-ons, and five transmitter/receiver devices.[61]

If only Sudan would open up transit rights, then the blockade on Orientale Province could be broken and a Soviet supply line would at least be techni-cally feasible. The Casablanca Committee sent a special delegation to Dar es

Salaam but they made little headway, in large part due to the strong U.S. pressure on Sudan to block passage rights to the eastern provinces of the Congo. Washington was particularly concerned about the favorable attitude toward Gizenga by the military governor of south Sudan. The United States petitioned its allies to "take a tough line" to prevent Sudan from becoming a gateway for communist aid for the Congo.[62] So far the pressure was holding.

With all of the positive news coming out of Africa, Khrushchev decided that he could afford to boost aid to Gizenga, at least indirectly. With prodding from Moscow, East Germany made plans to send aid to Gizenga. A Soviet deputy minister for Africa, V. A. Brykin, stressed to his counterpart in East Berlin the necessity of providing aid for Gizenga given the "international reasons" that served to limit Soviet aid and complicated the question of transportation. East Germany agreed to make a donation worth 300,000 deutsche marks consisting of medical supplies and clothes to be sent to Cairo at the end of January 1961.[63] In late January, the Soviet Red Cross chairman, G. A. Mitreev, asked that food and medical supplies be allowed to pass through Sudanese territory on the way to the Congo. Sudan, however, would refuse even this modest request. What proportion of the aid sent to Stanleyville actually made it there is uncertain.[64]

The crisis continued to escalate. Evidence surfaced during the second week of January 1961 that Mobutu was using Ruanda-Urundi as a staging ground for his attack on Stanleyville. Upon hearing the news, the Soviet Union immediately brought the Security Council into session again. Khrushchev charged that the secretary-general "knew in advance of the plans to attack the province of Kivu from Ruanda-Urundi" and even intervened on behalf of Mobutu. Ceylon, Liberia, and the UAR introduced a resolution condemning the Belgian buildup in Ruanda-Urundi, but it failed to win sufficient support.[65] Soon thereafter *Izvestia*'s correspondent Nikolai Khokhlov accused Belgium and "other" states (perhaps a reference to South Africa) of sending mercenaries to the Congo, and using Ruanda-Urundi and Northern Rhodesia as staging grounds to help Mobutu, while Hammarskjöld turned a blind eye.[66] Mobutu had seized the initiative, but the rebels were stronger than he bargained for, and if Lumumba were to escape now, the opposition would be a serious threat.

Assassination at the Big Tree

With so much military activity going on in the Congo, Ambassador Timberlake was on pins and needles and warned Allen Dulles that the crisis was on the verge of spiraling out of control. Dulles brought the problem to the NSC. A mutiny at Camp Hardy on the night of January 13 therefore easily heightened fears in Washington, Brussels, and Leopoldville of a coup in favor of Lumumba.[67] Kasavubu now agreed to get rid of Lumumba by sending him either to Kasai or Katanga, knowing of the danger that lurked for him in both places. It was Mobutu who officially brought him to the airport. Devlin had urgently warned Kasavubu about the mutiny and added that further problems could only be prevented by "drastic action." Devlin's "forceful intercession," in the words of a member of Richard Bissell's staff, therefore helped bring about the transfer.[68] Devlin soon learned that Lumumba was being sent to Bakwanga, Leopoldville's "slaughterhouse," and he knew that there, Lumumba would be assassinated. He did nothing to stop the transfer/murder, a policy he had been instructed to carry out.[69] A short while later Devlin learned that Lumumba's actual destination was Elizabethville, another place where he would certainly be assassinated. As Stephen Weissman noted, Devlin did not report his knowledge of Lumumba's transfer to his superiors until three days later.[70]

According to Ludo De Witte, a Dutch historian and sociologist, Brussels planned the assassination in advance of the mutiny at Camp Hardy and then worked hard afterward to shift the blame onto the Congolese. The Belgian Parliamentary Commission disputed the charges of premeditation. The minister of African affairs, Harold d'Aspremont Lynden, ordered Lumumba's transfer to Katanga, and Kasavubu swiftly agreed. In early January, Colonel Frédéric Vandewalle, former administrator of the Sûreté, arrived in Katanga to help orchestrate Lumumba's elimination. In the end, Vandewalle would keep a safe distance from the actual deed, carefully preserving his political usefulness. Belgian commissioner Frans Verscheure and Captain Julien Gat took over when the time was right. Tshombe also played an indispensable role by agreeing to the whole affair. There is some suggestion that he originally tried to refuse the plane landing rights, but the pilot, out of gas, simply landed the plane anyway. In the end, no one doubted Tshombe was glad to see the assassination of his archrival.[71]

During the day of January 17, according to De Witte, Lumumba, Okito, and Mpolo were tortured by Belgian officers and Katangan leaders. At nightfall the prisoners were driven fifty miles outside of Elizabethville and abused amid a circle of Congolese and Belgian soldiers. Captain Gat gave the signal to the firing squads around midnight, and after that the murderers tried to find a way to get rid of the physical remains of Lumumba to conceal evidence of the crimes.[72] The role of the Belgians, who knew they could never fully return to the Congo as long as Lumumba lived, effectively reveals the repugnant side of imperialism. The role of the Congolese accomplices, who simply wanted more power for themselves, was hardly less objectionable. Nor was that of the Americans, implicated by their knowledge and understanding of what was going to happen.

Exactly what the CIA did know is uncertain. What *is* certain is that the CIA, like the Belgian secret service, was still working toward assassination. How much responsibility should be borne by these organizations and the governments that supported them? The Belgian Parliamentary Committee has determined that the Belgians were "morally responsible for circumstances leading to the death of Lumumba," even though no Belgian official was known to have given the final order to shoot Lumumba.[73] The CIA was clearly an accomplice by knowingly failing to prevent Lumumba's murder. Although morality is not typically a major concern in foreign policy decisionmaking, there is a general consensus that the latter should at least be reflective of basic social values.[74] That they were not was clear in these darkest days of the Congo crisis. As far as Eisenhower and Dulles were concerned, Lumumba's assassination was as good as if he finally had fallen into that proverbial river of crocodiles.

Sometime before his transfer, Lumumba wrote his last words in the form of a letter to his wife, Pauline. They were familiar words to those who had listened to his messages over a year ago in Stanleyville in 1959, and upon independence in June 1960, only six months previously. "We were born to live in freedom, not in slavery as we did for eighty years. . . . History has proved that independence is never handed a people on a silver platter. It must be seized. . . . The forces of liberation always win out over that of oppression. . . . [A] radiant future is dawning on our horizon."[75] But first there would be a dark night. It would take three weeks before the world learned about his murder. The Congo itself would sink further toward civil war, limited only by the presence of the United Nations and the reluctance of the major powers to commit more resources to a crisis so distant on the horizon.

8. A "Cold War" Civil War

As the grim events of Lumumba's assassination were taking place, fanfare and hoopla immersed Washington with the final preparations for the inauguration of John F. Kennedy. Kennedy knew before that snow-laden and crisp Washington Friday of January 20 that he and Chairman Khrushchev would clash over many issues, including the third world. Khrushchev had already turned attention to the region with his speech on January 6, 1961 at a closed meeting in the Kremlin to party ideologues. He promised new Soviet efforts to help emerging nationalist movements overcome colonialism.[1] His speech was soon published and attracted the attention of the U.S. ambassador in Moscow, Llewellyn "Tommy" Thompson. Thompson quickly cabled Kennedy that Khrushchev's speech was a renewed "declaration of Cold War" and was "expressed in far stronger and more explicit terms" than before. Kennedy took the warning at face value and often quoted from the speech as indicative of Khrushchev's intentions.[2]

In a message of his own, Kennedy responded to what seemed to be a series of new challenges from the Soviet Union, including Khrushchev's speech. He promised to help "those people in huts and villages . . . struggling to break the bonds of mass misery" and pledged to set America on the right foot again. Several speeches later he added a sense of urgency by telling the American people that "the crises multiply" each day while "the tide of events has been running out—and time has not been our friend."[3] Kennedy's words foretold his own more activist approach.[4]

The New Administration Takes Charge

Crises in Cuba and Laos dominated the first days of the administration. Two weeks before he left office, Eisenhower broke diplomatic relations with

Castro's Cuba. He left Kennedy with covert plans to use a group of Cuban exiles to overthrow Castro, what ultimately became the bungled Bay of Pigs landing in April 1961. The episode haunted Kennedy for the rest of his administration as one he did not want to repeat.[5] Meanwhile, the situation in the small, almost forgotten country of Laos became extremely volatile. First, Kennedy made an attempt to improve the fortunes of the right-wing general Phoumi Nosavan. After this attempt failed, and against considerable bureaucratic resistance at home, Kennedy accepted the widely regarded neutralist Souvanna Phouma as prime minister. Souvanna in fact had regained power with the help of the Soviets and North Vietnamese who were heavily supporting his military operations thanks to his short-lived coalition with the communist Pathet Lao.[6] The Laotian example served as an important one because it raised the question of a neutralist option for the Congo.

Kennedy was clearly undecided over what to do in the Congo. As was his tendency elsewhere, he showed a general "readiness to enter into negotiations," in the words of historian Lawrence Freedman, and looked for ways to use diplomacy to smooth out the situation.[7] The real (although soon theoretical) problem, however, was what to do about Lumumba. Averell Harriman, heir of the Union Pacific fortune and a longtime Democratic Party politician and elder statesman, privately warned Kennedy not to "save Lumumba," who was on a mission to establish a strong central government.[8] But this is exactly what Kennedy's brother Edward suggested he do after a trip to the Congo. The younger Kennedy urged the release of all political prisoners, including Lumumba.[9]

Thomas Kanza was also trying to get the president to do just this. Kanza had opened a communication channel to Kennedy via Eleanor Roosevelt. He asked Kennedy for two things: (1) to support the reconvening of parliament, and if that parliament renewed its vote of confidence in Lumumba, then to support his return; and (2) to arrange for the United Nations to protect political prisoners. Via Roosevelt, Kanza believed that Kennedy had agreed to his first request and declined the second. Kanza also referred to an informal deal between Hammarskjöld and the president-elect, in which the two agreed that Lumumba should remain in Leopoldville (and by implication under house arrest), at least until Kennedy took office (figure 8.1). Whether Lumumba knew about any of these "deals" and how clear they were to Kennedy is unclear. What we do know is that Kennedy refused to intervene directly to protect Lumumba before he actually took over the White House.[10]

The promise of Kennedy's presidency certainly raised expectations. After his inauguration, Kennedy asked his incoming team to reassess the situation in the Congo. The two key problems were how to end the rebellion in Stanleyville and how to get the Belgians out of Katanga, both of which

Figure 8.1. Eisenhower and Kennedy in Transition, January 19, 1961

Source: John F. Kennedy Presidential Library; White House photograph.

were necessary to pave the way for reunification and, ultimately, peace. In the end, Lumumba's assassination temporarily sapped the rebellion in the east and gave Kennedy a breathing space. The question of Katanga was not quite as easy. Thomas Borstelmann has suggested that Kennedy "broke with Eisenhower by clearly opposing Katangan separatism" because he feared the "racial polarization" that Tshombe brought to Africa and the opening for the communists this would provide.[11] Kennedy's relationship with Tshombe was much more strained than Eisenhower's. Kennedy spoke out openly against the secession and pledged his support for Congolese unity. He did keep one thing in common with Eisenhower, and that was his reluctance to use force to end the secession.

Not yet knowing he would be freed from the messy issue of what to do about Lumumba, Kennedy asked his advisers to write a "new policy" for the Congo. The original draft of this policy began in the State Department's International Organizations division. It was here that the new policy picked up its call for "all principal political elements in the Congo" to be included in the new government with Joseph Ileo, not Lumumba, as prime minister. To appeal to the Afro-Asian states, the plan called for the "military neutralization of all Congolese elements" and a strengthened U.N. mandate.[12]

The draft was supported by the assistant secretary of state for African affairs, G. Mennen Williams; the undersecretary of state, Chester Bowles; and the ambassador to the United Nations, Adlai Stevenson. These three and others would become known for their support of an Africanist position and found themselves opposed to the Europeanists. "Soapy" Williams (his maternal grandfather had founded the Mennen brand of personal care products) had no Africa experience, but as governor of Michigan he had fought hard to promote civil rights. With a trademark green bow tie with white polka-dots and a usually cheerful demeanor, he talked a lot about the future of "Africa for the Africans." Bowles's support for the new policy was not surprising, since he was one of the most sympathetic Africanists of the administration. He had published his views in *Africa's Challenge to America* four years earlier. Bowles's influence was moderated by his rocky relationship with the Kennedy family, especially Robert Kennedy, which his characteristic lack of tactfulness tended to exacerbate. Adlai Stevenson's relationship with Kennedy was even more strained. Stevenson was a two-time presidential nominee who aspired to become secretary of state. He thought of himself as wiser than either the president or his choice to head the Department of State, Dean Rusk.[13] So while the Africanists often had early impact on policy statements, they almost certainly would be revised by those closer to the Oval Office.

More influential advisers, like Dean Rusk and McGeorge ("Mac") Bundy, had less interest in the Congo. Rusk had some previous experience in the Far Eastern Division of the State Department, and was well liked among top administration advisers, but was barely known beyond this small circle. According to historian Robert Dallek, Rusk, although more influential than the department he led, was not expected to take strong positions in policy debates.[14] He turned his attention to the Congo when necessary, and generally tried to limit U.S. involvement without surrendering too much to the Lumumbists. This in itself was greater than that of McGeorge Bundy, Kennedy's key foreign policy adviser, who seemed to take very little interest in the Congo. The lack of interest among Kennedy's top advisers would, of course, negatively impact the preparedness of the administration in dealing with the continuing crisis.

Early on, Secretary Rusk made several amendments to the "new policy" draft, the most important of which was to drop support for all the principal political elements of a new Congolese government. With a penchant for precision, Rusk supported Kasavubu's efforts to create a "middle-of-the-road" government with Ileo as prime minister, and if this failed, then he would accept the idea of a more "broadly based government" with "Lumumbist elements but not Lumumba himself."[15] Rusk's changes, which would become the final version, made support for a government with Lumumbist elements the "fall-back" position.[16] Rusk preferred to keep Lumumba under arrest "until the situation in the Congo has been sufficiently stabilized—politically and militarily."[17] Apparently, he did not see or clearly wanted to avoid a Laos-like solution for the Congo.

Rusk was in fact bridging a gap with many in the Defense Department who wanted to offer Kasavubu full U.S. backing without including a reference to the Lumumbists at all. He also voiced the interests of Europeanists in the State Department, an informal group who believed that the United States should better coordinate its policy with Belgium and try to negotiate a rapid solution between the Belgians and Congolese.[18] Rusk declared that the West "clearly could not afford [to] lose the Congo" but, as was typical of the Europeanists, he was more concerned about the damage to America's global position than to the lost prestige it might suffer in Africa.[19] Both he and George Ball, who would become undersecretary of state in November 1961, believed at least at this stage that the United States should disengage from the Congo as soon as possible.[20]

Compromise policies might have been inevitable, but that does not mean they would be successful, as Kennedy would find out. Africanists felt betrayed that his "new policy" was not bold enough in its support of a democratically elected government. Europeanists warned that the plan made too many concessions to the Lumumbists. By itself, the plan was indecisive on the problem of Lumumba, lacked a time frame, and was sure to face difficulties in gaining support abroad. It also involved the United States in supporting an as-yet-unknown administration in the Congo. So it is no wonder Kennedy "expressed anxiety" about his "new policy" for the Congo almost as soon as he had attached his signature to it.[21] The president now lamented that the "new policy" went too far in appeasing the Afro-Asian states on the issue of support for the Lumumbists, without any guarantees that they would return any favors.[22] This fear of betrayal in the third world would persist and contribute to his misgivings about the entire U.S. role in the Congo.

From the outset of the Kennedy administration the question on everybody's mind was: just how far should the United States extend itself in the Congo? Neither the Defense Department nor the CIA thought that the State Department had the right answers. The Joint Chiefs of Staff chairman, General Lyman Lemnitzer, warned Kennedy that "the United States is capable of successful military intervention in the Congo," but "our capability to conduct other similar type operations elsewhere in the world would be dependent on the extent of the U.S. commitment in the Congo." No doubt his advice was influenced by the fact that he and others were then working out the details of U.S. support for the anti-Castro landing at the Bay of Pigs. Instead, Lemnitzer recommended strengthening U.S. commitments to the United Nations as the best way to manage the crisis in the Congo for now. Oddly, he also warned his superiors that a pro–United Nations strategy probably would not work.[23] His underlying message seemed to suggest that the Congo was a no-win situation and the administration might consider it best to cut its losses while it still could.

CIA director Allen Dulles opposed the "new policy" altogether. A holdover from the Eisenhower administration and a true Cold Warrior, Dulles immediately told Bundy that the CIA was not asked to submit "intelligence considerations" about the draft plan. The CIA, he stated, would have "suggested certain changes in, or additions to, the actions proposed."[24] At a Congo Task Force meeting in early February, the CIA raised concerns about the effect of this "new policy" on U.S. allies in the Congo and warned that it might result in a "drift toward Gizenga."[25]

Alternatively, the CIA developed its own plan for the Congo, known as its Silver Bullets program. Virtually no documentation has been released about this program, except for one short editorial comment in the *Foreign Relations of the United States* series. The covert option apparently did appeal to Kennedy. One month after he approved his "new policy" for the Congo, Kennedy ordered the CIA to "expedite" its Silver Bullets program.[26] Although not directly linked by available evidence to the Silver Bullets, Stephen Weissman uncovered still classified documents showing that one week after the "new policy" was approved, the National Security Council's Special Group on the Congo authorized $500,000 for "political action, troop payments and military equipment" intended for "the people who had arranged Lumumba's murder," which he believed to be a continuation of Project Wizard.[27] If this additional money was indeed approved and if at least some of the money made its way to the Congo, it almost certainly involved strengthening Kasavubu and fortifying Mobutu's army, a line of action long favored by the CIA and Devlin. The money might also help explain why Mobutu, who did not have much public support from Kennedy during the early months of his administration, still remained favorable to Washington.

Kennedy also believed in the power of private diplomacy and personal relationships. Upon taking office, Kennedy built friendships with African leaders like Nehru, Nasser, and Nkrumah as his "weapon" to fight the Cold War in Africa—to use the words of historian Arthur Schlesinger.[28] Kennedy wanted to convince "principal segments"[29] of the Afro-Asian community to agree to support a "broadly based government" in the Congo.[30] The Casablanca group, however, including Egypt and Ghana, remained openly suspicious of the "new" U.S. policy since it did little to address the Belgian problem. They continued to threaten troop withdrawals.[31] Their failure to support what Kennedy considered an enlightened policy would leave the new president wondering if it was well-nigh impossible to work with third world radicals.

Of all the components of Kennedy's "new policy," the revised U.N. mandate was theoretically the easiest to achieve. Kennedy privately appealed to France, Britain, and Belgium to accept revisions in the U.N. mandate, but the results were disappointing. All three allies complained that Kennedy's new policy weakened Kasavubu and obstructed Mobutu's action against Gizenga.[32] Perhaps they were mollified if they were told about the covert policy and money designated for the Congo and ultimately Mobutu. The installation of a "middle-of-the-road" government hit a snag when the parliament refused to ratify Kasavubu's proposed government with Ileo as prime minister. On February 9, Kasavubu installed Ileo as prime minister anyway.[33] Up until this time, the world still did not know, officially, that Lumumba had been assassinated.

Finding Scapegoats

At the news of the assassination, President Kennedy seems to have gone, at least briefly, into crisis management mode. In the tense days after the February 13 announcement by Godefroid Munongo, interior minister for Katanga, Kennedy warned the Soviet Union against unilateral intervention and stressed that a U.N. failure now would not spell an end to the U.S. interest in the Congo. At the same time he alerted Americans as to the risks of war in the Congo.[34] The *New York Times* reported that plans were being drawn up for the dispatch of 80,000 troops, and a group of five U.S. naval vessels known as Task Force 88 (with 500 marines on board) assembled with instructions to wait near Port Matadi. There is no evidence that the plans existed, but the reports added to the anxiety at the time.[35]

All across the globe, people reacted with dismay to the news of Lumumba's murder. Rioting took place in major cities such as Moscow, Warsaw, Belgrade, Havana, Bombay, Jakarta, and Cairo. Attacks on the U.S. and Belgian embassies and a U.S. cultural center in Cairo were particularly bitter. Chinese authorities staged a massive protest over the murder of Lumumba with more than half a million demonstrators. Premier Zhou Enlai, vice premier and foreign minister Chen Yi, and Politburo member Pong Cheng led the rally in Beijing. Zhou Enlai strongly denounced U.S. action in the Congo; but, perhaps honoring a grace period for the new administration, he made no direct references to President Kennedy.[36]

At home, African Americans began to rally in defense of the Congo and Lumumba. Some African American voices, such as those heard in the *Defender*, portrayed Lumumba as a black nationalist hero. Even the more conservative *Baltimore African American* questioned the U.N. treatment of Lumumba and the reasons for his assassination. In New York, African

Americans staged a demonstration at the United Nations on the north side of 42nd Street. They included a leading proponent of nonviolence, James Lawson, from the United African Nationalist Movement, and Daniel Watts from the Liberation Committee for Africa. Singer Abbey Lincoln led the Cultural Association for Women of African Heritage in the demonstrations. Lumumba became a symbol of the "black man's humanity struggling for recognition." For a brief moment he became an international Emmett Till and all the other victims of lynching rolled into one.[37]

On February 15, about sixty protesters, poet Maya Angelou included, tried to enter the Security Council meeting, and the resultant scuffle injured eighteen U.N. guards. Angelou remembered the disappointment she felt when black leaders publicly rejected any association with the march and with a "communist" leader such as Lumumba. Even Malcolm X would only comment on the black community's discontent with official U.S. foreign policy rather than speak out on the assassination. With the U.S. civil rights movement still in its early stages, none of its leaders wanted to be tainted by any form of association with communism. Other African Americans had different reasons for silence. Ralph Bunche, for instance, deplored the protests at the United Nations, believing that the problems abroad were of a different scope and nature compared to those at home.[38] So while there was a growing sense that racism at home translated into racism abroad, the two issues still remained very much separate in the public realm.

Subsidizing Gizenga

The Kremlin doubted that Lumumba was safe ever since his arrest. *Pravda* reported on January 11 that Lumumba was probably already murdered and repeated Mobido Keita's charge that Belgian firms were offering 800,000 francs to anyone willing to execute Lumumba.[39] When the news of the murder surfaced, Khrushchev personally charged Hammarskjöld with responsibility.[40] Like the Chinese, Khrushchev did not implicate the new U.S. administration in Lumumba's murder. His own inaction in preventing Lumumba's murder already suggested that he did not want to be dragged further into the crisis. Finding convenient scapegoats was really all anyone, including the communists, wanted to do.

Khrushchev tried to blame the whole mess on the United Nations. On February 14, the Kremlin leader issued a statement with a series of demands unlikely to be seriously considered, including the arrest of Tshombe and Mobutu, discontinuation of the U.N. operation, dismissal of Hammarskjöld, and provision of aid to the lawful Gizenga government. "The colonialists seek at all costs to drown the national freedom of the Congo in blood. . . . It is essential that all possible help and support should be given to the national Government of the Congo in Stanleyville," the statement from Moscow read.[41]

The Soviet chairman had not entirely given up on an African partnership, especially with Egypt, and looked to see if they were ready to join forces. For the Kremlin, the problem of logistics remained real. In late January, Soviet deputy foreign minister V.S. Semenov had met with Nasser to discuss some of the problems of supplying aid to the eastern Congo. Semenov outlined Soviet goals: "The Soviet Government highly appreciated cooperation with the UAR Government and was ready to render any assistance to the legitimate Congolese Government [i.e., Gizenga]. The launching of guerilla warfare deserves consideration but in our opinion the trouble is that the Congolese leaders have no experience. We've made up our minds to send to Stanleyville an experienced person and we are going to send a group of diplomats there, including the military, but we haven't had an opportunity to transfer them yet. I also suggested sending Gizenga some persons having combat experience in Algeria." Nasser sympathized with the difficulties of sending in specialists, but then, according to Semenov's report, "dismissed the matter with a joke saying that parachuting our diplomats seems to be the only way to guarantee their reaching Stanleyville."[42] The Kremlin was still hoping that the Sudanese government of Ibrahim Abboud might allow the shipment of supplies, even weapons, through Sudan, but this optimism was misplaced. Abboud was unlikely to have any sympathy for the Soviet Union, having survived three coup attempts that were supported by the Sudanese Communist Party, and still heavily relying as he did on the British for support.[43]

In early February, Khrushchev urged East Germany to provide additional support to Gizenga. On February 14, East Germany informed Gizenga that they were in the process of approving a three-person team to help him with political, military, and economic planning.[44] As part of this exchange, Gizenga opened diplomatic relations with East Germany.[45] Khrushchev also sent Gizenga a note telling him that the Czechoslovakian government and people would aid him, suggesting that help might be coming from other sources as well.[46]

The Czechoslovakian government began to conduct negotiations with Gizenga. Czechoslovakian president Antonin Novotny was particularly interested in creating a civilian air transport service into Stanleyville. He planned to approach the Sudanese, even though he knew their attitude was negative, and he faced probable U.N. opposition as well. The Czechoslovakian government also planned to give £25,000 to Mulele.[47] However, a month later Czech representatives reported that they did not trust Mulele, and therefore money remitted to Cairo for him was not handed over. It was well known, they wrote, that Mulele lived "in easy circumstances" and was "surrounded by the company of very dubious persons" including possible imperialist intelligence agents.[48] The uncertainty surrounding the commitment of the relatively young and inexperienced Stanleyville opposition hindered (and discouraged) greater involvement by either radical nationalists or communists, who had so much less to lose.

A New U.N. Mandate: The February 21 Resolution

The Congo was on the brink of civil war, threatened by armed insurrection and ethnic unrest. Kennedy, barely a month in office, was not ready with an aggressive policy to manage the conflict in the Congo. When the Security Council reconvened on February 15, Adlai Stevenson took the floor, and, despite a two-hour interruption by gallery protesters, made a well-crafted case for moderate revisions to the U.N. mandate. He urged the reorganiza- tion (instead of the disarmament) of the Congolese national army, called for broadening the government, and supported the voluntary reconvening of par- liament.[49] Hammarskjöld supported Stevenson and Kennedy's moderate revi- sions.[50] Their combined failure to take any real action or confront Belgium only lent credence to the Soviet charges that ONUC was supporting the impe- rialists. Zorin submitted a draft resolution that placed "full responsibility" for Lumumba's murder on the "Belgian colonialists" who acted "in their hatred for the cause of . . . national liberation." His resolution, which called for an end to the U.N. operation and the dismissal of Hammarskjöld, was easily defeated, but showed the extent to which the Soviet Union was now willing to go in criticizing ONUC.[51]

The Afro-Asian states, led by Egyptian president Nasser, supported their own draft, which agreed with Stevenson's call for reorganizing the ANC and reconvening parliament, but also "urged" ONUC to evacuate non-U.N. (i.e., Belgian) personnel from the Congo. Fearing the spread of violence after the announcement of Lumumba's murder, the resolution also included for the first time ONUC's right to use force "if necessary, in the last resort" to prevent a civil war.[52] The phrase was an important and dramatic increase in ONUC's responsibilities, and was a clear expansion of the peacekeeping mission.

The big question was whether Kennedy would support a resolution that sanctioned any kind of use of force in the Congo. Initially the answer was no. Only after Stevenson personally called the president and urged him to accept it, did he relent.[53] Two factors worked in favor of U.S. approval. First, the Sudanese representative publicly announced that his country would not permit supplies to be transferred through Sudanese territory, thus sealing off the northern route for Soviet aid to Stanleyville.[54] Second, Stevenson learned that Jaja Wachuku's Conciliation Commission planned to support Kasavubu's nomination of Joseph Ileo as prime minister, suggesting that the leaders preferred by the United States had a real possibility of international support.[55] Perhaps just as important, U.S. support for the resolution gave Kennedy another chance to win back the badly shaken Afro-Asian support for U.S. foreign policy after Lumumba's murder, and this may have factored into his decision as well.

A Soviet veto would isolate Moscow from the Afro-Asian states and perhaps also move the debate to the General Assembly where there was even greater support for Hammarskjöld. Privately, Gromyko and the Soviet Foreign Ministry saw the resolution as a double-edged sword. On the one hand, the resolution was directed against Tshombe and Mobutu and would halt their growing campaign against Gizenga. But the added powers to use force would also give ONUC license to establish a greater presence in the Congo. The Soviet Foreign Ministry warned the African states that the so-called reorganization of the ANC in reality meant crushing Gizenga and his supporters.[56] Moscow wanted to be particularly careful, since its Chinese critics lurked in the background, and the Kremlin now did not want to be spotlighted as responsible for the demise of Gizenga.

Despite the problems and embarrassments a veto would have created, the Kremlin originally planned to do just that. According to an internal Soviet policy review, a joint petition from the UAR, Ceylon, Liberia, and the Congo delegations convinced the Kremlin to let the resolution go into force by abstention. Moscow still planned to veto the resolution if it in any way extended Hammarskjöld's powers or officially recognized Joseph Ileo or any other "imperialist stooge" as prime minister.[57] In return for dropping the veto, Zorin asked Egypt, Ghana, Morocco, Guinea, India, and Indonesia not to withdraw their troops or personnel from the Congo. He stressed that since any U.N. plan of disarmament or neutralization of the ANC would be controlled by the United States or NATO, it was all the more important to keep their forces, and eyes, in the Congo.[58] In making this request, Zorin ironically solved one of Hammarskjöld's toughest problems—keeping enough troops in the Congo, since many of ONUC's soldiers were from Casablanca states. Egypt, Morocco, and Indonesia withdrew their troops from ONUC by the end of February, but other key states such as India and Ghana agreed to keep theirs in, at least for the moment. The way was now cleared for the Security Council to adopt the new resolution, with the Soviet Union abstaining.[59]

Hammarskjöld, whether he wanted it or not, now had the power to prevent a civil war in the Congo. The very threat of greater U.N. involvement seemed to be enough to keep the Congolese rivals at bay for the time being. Mobutu's troops had been poised for weeks waiting for the right moment to attack Gizenga. To prevent the attack, ONUC Commander General Sean McKeown (von Horn's successor) negotiated with Mobutu a neutral zone to keep his troops away from Gizenga's, who were now under Lundula's command. The CIA had helped Mobutu prepare for the attack, but after the February 21 resolution it muted its support to avoid the risk of a confrontation with the United Nations. As was the case earlier regarding plans for Lumumba's assassination, the U.S. dependence on the United Nations to shield its presence in the Congo helped restrain CIA activity. In this sense, the U.N. troops did protect the Lumumbists, as the Soviets had hoped. On the other hand, the neutral zone helped reinforce Mobutu's blockade of Orientale Province. The situation remained as fluid and as volatile as ever.

A Most Persistent Opposition

Along with the protective U.N. presence, Gizenga also won some important international recognition. By the end of February, Guinea, Ghana, Morocco, Mali, China, and the Soviet Bloc recognized Gizenga's regime in Stanleyville. The early successes, however, might have caused Gizenga to overplay his hand. In late February, Gizenga regrouped his forces and launched a three-pronged counterattack against the Leopoldville regime. Gizenga's columns set out westward, one to Luluabourg, one to Coquilhatville (the capital of Equateur), and a third to Port Franqui.[60] The advances were short-lived. Not only did he run into Mobutu's well-supplied counteroffensive but had to retreat to defend his leadership against a major challenge led by Bernard Salumu. The rivalry between his close ally Christophe Gbenye and Anicet Kashamura, now a renegade ruler in Kivu, also helped to sidetrack his offensive.[61]

Gizenga continued to bombard Khrushchev with requests for aid. His newest request for aid came on February 21, the day of the new U.N. resolution. Pierre Mulele, from Cairo, seconded the request. He also asked the Soviet Union to send a mission to Stanleyville.[62] The very next day, February 22, Gizenga asked for humanitarian aid and several days later requested greater military aid including aviation equipment and long-term credit.[63] Perhaps stung by the seeming lack of a response and wanting to emphasize the urgency of his situation, Gizenga ousted four pro-Soviet communist newsmen. Clumsily using the same carrot-and-stick approach that Lumumba had used, Gizenga sent a message that the Kremlin's influence was not free.[64]

Although seemingly shortsighted and petty, the tactic just might have worked. On February 28, East Germany secretly approved sending a consultant and chargé d'affaires, Kurt Böttger, to Stanleyville, at least partially fulfilling its earlier promise to help Gizenga. The chargé's job was to help determine how East Germany could provide further aid and assistance.[65] Aid was not coming fast enough and Gizenga knew it. A few days later on March 4, Gizenga sent the Soviet Union a rather stilted letter, perhaps for propaganda purposes. He acknowledged the Kremlin's February 14 telegram of sympathy regarding Lumumba, and replied that he was convinced that moral and material aid would soon follow.[66] It was back to the carrot approach.

By this time Gizenga was on the verge of collapse. He had little money or supplies, especially ammunition and gasoline. In documents obtained by Sergey Mazov, Czechoslovakian newsman Dushan Provnarik reported on the growing disaffection of Gizenga's army. The roughly 8,000 soldiers had "relatively modern" Belgian arms, and were still loyal, but without wages they would refuse to fight. It was hard enough to send supplies, but just as hard to get cold, hard cash to the "legal" government in Stanleyville. Probably sometime in late February 1961, Moscow sent $500,000 to aid Gizenga in two installments of $250,000 each. The first installment was used to pay the soldiers and restore order in Orientale, Kivu, and northern Katanga, at least for a time.[67] The second installment never made it to the Congo and became subject to a true spy-versus-spy drama. CIA chief Lawrence Devlin learned from an agent close to Mulele that the payment was to be made via courier through Sudan. He sent a CIA operative to distract the Congolese courier at the Khartoum airport and snatch the suitcase.[68]

In the shadow of activity going on at the United Nations and in the Congo, Mulele quietly made a trip to Moscow on March 7. His visit came after the series of exchanges between the two countries and was a positive sign that at least something might be forthcoming. Over the next few days, Mulele met with deputy minister of foreign affairs, Vasili Kuznetsov, and other officials. Discussions focused on logistical and supply-line problems, an issue that would ultimately determine the nature of cooperation between the two states. Mulele proposed buying Soviet civilian aircraft with Congolese wing markings for transport either via Cairo-Stanleyville or via Accra to the mouth of the Congolese river. The latter route would require longer-range planes, and Mulele suggested several Ilyushin-18s. According to evidence found by Sergey Mazov, the head of the Foreign Ministry's Africa Department, Vladimir Brykhin, cited "political" issues and directed Mulele to negotiate transport routes with the African states since the United Nations would be unlikely to let Soviet planes fly over the Congo. Soviet defense minister Rodion Malinovsky said that in fact Soviet planes were ready to fly to the Congo, but U.N. forces would shoot them down—a response, Malinovsky said, that the

United Nations had made "quite clear."[69] For the moment, the logistical difficulties gave Khrushchev another convenient scapegoat. When African countries could agree to help overcome some of the obstacles of getting aid into the Congo, then, the communiqué suggested, the Soviet Union was ready and waiting to supply greater material aid. In fact, the communiqué pointed out, the Soviets had provided six airplanes and were considering granting long-term aid and radio matériel.[70] Khrushchev did not cut off aid entirely, but again leaned on propaganda in an effort to protect his anti-imperialist leadership. But greater material aid was now regarded as impractical, and as Sergey Mazov argued, Khrushchev was "inclined to back off" and remove some of the dangers of escalating the crisis. This was the likely turning point at which he began to see the Congo crisis as a setback for his goals in Africa.[71]

Gizenga also looked to China for support, but again with limited results. On the positive side, Chinese contempt for the U.N. operation ran deep, and this sentiment was expressed in *Renmin Ribao*, the official communist newspaper. "Some naive people," commented the newspaper in what was an obvious jab at Khrushchev, "were inclined to believe that the U.N. intervention could help the Congolese people. . . . They did not realize that the [United States] has always used the [United Nations] as an instrument for aggression, and that inviting in the [United Nations] means letting in U.S. imperialism."[72] China also continued to support general aid for the national liberation movement, but just what its intentions were in the Congo remained unclear.

A secret Chinese analysis written in late January suggested that Beijing was not ready to support Gizenga any further. The report noted that "at present the national liberation movement of the Congo is mainly led by the capitalist [bourgeois] nationalist elements. Among them wavering and compromise prevail and so they cannot undertake correct and firm leadership." The analysis predicted that either the proimperialists would form a weak central government, or the Lumumbists would overcome their weakness and win control of the country. "The nationalist party headed by Lumumba and Gizenga" needed "to overcome continuously its own wavering and utilize correctly all internal and external revolutionary forces" available to it. Once this was achieved, the report counseled, the movement should "use the Orientale Province as a base" and then "fight back from Stanleyville to Leopoldville to unite the whole Congo."[73] For now, Chinese influence in the Congo remained minimal, as even the vice president of the Congo-China Association admitted by the end of the year in a radio broadcast.[74]

The unraveling of the situation in the Congo made more uncertain both the U.S. and Soviet positions, but the assassination of Lumumba ultimately weakened their interest in the Congo. With Lumumba gone, exactly how the superpowers would respond was unknown. Gizenga tried and tried to squeeze out more aid, but he was not convincing enough. Khrushchev kept Soviet aid minimal and piecemeal. If his failure to support Lumumba more firmly can be considered a mistake, so was his failure to offer more aid to Gizenga (even if the latter was of smaller magnitude). Lumumba's assassination was a setback, and if Khrushchev had really wanted to do more to improve the Soviet position in the Congo and contribute to decolonization he should have done more to prevent it. With the crisis moved off the front burners of the Cold War, in many ways the Soviet Union enjoyed greater freedom of action for the future. Still, Khrushchev was not ready to use this latitude. The basic problems that had created the Cold War crisis in the Congo were not yet resolved. Neither Khrushchev nor any of his advisers had any creative thinking to offer and instead continued to blame the United Nations for their problems. President Kennedy could certainly boast of more energy in this regard, but his "new policy" was hindered by its compromise nature and the fact that his vision for a government in the Congo was never clearly defined. Kennedy was left to sort through the series of recommendations offered by different factions in his administration regarding the best type of government for the Congo and then figure out how to get it in place and working effectively. The remaining task for all involved was nothing less than to unite a country that had never truly been united.

9. No Silver Bullets

There were no silver bullets, no magical solutions, for the Congo. For Eisenhower, Lumumba's assassination promised to clear up the problem of the Congo, at least temporarily. With Lumumba gone, and the Congo looking like it was safely in the Western camp, Eisenhower assumed that the West had won—and Khrushchev had lost—this battle in the Cold War. Eisenhower had so personalized the problems in the Congo that he failed to see the underlying causes of nationalism that had generated the crisis. That was where Kennedy's approach left the United States better equipped to handle the Congo. Key reports, including the now-famous "Analytical Chronology" of the crisis compiled at the outset of the new administration, emphasized the need to find a constitutional way bring the Congo back together and not leave the richest half of it in the hands of the imperialists. Kennedy wanted to find a nonviolent, even nonconfrontational, way to eliminate the monster of secession. While his insight and analysis could be crisp and new, his approach was muddied by reliance on the old tactic of covert operations.

Kennedy's New Approaches

Kennedy's emphasis on reunification for the Congo stressed that he had not abandoned Eisenhower's Cold War goal of denying influence to the Soviet Union. In fact, the Cold War continued to shape how the administration viewed and handled the crisis. In February 1961, U.S. ambassador to Moscow Llewellyn Thompson returned to Moscow with a private letter for Khrushchev from Kennedy.[1] Thompson told Khrushchev that Kennedy did not want to see their differences in the Congo "develop into a serious obstacle" in their overall relations. Although trying to minimize the importance of the Congo, he also implied a direct U.S. intervention if the U.N. solution did not work.[2] Khrushchev surely must have wondered what difference a United States–led intervention, versus ONUC, would make.

The Kremlin was not ready to hand over the Congo so easily. Khrushchev responded that the U.S. and Soviet positions were so "completely contradictory," that "prospects were not exactly bright" for an agreement. He reiterated his charges that Lumumba had been murdered with "Hammarskjöld's connivance." The Soviet leader seemed genuinely concerned about U.N. bias. "If our side had [the] Secretary-General, he asked, could you rely on us?" He hinted strongly at his continued interest in U.N. reform. Thompson tried to dismiss the issue by again arguing that "nothing in [the] situation there [the Congo] is basic to U.S. or Soviet interests."[3] While Thompson was probably trying to marginalize a country that to him did not seem worth the effort, Khrushchev obviously feared the crisis in the Congo was indicative of trends in the third world, the region where the Soviet Union had the most to gain.

Kennedy had more luck improving cooperation with Brussels. In March, a coalition Christian Socialist government led by Théo LeFèvre and Paul-Henri Spaak as foreign minister took power in Belgium. Spaak, a serious politician, balding and with heavy-rimmed glasses, was a stalwart in European diplomatic circles. For the previous four years he had served as NATO secretary-general. The LeFèvre-Spaak team had promised to adopt a more moderate Belgian policy on Katanga, and Spaak was much more conscientious about international cooperation than his predecessors had been. For Kennedy this was good news and in itself guaranteed a better understanding between Belgium and the United States.[4] Even with Belgium on board, cooperation on the Congo had to come from within the United Nations, and that had to be worked out and negotiated.

The United Nations at a Crossroads

The United Nations was coming under great pressure, particularly from the Afro-Asian states, to end the Katangan secession. They wanted Kennedy to use the resolution of February 21 to retake Katanga by force and threatened to quit the Congo altogether if a solution was not found quickly. Kennedy felt the pressure, and a major goal of his "new policy," which was not so new, was to buy time for the United Nations in the Congo. Actually what did buy time was a series of three conferences in Tananarive, Coquilhatville, and Lovanium. In the process, the United Nations abdicated its initiative on Katanga, and while perhaps dealing with problems in the east, found itself in a much weaker position to the south.

The other major goal of Kennedy's "new policy"—that of finding a middle-of-the-road government—was in shambles. The president watched as the government led by Ileo failed to win general or parliamentary support as the legitimate government. In helping to design a new government for the Congo, the United States had sidelined the Kasavubu-Mobutu team. In retaliation, Kasavubu and Mobutu strengthened their personal alliance and became increasingly antagonistic toward the United States and the United Nations.[5] Mobutu ordered the ANC to fire on anyone who opposed them. His troops first fired on a group of four Canadian ONUC soldiers, and then on March 5 attacked a Sudanese contingent located at Port Matadi, the first attack on African soldiers. The very next day Sudan pulled its troops out of ONUC.[6]

In this tense milieu, Ambassador Timberlake feared a confrontation between ANC forces and U.N. troops.[7] The ambassador ordered a U.S. Navy task force of five ships, called the Solant Amity, sailing off the coast of Africa to reverse course in case the United Nations needed help. Timberlake's orders violated the chain of command, and so angered Kennedy that his eventual removal as ambassador became a certainty.[8] For a time, the Congo was left without a reliable ambassador, which increased the disconnect between Washington and field hands in the Congo.

From the Congolese perspective, Kennedy was unrolling his new plans without considering their interests. Kasavubu feared his time was running out and tried a new strategy of his own. He announced that he would meet with Tshombe at Tananarive, in the Malagasy Republic, from March 8 to 12 to negotiate an alliance against the twin enemies of "communist tyranny and United Nations tutelage."[9] Kasavubu gravely miscalculated[10] and Tshombe dominated the meeting. The final agreement at Tananarive was a shock to both the United Nations and the United States. The agreement provided that the Congo would become a loose confederation of sovereign states with Kasavubu as president. Kasavubu and Mobutu agreed, in principle, to work with Tshombe and suspend cooperation with ONUC.[11]

As soon as the conference was over, Kasavubu looked for ways to escape the lopsided agreement. The Kennedy administration now tried to use the influence of the left to balance the right. Perhaps the administration took its cues from Laos, or perhaps it was just the quickest way to slow Tshombe down. On Timberlake's advice, Kasavubu suggested that Gizenga attend the follow-up conference in Coquilhatville under U.N. auspices. Gizenga could help tilt the ideological scales back toward the middle.[12] The once-ignored Gizenga clearly relished the attention. He also must have been weighing his future prospects without Soviet aid. Gizenga invited Frank Carlucci, an American Embassy officer, to Stanleyville and, according to one cable, gave Carlucci the "red carpet treatment" while also emphasizing that he was not a communist. The young—but even then tough—Carlucci had worked in the Congo for the previous two years and was knowledgeable about Congolese politics. Secretary Williams tried to reassure Gizenga by making a public announcement that he must be represented in a new federal government. Still, Gizenga's cooperation was erratic, making the future of negotiations more uncertain.[13] The negotiations at Coquilhatville began on April 24 and were clumsily handled. Tshombe made a series of demands at the outset that resulted in the United Nations putting him under house arrest for the duration of the meeting. The conferees agreed to a federal republic and the election of a government by parliament, scheduled for a month later at Lovanium University, just outside of Leopoldville.[14] There was much anticipation as to what the next conference would bring.

The growing anti–United Nations sentiment in the Congo in April pushed Hammarskjöld and Kennedy closer together. Hammarskjöld asked Kennedy to increase his public support for the U.N. operation to help boost ONUC's flagging reputation.[14] Kennedy offered a quid pro quo: remove Dayal and he would.[15] It was a lot to swallow for Hammarskjöld, who feared that dismissing Dayal would jeopardize Nehru's promise to bolster the Indian contribution beyond the 5,000 troops already committed.[16] Hammarskjöld first decided to shore up the U.N. position in the Congo. He signed an agreement with Kasavubu[17] and then Mobutu to let U.N. troops return to Matadi. With the United Nations on firmer ground, Hammarskjöld now removed the unpopular Dayal, announcing his "temporary" recall to New York. The decision to remove Dayal had gotten easier, since he was no longer on speaking terms with either Kasavubu or Mobutu and had endured a stream of assassination threats.[18] Dayal's withdrawal helped boost the position of Kasavubu by removing one of Gizenga's strongest international supporters. Kasavubu now agreed to begin drafting a new constitution to prepare the way for the parliamentary gathering at Lovanium the next month when a new government was to be elected.[19] True to form, Tshombe was already refusing to participate. Lovanium seemed to promise little.

Gizenga remained unenthusiastic about the upcoming parliament but, under some pressure from Nasser, agreed to participate.[20] In fact, Gizenga had few real options. As of yet there were few signs of any long-term support from the Soviet Union. True, Soviet diplomats were in the early stages of setting up an embassy in Stanleyville, but they showed little enthusiasm for their new location. Leonid Podgornov, the KGB agent who had helped set up the Soviet embassy in Leopoldville a year earlier, now led the new Soviet mission to Orientale. He arrived with Oleg Nazhestkin and an inconsequential sum of aid. Their biggest accomplishment was to set up a makeshift radio station. Instead of giving encouragement to the opposition, the Soviets seemed to want Gizenga to return to Leopoldville to find more influence there. Nazhestkin even stated that the Soviet mission worked to bring about a compromise among the Congolese.[21] Finally, Gizenga agreed in principle to cooperate. He announced his decision to attend the upcoming Lovanium conference and therein took the first step toward rejoining the government in Leopoldville.

The Chinese were appalled at Gizenga's decision. The Chinese chargé d'affaires Chang Tung had also recently arrived in Stanleyville.[22] To the dismay of both himself and China's foreign minister Chen Yi, Gizenga, in their view, verged on reconciliation with the imperialists. The Chinese blamed the Kremlin. Soviet leadership, they charged, had transgressed all lines of respectability when it "persuaded Gizenga to attend the Congolese Parliament . . . and to join the puppet government."[23] When the Sino–Soviet dispute became public, the Chinese asked in an open letter: "Does the leadership of the CPSU feel no responsibility for all this?"[24] Zhou Enlai had charged that the Lovanium conference was simply a new U.S. plot to control the Congo.[25] The Kennedy administration, it said, along with "compromising countries in the Afro-Asian bloc," including the UAR and Ghana, all worked to convince Gizenga to capitulate at Lovanium.[26]

The Chinese attack begged the question of what Moscow hoped to gain. Had Gizenga stood his ground more firmly, Moscow might have gained an ally, even a weak one, in a central Congolese government at Leopoldville. But without a firm Soviet commitment in the first place, Gizenga got cold feet. That left an unexpectedly easy opportunity for Washington to secure its preferred outcome at the Lovanium parliament, which was just preparing to meet outside the capital city.

The Lovanium Parliament

As late as June 1961, Kennedy remained undecided about whether to support the upcoming Lovanium gathering. Leaving so much up to the Congolese still seemed risky. Kennedy's Congo Task Force was asked to find a response. The group was headed by Secretary Williams, and included Chester Bowles, Edmund Gullion, Kennedy's newly appointed ambassador to the Congo, and McMurtrie Godley, who would remain the chargé d'affaires until Gullion could take up his duties. The Task Force recommended U.S. support for the parliament at Lovanium as well as support for the formation of a new government that included several token Lumumbists; that is, only if real power fell into the hands of a pro-Western ally.[27] To ensure this, the Task Force looked to Adoula, having decided that Ileo was too "weak" a prime minister.[28] Adoula was a native of Leopoldville and had secretly aligned himself with the pro-Western Binza group.[29] Godley suggested that Kasavubu present the conference with an Adoula government as a fait accompli. Kasavubu refused, pleading that he could not get Ileo to agree.

The generally harder-line Europeanists in the State Department wanted a more solidly Western outcome guaranteed. Secretary Rusk looked to Tshombe to shift the Lovanium proceedings to the right and petitioned Belgium, Britain, and France to help convince the maverick Katangan to participate.[30] As usual Tshombe was refusing to go along, this time citing the fiasco at Coquilhatville. Without a clear win for Adoula and failing to bring America's European allies on board, Rusk and others had a delicate task at hand. Rusk knew one thing he did not want: a compromise with Gizenga. He thought that the United States should be doing more to weaken the Lumumbists.[31] Thinking he needed more time to do this, he instructed Godley to have Kasavubu stall the opening of the parliament. Godley boldly refused, fearing that such a move would undermine the whole parliament.[32] Just as the conference was starting, Kennedy had another unruly diplomat on his hands.

On July 13, all 188 (out of a total of 221) deputies from the Congolese Chamber and Senate (minus those from Katanga) gathered at the campus of Lovanium University. The meeting was closed, literally fenced off from the world—meaning no liquor, no money, no weapons, and no women. The major task at Lovanium was to organize a new government. Very quickly it seemed like the conference would be a victory for the left. Votes for the Chamber presidency went to the pro-Lumumbist Henri Kasongo, who had held that position in July 1960.[33] Rumors spread that Gizenga was likely to be voted prime minister.[34] Inexplicably, Gizenga refused. Perhaps he feared for his safety, or perhaps he realized the United States would never accept his government anyway. Cleophas Kamitatu later recalled the all-night negotiations between the pro-Gizenga nationalist bloc and Adoula, whom the bloc saw as the "least evil" alternative of pro-Western candidates. A deal was made to support Adoula as prime minister. Perhaps fearing to be cut out of power altogether, Gizenga accepted the post of vice prime minister.[35] It was another classic example of the Congolese ability to cooperate. Gizenga's nationalist bloc retained thirteen ministries, twelve went to their pro-Western opponents, and one to Jason Sendwe of Balubakat (as second vice prime minister). Ten ministers held the same jobs they had in the Lumumba government, and two others held different ministries. Seven each had served in the Gizenga and Ileo governments. Gbenye became minister of the interior, Bomboko remained foreign minister, and Ileo became minister of information.[36]

So, in the end, Lovanium turned out to be a victory for the United States and the United Nations.[37] The CIA reportedly spent $23,000 for its activities during the parliament.[38] Historian Richard Mahoney has chronicled how CIA operatives got around the fenced-off area at Lovanium by using underground tunnels to actually distribute handsome amounts of cash to anyone who would promise to change their vote to Adoula, although no documentary evidence about this activity has surfaced.[39] Devlin does mention that he personally met with Adoula regularly, and he and other CIA agents met with as many other parliamentarians as possible to "recommend" that Adoula be elected the next prime minister.[40] At the end of the conference, the president's special assistant Walt Rostow wrote to the president that "there is optimism all over" Washington in the hopes "that the Congo situation is on the way to solution."[41] Had he limited his optimism to the problem of the Lumumbists and Gizenga, then the statement might have been more accurate.

Gizenga Quivers, Moscow Snaps

After Lovanium, Gizenga dissolved his Stanleyville regime, as he had agreed. Yet he showed no signs of leaving Stanleyville or actively cooperating with Leopoldville. The dissolution freed the states that had recognized Gizenga to then establish relations with Adoula. Of all the former Gizenga allies, only the Chinese packed their bags for home. China was contemptuous of Gizenga and simply closed its embassy in Stanleyville on September 16, "in view of the fact that the lawful government of the Republic of the Congo has announced its own termination."[42] The Kremlin chose to recognize the new Adoula government as the legal successor to Lumumba. The Soviet mission returned to Leopoldville on September 24, and their allies, including the East Germans, followed suit.[43] Podgornov did not find a warm welcome in Leopoldville. First, Devlin had installed some wiretaps in their building and then "to make life difficult for them" hired a *feticheur* to chant a curse for hours, warning away anyone who wanted to enter the property.[44] Although the Lovanium parliament had voted to accept the Stanleyville foreign diplomatic missions, the foreign minister, Justin Bomboko, demanded that they return home for proper accreditation. He finally relented under pressure from the interior minister, Christophe Gbenye, and the Soviet mission was received on December 2, 1961.[45]

At the time of the Lovanium conference, Khrushchev was reviewing his entire strategy toward the Congo and Africa in general. By the summer of 1961, global strategic concerns had pushed the Congo closer to the bottom of the Kremlin's list of priorities. On July 29, KGB director Shelepin sent Khrushchev what historian Vladislav Zubok has referred to as "mind-boggling array of proposals" to try to tie down U.S. forces in various part of the world "during the settlement of the question of a German peace treaty and

West Berlin." Shelepin's plan, adopted by the Central Committee on August 1, was supposed to show the United States a military conflict over West Berlin would weaken the U.S. position not only in Europe but also in Latin America, Asia, and Africa. Specific measures included providing weapons and help organizing anticolonial uprisings in Latin America and in Africa, including Kenya, Rhodesia, and Portuguese Guinea.[46] The obvious failure to mention the Congo is indicative of the Kremlin's loss of interest in becoming further involved in the crisis. At the same time, the strings attached to aid for Africa were also becoming more knotted. The Twenty-Second Congress's new program for the party (formally adopted in November 1961) emphasized that "young sovereign states" must "extricate themselves from the capitalist world economy," implying that this must happen if they wanted enhanced aid from the Kremlin.[47]

So with the Soviet Union looking elsewhere and tightening its aid policy, the problem for Washington of what to do about Gizenga seemed to be subsiding. Even if Gizenga was not cooperating with Leopoldville, he was isolated in Stanleyville and without measurable influence. Greater problems still brought attention to the south, toward Katanga.

The Katangan Round One Ends in Tragedy

Kennedy understood that the "victory" at Lovanium did not solve the problem of Katanga. Adoula remained politically and militarily vulnerable as long as the secession continued. Adding to the administration's problems, the communist and Afro-Asian states were increasing pressure on the United Nations to end the Katangan secession.[48] Hoping to ride the coattails of success at Lovanium, the administration was making "great efforts," in Rusk's words, to win Tshombe's cooperation with Leopoldville.[49] Kennedy had his new ambassador on board, who spent a lot of his time trying to convince Adoula and Bomboko to negotiate with Tshombe. Again, the problem lay with Tshombe, who rejected the American efforts. In a show of his contempt, the Katangan leader had his gendarmerie attack the Baluba in Elizabethville for supporting the Lovanium agreement.[50]

Hammarskjöld could not let Tshombe's attack on the Baluba go unanswered (figure 9.1). The United Nations was on the brink of success in managing the unrest in the east, and the Afro-Asian states were demanding equal action on Katanga.[51] The new director of U.N. operations in Katanga, Conor Cruise O'Brien, a former member of Ireland's Department of External Affairs, and Mahmoud Khiary of Tunisia and head of the U.N.'s civilian operations, "invited" all unauthorized persons to leave the Congo. The invitation won

Figure 9.1. Refugees Flee from Tshombe, September 8, 1961

Source: United Nations photograph.

few responses, and only a handful of Belgian civilians actually volunteered to leave. O'Brien and Khiary, with Hammarskjöld's approval, launched Rumpunch on August 28 to speed their exit.[52] ONUC forces, led by Indian gurkhas, seized the headquarters of the gendarmerie, the radio station, and other communications buildings in and around Elizabethville. Other ONUC forces, supported by its Military Information Branch, helped destroy the Katangan air force and began disarming Tshombe's soldiers.[53]

Within hours Tshombe and the Belgian government agreed to cooperate with the withdrawal request. O'Brien halted the operation.[54] In fact, Rumpunch did little to stop UMHK's support of Tshombe or his ability to regroup.[55] Within days a fresh supply of mercenaries arrived from Rhodesia, the French colonies in Africa, South Africa, and even Belgium. These new mercenaries, instead of being Belgian patriots, were of dubious background and often had criminal records.[56]

O'Brien and Khiary quickly realized that the operation had been halted too soon and urged Hammarskjöld not to let the U.N. advantages slip away. Despite serious legal doubts, Hammarskjöld approved Operation Morthor, the Hindi word for "smash," but warned his ONUC chief Sture Linnér to proceed cautiously.[57] The new operation began on September 13. Again, ONUC forces seized control of key outposts in Elizabethville and made moves to arrest Tshombe, Munongo, the minister of foreign affairs Evariste Kimba, and others.[58] Prematurely, O'Brien announced that Egide Bocheley-Davidson, a former MNC-L representative in Orientale, and now a Gizenga supporter, would take over provincial leadership in Katanga.

Tshombe was now in Northern Rhodesia, where the prime minister, Roy Welensky, was ready to help. In another of his classic misjudgments, Welensky sided with Katanga. The one remaining Katangan Fouga Magister aircraft, along with several Rhodesian planes, bombed the U.N. troops and caused a number of casualties. The makeshift Katangan force surrounded the U.N. troops in Jadotville, bringing the U.N. campaign precariously close to defeat and leaving everyone wondering what had gone so wrong.[59]

President Kennedy was "extremely upset" about the action in Katanga.[60] Kennedy paled at the thought ONUC might "get licked" only six months after his humiliation at the Bay of Pigs.[61] He met with Dean Rusk, who then called Bunche at the United Nations in New York. Neither the president nor Rusk could believe that the United Nations would take such an extreme action without "prior consultation" with Washington. Their main point of concern was the substitution of the "Gizengist left winger" Bocheley-Davidson for Tshombe. Rusk added that if the U.N. operation led to communist control of Katanga, congressional reaction would send him back to "cotton picking in Georgia." Rusk promised to come to New York on Sunday evening.[62] In a show of displeasure, the president abruptly declined to assist in the further transport of troops.[63]

Hammarskjöld ducked the protests. He boarded a plane for Leopoldville on Sunday afternoon, several hours before Morthor began.[64] The secretary-general would still have to encounter Ambassador Gullion, whom Kennedy ordered to meet with Hammarskjöld and express Washington's "dismay" at the U.N. operation (figure 9.2).[65] Rusk had warned Hammarskjöld that Britain was "equally upset," and Britain let its sentiments be known. Macmillan publicly threatened to terminate British support of ONUC. Other European allies added their voices, while De Gaulle accused Hammarskjöld of exceeding his mandate.[66]

Hammarskjöld's private reaction is surprising. In a letter to Bunche (published by *The Guardian*) he asked rhetorically whether the U.S. administration supposed that implementation of the February 21 resolution "should be conditioned on whether or not we may meet resistance or on whether or not the final outcome may be one which does not suit their political taste?" He continued, "It is better for the U.N. to lose the support of the US because it

Figure 9.2. Kennedy Confers with Ambassador Gullion, August 18, 1961

Source: United Nations photograph.

is faithful to law and principles than to survive as an agent whose activities are geared to political purposes." What is equally stunning is that he seemed to have acquiesced in the selection of Bocheley-Davidson for Katanga. In the same letter to Bunche, Hammarskjöld stated that "we did what we could through Mr. Linnér . . . to avoid the personality of the Commissaire Dëtat, but that this was not successful. However, the Commissaire is accompanied by 2 Katangan moderates."[67] Thus, Hammarskjöld appeared ready to bear the brunt of the controversy surrounding these decisions.

Hammarskjöld was equally frustrated that the problem of Katanga had been dumped on him. The only U.S. solution seemed to be to get Adoula and Tshombe talking again, although as Hammarskjöld complained, they had done nothing to actually "bring Tshombe to his senses."[68] He left New York convinced he had to do the job alone, with no firm guarantees that Tshombe would meet with him. The Katangan finally agreed to meet, and on September 17, Hammarskjöld flew to Ndola, just a few miles into Northern Rhodesia.[69] Hammarskjöld's plane, the *Albertina*, crashed into the side of a mountain just miles from its destination. There were no survivors.[70] With the United Nations at one of the darkest points in its history, it has been hard to believe that his death was a coincidence. There is evidence that the crash was an accident, perhaps a faulty map or landing instructions. Accusations of foul play were, and are still, rampant. Primary suspicion naturally falls on the Katangan gendarmerie, since they were waging an undeclared war against the United Nations.[71]

For the Congo, Hammarskjöld's death was earth-shattering. What would happen to ONUC? Kennedy's more liberal supporters, like Senator Jacob Javits of New York, called for the United States to back the United Nations "with troops if necessary" to complete U.N. objectives.[72] Javits remained a lone voice, and few in Washington wanted more military activity, although they had no real alternatives of their own.[73] The United Nations immediately negotiated a provisional cease-fire with Tshombe. *Pravda* ludicrously charged that the near defeat of ONUC was staged. Zorin denounced the cease-fire negotiations with Tshombe and announced that stopping the military activity was illegal and needed Security Council approval.[74] The Soviet outcry was pitifully inconsistent with previous policy and its timing more designed to influence the selection of a new secretary-general for the United Nations.

Predictably in such circumstances, the selection of a new secretary-general was animated. By early November, the political dust was settling, and the General Assembly selected U Thant to succeed Hammarskjöld. U Thant was a mild-mannered Burmese schoolteacher and journalist who had worked closely with Hammarskjöld and supported his commitment to end the Katangan secession.[75] He was a moderate neutralist who preferred quiet diplomacy and tended to rely more on superpower initiatives. Perhaps most fortuitously, he did not generate much opposition from any side. Although later he would adopt a more forceful policy in the Congo, for now he endorsed the cease-fire. Once again ONUC gave up hard-won gains and left everyone wondering if the United Nations would ever have the will to succeed.

Another Gamble: Round Two

Unexpected events often bring new opportunities. George Ball, who had always wanted out of the Congo as soon as possible, now urged the president to increase U.S. aid to Leopoldville.[76] The hope was to save some of the U.N. achievements in Katanga. Kennedy agreed to send C-130 transport planes under U.N. auspices to strengthen Adoula. The support was moderate enough to make a point, but not intended to encourage Adoula to attack Katanga.[77] Intentions aside, Adoula proved to be another unmanageable ally and as soon as he received the planes, sent ANC troops to Katanga to "complete" the U.N. action. The two ANC battalions were easily rebuffed by Tshombe's army, numbering as many as 13,000, and assisted by new Fouga Magister aircraft and crews from France. Tshombe continued to collect $44 million in revenue from UMHK and other companies, and much of this went to military expenditures.[78] The president was now right back at the start, with Adoula and Tshombe refusing to come to terms with each other and no solution in sight.

The majority of Afro-Asian states were hopeful that the end of secession might be in sight. In the Security Council on November 12, Ceylon, Liberia, and the UAR proposed a new resolution authorizing the use of force to end the Katangan secession.[79] Washington, of course, threatened to use its veto. However, Adlai Stevenson helped rewrite the original version so that it included a clear statement on the illegality of the Katangan secession but provided for no additional use of force. The final version called on the secretary-general to take whatever action was necessary to deport all foreign military personnel who were not with the United Nations.[80] Kennedy withheld his support until another urgent phone call from Stevenson. The latter convinced Kennedy that he was not really agreeing to anything new.[81] Again the president made what he thought was a major concession to the Afro-Asian states in the hopes that they would strengthen their support of U.S. policy.

Kennedy's gamble with the Afro-Asians drove a wedge in his relations with Britain and France, both of whom abstained on the U.N. vote.[82] Neither NATO ally could tolerate what they believed was another step toward the use of force by the United Nations, in what was essentially a crisis of decolonization.[83] France's negative vote was consistent with its past policy of rejecting U.N. intervention in Congolese affairs.[84] The British tacitly supported Tshombe and did not want to see the use of force in the Congo, although there are signs they were growing weary of the whole affair. They now convinced Welensky to help appeal to Tshombe to negotiate with Adoula, especially before a "likely" strengthening of the U.N. mandate.[85] NATO criticism and the rift with Britain and France, in fact, would help clear the way for a more independent U.S. policy, although Kennedy would never abandon trying to keep the alliance stitched together.

Kennedy also had to contend with a significant segment of American society who followed Europe in support for Tshombe. Few Americans were interested in military activity in Africa, and now the pro-Tshombe supporters had a new anti-war–minded audience. The pro-Tshombe movement was led by a northern Democrat, Senator Thomas Dodd of Connecticut. Dodd was a close friend of Vice President Lyndon Johnson and a member of the Senate Foreign Relations Committee. He spoke out strongly against "godless" communism, which he equated to Nazism, an ideology he had helped outlaw at the Nuremberg trials. In the 1950s, Dodd had once lobbied for Guatemala's dictator, Carlos Castillo Armas, and largely because of these efforts the U.S. House of Representatives agreed to send that country $15 million.[86] Information has also surfaced recently that UMHK paid Dodd a $10,000 monthly stipend for his efforts in Katanga (although how long this arrangement might have continued is unclear).[87]

Dodd developed close connections with Michel Struelens, who had worked as a colonial administrator and later for UMHK. Struelens was a Belgian citizen and a former colonial administrator in the Congo. He set up the Katanga Information Services, based in New York, which represented the Katangan government and sponsored the Committee for Aid to Katanga Freedom Fighters to lobby Congress in December 1961. The committee was directed by Max Yergan, an African American intellectual and converted leftist, and supported by such eminent conservatives as Senator Barry Goldwater (R-Arizona), and William F. Buckley Jr., editor of the journal *National Review*, which became the primary vehicle of the growing conservative movement. Buckley, briefly a CIA officer, was controversial in his views that championed white superiority but popular for his charisma and humor.[88] Other prominent members or supporters included former president Herbert Hoover, Republican National Chairman William Miller, and General Albert C. Wedemeyer, the celebrated World War II hero and who had been one of the first to warn of China's fall to communism in 1949. Dodd also found strong support among congressional members from the South. Leading congressmen—including senators Strom Thurmond (R-South Carolina), Harry F. Byrd (D-Virginia), Thurston Morton (R-Kentucky), Frank Lausche (D-Ohio), Bourke Hickenlooper (R-Iowa), and Senate minority leader Everett Dirksen (R-Illinois)—all voiced pro-Katangan views.[89]

If the American public could not understand or fully rationalize support of Tshombe, they certainly could relate to the criticism of the United Nations. The *Christian Science Monitor* called the situation a "thorough mess." Even the influential *New York Times* political analyst Arthur Krock questioned what he saw as Washington's vendetta against Tshombe. Other newspapers such as the *Wall Street Journal* asked why the United Nations was even trying to subdue Tshombe in the first place. The *New York Daily News* called on the United States to stop bankrolling ONUC, while the *Dallas Times Herald* asserted that the United Nations was "looking worse and worse in what at best is a sorry spectacle."[90] These criticisms poked holes in the administration's policy by questioning why Kennedy (along with the United Nations) was fighting an avowedly anticommunist regime when the central government in Leopoldville seemed weak and inept.

Still, Kennedy temporized. He sent Tshombe a message to soften the impact of the latest U.N. resolution of November 1961. Kennedy's message urged "calm and moderation" and was delivered, appropriately, by Senator Dodd, who was then visiting Elizabethville. The message gave Tshombe yet another signal that the United States was not ready to use force against him.[91] Tshombe tested Kennedy's mettle even further when Katangan gendarmes in Elizabethville roughed up U.N. representatives Ian Smith and Brian Urquhart. Tshombe's troops then clashed with the ANC in Kongolo (near the Kivu border), and on December 3, Katangan and U.N. troops battled at the Elizabethville airport, and several U.N. planes were fired on.

U Thant, tired of Tshombe's provocations, was ready to act. So was Kennedy, or least he was ready to *say* he was ready. U Thant ordered ONUC to take any air or ground action necessary to defend the U.N. position. Thus began Round Two (after the Round One Rumpunch and Morthor operations). U.N. strategic plans for Round Two included seizing key points in Elizabethville, including the airports and military bases, and preventing Tshombe from reinforcing his troops. Kennedy approved limited military aid in support of Round Two, including the use of planes to transport troops if the flights could be made without risk of being shot down.[92] On December 12, 1961, U Thant accused UMHK of protecting the mercenaries and manufacturing bombs and armoring trucks for them, and in retaliation ONUC forces bombed UMHK's installations.[93] Despite all indications that events were moving in this direction, Kennedy was not ready for this escalation in the fighting. Even Undersecretary of State George Ball supported a stand-down and immediately demanded that "every reasonable attempt" be made to bring Adoula and Tshombe to talk. Sensing the wedge, Tshombe appealed for a cease-fire two days after the action began against UMHK.[94] The United Nations was incredibly close to winning control of Katanga, and U Thant knew it. In a daring move, he authorized another air strike against UMHK's buildings.[95]

After some arm-twisting by U.S. ambassador Gullion, Tshombe finally agreed to go to Kitona, a resort close to the Atlantic Ocean, to sign a cease-fire.[96] Here, on December 21, Tshombe and Adoula signed the Kitona Accords. By signing this document, Tshombe recognized the unity of the Congo and the Loi Fondamentale as the Constitution. As soon as Tshombe returned to Elizabethville, his ministers charged that the Kitona document had been imposed on Tshombe and he would not honor it.[97] After even more arm-twisting, Tshombe was again made, in early January 1962, to express his support for the Accords that he had already signed. This time he agreed only to the clause in support of unity and rejected allegiance to the Loi Fondamentale, which would have required that he cooperate to reestablish the integrity of the Congo, as outlined by this 1960 law.[98] Everything was in place for yet more problems with Tshombe.

Gizenga's Arrest

The tentative end of Round Two gave Khrushchev another chance to poke holes into U.S.–European policy. The Soviet Union criticized the premature end to the action, an argument the Afro-Asian states would find hard to ignore. "Who gave them [i.e., the U.S., British, and French colonialists] the right to stop the U.N. operations?" *Pravda*'s correspondent Tomas Kolesnichenko asked. In fact, he suggested, the near victory in Katanga had promised to bring an end to secession and finally fulfill the wishes of the Congolese people.[99] Stopping short of this was further evidence that the United Nations was not working in the interests of the Congolese people. These random criticisms coming from the Soviet Union only emphasized the ineffectiveness of Moscow's policy at this stage and the hollowness of its support for Gizenga.

Nor were the Congolese ready to let Gizenga cause more trouble. After Gizenga strongly criticized Adoula from his outpost in Stanleyville, twenty-five members of the Congolese parliament, including ten MNC-L members, demanded that he return to Leopoldville. Gullion urged Adoula to put Gizenga in "protective custody" after forces loyal to Gizenga captured and killed ten Italian airmen in November.[100] In early December, Lundula, the longtime Lumumbist commander in chief of Gizenga's forces, defected and returned to Leopoldville, and the Chamber announced its intention to arrest Gizenga,[101] Christophe Gbenye, now serving as Adoula's interior minister, and meeting with Devlin on the side, also signed the arrest warrant.

President Kennedy had no more interest in dealing with Gizenga. Ralph Dungan, a special assistant to the president, told George McGhee, undersecretary of state for political affairs, that Kennedy "was very anxious to get word to Adoula that we think it is important that Gizenga be thrown out."[102] On January 19, almost exactly one year after the assassination of Lumumba, Gizenga was captured and this time brought to Leopoldville in a U.N. plane. He was put under house arrest and eventually imprisoned on the island of Bula Bemba near Leopoldville.[103]

Upon hearing of Gizenga's arrest, the Soviet Union began a campaign of protest that seemed more obligatory than angry. But the campaign was also surprisingly persistent, even in the view of Soviet friends such as the UAR's ambassador in Moscow. The Central Committee prepared a plan to defend Gizenga that was extensive and included the Foreign Ministry and the press.[104] Zorin began by trying to call another Security Council meeting. Soviet publications protested Gizenga's poor treatment and warned that he would meet the same fate as Lumumba. Prominent Soviet academics such as Bobodzhan G. Gafurov, and even Dmitri Ol'derogge, the aging doyen of African studies in the Soviet Union and the mentor of the leading Africanist Ivan Potekhin, made special pleas for Gizenga's life. Soviet and African students marched in front of the University of the Friendship of Peoples in support of Gizenga.[105] A *Pravda* journalist, Lev Volodin, decried the arrest and questioned his safety but did not single out Adoula for special condemnation.[106] In response to these criticisms, Adoula allowed foreign correspondents, including Georgii Fediashin, to visit with Gizenga on April 21. The journalists found little of substance to criticize about his treatment.[107]

The Soviet assessment of the situation in the Congo would reach a new nadir after the arrest of Gizenga. Christophe Gbenye and Joseph Kasongo, the two leading Lumumbists left with any influence, had joined everyone else in Leopoldville. In January 1962, Podgornov had denounced Kasongo as an imperialist agent after he criticized Gizenga and called his arrest justified. Podgornov argued that a better candidate for support was Egide Bocheley-Davidson, and that the Soviet Union should support him as a replacement for Kasongo as president of the Chamber of Representatives. But the opposition now suffered from a lack of direction, as the MNC-L, the PSA, and Cerea were all fragmented or torn apart and without a leader or voice.[108]

Gizenga's arrest came on the heels of several serious setbacks for the Soviet Union elsewhere in Africa, and the lackluster Soviet response is indicative that Khrushchev was downgrading Africa. In December 1961, President Sekou Touré sent the Soviet ambassador Daniel Solod home after suspecting him of encouraging students to protest against the government. Touré's actions were an expression of disillusionment with Soviet aid. Another strike against Soviet prestige in Africa occurred after Kennedy decided to go ahead with funding for the Volta Dam project in Ghana and improve relations with Nkrumah.[109] In Egypt, Nasser had also begun to retreat from his radical stand on the Congo as he turned his attention to Arab problems and searched for more cooperation with the United States.[110] Against the backdrop of these challenges for the Soviet Union, Gizenga's arrest accentuated the growing superficiality of Soviet influence in Africa and helped call into question Khrushchev's promises that a foreign policy of expansion would increase the security of the Soviet Union.

Taking a Stab at ONUC Financially

Still, the Soviet Union managed to find some small leverage. Khrushchev wanted to see the end of ONUC, and the sooner the better. He had long opposed the continuation of the operation and for over a year had refused to pay financial assessments for ONUC. Soon the whole issue of paying for ONUC began to take on a life of its own.

The Budget Committee of the United Nations had decided in 1960 that the expenses for the operation were to be borne by the entire U.N. membership on a percentage basis. Enforcing payment was difficult. As a result, the United States had periodically made voluntary contributions to keep the United Nations solvent and able to continue to carry out the operation in the Congo. Funding for ONUC had been secured until the end of 1962, but after that it was clear that financial shortfalls would force downsizing of the operation. The Soviet Union had consistently opposed extra assessments for ONUC, arguing that they had not been subjected to the Security Council veto.[111] Soviet strategy questioned the viability of any new military action in the Congo without the financial ability to support them. These budget problems made it all the more apparent that time was running out for ONUC.

The Soviets were not alone in their distaste for spending more money on ONUC. A group of U.S. members of Congress, led by Representative Omar Burleson (D-Texas), complained that the United States was bearing too much of the U.N. financial burden, especially in the Congo. Because of such criticism, U.S. allies and strong proponents of the United Nations—like Britain, Canada, and Ireland—felt added pressure to increase their contributions, which they did. France sided with the Soviet Union in arguing that the peacekeeping budget should not be mandatory. Belgium, not wanting any more unwelcome international attention, tried to hide from the entire debate.[112]

Questions about financing ONUC would continue to simmer, not yet to the point of boiling over into mainstream discussions about the operation or peacekeeping. Yet everything about ONUC now seemed halfhearted, and it was only a matter of time until the operation would have to come to an end. Would it simply cease to be? Would it be replaced by something less ambitious? Would something more dramatic happen to bring it to an end? The operation itself was indeed at an important juncture in its history, the history of the United Nations, and the history of the Cold War in the Congo.

10. Force and Reconciliation

Diplomacy to solve the Congo's problems was not working. Tshombe continued to flout the Kitona Accords, which kept the crisis simmering. In an effort to implement the accords, the United States and the United Nations supported a series of talks.[1] The endless discussions only accentuated Tshombe's insincerity. Although the Katangan leader repeated his promises to cooperate, he refused to follow up with any meaningful action. President Kennedy looked to his European partners, especially Spaak and Macmillan, to help convince Tshombe to actively support reunification of the Congo.[2] Kennedy, however, found neither Belgium nor Britain ready to push Tshombe too hard. At their two-day meeting in Bermuda on December 19–21, Macmillan tried to impress on Kennedy that the United States had "over-rated" Adoula and the United Nations.[3] A few months later, in May 1962, Macmillan curtly made clear to Kennedy that if the talks with Tshombe broke down, Britain would not support another round of U.N. military action.[4]

If neither Tshombe nor his European partners wanted Kennedy to act, Prime Minister Adoula did. Despite the criticism that had fallen on Lumumba for his trip to Washington, Adoula tried a trip of his own in February 1962. He met with President Kennedy and subsequently with Secretaries Ball and Williams and urged support for the Kitona Accord (figure 10.1). With growing impatience, Ball turned the tables and pressed Adoula to compromise with Tshombe and support U.N. retraining of the ANC. Adoula blamed the retraining delay on Mobutu, who, he said, did not want a United Nations–managed program.[5] Taking another cue from Lumumba and probably hoping to shake Washington into action, Adoula also met with the Soviet U.N. representative, Vladimir Zorin. When the prime minister returned to the Congo,

Figure 10.1. Adoula Meets with Kennedy in Washington, February 5, 1962

Source: John F. Kennedy Presidential Library; White House photograph.

he announced that Zorin had invited him to visit the Soviet Union and that he had accepted the invitation.[6]

With few other tangible benefits from his trip, Adoula appealed to the international community and asked for a new Security Council meeting to discuss implementation of Kitona.[7] Kennedy opposed reconvening the Security Council because he feared that it would mandate the use of force against Katanga.[8] Adoula had the sympathetic ear of U Thant, who believed that at this stage the Security Council should review the entire U.N. operation in the Congo. News coming out of Katanga only reinforced his position. Tshombe had reportedly goaded 10,000 women and children to storm a U.N. roadblock and continued to defy the Kitona Accords. Once again, the prestige of the United Nations was under fire and U Thant wanted a clear mandate or out of the Congo business entirely.[9]

It was becoming apparent from all angles that Kennedy would have to act or cut his losses in the Congo. Now that the United States was so deeply involved, the latter option of disengagement would cost a lot more in terms of goodwill and progress in Africa than it would have over a year and a half ago when General Lemnitzer suggested the option. Instead, Kennedy reaffirmed his support for "all possible measures" short of war to end the secession. Resorting to a favorite tactic, the president sent Colonel Michael J. L. Greene to the Congo to evaluate the military needs of the ANC and devise a plan for its retraining. More generally, the mission was intended to emphasize the U.S. commitment to end the secession. From the Congo, Ambassador Godley warned Kennedy that the mission might end up being counterproductive if no aid was ultimately forthcoming. Congolese suspicion of the U.S. mission ran so high, he warned, that the ANC rank-and-file would interpret Greene's visit as a spy mission.[10] So would Tshombe.

Composing the U Thant Plan

Looking for a way out of the deepening imbroglio, the African Bureau of the State Department drafted a plan for national reconciliation in the Congo. The plan, which was hammered out with U.N. officials, was eventually accepted by U Thant and became popularly known as the U Thant Plan (figure 10.2). Theoretically, the plan ensured that the United States would take the lead in finding a solution to the Katanga question and therefore avoid any undesirable U.N. military action.

The intention was to reunite the Congo through a series of progressive measures. A new constitution was to be drafted in stages and approved by the Congolese parliament. To facilitate reunification, Katanga would transfer revenues received from UMHK to Leopoldville. Then the ANC would be regrouped and retrained, and finally members of Katanga's strongest political party, Conakat, would be brought into the central government. UMHK agreed to make payments to the central government, with the caveat that Tshombe freed them to do so. That caveat, obviously, was problematic.

The plan had no specific timetables but rather four phases intended to guarantee timely implementation. If progress was not made in the drafting and approval of the new constitution (phase one) or in Katanga's acceptance of it (phase two), then economic sanctions (phase three) were to be invoked. Sanctions would include an international boycott of copper, 75 percent being imported by Belgium and, at the Belgian government's request, a boycott of cobalt, 75 percent being imported by the United States. A British agreement to go along with sanctions was conspicuously absent, suggesting another major flaw in the plan from the outset. Finally, if economic sanctions did not work, the drafters included an oblique threat of military coercion (phase four) to ensure its implementation.[11]

For a fleeting moment, Kennedy's advisers were united and favored the plan, although they differed in their enthusiasm and their understanding of the

Figure 10.2. Kennedy, U Thant, and Stevenson, January 1962

Source: John F. Kennedy Presidential Library; White House photograph.

risk of force involved. Secretary Rusk believed that the U Thant Plan offered a possibility of ending the constitutional crisis, but he wanted to avoid any use of force. He did not think the United Nations would be "able or willing" to impose a "political solution by military action" nor did he believe that the United States could control any fighting once it broke out.[12] Ball and Williams seemed less concerned about the use of force and were more enthusiastic about ending the crisis.

Regardless of the possibilities, the risk of the use of force was clearly understood at the highest levels. The minutes of the meeting with the president on July 25 recorded that "the actions contemplated would realistically involve the risk of fighting" but "under no circumstances will the United Nations take a military initiative. . . . Such actions would have to be done at the request of the Government of the Congo," thus implying that Kennedy, through daily intimate working relationships, would have the final say.[13] Ball believed that this risk would only materialize if negotiations were handled clumsily, and called the plan a "reasonable solution" based on "constitutional principles" and "practical measures."[14] The "ultimate weapon" against Tshombe, he held, was the tax-collection (or revenue-sharing) scheme, which would redirect UMHK's resources.[15] After the past two years of fruitless negotiations with Tshombe, the administration inexplicably failed to consider what had been at the heart of its difficulties— Tshombe simply did not believe that the United States would support the use of force to end Katangan secession. And as long as Tshombe was in power in Katanga, he had no incentive to "free" UMHK from making payments to him, and UMHK continued making those payments.

Kennedy gave the plan general approval by August 5, but with one crucial modification. Phase four of the original plan presented to Kennedy had referred to "more stringent measures," implying the use of force, if sanctions failed. Kennedy watered down even that threat, so that phase four of the official plan referred only to "measures that could be taken" after sanctions.[16] Everyone could read between the lines.

Kennedy's continued reluctance to commit to the use of force concerned U Thant. The secretary-general did not want to involve the United Nations if he was not assured of U.S. and European support for "his" plan or the freedom to execute it as outlined. To assuage his fears about Kennedy's modifications, Ball assured U Thant that there was a general agreement among the United States, Belgium, Britain, and France that they were willing to back him up "in pressing [the] two sides [to] reach agreement."[17] This statement was a stretch, since the three U.S. allies still opposed the use of force in the Congo. U Thant, as optimistic as anyone, overlooked the exaggeration in the hope that the plan was a road map to solving the Congo problem. With Ball's guarantee, he dropped the idea of reopening the Security Council debate and accepted the plan.[18]

Both Adoula and Tshombe formally accepted the U Thant Plan, but only under great pressure. The plan, after all, was drafted by foreigners and had no Congolese involvement or imprint. Adoula agreed to the plan on August 23, and after some wrangling by Undersecretary of State George McGhee, Tshombe agreed to the plan on September 3. McGhee, a wealthy Texas oilman who had a reputation for his pro-Katanga sentiments, boasted that the new constitution would grant more responsibility to the provinces and "would in effect paraphrase the U.S. Constitution."[19] Adoula could rationalize the plan as a way to finally end the secession and reunify the Congo, while Tshombe had little option, given the Belgian and UMHK agreement, at least verbally, to go along with it.[20] In any case, Tshombe's history of reneging on agreements did not bode well. Besides, all the plan meant for the moment was another round of negotiations.

Surprise, But No Surprise

Suddenly in early September, everyone seemed to recognize the high stakes that the plan entailed. Barely a week after formal announcement of the U Thant Plan, both Rusk and Ball seemed surprised by the risk of force it entailed. Ball now berated the "mush" coming from the African Bureau where it was assumed that force was the only way to end the secession. He promised Kennedy that he would take over management of U.S. policy in the Congo. For direct information he called the quick-thinking Lewis Hoffacker, who had just been transferred from the U.S. Consulate in Elizabethville to the embassy in Leopoldville. Ball discovered that Hoffacker had been opposed to the plan because of its commitment to use military force, but that the White House had not been informed of his views. Ball now lamented that "we were going to have to do some very careful and adroit disengaging from this," that is, from the commitment to use force.[21] Rusk agreed and tried to bring U.S. ambassador Gullion and others in the Congo in line. "We should be clear in our own minds" he wrote the ambassador, "that the resumption of military action between ONUC and Katangese would have disastrous consequences for both U.N. and for U.S. policy and we should be careful not to give it encouragement."[22]

As the U Thant Plan came under increased scrutiny, so did the administration's policy in the Congo. The general American public was at best lukewarm toward the use of force against Tshombe. Particularly irksome to the president was the *New York Times* columnist Arthur Krock's direct attack on Kennedy's policy as "confused" and ineffective.[23] The criticism had a ring of truth as Kennedy seemed unable to explain what he was doing in Katanga. The president also continued to waffle on the best approach to Tshombe. Senator Dodd and the Committee for Aid to Katanga questioned why Kennedy would want to undermine Tshombe's efforts to save Katanga from communism. Appealing to Dodd's ego, and trying to use Dodd for his own purposes, Kennedy asked the senator to deliver another letter to Tshombe. Gullion strongly opposed the overture, which he said sent the wrong message, but Ball and Rusk overrode his objections. The letter reassured Tshombe that the United States had no hard feelings toward him personally and tried to persuade him to mend his differences with Adoula.[24] To dull some of the criticism, Rusk gave a rare press conference to support the U.N. operation as the best way to end the crisis peacefully.[25] What else was Tshombe to think?

It was no surprise that Moscow disliked and denounced the U Thant Plan. Before the plan's release, U Thant traveled to Moscow to meet with Khrushchev and win his support. Khrushchev not only rejected cooperation with the plan but publicly denounced it as another Western-led conspiracy.[26] U Thant was visibly shaken by the rebuff and responded that the Soviet leaders let "fear and suspicion" dictate the Kremlin's policy.[27] Instead, the Soviet Union advanced its own plan to end secession. The Soviet plan, designed to point out the weaknesses of the Western scheme, called for an end to the Katangan secession, the expulsion of foreign mercenaries, provided for aid to the central government, and finally called for the withdrawal of ONUC forces.[28] As if to emphasize its willingness to take on a more vigilant role, Khrushchev mended fences with Adoula and reopened the Soviet Embassy, which had been closed for a year. Moscow now appointed a new ambassador, Sergei Nemchina, to the Congo.[29]

By the summer of 1962 it was becoming more apparent that the Soviet Union would not so easily escape assessments to pay for ONUC, and this might have given Khrushchev added incentive to keep a footing in the Congo. In June of that year, the International Court of Justice issued its ruling supporting the legality of the special assessments to pay for the Congo operation. The ruling stipulated that *all* members were responsible for paying for peacekeeping operations or go into arrears under Article 19. The court also upheld the legality of the sale of $200 million in U.N. bonds to help cover the U.N. debt.[30] The Soviet Union rejected the court's ruling and continued to ignore assessments. On September 21, 1962, Gromyko repeated that the Soviet Union would stand by its policy of nonpayment.[31] Eventually, however, if Article 19 were applied, it would mean the Soviet Union would lose its voting rights in the General Assembly.

Nor were the Congolese comfortable with what the U Thant Plan meant for them. By October 1962, unrest had spread all over the country in anticipation of what the U Thant Plan really meant for power sharing between the central government and the provinces. Unrest also plagued Kasai, where in mid-October, Albert Kalonji briefly escaped from jail and stirred up opposition to Adoula.[32] In Kivu, Anicet Kashamura announced formation of the Mouvement de Résistance Congolais, a combination of Cerea, MNC, PSA, and Sendwe's Balubakat with the objective of overthrowing Adoula. Adoula retaliated against the movement by arresting Gbenye, whom he managed to keep in jail for about six weeks, ultimately doing more harm to his popularity than good.[33]

Implementation of the plan was in serious jeopardy almost from the day of its adoption. Adoula had agreed to the new constitution drafted by U.S.–U.N. legal experts but demonstrated little enthusiasm in getting it passed by the Congolese parliament. Ball concluded that the new constitution was "over-sophisticated and probably unworkable," but felt its ratification by the Congolese parliament was necessary to avoid invoking sanctions.[34] Hoping to jump-start the stalled negotiations, McGhee made a second trip to the Congo.[35] Tshombe, however, refused to negotiate while Mobutu was still conducting a three-week-old offensive against Katanga. Meanwhile, the Katangan leader was building up his air strength and hiring more mercenaries. Frustrated with the lack of progress, Adoula suddenly called for a move to third-stage economic sanctions. The date was October 20, 1962.[36]

His timing was disastrous. Adoula could not have known that President Kennedy was consumed by what was yet the fiercest of Cold War crises. Unknown to the world, on October 15, U.S. intelligence had detected Soviet construction of a ballistic missile site in Cuba, beginning a week of intense discussion at the White House. On October 22, Kennedy announced a quarantine to keep Soviet offensive hardware from reaching Cuba. Minute by minute the world waited to see whether Soviet ships would challenge the blockade. The problems did not stop there. On the other side of the globe, and making U.N. military action in the Congo even more unlikely, India had become embroiled in a border war with China. Indian prime minister Jawaharlal Nehru would eventually announce the recall of his 5,700 troops serving in ONUC, almost a third of the force. Indian troops would not actually leave the Congo until February 1963, but the writing was on the wall.

With the prospect of stage-three sanctions looming, Kennedy faced a serious dilemma. Was the U Thant Plan about to entangle the United States in a military confrontation that it did not want? And without key Indian support? National Security Council staff member Carl Kaysen, who had been a lone voice in Washington against the U Thant Plan, warned that if the United States failed to honor its commitments, the Adoula government would fall to a more radical one and the majority of African states would come to the support of Leopoldville, while Portugal and the white-minority regimes in the Central African Federation and South Africa would come to the aid of Tshombe. The result, wrote Kaysen, would create "something like [a] White-Black war in Africa" with the United States caught in the middle.[37] Kennedy still felt that he could not risk the use of force, especially in light of events in Cuba and India. Instead, he revived the Greene Plan for retraining the ANC forces. Kennedy now tied aid for the retraining to Leopoldville's willingness to facilitate the reintegration of Katanga.[38] It was a last-ditch effort to stall the move to phase three.

U Thant was not sympathetic to Kennedy's second thoughts about the use of force. Exasperated with the lack of progress, the secretary-general now took the initiative. He announced that he would call for economic sanctions if no headway in the constitutional negotiations had been made by November 15.[39] Aghast, Kennedy had not expected the announcement. But Adlai

Stevenson warned him that if the administration continued to obstruct economic sanctions, eventually U Thant would take even "more risky measures." If blocked further, Stevenson predicted that the secretary-general was ready to pronounce ONUC a failure and dump the entire mess on the United States.[40]

Probably sometime in late October or even early November, the Kennedy administration began taking some covert steps to strengthen the air force in the Congo. According to historian Leif Hellström, the CIA began to create its so-called "instant air force" in the Congo. Air strength remained key to the stability and power of any government in Leopoldville. In mid-1962, Leopoldville bought six trainer T-6 aircraft from the Belgian government. Soon afterward they approached the United States for pilots and then asked for rockets for the aircraft to help block the Katangan air offensive. In an interview, Lawrence Devlin told Hellström that U.S. ambassador Gullion supported the initiative to hire pilots. Devlin also met with Adoula at the beginning of November. Two weeks after this meeting, documents (dated November 15) refer to six Cuban pilots who were trained by the Miami-based, CIA-backed Caribbean Aero-Marine to fly the T-6s for the Congolese.[41] The hope at this point was to boost the Adoula government and with luck prevent its collapse on the eve of what increasingly looked like another possible U.N. intervention.

Sanctions according to the U Thant Plan had been set in motion and the November 15 deadline came and went. In Leopoldville, Congolese leaders were beginning to doubt the U.S.–U.N. commitment to the full implementation of the U Thant Plan. Kasavubu's own political party, Abako, openly debated calling for the plan's suspension, which would allow Leopoldville to resume its attack on Katanga.[42] In a conversation with Devlin, Mobutu warned that the Soviet Embassy was in the process of drawing up a "shopping list" of military supplies. Simultaneously, Adoula told Ambassador Gullion that he would be under great pressure to accept such aid if that is what it took to end the secession.[43] Although obviously a tactic to get the Americans moving, it was understood as a real possibility because the Soviet Union had shown a willingness to provide aid in the past.

Adoula's government would not last long without some kind of action on Katanga soon. On November 25, the Congolese prime minister narrowly survived a vote of no confidence. Had he lost, the Chamber planned to put forward a new government slate with the moderate Lumumbist, Alexandre Mahamba, as prime minister, who almost certainly would have asked ONUC troops to leave the Congo. On the same day as the parliamentary vote, the U.S. administration privately approved sending a "reasonable quantity" of rockets for the instant air force, although some "technical details" would have to be worked out.[44] The news did not change the internal situation, which continued to deteriorate. In order to appease the Lumumbists, Adoula lifted the state of emergency in Leopoldville and granted amnesty to political prisoners. Still, the anti-Adoula alliance threatened to seek Adoula's resignation if economic sanctions were not invoked.[45] The crisis mounted.

U Thant and his advisers were nearing the end of their rope in support for the plan of national reconciliation, at least as it was being implemented thus far. At a dinner party on November 26, Ghana's U.N. representative, Robert Gardiner, pulled aside the deputy assistant secretary of state for public affairs, Carl Rowan, and accused the United States of "betraying" the people of the Congo "while using the [United Nations] as a shield" to hide from further action. Gardiner expressed the full extent of African and Asian disillusionment with the failure to implement the U Thant Plan. He told Rowan that the United Nations would go along with the United States for another month, and if nothing had improved, "the [United States] will be free to deal with [the] Congo all by itself." The real shame, Gardiner lashed out, was that "Tshombe has built up his air force, his offensive capacity . . . while . . . our hands have been tied by U.S. evasions [and] timidity." Gardiner also warned that the Soviet ambassador had already offered Adoula "everything he needs" and that if he (i.e., Gardiner) were Adoula he would take the offer. Stevenson confirmed that Congolese foreign minister Justin Bomboko had privately expressed opinions similar to Gardiner's.[46] Bomboko was traditionally pro-Western, and his occasional threats of defection were signals of serious discontent.

Bombarded with such pessimism, and realizing that events in the Congo were at a turning point, Kennedy reluctantly agreed to sanctions. He gave Tshombe an ultimatum to allow 50 percent of UMHK's revenues to go to the central government, or face "severe economic measures."[47] Tshombe turned up pressure on UMHK, still willing to call Washington's bluff. He threatened a "scorched earth" policy, daring Belgian interests to face the losses that they would incur if they abandoned him.[48] Tshombe benefited from the fact that the United States and Belgium were still woefully disunited, even after a series of negotiations (figure 10.3). Belgium did little to actively support Kennedy's ultimatum, despite its profession not to want another bad year for copper. Britain still refused to go along with sanctions after an intense round of U.S.– British negotiations, striking another blow against their effectiveness.[49]

Meanwhile, Adoula struggled desperately to remain in power. He claimed that his government was "in ruins" and Tshombe was attacking his troops and villages daily while the United States and the United Nations did nothing.[50] On December 11, the Congolese prime minister decided that the only way to save his position was to get the U Thant Plan back on track. He sent a letter to seventeen nations calling for an embargo on copper and cobalt, in

Figure 10.3. Kennedy Meets with Belgian Foreign Minister Paul-Henri Spaak, November 27, 1962

Source: John F. Kennedy Presidential Library; White House photograph.

effect single-handedly invoking phase three of the U Thant Plan. U Thant felt he had few alternatives.[51] The secretary-general was under great pressure from African and Asian states, including moderate states like Nigeria, to make some progress on implementation of "his" plan, regardless of the U.S. position.[52] Thus, he supported the embargo, thus finally implementing phase three sanctions.

A New "New" Policy and Round Three

With U.N. actions running ahead of expectations, and the Adoula government near collapse, Kennedy's top advisers pushed hard for a clear demonstration of the U.S. commitment to end the crisis. To thrash out a new "new policy on the Congo," Kennedy, Rusk, Ball, McGhee, Williams, Bronson Tweedy from the CIA, deputy secretary of defense Roswell Gilpatric, director of the State Department's Bureau of Intelligence and Research Roger Hilsman, Bowles, Cleveland, and Colonel Greene, among others, attended a series of meetings on December 14 and 17. At the first meeting on Friday afternoon, everyone accepted the fact that diplomacy had failed and agreed that Katangan separatism tarnished U.S. policy as neocolonial. George Ball endorsed a show of force to reunite the Congo. The United Nations, he said, needed "to make a more impressive show of force than it has yet done." Ball recommended U.S. aid for a U.N. attack on Katanga, including a U.S. fighter squadron with eight fighter jets and several reconnaissance aircraft operating with U.N. ground support.[53] Even the usually pro-Katanga McGhee agreed, while Williams, Bowles, and Stevenson (from New York) advocated greater support of United Nations–directed military action. Conspicuously absent from discussions was the issue of cooperation with the European powers, necessary to convince Tshombe that his time had run out.

The axiom "image is everything" was important for Kennedy, who needed to persuade his domestic critics to go along with his Congo policy. He now put his advisers to the task. Kennedy never seemed to doubt that Katangan independence left an opening for Soviet infiltration into the Congo, but wanted to know how he should frame the problem with Tshombe. Part of his concerns lay in the unanswered question of Tshombe's future after the secession was ended. Bundy and Kaysen suggested portraying military action as a way to "guarantee" the anticommunist Tshombe a place in government, which would placate his supporters like Senator Dodd. Bowles more naturally suggested making Tshombe out to be the "bad guy" whose policies invited the Soviet Union to meddle in the Congo.[54]

By Monday morning doubts about the proposed use of force had surfaced. What would happen, Rusk asked, if the show of force still had no effect on Tshombe? "Would we go in further with whatever force is needed?"[55] Kaysen also weighed in with a memorandum to Kennedy opposing the fighter squadron without exploring other alternatives first. These and other growing questions appear to have had some effect.[56] Later that day Kennedy wondered whether the United States could "get out" when it wanted after committing the prestige of its personnel. Still haunted by the Bay of Pigs, Kennedy again insisted that there would be "no fight if we can't win" in the Congo. The president decided to wait to take action on the air squadron and instead agreed to tell U Thant that the United States would provide him with the military hardware (fighter aircraft, armored cars, trucks, technicians) that he had requested to help out ONUC forces.[57]

Additionally Washington agreed to beef up its "instant air force" in the Congo. In the first days of December, Kennedy approved the delivery of rockets for the T-6 Cuban-piloted aircraft. They arrived on December 17, and were outfitted quietly and as quickly as possible by U.S. Air Force technicians in civilian clothes. The force was preparing for a possible strike as early as mid-January. The United States kept close control and it could pull the plug at any time through its control of the Cuban pilots. Ultimately they were not needed, but the Cubans were left in place and they continued to fly the T-6s around Leopoldville to show U.S. support for the Congolese government.[58]

Kennedy remained undecided over the best course of action in the Congo. If Tshombe was "not cowed" by the newest U.N. effort, or by the threat of a U.S. air squadron, Kennedy told his circle of advisers that "we would then decide on further actions in the light of the requested military appraisal."[59] The fact that neither the administration nor Kennedy could articulate what they wanted to achieve or how—beyond a unified, anticommunist Congo—is baffling. Perhaps most troubling is the failure of the administration to consider prodding the European powers to convince Tshombe to cooperate. Without its European allies on board, Washington would never be able to convince Tshombe that it was ready to use force.

U Thant was also experiencing doubts about the offer of a U.S. fighter air squadron, and on December 21 asked Kennedy to defer any final decision.[60] He told Washington that he did not want to jeopardize U.N. neutrality or his relations with the Soviet Union. Perhaps U Thant was infected with the same optimism as Kennedy, and hoped that a show of force was all that was needed. Charles Yost, a deputy to Stevenson, told Secretary Ball that U Thant and Bunche "think that the mere display of this force will be sufficient to cause Tshombe to give way." Ball reacted positively. "This may not be too bad a solution," he mused.[61] U Thant also asked the Royal Canadian Air Force air commander H. A. Morrison to organize an air force. Morrison assembled fighter jets from the Swedish and Ethiopian air force, transports from Italy, and Canberra bombers from India. The Canberras were controversial because they were capable of dropping 1,000-pound bombs, and although there are suggestions that Washington nudged the United Nations to call on London to supply twenty-four of the 1,000-pound bombs, none were ever used against Katanga.[62]

Kennedy decided it was time for another military mission and sent General Louis W. Truman to the Congo to review the situation. Truman's real task was to figure out what to do if Tshombe would not surrender. His mission, announced on December 18, seemed to be another delay by Kennedy to avoid a difficult decision.[63] Tshombe again took advantage of the time he had and went into action. He dispatched his *jeunesse* warriors to instigate sporadic riots around Elizabethville (although he would subsequently agree to a truce). Then, on Christmas Day, members of the Katangan gendarmerie, drunk from their extra beer ration, began reveling on top of a copper heap and thought they were under fire from U.N. troops and fired in return. U Thant demanded that the gendarmerie withdraw and give the U.N. troops their rightful freedom of movement by 3:00 p.m. on December 28, 1962.[64] The deadline passed with no response from Tshombe. Thus began Operation Grand Slam, also referred to as Round Three, aimed at ending the secession.

Engaged in this newest emergency, the United Nations officially requested a fighter squadron from the United States. The U.S. Air Force began planning to move a squadron of F-84s into the area, although events would ultimately supersede the plans. ONUC forces were also better prepared this time around. Without the hesitation it had exhibited in the past, the United Nations' Swedish air unit attacked the Avikat, the Katangan air force base, at Kolwezi, and destroyed all but a few aircraft. U.N. ground forces commanded by India's popular Dewan Prem Chand moved in and soon took control of Elizabethville. All along the way, U.N. forces encountered very little popular resistance. ONUC soldiers headed for the Lufira River, beyond which lay the prizes of Jadotville and Kolwezi, the location of UMHK's installations.[65] Jubilant, ONUC's chief of operation in the Congo, Robert Gardiner of Ghana, promised that "we are not going to make the mistake this time of stopping short."[66] Meanwhile his boss, who believed the threats that Tshombe would blow up all the mining installations, had promised the Belgian ambassador that U.N. troops would not cross the Lufira.

Both Rusk and Stevenson sought reassurances from Bunche that current U.N. military plans were limited.[67] Sensing Washington's uneasiness, Ambassador Gullion, from Leopoldville, single-handedly tried to discourage any deals with Tshombe and emphasized the fragility of the Congolese government. Rusk was deaf to any such appeals. Instead, and with Kennedy's approval, Rusk made a telephone call to U Thant to urge the secretary to "call all parties to agree to [his] plan" and end the fighting.[68] As if that was all that was needed! His unrealistic expectations demonstrated Kennedy's willingness to do anything to avoid the use of force. The communication, or miscommunication, left a gulf between Washington and New York. On December 31, the secretary-general made a statement on the recent U.N. action in which he said he regretted the use of force. He agreed to give Tshombe two weeks to allow him time to ensure cooperation of his forces with the United Nations, but refused to meet with him.[69]

A political settlement was nowhere in sight. Rusk did manage to get a pledge from Belgium and Britain to help persuade Tshombe to return to Elizabethville (from a sanctuary in Kolwezi) and resume negotiations. Tshombe agreed to renew his commitment to the U Thant Plan, but by this time there was a lot of pressure on Adoula to abandon that failed initiative. In truth, resuming negotiations assumed that he (Adoula) would make more concessions than his rebellious parliament would tolerate. With the military settlement teetering on the brink of disaster, Adoula prorogued parliament and saved himself an impending battle for office.[70]

What happened next surprised everyone. Instead of halting, U.N. commander Prem Chand marched his troops across the Lufira River. U Thant blamed the advance on a breakdown in communications. Some suggest that Prem Chand simply ordered all radios shut off while Brigadier Reginald Noronha led his men across the river by using the twisted steel remains of a railway bridge.[71] Before they knew it, literally, Noronha was in Jadotville and the mercenaries had fled.[72] Upon hearing the latest news, Dean Rusk called U Thant, and in a clearly difficult conversation expressed the "deep concern" in Washington and suggested new talks with Tshombe. U Thant rejected this course and instead gambled on success.[73]

At least by January 9, the secretary-general had made the decision to continue the U.N. offensive right into Kolwezi. Kolwezi was home to two of the province's key dams and its power generators, and the Western powers were loath to inflict damage there. Tshombe continued to refuse their peaceful entry. But on January 14, a group of Katangan ministers declared they were ready to end the secession and allow the United Nations freedom of movement throughout Katanga. With his support crumbling, Tshombe agreed to go along and renounce the secession, but that, of course, did not guarantee his cooperation. The next day UMHK signed an agreement with Leopoldville to turn over all its receipts in foreign exchange in return for an agreed-upon amount of Congolese francs. It was the signal that Belgian business interests were finally ready to cooperate. U Thant pushed forward, and on January 21, 1963, U.N. troops entered Kolwezi.[74] Although Tshombe did not yet surrender, the secession of Katanga had been broken, at last. With that Grand Slam force, and barely a whimper in response, the three-year secession was over.

Two days later, Senator Joseph Ileo arrived in Elizabethville as a representative of the central government. U.N. forces then began a sweep of Katanga to rid that province of mercenaries.[75] An estimated 8,000 mercenaries lingered in Katanga, although they were quickly dispersed. Tshombe went into hiding, fearful that his life was in danger from several different quarters. In and out of Katanga from secret locations, often in Northern Rhodesia, Tshombe maintained his bid for leadership of Katanga. He also began to put out feelers to find a post in Leopoldville. On May 31, Tshombe escaped to Spain to avoid arrest as U.N. troops finally brought the last holdouts in Katanga under control.[76] For the time being, he was forced to let emotions subside.

Reunification without Rewards

Unfortunately for Adoula, the benefits that were supposed to have devolved on him with the end of the Katangan secession and "reunification" failed to materialize. Unrest developed throughout the entire Congo, but particularly in Kasai. Although Kasai's attempted secession had been brought to an end about a year ago, the province remained in rack and ruin. Ethnic fighting, dislocation, and economic troubles were rampant. By March 1963, about 3,000 Balubas were dead and 150,000 had fled into the forest with the destruction of the town of Mtabi. The unrest continued until a greater U.N. presence established some degree of control. Unrest would return to Kasai in June and would continue to add to Adoula's problems as he struggled to retain power.[77]

Adoula also had to contend with all the economic problems associated with decolonization and civil war. Political problems continued to mount, threatening government breakdown. Adoula set out to handle the political crisis he faced, knowing he had the most leeway here. He first tested the possibility of an agreement with the leftists, and in April released Gizenga from jail. The overture was not enough for the Congolese parliament. The Chamber passed a vote of no confidence in Adoula, threatening new elections, but the vote was overturned by the Senate. In defiance, Adoula adjourned parliament for a month.[78]

Security issues continued to afflict the United Nations, at least for the next few months. After the success of Grand Slam, Kennedy wanted to keep ONUC in the Congo for a little while longer. His hopes hinged on a U.N.-sponsored retraining program for the Congolese army. Had Hammarskjöld still been alive he might have had more luck persuading the international community to support such a venture. U Thant soon made it clear, however, that he thought this was out of bounds for the United Nations.[79] He wanted to bring an end to the U.N. mission in the Congo as quickly as possible. In May 1963, U Thant announced that he was reducing the U.N. force and planning for its withdrawal by the end of 1963, and asked for $33 million to wind up the operation. Even this request caused a storm of protest from the Soviet and radical African states, but a U.N. special session voted in June to approve the additional sum.[80] Kennedy considered the time frame too hasty.[81] At Kennedy's urging, Adoula requested that U.N. troops remain in the Congo after December, and eventually he would win a six-month extension. The last U.N. troops would finally leave in June 1964.[82]

Kennedy began looking for ways to reduce the U.S. role in the Congo, not wanting to be left holding the bag after an ONUC pullout. He sent Harlan Cleveland, his assistant secretary of state for international organizations, to the Congo to find a way to reduce the U.S. presence. In his public report to the

Figure 10.4. Kennedy and Mobutu in the Oval Office, May 31, 1963

Source: John F. Kennedy Presidential Library; White House photograph.

president, Cleveland recommended "multilateral coordination" with America's allies and suggested that "in a few years time" the Congo "should no longer require substantial outside aid."[83] Kennedy subsequently urged Brussels and London to follow the United States and boost their direct aid to the Congolese government to compensate for the scheduled ONUC phaseout. In March, Adoula signed military agreements with Belgium, and then signed agreements with Israel and Italy. The Belgian military mission, CAMAC, provided the ANC with a temporary officer corps and helped train the ANC. Israel would help train paratroopers, and Italy would help train the air force.[84]

Belgium agreed to contribute $40 million to the aid program, and the United States would provide $80 million.[85]

The ANC retraining program helped elevate Mobutu as a key figure in the Congo. Mobutu now decided to travel to the United States and met with Kennedy on May 31 (figure 10.4). His meeting symbolized the Congo's new relationship with the United States. As guest of the Department of the Army, Mobutu toured U.S. military complexes for two weeks.[86] During the now famous but rather formal encounter with President Kennedy, Mobutu promised that with U.S. aid he could keep order in the Congo. When the two moved out to the Rose Garden, Kennedy complimented Mobutu (within earshot of the press corps) with his famous words: "General, if it hadn't been for you, the whole thing would have collapsed and the Communists would have taken over." Kennedy's compliments were an obvious exaggeration. The president next asked about what to do with Gizenga, but Mobutu, ever the fox, strived to keep his image as uninterested in politics and replied that was a problem for the government, not the military.[87] In reality there was still a lot of apprehension about ANC retraining, which would remain a focus for the foreseeable future.[88]

Two months later, on July 19, Kennedy approved a military assistance program for the Congo and sent a small military assistance advisory group to the Congo. The mission, known as COMISH under Colonel Frank Williams, was attached to the U.S. Embassy in Leopoldville. Its main purpose was to supply vehicles, aircraft, and communication equipment to the ANC. In addition, it coordinated the operations carried out by the CIA-recruited Cuban exiles who constituted the "instant air force."[89] By way of comparison, in 1952 Eisenhower had sent a similar group to Vietnam, and by the end of 1962 it had become the crux of Kennedy's policy there with 9,000 "advisers."[90] Nothing of that scale would ever be reached in the Congo, but by sending military advisers and offering bilateral military assistance, Kennedy sent the United States down the road of involvement in another postcolonial civil war. His greatest concern had been the ability to get out of the Congo when he wanted, but his policies worked against this ability in the long run.

The Shifting Sands of Soviet Politics

The word "contradictory" best describes the Soviet response to the Congo crisis in 1963. At the United Nations Zorin, again seeking any international influence he could find and without regard for consistency, called the latest military action illegal, rather ironic after the Soviet offer of military aid to U Thant. As soon as the Soviet Foreign Ministry recognized ONUC's military success, it called on U Thant to take even further action and evict the

Belgians from the Congo for good.[91] The Soviets were always uncomfortable with the U.N. activity. Evgenii Primakov, then a young and hard-working analyst, predicted that talks with Tshombe would never lead anywhere and charged that the United States, Belgium, and Britain actually held a trusteeship over the Congo. Western powers, he warned, with his characteristic sharpness, planned to keep the U.N. forces in the Congo as long as possible to better control events.[92]

The moment the fighting ended, the Soviet Union revived its campaign to terminate ONUC. The Africa Department of the Soviet Foreign Ministry sensed that U Thant was not anxious to extend the U.N. role in the Congo. A ministry report quoted U Thant as saying that to resolve the Congo crisis it was necessary to put an end to Western interference and terminate the U.N. mission.[93] Soviet representative Nikolai Fedorenko delivered a statement to U Thant denying that the United Nations had any responsibility to maintain law and order or retrain the ANC once the secession was ended. Instead, the statement insisted, a Congolese parliament should determine its own affairs.[94] The emphasis on the revival of the parliamentary role reinforced the estrangement between the Soviet Union and Adoula.[95] When ONUC finally became politically impossible for U Thant, the Soviet Union congratulated itself for thwarting U.S. plans to reorganize the ANC under the U.N. flag.[96]

The debt from the Congo crisis put the United Nations on the verge of bankruptcy. Khrushchev still publicly defended his decision on nonpayment in both political and legal terms.[97] The arrears of the Soviet Union and France almost equaled two years of payments, and they were in danger of being denied voting privileges in the General Assembly under Article 19. Fedorenko threatened that the Soviet Union might even walk out of the United Nations if new assessments for ONUC were approved. He argued that only a two-thirds vote by the Assembly could deny a member its voting rights.[98] Any denial of Soviet participation in the United Nations would challenge the integrity of that organization, he warned. The Soviet Union gambled that in these circumstances the international community would blame the United States for destroying the United Nations, and that the United States would try to avoid this.

Regarding its actual policy in the Congo, the Soviet Union shifted between supporting the Gizenga opposition and normalizing relations with the central government, just as it had tried to do previously in the aftermath of the Lovanium agreement. Official Soviet analyses of the crisis concluded that "the political situation remains very unstable."[99] Soon, however, Moscow suspected that the fall of Adoula was imminent, and distanced itself from the weak prime minister. In late April, the Kremlin withdrew its invitation to Adoula to visit Moscow, saying that the time was inopportune. The whole affair soured relations with Adoula, who fumed at the Soviet attempt to spread a rumor that he had been pressured by the West not to go to Moscow.[100]

Meanwhile, Moscow made a gift of medical supplies to the Congo, although the offer was made outside the limits of the U.N. operation (to which it technically still subscribed). In July, François Fumu, the moderately radical second vice chairman of the Congolese Chamber of Representatives, led a delegation to Moscow for three weeks in July. Fumu met with Leonid Brezhnev, the Politburo member with the most interest in African affairs.[101] Overtures to even more radical members of the government were forthcoming. The Kremlin invited the minister of information, Anicet Kashamura, to visit the Soviet Union. At the same time Soviet newspaper correspondents showed continued interest in the rebel cause. Khokhlov, *Izvestia*'s correspondent who attended a parliamentary session in the Congo, suggested that the Gizengists were waiting for the right opportunity to act.[102] He was not blinded as to the difficulty the rebels faced. In a report on his visit to UMHK's facilities in Elizabethville, Khokhlov indicated that the conglomerate had retained a great deal of power and influence over the course of events.[103]

As the Soviet Union waited for the end of ONUC, developments across the river in Congo-Brazzaville hinted that a more active policy would reap greater rewards. In August 1963, the incompetent and corrupt regime of Abbé Youlou in Brazzaville was ousted in the wake of labor riots. His successor, the leftist Alphonse Massamba-Débat, associated with the radical African states and sought assistance from China and the Soviet Union.[104] Brazzaville, in fact, had relatively good relations with China. China had resuscitated its interest in Africa and criticized Soviet indifference to the national liberation movement in Brazzaville. The ability of a popular protest to overturn a government and establish a revolutionary regime in the heart of Africa proved that radical change was possible.

Could the same scenario repeat itself in Leopoldville? At first the Soviet Union did not seem to think so. The weakness of the Gizengists led Soviet specialists to question whether "uprisings" in Kasai or Kivu were truly revolutionary in nature. *Izvestia* charged China with misinterpreting the rebel movement and elevating it to a higher level of ideological sophistication than it had in fact attained.[105] The Chinese, Moscow charged, believed that rifles and guns were the best means of advancing communism, when in reality economic development was the answer.[106]

Ignoring its own advice, the Soviet Union avoided addressing economic issues and tried to find greater political influence. If the Soviet Union was to preserve any influence in Africa, a report for the Central Committee in March suggested that it needed to combat Western anticommunist propaganda. It was an old problem, and the remedies suggested were familiar but had never really brought about many results. They included a greater distribution of literature about the noncapitalist path of development in forms accessible for Africans. Measures also continued to promote the People's Friendship University, now popularly known as Patrice Lumumba University. The Soviet Union also tried once again to encourage a sense of unity among Africans, hoping not only to create solidarity against European and U.S. capitalists but also to undercut Chinese propaganda.[107] All of this points to the fact that by 1963 the Soviet interest in the Congo was minimal, but was capable of reblossoming.

For now the end of the Katangan secession removed a dangerous source of instability in the Congo, at least from the perspective of the United States and the majority of African states. Huge injections of aid from the United States and Europe went to strengthen the Adoula government and help Mobutu and the ANC to destroy whatever resistance still existed in Katanga. The Soviet Union seemed ambivalent toward the political configuration in Leopoldville, and paid relatively little attention to the faltering radical movement in the eastern provinces of the country but still kept some lines of communication open. Although a few pro-Lumumbist pockets still existed in Stanleyville, no one foresaw their ability to mount a concerted attack on the government within a year.

11. Johnson's Distraction

In mid-1963 virtually everyone involved in the Congo crisis had hoped that it was over, but that hope was misplaced. In Leopoldville, the fragile economy worsened as rampant unemployment, decay of infrastructure, corruption, a thriving black market, and failed monetary reform stifled development. Strikes were a principal form of protest. Ambassador Gullion warned Washington that although Adoula had presided over the end of the secession and greatly improved his international support, the "masses cannot . . . buy or sell or eat these" victories. If unrest did flare up again, Gullion wrote, the unruly and disorganized ANC would only make matters worse.[1] Additionally, the antici-pated withdrawal of ONUC troops emboldened the numerous, albeit fractured, opposition movements. Gizenga no longer commanded any effective loyalty, but radical leaders such as Pierre Mulele, Gaston Soumialot, and Christophe Gbenye quickly picked up where he left off in the countryside. Adoula tried to undermine the opposition by redividing the country into twenty-one prov-inces, which forced provincial leaders and political groups to build new bases of support, but this too only brought increased dissatisfaction.[2]

President Kennedy's attention to the Congo crisis had peaked during the military operations of the U Thant Plan, but dropped quickly afterward. The lack of direction from the White House rekindled departmental rivalry between the Africanists and Europeanists. Of particular concern was how to respond to the growing opposition to Adoula and the ever-larger rebel move-ment in the east. Africanists wanted to see a greater direct role for the United States in resolving the political problems, while Europeanists emphasized the importance of the ANC retraining program and providing military assistance with the involvement of U.S. allies such as Belgium and Britain.

The Opposition Regroups

Two centers of opposition to the Congo central government formed, one in eastern regions of the province of Leopoldville and one in the eastern provinces of Kivu and Orientale. Both were potent hot spots. Although very different in form, leadership, and goals, both wanted to see an end to lopsided Western influence. They maintained minor contact with each other, but there were no serious efforts to unite the two.

In July 1963, Pierre Mulele, the former Parti Solidaire Africain (PSA) vice president and minister of education in the Lumumba government, returned from his tour of China, Eastern Europe, and Egypt. He had been well received and trained in revolutionary activity and warfare along the way. From Kwilu, the eastern region of Leopoldville Province, Mulele and his supporters called for an end to government suppression and demanded new elections. According to historian Ludo Martens, Mulele organized the peasantry into small, independent partisan cells and provided ideological training. Mulele demanded that his troops show strong discipline, respect, and honesty. He prepared his cadres for a class war and promised an equitable new society free from foreign exploitation. The influence of Maoist thinking and his experiences in China were apparent. And where ideological training would have less impact in the forests of the Congo, Mulele was also able to build a strong personal following.[3]

By September 1963, the opposition movement in the eastern provinces had coalesced into the Conseil National de Libération. Christophe Gbenye, the CNL's nominal leader, and Gaston Soumialot organized the main branches of the movement. The CNL was most active in the provinces of Orientale, Kivu, and northern Katanga, spilling over into Kasai and Equateur provinces. They won most of their outside support from Soviet and African allies. A smaller CNL faction was led by Egide Bocheley-Davidson who, ironically, relied more on Chinese aid and wanted to create a broader-based movement rooted in peasant support.[4] The new leftist president of Congo-Brazzaville, Massamba-Débat, offered the CNL sanctuary, a freedom that allowed it to expand international contacts. The CNL sent emissaries to sympathetic African states to look for material support. In January 1964, Soumialot went to Bujumbura, Burundi (formerly part of Ruanda-Urundi), where he organized the eastern resistance and recruited thousands of Tutsi exiles in southern Kivu. In addition to Burundi, the CNL organized camps in Uganda and Tanzania, probably with the help of the Chinese who had a relatively large embassy in Uganda.[5]

CNL leaders tended to clash easily and relied heavily on the hero worship of Lumumba as a uniting force. In the heart of Stanleyville, a monument to Lumumba was used as a place to mete out justice and remind the population that they had been commissioned to continue their hero's work. Within the CNL, ideology generally was less pronounced. The group relied more on anti-imperialist, anti-American propaganda.[6] The Stanleyville newspaper *Le Martyr*, published from August through November 1964, regularly included severe anti-American tracts, the language belying a Soviet or communist hand in their drafting.[7]

Both the Mulelist and CNL (or Simba) movements included a mixture of demagoguery, superstition, and magical beliefs. In Kwilu, soldiers chanted "Lumumba mai, Mulele mai" evoking *mai*, or the magic water that would protect them from their enemies' bullets. CNL soldiers were popularly known as the Simbas, meaning "lion" in Swahili and feared for their brutality. Despite the reportedly large numbers of weapons in the area, the soldiers were often untrained and reckless youth. They prepared themselves for battle by a mixture of abstinence the night before, drugs, and mysticism. The *dawa*, a magical belief in invincibility, gave Congolese youth unwarranted confidence in facing their often better-armed government opponents.[8]

Moscow did not actively support any of these early reorganization efforts, but was interested. The Central Committee (by way of its highest authority, "the Instantsia") ordered a KGB operative in the Congo, Boris Voronin, to establish and maintain contact with the opposition parties. Voronin thought this would lead to "no good," and complained that the parties were poorly organized and had no experience working clandestinely. He believed his time would be better spent maintaining contacts with agents among representatives of Western countries. It *was* particularly difficult to maintain contact with the opposition since they were still operating outside Congolese territory. Voronin feared that such risky contacts would lead to a scandal, or perhaps even another diplomatic expulsion.[9] His concerns were prescient.

Saving Adoula, for Now

The growth of the opposition caused disgruntlement within Adoula's main pillar of support, the Binza group. They questioned his unwillingness to ally more firmly with them and act against the so-called procommunists. They also wanted more done about economic problems. The Binza group—including Joseph Mobutu; the head of the Sûreté Nationale, Victor Nendaka; the minister of justice, Justin Bomboko; and, loosely tied with them, the national defense minister, General Jerome Anany—were becoming more outspoken now that the Katanga secession had ended. They were growing less heedful of specific Western interests and wanted to see more progress at home. They all feared that Lumumbist demands would continue to escalate and counseled Adoula to immediately suppress the opposition with force if necessary.[10]

By mid-October 1963, the Binza group was close to taking full control of authority and pushing Adoula to the sidelines. On October 20, amid strikes and a new army revolt, the government declared a state of emergency.[11] Gullion suspected a plot to overthrow Adoula, and believed that a Binza-led action against the protesters was the prelude to what was in fact a coup d'état. He cabled Washington that if the Binza group demanded a crackdown, it would result in either a government collapse or a Binza-led grab for power. The latter would be undesirable, according to Gullion, because the Binza group had no legitimacy and even less talent for compromise than Adoula, and a takeover by them would further stir the opposition.[12]

The Binza group resolved to expel Soviet diplomats from Leopoldville for a third time. Even Washington did not think the Soviet Union posed enough of a threat, and argued that expulsion of the Soviets would further isolate what was already seen as a Western-biased leadership. It is possible the Binza group was taking preemptive action against what they saw as a strong regrouping of the opposition, who were sure to approach the Soviet Union for material aid. After General Anany told Gullion on October 25 that the communist embassies were soon to be expelled (with the exception of Yugoslavia), Gullion tried to dissuade him. The U.S. ambassador defended the moderate position of Adoula, and warned Anany that the adverse reaction of the international community, and especially the nonaligned states, would further isolate the Congo and make it harder to find support.[13]

Undersecretary of State George Ball accepted that the United States could do little to stop the expulsion of the Soviet diplomats. All he asked was that it "would be helpful externally to relate reasons for [the] exclusion." In this way it would be easier for the United States to disassociate itself from the move.[14] The Binza group waited for a reason to justify the expulsion, and on November 19, they found one. That day, KGB operative Voronin, under cover as a Soviet Embassy counselor (and with a passport), and press attaché Yuri Miakotnikh were returning from Brazzaville after a meeting with the opposition rebels. Congolese soldiers broke into their car and roughed up the two Soviets, who were trying to tear up the documents. They snatched the diplomatic pouch and found what were described as incriminating documents.[15] That same day ANC troops also arrested Czechoslovak diplomats who were waiting in their car in front of the Soviet Embassy.[16] Adoula and the Binza group held an emergency meeting to discuss what to do. The meeting reflected their differences over suspending relations with the Soviet Union.[17] In the end, the hardliners won and Voronin and Miakotnikh were declared personae non gratae and expelled.

The Kremlin had become aware that some action against its diplomats was being planned. *Le Progrès*, a Congolese paper, published an article three weeks before warning of the pending expulsion of Soviet, Czech, and Egyptian diplomats.[18] After the arrest of the embassy personnel, Foreign Minister Gromyko delivered a note to the Congolese chargé in Moscow, Sébastien Kini, expressing indignation at the violence and demanded the release of Voronin and Miakotnikh under the Vienna Convention on Diplomatic Relations. On November 24, Gromyko sent a second note to the Congolese government charging that Mobutu and Nendaka had manhandled the diplomats and protesting their continued detention. The note indicated, however, that the Voronin and Miakotnikh affair had not been understood as a break in relations.[19] Overall, the weak international response to treatment of the diplomats told of international apathy toward the Congo, and could be taken as a dangerous sign of things to come—had anyone been looking for them.[20]

While the Binza group was flexing its muscles, Adoula's weakness was causing the White House to flinch. As usual, administration members were divided on how to handle the prime minister. Ball was becoming increasingly impatient with Adoula's inability to command the government. However, from the field, Gullion had repeatedly urged Washington to support Adoula against the Binza group and to oppose the return of Tshombe, who was sending out feelers from his Spanish hideaway. Gullion's views seemed more in line with New York than Washington. Ralph Bunche, who had resumed his post as undersecretary for special political affairs at the United Nations, supported Gullion. He believed that Mobutu had "completely disavowed Adoula's policy" of seeking cooperation with the West, evidenced by Mobutu's announcement that he could maintain order without foreign aid. The Binza group, Bunche agreed, was pushing Adoula aside and causing dangerous new tensions in the Congo.[21]

At this moment, Kennedy decided to pull Gullion from the Congo, "for reasons which remain obscure," in the words of historian Stephen Weissman. It is possible he was pulled because those in charge of Congo policy no longer believed his messages. Gullion's replacement was G. McMurtrie "Mac" Godley, who had served as one of his counselors at the embassy in 1961 and 1962. Godley had been the one to reject Rusk's orders to urge Kasavubu to delay the opening of the Lovanium parliament, so given the past unruliness among his diplomats, Kennedy's choice here seems peculiar.[22]

Godley would not arrive in the Congo for a couple of months, and again at a crucial moment, this time during the matter of the Soviet diplomat's expulsion, the United States had no ambassador in the Congo. In the meantime, major reports from the embassy in Leopoldville were sent by the young embassy officer Monteagle Stearns. Stearns protested any efforts to get the Soviet diplomats released as "counter productive."[23] He believed that the

Soviet presence was more of a danger than did either Ball or Gullion. The new aide in Leopoldville urged that he be allowed "to exploit to fullest evidence of Soviet subversive actions against Adoula," and give to U.N. officials all the supporting information he could without compromising the sources of information.[24] However, Stearns's effort to take a stronger stand against the Soviet Union would have to wait.

Johnson Takes Over

Everything changed on November 22, the day President Kennedy was shot in Dallas. Lyndon Johnson suddenly became president and was not prepared to deal with foreign policy crises, especially in the Congo. He attended only a few high-level meetings on the Congo and actively participated in none.[25] From the beginning of his presidency, he did not consider the Congo a "favorite" subject.[26] It was instead a "distraction" from his Great Society legislation and the deepening U.S. involvement in Vietnam.[27] In Saigon, just three weeks before Johnson took office, a military junta assassinated President Ngo Dinh Diem, and Kennedy had increased the number of military advisers to South Vietnam to 16,000. Johnson would continue to increase the U.S. presence in Vietnam and devote most of his attention to finding a strategy for a Cold War victory in Asia.

Ominously, top administration members compared the Congo and Vietnam, even though the reality was apples and oranges. Soon after Johnson took the oath of office, Carl Rowan, director of the U.S. Information Agency and NSC member, sent Johnson a message. "There is an ever-increasing likelihood that we may be faced with the need to mount an informational-psychological offensive" in the Congo "of the magnitude we now are undertaking in Viet-Nam." Rowan elaborated: "As in Vietnam, the basic problem continues to be security. . . . A military solution will not be possible unless an energetic political, psychological, and informational campaign is promptly undertaken designed to obtain the active support of the local tribal leaders and their followers to the central government."[28] So while Eisenhower and Kennedy had talked about winning hearts and minds of the people if any military security were to be found, now a "psy-op" was needed to win the military battle.

Johnson's initial approach to Africa was very general and reflected his lack of knowledge about the continent. His first messages to Africa were filled with platitudes as he promised to work toward "justice, freedom, and peace" and help the newly independent countries strengthen their foundations. At their broadest levels, his goals were to discourage "excessive fragmentation" and "remove risks of great-power confrontation."[29] Such an approach, unavoidable for the moment, left him vulnerable to crisis management.

Johnson's interest in the Congo was discouraged by the confused legacy he inherited. Kennedy had tried to find a political solution for the Congo, but after the U.N. withdrawal he increasingly looked to bilateral military assistance to replace the efforts of the international organization. Johnson naturally picked up where Kennedy had left off. Yet Johnson had his own style and ultimately his own policy. Kennedy had some interest in a moderate government. Johnson seemed not to care at all. His disposition made him unlikely to become interested in the nuances of Congolese politics. Virtually throughout his administration, Johnson tried "to keep Africa off the agenda," as historian Terrence Lyons has shown, and when he could not, seek quick solutions.[30] Those solutions, however, often lacked political and social depth and left problems simmering.

Try as he might, Johnson could not always keep Africa, or the Congo, off the agenda. Rebel activity and the growing power vacuum in Leopoldville along with renewed Soviet and Chinese interest moved the situation toward another crisis. Despite Johnson's ambivalence about the Congo, his administration remained determined to prevent any victory for the communists there. The scheduled end of ONUC and the withdrawal of all U.N. troops by June 1964 denied Washington the use of the United Nations as an umbrella for U.S. policy. The United States now looked to the Europeans, especially the Belgians, to take over the principal responsibility of fighting the Cold War in the Congo.

If Johnson was insecure and defensive about his ability to control foreign policy in the early days of his administration, he seemed more willing to let his advisers search for a policy for Africa.[31] Johnson asked the National Security Council's Special Group on Counter Insurgency to consider the problems in Africa and provide guidelines for U.S. policy. The NSC Special Group approved an action memorandum that emphasized an improvement in U.S. intelligence and the provision of direct U.S. assistance to African internal security forces as well as economic assistance programs. Hoping to count on the support of NATO allies, it also endorsed the expansion of multilateral aid to problem areas.[32] Around the same time, ambassador-at-large Averell Harriman visited the Congo, and according to a Department of State summary, "recommended to the President that the United States give increased military assistance to the Congo." His recommendations were approved, and the United States sent equipment, including T-28 aircraft piloted by the CIA-recruited Cubans.[33] In June, Harriman was given responsibility to oversee Africa policy.[34]

The Peacekeeping Debate

By 1964, the Cold War debate over peacekeeping was intensifying.[35] The actual discussion was still about responsibility for costs of ONUC, but the underlying significance for the future of peacekeeping was clear. Soviet spokespersons made the dubious argument that because the U.N. force was illegal (even though they had originally voted in favor of it), so were the mandatory financial assessments designed to pay for it. By fall 1964, the debt of the Soviet Union and six other bloc countries would total two years of dues to the United Nations. By January 1965, France and twelve other countries were slated to join them. All could lose their vote in the General Assembly if Article 19 were invoked.

Rhetoric from both sides was conflicting but serious. In January 1964, President Johnson and Premier Khrushchev exchanged letters indicating that each preferred to find a peaceful settlement to U.N. financial problems and the future of peacekeeping. Stevenson opened discussions with his counterpart Nikolai Fedorenko to search for a way for the United States and the Soviet Union to settle their differences. The United States would not yet budge on the "uniting for peace" resolution or the applicability of Article 19 in this case.[36]

Washington was generally uneasy with the precedent of nonpayment and contended that the defaulters should lose voting rights. Former president Eisenhower counseled firmness with the Soviet Union and weighed in favor of invoking Article 19. "The USSR has stubbornly refused to pay its share of the United Nations costs thus incurred," he wrote, and "it seems to me that the United States must continue to insist that the USSR lose its voting rights in the United Nations if it fails to meet its financial obligations to the organization."[37]

International opinion divided over applicability of Article 19. In March 1964, the United States and Britain suggested that in return for minimal Soviet payments (to prevent invoking Article 19), proposals for funding future peacekeeping operations would be submitted to the Security Council.[38] The Soviet Union rejected the offer and denounced the talk of applying Article 19. The Kremlin further threatened that depriving the Soviet Union of its General Assembly voting rights by inappropriately invoking Article 19 could wreck the United Nations and would be considered an unfriendly act toward the Soviet Union.[39]

Whatever the results, peacekeeping in the Congo was over. The last few U.N. troops were scheduled to leave the Congo on June 30, 1964. On the eve of their departure, U Thant declared the U.N. operation a success in preserving the territorial integrity of the Congo, in overseeing the eviction of foreign military personnel, and in preventing civil war. "The [United Nations] cannot permanently protect Congo from internal tensions and disturbances created by its own organic growth towards unity and nationhood," he said. The Congolese themselves, U Thant urged, must "merge their factional interests in a true effort toward national reconciliation." U Thant was cautious and stated that "even though there have been some recent events which have not been very encouraging," especially in Kivu and Kwilu, efforts at national reconciliation were being made. These efforts included talks with Tshombe and a possible reconciliation with Gizenga, whom Adoula had promised to release from prison. The secretary-general acknowledged the importance of retraining the ANC, but offered no thoughts on how that training should take place. He did not believe it to be a job for the United Nations.[40] He thus washed his hands of the Congo problem.

U Thant's broad-brushing over the real difficulties in the Congo was, perhaps, a contrived effort to force the Congolese to deal with their internal divisions. It did not prepare the international community for what to expect in the aftermath of a U.N. pullout. There was no system in place to help address those problems fostering division. The CNL rebels had amassed their forces and were ready to make a strike, planning to reach Stanleyville as soon as they could. Adoula's weak government could not match that challenge by itself.

First Skirmishes in a New War

Although exactly what Lyndon Johnson knew as vice president is unclear, by February 1964 it was brought to his attention that communist Cuba was training guerrillas for Africa, and the Congo was an obvious place for their deployment. Special assistant to the president Bill Moyers forewarned Johnson that nobody "was giving any thought to that," meaning Cuba's activity in Africa. He urged the president to designate some of his advisers to monitor the situation.[41] While Algeria had been Cuba's first venture, Captain Pablo Rivalta and a few others arrived in Tanganyika (which united with Zanzibar and became Tanzania in April 1964), with the support of Julius Nyerere, who let the eastern Congolese rebels use the area as their main rear guard. Nyerere's interest came late, in part because Tanganyika only won full independence in December 1961.[42] For now, however, the administration did not seem too concerned about the potential role of Nyerere or the Cubans in the Congo.

By early 1964, the successes of Mulele's resistance movement in Kwilu Province exposed the central government's lack of control in the countryside. The *New York Times* reported that the guerrillas were better organized than in the past, and on February 12 successfully mounted an attack on the local capital of Kikwit. Mobutu sent ANC troops to the Kwilu area, but U Thant denied cooperation of U.N. forces in quelling the rebellion, and government forces alone were not very effective. After the United Nations declined to help, the CIA stepped in.

Johnson, like Eisenhower and Kennedy, relied on the CIA to fill the holes in his policy in the Congo. But there was a significant difference. Eisenhower had used the CIA to get rid of Lumumba and to help find an alternative leader—both objectives that were beyond U.N. goals—while Kennedy continued to use the CIA primarily as way to achieve political goals in connection with the United Nations. After departure of ONUC, Johnson used the CIA as a tool by which to manage political but primarily military problems. Johnson's strategy deepened U.S. investment in the long-term stability of the Congo. The first target was the smaller rebel movement in Leopoldville Province. Mobilizing the "instant air force," Cuban exile pilots flew T-6s for the CIA from a base near Kikwit and repulsed the rebel attack on the city. Although Mulele and his men were forced back, they quickly regrouped. The well-seasoned Colonel Frederic Vandewalle (now an observer in Belgium) concluded that the air attacks accomplished little in terms of hindering the rebels, and may even have further increased hostility toward foreigners among the local population.[43]

By spring the main theater of activity had shifted eastward where a larger, less coherent opposition had taken hold. Soumialot had moved the center of his operation away from Brazzaville to Bujumbura. In mid-April, there was serious rioting in Bukavu (the capital of Kivu, a province that bordered on Burundi), and in mid-May, the CNL seized the city of Uvira in Kivu. At Uvira, the ANC troops were thrown into a panic and fled the area, unable to count on support from the population they had alienated by their previous plundering. Rebel successes convinced many ANC troops that the *dawa* magic was superior to their weapons, and they would not advance toward rebel lines.[44] In June, Soumialot turned southward and by the end of the month was closing in on Albertville.[45]

The United States sped up its efforts to supplement Mobutu's security forces with anti-Castro Cuban volunteers. The Cuban volunteers won a quick reputation for being strong and powerful, and the Lingala term "makasi," meaning strong, became their nickname.[46] So when several key Cuban pilots refused to fly without weapons, they sent a clear message to Washington. Dean Rusk lifted his ban on arming the T-6s, and the CIA and COMISH worked to outfit the T-6 fighter force. Devlin himself recalled that "once the planes were armed, they [i.e., the Makasi pilots] became an invaluable aid to support the government. Without them the [Congo] government would have fallen."[47] In the meantime, the CIA with the Defense Department brought in six more T-28s and began training more Cuban pilots. While they were training, two American pilots filled their seats and bombed the Ruzizi Valley, in the eastern Congo at Lake Tanganyika. The aerial bombings were intended to clear the way for government and mercenary troops to retake control of the area from the CNL, which was closing in on Albertville.[48]

On June 14, the news leaked that American pilots were under contract to the Congolese government. The Johnson administration was immediately pelted with questions from the press. The State Department first announced that U.S. planes flew missions but were not involved in combat. The next day it conceded that, on supposedly new information from the embassy, U.S. pilots had indeed flown the planes in combat missions, but added that further involvement was banned.[49] The growing tension and activity in the Congo naturally reflected the strengthening of the opposition movement.

Tshombe Returns

In Leopoldville, Kasavubu and Adoula competed for control of the government. Kasavubu made a bid for more power by pushing through a new constitution. A year earlier he had called on parliament to draft a new constitution, but the issue of power sharing deadlocked any discussion. Kasavubu dismissed the parliament for a "holiday" and then appointed a commission to draft a new constitution. In June 1964, the commission released the new document. The new constitution decreased the powers of the national parliament, ratified the creation of twenty-one new provinces, and increased the powers of the provincial governments. It allowed the president to dissolve a government and appoint a caretaker government until elections were held. The office of the prime minister was thus weakened, leaving Adoula sidelined. Kasavubu claimed that a referendum at the end of June had approved the Constitution, but there is no evidence that one was ever held.[50] At the stroke of a pen, the new constitution rescinded the Lovanium agreement on the very eve that the United Nations prepared its withdrawal. It was obvious that Adoula's days were numbered.

Four days before ONUC was formally ended, Tshombe returned to Leopoldville. With dim prospects facing the Adoula government, Mobutu welcomed Tshombe back and guaranteed his safety.[51] On July 9, Kasavubu, after a brief hesitation, asked Tshombe to form a transitional government.[52] Adoula barely made a whimper. Tshombe, who agreed, suddenly found himself "captain of a ship that was leaking everywhere." He estimated that three-fifths of the country was controlled by rebels and promised to reunite the Congo once again. In a show of purported good faith, he toured Leopoldville with Gizenga (among the political prisoners whom the cabinet had just released[53]) and Albert Kalonji. He lifted the state of emergency in Kivu and called on the Lumumbists (i.e., Simbas) to quit their rebellion. But when it came to power sharing he would not bend. He himself would fill six major offices—prime minister, foreign affairs, trade, commerce, planning, and information—and his longtime aide Godefroid Munongo would resume his position as minister of the interior. Together Tshombe and Munongo controlled eight of eighteen posts, with the rest of the posts held by virtual unknowns.[54]

A surprising choice at first glance, especially from the view from the White House, many factors came together to seat Tshombe. After Tshombe had refused to cooperate with the U Thant Plan, the Kennedy administration had refused to have anything to do with him and had little contact with him during his years in exile. A State Department summary a few years later stated that the United States "was not privy to this decision" about Tshombe's return.[55] U.S. ambassador McMurtrie Godley, in fact, thought this was the "most bizarre way of finding employment for him [Tshombe]." It is also clear that Kasavubu was unlikely to have acted on his own. Godley believed that Belgium was behind the move, and warned that the United States would not want to be drawn too closely to its ally on this account. Embassy officials worried that Tshombe would become the next African "Uncle Tom" and described him as biased "in favor of the Belgians."[56]

Tshombe indeed had strong Belgian support for his return to power. Société Générale, UMHK, and business interests in general certainly wanted to see Tshombe return to the Congo. Even the wary officials in Leopoldville hoped the promise of normalizing economic production in Katanga would help fill their near empty coffers. Tshombe's circle of advisers included many of those who had served him earlier; of particular note was the inclusion of René Clemens. Tshombe, a lover of ironies, named Michel Struelens, who had been evicted by the Kennedy administration in 1963, as his special representative to the United States, and told McGeorge Bundy he would be, for all intent, "acting foreign minister" of the Congo. Struelens, of course, was a Belgian national with ties to UMHK.[57]

Tshombe immediately accepted Belgian military aid. The Belgian military assistance program became, according to a State Department document, the "backbone of the ANC."[58] Tshombe also brought with him an array of mercenary support. He still commanded a small army of mercenaries who had lodged themselves in Angola and who could help the ANC deal with the rebels, and he now brought these men to the Congo. Tshombe maintained important contacts with the Rhodesians and South Africans who were known to be friendly to the idea of supplying mercenaries. He also called in the infamous "Mad Mike" Hoare from South Africa to organize about two hundred and fifty soldiers in the Fifth Commando (nicknamed the "Wild Geese") to help the ANC fight the Simbas. Hoare was an Irish-born English mercenary who had fought previously in Katanga.[59] With the ANC in shambles and retraining not likely to have an effect for months if not years, the use of mercenaries seemed not only appealing, but even necessary.

For two weeks after Tshombe's return to Leopoldville, Johnson maintained an uncomfortable silence on the issue of recognition. In the meantime, Henry

Luce's *Life* magazine published an article calling on the president to recognize that Tshombe was the "best bet" in the Congo. Johnson was incensed that Luce seemed to be challenging his prerogatives as chief of state.[60] Just a week earlier, Harriman had advised Johnson to "quietly" continue economic and military aid to Tshombe. Now having to appear as if he were pushed by journalists, Johnson called a press conference to announce that he would recognize the Tshombe government. "We have every intention of being understanding and cooperative" with Tshombe, Johnson said.[61] Johnson's sudden overture to Tshombe does not seem to have been preceded by a comprehensive review of policy, but was decided on the basis of expediency.

Johnson was left to convince the State Department to support his decision. Tshombe was considered an old foe in the State Department, whose desks were still dominated by Kennedy's appointees. Thanks to the efforts of Senator Dodd, Tshombe had considerable popular support within the United States and the Congress. Dodd deplored the "negative and laggard attitude" of the State Department toward Tshombe and seems to have been instrumental in convincing Johnson to accept Tshombe. Dodd was also behind a meeting between Michel Struelens and Mac Bundy that ironed out at least some of the difficulties between the administration and Tshombe.[62] Perhaps because of his lack of concern for Africa, Johnson determined this case innocuous enough on which to appease the conservative wing of his party and recognize Tshombe.

While there was support for Tshombe among white Americans, a growing number of voices from the African American community were opposed to him. In fact, of all foreign policy topics, the crisis in the Congo continued to receive the most noteworthy attention, and was comparable to the growing criticism of apartheid in South Africa. Malcolm X now regularly spoke out against events in the Congo. He fulminated against the return of Tshombe, "a paid killer" who everyone knew was implicated in the murder of Lumumba. He was "the worst African ever born" and now thanks to the imperialists (and their use of tax dollars) ruled the biggest (and possibly richest) state in center of the continent.[63]

Ultimately, Johnson was left to deal with the ongoing crisis left by Kennedy. He put U.S. bilateral relations with the Congo on a military footing, and then turned the crisis over to the State Department. The opposition movement, whose grievances had never been addressed, regrouped over the course of the year. The rebels were more anti-imperialist and more anti-American with every passing day. Johnson would find it easy to toss aside the idea of a moderate government as his new administration picked up where Kennedy left off. In doing so, he significantly altered U.S. foreign policy in the Congo, to the point that it relied heavily on the use of force, albeit a mercenary one, and waited for the larger crisis to come.

12. "Carrying the Burden" in the Congo

No one in the Johnson administration wanted to talk about direct U.S. intervention in the Congo. Secretary of Defense Robert McNamara and Deputy Secretary Cyrus Vance repeated the belief, long held in the Pentagon, that greater U.S. involvement should be only an extreme last resort. Johnson himself questioned whether U.S. intervention would even be possible. With so much unrest and uncertainty in the Congo, Secretary Rusk warned that a communist takeover in the Congo could occur even after all that had been done to prevent it. The president agreed with Rusk and worried that "time is running out and the Congo must be saved" from communism.[1] Despite the magnitude of the problems in the Congo, his administration seemed to have no independent ideas of how to help stabilize the country.

Instead, Johnson looked to Europe. The president told his European allies that it was now "their responsibility" to help contain the crisis in the Congo. He warned that if the Europeans abdicated that responsibility, then the United States could not continue to "carry the burden alone in the Congo."[2] Privately, he mused over the unpleasant irony that, after "running the Belgians out," the United States would have to return to the Congo only to be seen as "wrapping the colonial flag" around itself and "acting unilaterally."[3] Johnson's greatest victory, however, if it can be called that, was to convince the Europeans to carry out his policy and serve U.S. Cold War interests.

The Communist Factors

The simmering Sino-Soviet split again worsened in late 1963 at a crucial time for the Congo. As part of China's Afro-Asian solidarity campaign, Mao accused the Soviet Union of "great power chauvinism" similar to the traditional white imperialists. The Soviets responded, in the caustic words of Boris Ponomarev, by denouncing Chinese "nationalist arrogance." In February 1964, the CCP took a step further and declared itself "in the vanguard of the international communist movement" and charged Moscow with betraying the national liberation movement. The charge infuriated Khrushchev and only fueled the polemics between the two communist giants.[4]

As if to underline its charges, by early 1964 China was openly supporting the Kwilu and Stanleyville revolutions. The renewed Chinese interest in Africa was expressed by Zhou Enlai's tour of Africa in early 1964, including a stop in Burundi where some Congolese rebels had exiled themselves.[5] In May, *Renmin Ribao* applauded Mulele's military efforts since "it is impossible for the Congo to achieve national liberation through so-called parliamentary struggle, but only through armed struggle."[6] Several months later, in September, the Chinese premier and second in command, Liu Shaoqi, reaffirmed the pledge to support the rebels although he vehemently denied charges of Chinese intervention.[7]

On August 5, Chinese defector Tung Chi-Ping told reporters that Beijing planned to "take over" the Congo. He claimed to have been present at the briefing of the Chinese ambassador-designate to Burundi and quoted Mao as saying that "if we can take the Congo, we can have all of Africa." Tung credited Chinese guerrilla Kin Me for rebel successes in the east.[8] His widely publicized statements raised the general anxiety in Washington that the rebels were controlled by Beijing and Moscow (it still made little difference which one). The language was, of course, extreme, but if China could win a major place of influence in the Congo, it certainly was possible that China would then have gained entrance into much of Africa and, in fact, win an international diplomatic clout it was still lacking.

The Soviet Union, after watching the growing opposition movement in the Congo and the heightened Chinese interest, reversed its initial assessment that the rebellion was again premature.[9] Soviet reports dismissed American contentions that the rebellions had little local support.[10] Unrest lay deep in the countryside, the communists argued. A major reason, Soviet writers explained, was the lingering presence of the United Nations, as it managed its long withdrawal. Nikolai Khokhlov even told *Izvestia* readers that the United Nations caused the current economic crisis by encouraging the black market in the Congo.[11] The Soviet representative at the United Nations Nikolai Fedorenko soon shifted to blaming the United States and Belgium for the poor state of economic affairs in the Congo.[12]

The Soviet Union supported the rebels with a token amount of aid. The historian Piero Gleijeses quoted a document from the former East German archives in which an official was asking about the possibility of Soviet aid to the revolutionaries. In response, according to this document, "comrade K" replied that aid to the Congo was "extraordinarily problematic" because there is no cohesive leadership. Moscow did, however, supply small arms and weapons, boats, and other support matériel to the revolutionaries. The soldiers, however, often did not know how to use the weapons, and so their effectiveness was often limited.[13] Still, the outside aid allowed the opposition the basic starting point from which to challenge the central government at least momentarily, and had it been able to translate its success into political gains, it might have won more for itself.

The Fall of Stanleyville

By mid-1964, the CNL Simbas set out to take control of the land and villages in the eastern provinces. Simba soldiers, often very brutal, proved to be a match for the demoralized government troops. Just the news of the Simbas approaching often frightened local officials enough to surrender.[14] The CNL "popular army of liberation," led by General Nicolas Olenga, seized Kongolo in mid-July, and then took Baudouinville and moved north to Albertville. After the CNL took Albertville, they began the march toward Stanleyville. As Olenga plunged forward, joining him were bands of *jeunesse* warriors, whom today we would simply call "teen soldiers." By the time he closed in on the city, his army was "in the thousands." The ANC garrison in Stanleyville numbered 1,500 of some of the most disciplined and well-armed government troops. At the very moment the Simbas arrived, however, their leader, Colonel Leonard Mulamba, was not present. He had been sent by Mobutu to rescue the government position at Bukavu.[15] So here, too, the ANC defense disintegrated at the sight of the arriving Simbas. (See figure 12.1 for a map of these rebellions.)

Stanleyville fell dramatically on August 5. It was a bloody affair, and the rebels, heady with victory, attacked, raped, and killed anyone they suspected of association with the West. The American consul in Stanleyville, Michael Hoyt, watched from the consulate window as the ANC troops clashed on the streets with the Simba rebels. In addition to Hoyt, the nominal vice consul, David Grinwis, who was in actuality the CIA station chief, and three other personnel were the only official Americans who remained.[16] In the afternoon, the Simbas attacked the consulate itself, and Hoyt and others hid in a dark vault while the rebels tried to shoot down the door. Ambassador Godley and COMISH chief Frank Williams assembled a small rescue force and planned Operation Flagpole to land a helicopter at the consulate and evacuate the Americans. Fearing reprisals, especially from the erratic General Olenga, Hoyt canceled the

Figure 12.1. Map of the 1964 Rebellions

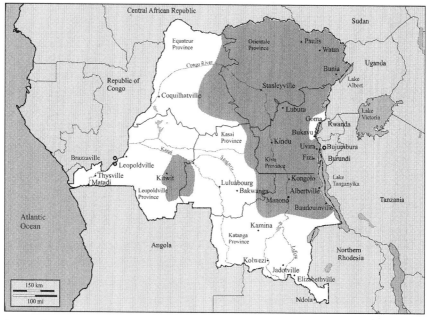

Source: Author's data; base, d-map.com.

operation. Upon their arrival in Stanleyville, Soumialot and Gbenye ordered the arrest of Hoyt and his aides and kept them in prison where, off and on, they were subjected to rough treatment. The Simbas soon made clear they would not let the remaining roughly 1,600 whites leave the city. Eventually several hundred additional white hostages, mostly Belgian, but including some American and British citizens as well, were brought to the Victoria Hotel. The CNL suspected that any departure of whites would clear the way for air raids on Stanleyville in support of an ANC advance.[17] They were right.

The Soviet press and radio cheered the capture of Stanleyville by the CNL. Khokhlov gleefully reported that the opposition movement was engulfing the whole country, and suggested that Mulele and Soumialot were advancing so rapidly that, even from virtually opposite sides of the country, they could soon join up together. However, in a more somber radio newscast, Khokhlov warned that the opposition lacked cohesion, suggesting that its success was not guaranteed.[18] Even the generally cautious Evgenii Primakov ventured that the rebels had taken Manono and were on their way to seize Elizabethville—a rather unlikely objective at this early stage in the rebellion.[19] Soviet reports mentioned little regarding the sources of rebel support, but on August 17, the

New York Times reported that two Soviet-made planes landed in Stanleyville laden with supplies, suggesting that there was an open and active supply line, at least for the moment.[20]

The Kremlin's justification for the aid came two weeks later. At the end of August, a TASS statement blasted the United States for "moving hundreds of combat ready paratroopers and heavy military equipment into the Congo." Referring to foreign sources, perhaps using wild reports from Uganda, the article confirmed that "American military planes have started battle operations . . . against the Congolese." A final warning stated that those "who infringe upon the freedom of the Congolese people know that the continuation of armed intervention . . . may lead to a broadening of the conflict. The Congolese people have true friends in Africa, and not only in Africa, who are able to render them the necessary support."[21] The Soviet Union still wanted greater African support, and this time it would see a greater number of African states willing to align themselves with Moscow.

In Washington, too, the fall of Stanleyville was a surprise, but its news competed for attention amid other crises at home and abroad. The day before the rebels took Stanleyville, the administration announced the second North Vietnamese attack on the U.S.S. *Maddox* in the Gulf of Tonkin. A retaliatory bombing strike against North Vietnam took place the very next day. Several days later Johnson used the Tonkin Gulf incident to push through Congress a resolution that allowed him to take whatever actions necessary, including the use of armed force, to prevent further aggression against South Vietnam. Domestic upheavals also competed for attention. In mid-July, Johnson had signed the Civil Rights Act, which opened public facilities to all Americans regardless of race. In late July, riots rocked Harlem, Brooklyn, and Rochester. By the second week of August, riots spread to New Jersey and Chicago, and in Mississippi three civil rights activists had been found dead, killed at the hands of the Ku Klux Klan.

With the presidential campaign heating up that fall, the dramatic decisions the country faced forced Johnson to answer to the conservative Republican Party candidate Barry Goldwater of Arizona. Goldwater railed about failures in Berlin, Cuba, Laos, and Vietnam, and promised to stop "the tide" that has been "running against freedom" even if that meant taking extreme actions.[22] Johnson retaliated with the famous advertisement of a little girl counting daisy petals, which became a nuclear countdown to warn of the recklessness of Goldwater's policies. Yet crises like the taking of hostages in the Congo fed into Goldwater's criticism that Johnson had failed to defend freedom around the globe. Criticism from the opposite end of the spectrum also came from within the Democratic Party. A week after the Tonkin Gulf Resolution, senators John Stennis

(D-Mississippi) and Mike Mansfield (D-Montana) warned that U.S. military aid to the Congo might lead to a slippery slope ending in an undeclared war in the Congo.[23] Johnson indeed walked on the edge of the Congo slope, trying to avoid a major crisis that could further divide his party right before an election.

Belgium and the Mercenary Option

The fall of Stanleyville pushed Johnson into action. Johnson put Averell Harriman, now undersecretary of state for political affairs, in charge of following the situation. Harriman acted quickly. First, he convinced Johnson to approve Joint Task Force–Leopoldville, a plan designed by General Paul D. Adams, commander in chief of the U.S. Strike Command, described as a small military force "to conduct rescue operations . . . as might be required by the Ambassador." Harriman then hopped on a plane to Brussels. In advance of Harriman's trip, Rusk had cabled Belgian foreign minister Paul-Henri Spaak that the United States wanted Belgium to provide "tangible specific measures to save the Congo." He asked Spaak to support the creation of a military force, 4,000 strong with 200 white officers. Harriman discussed this plan with Spaak, an old associate of his, and Harriman expressed his hopes for international support. Spaak rejected any talk of a Belgian-led military intervention to save the hostages and brushed aside Harriman's idea that the CNL was under communist control. Neither the Belgian public nor the business community, still stung by the U.N.'s Round Three destruction, was interested in intervention. Spaak finally agreed to send advisers and provide additional logistics and supplies for the ANC, while the United States would provide three additional unarmed C-130 transport planes and their crew. But the force itself was to be primarily Congolese along with some mercenaries. Spaak also agreed to help find an international cover for the new activity, but he repeated to the U.S. ambassador in Brussels, Douglas MacArthur II, and to Harriman that no European state would ever agree to send troops (and hence he did not want to become bogged down in begging neighbors to do so).[24]

Despite the caution Spaak expressed to Harriman, he immediately summoned the legendary Colonel Vandewalle and asked him to return to the Congo. Vandewalle was on a plane to the Congo the next day. As soon as he arrived, he began to organize the Fifth Mechanized Brigade, a group composed of foreign volunteers, the old Katanga gendarmes, and the ANC. The brigade was nicknamed named "the Ommegang," meaning procession in Flemish, and the name of a popular festival. Vandewalle immediately developed a plan to retake Stanleyville. He organized his 4,200 troops, including 62 Belgian advisers and 390 mercenaries (most from Angola and Rhodesia), and ANC troops into three columns and prepared to recapture rebel territory piece by piece and converge on Stanleyville from three directions.[25] According to Tshombe, he also "counted on American aid to permit rapid equipment of this brigade" and he worked closely with COMISH.[26] More savvy than in 1960, Brussels began a public relations campaign that stressed no Belgian mercenaries would be authorized to serve in the ANC.[27] Spaak tried to downplay Vandewalle's mission and deflected any fears of a repeat of the intervention in Katanga.

The uneasy alliance between Tshombe and Mobutu now had a drastic impact on strategy. From Leopoldville, Tshombe pleaded for more material support for the ANC and for the mercenaries. Tshombe enjoyed loyalty among the mercenaries since his days in Katanga and once again had the help of Mike Hoare. Yet assembling a new mercenary force would take time, and Mobutu's ANC forces (albeit unruly) were ready to deploy right away. Tshombe therefore agreed to ask for more equipment for the ANC, but did not want foreign troops (presumably under Mobutu's command) to join in the fight against the rebels.

A few days after the fall of Stanleyville, government forces retook Kongolo to the south, but they were forced to withdraw from Manono, and were thus unable to hold the center. The government-led forces had more luck farther to the east, taking Baudouinville. With help from the mercenaries and the Cubans, the ANC led by Mulamba held onto Bukavu after the attack by Olenga's soldiers. The battle for Bukavu also intricately tied the United States to the fighting after three Americans—Colonel William A. Dodds, who was the U.S. Strike Command's senior representative in Leopoldville, Lieutenant Colonel Donald Rattan, and a young service officer Lewis Macfarlane—were cut off by the rebels and disappeared for a few days, raising questions about their activity and safety. After a botched raid by Hoare, the ANC retook Albertville, a key objective, at the end of August. Undaunted by these losses and still holding onto half the country, the opposition made the daring decision to begin the trek to Leopoldville. The groundswell of support they expected did not appear. The decision to go to Leopoldville would ultimately spread the opposition too thin, and they would not be able to hold on nor gain enough support in the countryside.[28]

The White House shied away from public comment on the presence of mercenaries or the role of its own advisers. Secretary Williams arrived in Leopoldville on August 11, along with the four C-130 transport planes of the Joint Task Force–Leopoldville and instructions to get Kasavubu and Tshombe to cooperate with the United States and keep them informed. Williams found his task to be a tough one. He learned that Tshombe not only wanted to increase his mercenaries, but had already asked South Africa for direct military assistance including air combat forces. Tshombe hinted that if the South Africans were forced to leave the Congo, he would publicly ask the United States for parachute battalions to retake Stanleyville. Both Williams and Secretary Dean Rusk were unhappy with Tshombe's tactics. However, they offered him seven more T-28s and seven B-26 bombers. Williams prodded Tshombe to find credible African allies and announced that the United States would pay for troops from other African nations to aid the ANC, if any were willing. That would have at least given some legitimacy to Tshombe's regime and U.S. efforts to stabilize it. At the same time, more able forces under Mobutu's command would have the additional benefit of strengthening his hand in Leopoldville.[29]

On August 29, Dean Rusk announced the formation of a new interagency task force, the Congo Working Group (CWG). The working group was headed by Joseph Palmer II and included members of the White House, Defense Department, CIA, State Department, and several other agencies. Averell Harriman remained the dominant figure in the CWG and he worked closely with the national security adviser, McGeorge Bundy, to implement the Spaak-Harriman agreement.[30] Despite the support for a new military force for the Congo, the group voiced a preference to minimize American involvement and emphasized the need for an internationally based end to the crisis.

To appease the Americans, Tshombe himself made several halfhearted measures to search for African allies and portray himself as an ordinary African leader. He declared a policy of neutrality and appealed to African states for aid in dealing with the rebellion. His efforts were futile. Nigeria, Ethiopia, Senegal, and the Malagasy Republic, all with long histories of supporting Leopoldville, responded that any aid should be channeled through the new Organization of African Unity (OAU), which clearly had an anti-Tshombe bias.

The effort by the CWG to seek a greater international effort to end the crisis was hampered most prevalently by the disconnect between the United States and Belgium on how to deal with the rebels. Harriman believed that he had won assurances from Spaak that he would not "do business" with the rebels. Despite this, Spaak would contact and meet with Gbenye in secret twice during the first half of August 1964.[31] Around the same time, the CNL publicly proposed negotiations with the Americans, but Johnson rejected the offer. Soon thereafter the CIA, in efforts to free the hostages, began covert talks with the rebels.[32] Gbenye reportedly met with Devlin in late August in Bujumbura, and the two, according to Gbenye, were "about to reach an agreement about what should be done with the American consular staff," but he left abruptly to visit Uvira after it was "bombed by an American airplane." He returned, but "did not see him [Devlin] again."[33] The CNL leadership was convinced after this battle that American aid was to blame for their recent setbacks and this made them more reluctant to free the hostages and lose their only bargaining chips.

The Simbas were still in control of half the country. Gbenye took advantage of the CNL successes, and declared a People's Republic of the Congo on September 5, the same date on which four years earlier Kasavubu had dismissed Lumumba. Gbenye was to become president, Soumialot defense minister, Olenga head of the armed forces, and Thomas Kanza foreign minister. The new "state" was virtually stillborn. The new government and the CNL revolution were flawed from the start in too many ways. Internal squabbling, grandiose promises, and loud anti-imperialism in lieu of mobilizing popular opinion or motivating the people behind basic ideas of social reform or intellectual advancement, reliance on an undisciplined force, and weak international connections or support worked against the movement.[34] For a brief moment in September, however, the People's Republic captured the imagination of radicals around the world.

The Johnson administration turned to the OAU, hoping that it might provide an international peacekeeping force and give the Spaak-Harriman intervention a humanitarian cover. The OAU called a special session on the Congo on September 5. Tshombe agreed to attend, and while in Addis Ababa promised to dismiss mercenaries if African states provided assistance. Tshombe's proposals lacked seriousness and his relations with African states in fact plummeted to new depths. The OAU appointed Jomo Kenyatta to head a Conciliatory Commission on the Congo. The Americans hoped that this was the detached African commitment they sought, but they soon found out otherwise. Kenyatta first seated a CNL delegation headed by Bocheley-Davidson. He then announced he would work to find a cease-fire and open negotiations between the government and rebel forces. The commission immediately sent a delegation to Washington to urge President Johnson to withdraw all U.S. military supplies from the Congo.

The OAU delegation to Washington included representatives from Ghana, Guinea, and Egypt and left for the United States without prior guarantees of a meeting with the president. U.S. ambassador to Kenya William Attwood sensed the pending disaster if the delegation were ignored by the White House. Attwood convinced Secretary Rusk to meet with some members of the group as Kenyatta's personal representatives. The rebuff offended the OAU, which charged that Washington's insensitivity threatened to exclude Africans from finding solutions to African problems.[35] Johnson in fact treated the OAU delegation as no more welcome than Luce's article about what to do in the Congo several months earlier.

The hostage crisis continued and the international avenues did not seem to be panning out, while pressure to find some kind of solution kept mounting. The CWG was still hoping to find an alternative to a solely U.S. intervention, but just in case things took a turn for the worse, they asked the Joint Chiefs of Staff (JCS) for a plan to save the hostages. On instructions from the assistant secretary of defense, Cyrus Vance, the JCS asked General Adams to prepare another plan to rescue the Americans in Stanleyville. Adams recommended that a covert plan to rescue the hostages by a Special Forces team be combined with an overt plan to take Stanleyville and evacuate the entire foreign population. The combined JCS plan, as it was worked out, seemed too drastic, and it was set aside for the time being. Ultimately, the plan would be rewritten as Dragon Rouge, meaning Red Dragon, the Americans being the dragon, with the Belgian paracommandos as its breath of fire.[36]

Dragon Rouge

By October 1964, the Johnson administration had reached its own crossroads in the Congo. The White House was receiving reports that time was running out and the rebels had threatened to "kill all the Americans" if they were attacked.[37] Still, Ball and Bundy believed that there was plenty of room for cooperation with the Europeans to avoid military action by the United States. McNamara and Vance were less convinced. They warned that the administration might have to act on its own accord or, in the words of William Brubeck "tolerate publicly Americans being killed in a situation of primitive anarchy without timely response on our part."[38] They feared that if the United States stood by and watched while their citizens and diplomats were abused in Stanleyville, Washington would again appear weak and spineless when facing extremists. Up to this point, the Europeans had been less enthusiastic about cooperating in a military action against the rebels because their nationals were not under the same threat, and cooperation with the United States might induce similar wrath on their citizens.

Albeit reluctantly, the Belgians agreed to discussions, and on October 5 the National Security Council approved formal U.S.–Belgian planning of a rescue operation. Although they used General Adams's draft as their starting point, Adams himself (and to his chagrin) was not invited to participate in the discussions. Ironically, the discussions were made a lot easier by the rebels, who by mid-October were now taking Belgians and other Europeans hostages as well. At this point, Spaak himself seemed to have a change of heart, and visited Washington in early November. During this visit one of his aides suggested to William Brubeck that with U.S. planes, Belgium was ready to lend a battalion. Formal plans for Dragon Rouge were finally worked out. The operation was to be conducted primarily by Belgian paratroopers, flown into the Congo on U.S. planes.[39] In reality it was not strictly a rescue operation, given that it was designed as much to end the opposition as it was to rescue Hoyt and Grinwis.

By this time, there was also the tantalizing prospect of a Vandewalle victory that just might obviate the need for a rescue. His Ommegang forces had been closing in on the rebels from three directions. By November 16, Vandewalle's column of seven hundred men was inching northward, a band of mercenaries in front, followed by a joint column of the Cuban exiles and the Katangan gendarmerie, and with the ANC bringing up the rear. Bundy and Ball believed that the Vandewalle force, with support from the other two columns, might succeed in retaking Stanleyville. Harriman and the Belgians were more pessimistic that Operation Dragon Rouge could not be avoided and would have to rescue Vandewalle along with the hostages.[40] That pessimism increased over the next two days.

The Simbas were aware of Vandewalle's movement and knew that he would challenge their position. Tensions ran high. Gbenye threatened once again that if Stanleyville was attacked, all Americans and now Belgians too would be killed. He announced that "Major" Paul Carlson (actually no major but a young American doctor) had been condemned to death by a military tribunal as an American spy. On November 18, Hoyt and Grinwis and six other Americans were brought to the Lumumba monument and ritualistically prepared for sacrifice. Simba rebels joined the crowd in shouting the traditional anti-American slurs and manhandled the captives. The Americans were rescued at the last minute, thanks to the intercession of Gbenye.[41]

The day before the ritualistic torture, Johnson moved closer to authorizing Dragon Rouge. He approved the assembly of Belgian paratroopers on Ascension Island, a British possession that London had finally agreed to offer as the staging point for the operation.[42] Spaak now wanted the military rescue to proceed. Rusk recommended one last effort to appeal to the CNL "for the record," even though it was unlikely to yield results. He promised Johnson that the talks would not be used to prejudice or delay military action and noted that Vandewalle was four or five days away from Stanleyville.[43] It is possible that Rusk wanted to use the talks to give Vandewalle time to reach and enter Stanleyville if he could. As it was, talking with the CNL did not buy much time. Gbenye refused to work through Ambassador Godley. Instead, Ambassador Attwood met with Kenyan president Jomo Kenyatta and Thomas Kanza. The talks were tense, and culminated in a "confrontation" between Attwood and Kanza, with no real results.[44]

Internal CNL dissension hastened its fate. Olenga arrested Soumialot's entire staff because the latter had supposedly fled during fighting.[45] The dissension not only weakened the movement but left valuable aid unused. A Soviet-made Algerian plane was seen unloading more weaponry on November 18. More support was in the pipelines and on November 27, several Soviet planes landed in Ghana on their way to resupply the Congolese rebels.[46] The U.S. Embassy suspected a communist Cuban presence, and Hoare found stashes of Chinese weaponry left behind by rebels.[47] Also later found in Stanleyville were piles of undistributed pamphlets printed in Beijing outlining plans for a communist state for the entire Congo.[48] Ultimately, however, the strength of the rebel forces was unknown, encouraging the indecision about whether to go ahead with the rescue.

It was probably on November 20 or 21, during their regular morning meetings, that "the eight" decided to launch Dragon Rouge. According to Brubeck, the eight included Rusk, Ball, Harriman, Bundy, JCS Chairman General Earle Wheeler, Vance, former ambassador to Nigeria Joseph Palmer, and Brubeck himself. Harriman and Vance tended to lean toward the position that the rescue should proceed, while Bundy and Ball had more reservations about the plan. All were agreed, however, that Spaak's judgment of events was critical. Although it has been suggested that the Johnson administration abdicated the decision for the rescue to Spaak, virtually everyone was aware of the Belgian minister's views in favor of action.[49] A message from Spaak indeed clarified that he was in favor of proceeding. Hours later on November 21, Johnson approved Dragon Rouge but not the final timing of the launch.[50] The plan involved the restationing of paratroopers at Kamina, but left open the exact time of their arrival in Stanleyville. Johnson's decision, therefore, still gave Vandewalle time to arrive in Stanleyville and presumably liberate the hostages first (and bear the brunt of whatever aggression the rebels might have left).

The administration paid very close attention to the advance of Vandewalle. Johnson was focused on winning at the least cost possible. The administration also desperately wanted their activity to look more selfless than it really was. No one wanted the operation to be seen as another military adventure done for the sake of power and control. "There is an advantage in having this look not like a military operation but a humanitarian operation" Ball told the president. After all, Ball argued, "we were motivated by the fact that the sit[uation] in Stan[leyville] was deteriorating so rapidly, although . . . [there] has been no evidence that the sit[uation] is falling apart any more."[51] Thus Ball adroitly added a post hoc humanitarian justification to what was conceived as a military intervention to quash the rebellion.

The question of the actual timing of the paratroop drop still remained to be decided. In Washington, top decisionmakers closely tracked the progress of Vandewalle. Vandewalle had regrouped his mercenaries in Lubutu, and the next day, in what author Sean Kelly called "one of the best kept secrets of the whole operation," a CIA special unit joined him. The CIA unit was headed by William Robertson and included U.S. lieutenant colonel Donald Rattan and anti-Castro Cuban exiles.[52] At this point, his advance seemed to have stalled. Author Paul Semonin plausibly suggested that Vandewalle's troops were unable to enter Stanleyville without the additional U.S.–Belgian air cover. Vandewalle himself told of a violent attack by the rebels that delayed their final entry. Weather also played a role. By the morning of November 23 he was on the move again.[53]

Just after lunch on November 23, Johnson decided that without Dragon Rouge the situation would become worse. At 3:30 in the afternoon on November 23, Spaak and the JCS gave their dual "PUNCH" approval, which meant the paratroopers would take off for Stanleyville in about four hours, arriving in the early morning of November 24.[54] Thus, they would arrive just before Vandewalle. This gave the United States and Belgium ascendancy in Stanleyville, but also additional manpower if needed to secure the city. At daybreak on November 24, ten C-130s flew 320 Belgian paratroopers into the Stanleyville airport, which they secured very quickly. Within an hour, a Belgian rescue team rushed to Hotel Victoria at the city center where the hostages were being kept, shielding themselves from what was only light weapons fire (figures 12.2 and 12.3). The rebels had lined up two hundred and fifty hostages in V-formation on the road to the airport. When the paratroopers appeared, the Simbas fired on the hostages and thirty-nine were killed or later died from their wounds, including Paul Carlson. Hoyt, Grinwis, and the other Americans saved themselves by running in between buildings. Overall, about 1,600 hostages were flown out of Stanleyville. The roughly 600 Westerners, mostly missionaries, who remained in Orientale Province did so at their own risk, and about half perished in the violent aftermath to the rescue.[55]

According to the original plans, the Stanleyville rescue was to be followed by three other rescue operations, one each at Paulis, Bunia, and Watsa. Only the one at Paulis proceeded. President Johnson, the JCS, and Ambassador Godley wanted to go ahead with the others, but Spaak insisted that all the operations be stopped. Dean Rusk agreed and convinced Johnson to halt the other rescue plans. While perhaps not as comprehensive as Johnson might have preferred at the outset, Dragon Rouge did manage to break up and scatter the CNL leadership. Gbenye and Olenga fled to Sudan and Soumialot went to Egypt, leaving Laurent Kabila to emerge as the new leader.[56] Kabila had served as third in command. He was only twenty-six years old. Kabila was born in Katanga to a Luba father and had joined the Jeunesse Balubakat

Figure 12.2. U.S. Air Crews at Kamina, November 1964

Source: U.S. Air Force photograph.

Figure 12.3. Belgian Paratroopers Escorting Simba at Stanleyville Airport, November 1964

Source: U.S. Air Force photograph.

faction to fight Tshombe's secession. After Lumumba's assassination he gravitated toward the CNL opposition.

A White House statement explained that the purpose of its action was "to save the lives of innocent men, women, and children, both Congolese and citizens of at least eighteen countries." It argued that more hostages would have been killed had the operation not proceeded.[57] From his ranch in Texas, the president defended the rescue as humanitarian: "[W]e have to act promptly to save hundreds, even thousands of lives." He explained that "the Congo has been an arena of power struggles and ideological wars. I hope now that it can have at least a chance for peace." Then he assured listeners that "we have no economic gain to be served in the Congo. We seek to impose no political solution, neither our own nor that of some outsider. We have tried only to meet our obligations to the legitimate government and its efforts to achieve unity and stability and reconciliation in the Congo."[58]

Reality belied the idea that the operation was intended to save Congolese lives. They were given almost no protection. Within hours after the paratroopers had landed, Mobutu made sure his ANC units were in Stanleyville. He gave command to Victor Nendaka, whose wife and children had reportedly been executed by the rebels. Nendaka was "not at all charitable or compassionate," recalled U.S. lieutenant colonel Rattan.[59] Between ten thousand and twenty thousand Congolese lives were taken in retribution by the government troops in Stanleyville.[60] Godley recommended limiting the presence of the ANC, but this proved impossible, politically and militarily. Washington instructed the ambassador to make sure that there was as little contact as possible between the ANC and paratroopers in order to stem speculation that the joint arrivals were anything but coincidental.[61]

Mainstream American media coverage of the original rescue hardly questioned its humanitarian intent. The persuasiveness of the humanitarian motive is evident in the fact that the rescue has become the exemplary case in contemporary international law to illustrate the humanitarian justification for intervention.[62] The emphasis on humanitarian motives has masked the military side of the operation and the intention to use the paratrooper drop to defeat the rebels. White Americans focused on the plight of the hostages. After the hostage story subsided, the media turned its attention to the brutality of the Congolese, "of which there was plenty," as if to suggest that the "rescue" had been mandatory.[63] Reporters cited abuse after abuse by the rebels. Most, like *Time* magazine, asked whether "Black Africa can be taken seriously or not." The magazine detailed the murder of religious and priests, children, and women. Most of the mercenaries were fighting "out of conviction," while the rebels were "drunk and high on hemp."[64]

Not all members of the press corps praised Johnson's handling of the rescue. Publisher Frederick Praeger sent a letter to Bundy protesting the manner in which the rescue was handled, suggesting that the president should have stood firm once his decision to do the rescue had been made, used a Marine drop, explained his decision to the American people, and coordinated the activity "with enormous fanfare in the United Nations" and not hide behind the Belgian mercenaries.[65] Johnson did not take kindly to the "friendly" advice. "Three weeks ago," he stormed, "we had to be gentlemanly" toward advice from the press, recalling Luce's *Life* article. Now, after the election, he had no intention of being so harassed.[66]

Criticism coming from the African American community was stronger than it had been in the past. Martin Luther King, while in Oslo accepting the Nobel Peace Prize, expressed his own regret at the need for the rescue and its aftermath, but he hewed close to his message of nonviolence. Malcolm X denounced Washington's support of Tshombe, a traitor to Africa, and who was a murderer paid for by American dollars. American policy and the hostage rescue were extremist, he declared, and did not result in defense of liberty but rather the bombing of villages where women and children remained. He accused Washington of caring more for the "white" hostages (as he so perceptively pointed out was the term for the captives in the press) than the poor black Congolese who were held hostage on so many other levels.[67]

The need for the rescue showed the ineffectiveness of the administration's crisis management and failure to find real solutions. In effect, Johnson was dealing with the failure of Lovanium to find a way for the Congolese leftists to channel their differences in a political way rather than a military one or to participate in any real power sharing. Gizenga's role reflected the superficiality of Lovanium. The results further separated and divided the Congolese, and this time around no one was talking about a constitutional solution, but resorting only to guns and brute force.

13. Reaction and Mop-Up

Communist Reaction

The Soviet reaction to the airdrop was predictably harsh. Soviet monitors knew something was being planned as soon as they saw the paratrooper movement to Ascension Island. On November 23, Anatoly Dobrynin approached Dean Rusk about the flurry of activity. The Soviet Foreign Ministry delivered to the Belgian and American ambassadors an official protest. On November 25, Fedorenko called the airdrop a "flagrant act of armed intervention." Radio Moscow charged that the real purpose was much more than to rescue a few hostages but rather to save the Tshombe regime and suppress the national liberation struggle.[1] The statement deplored the "new act of armed intervention in the domestic affairs of the Congo on the part of Belgium, the U.S.A. and Britain."[2]

A din of protest came from all over the African, Asian, and communist regions of the world in response to the intervention at Stanleyville. In Moscow, students attacked the U.S., Belgian, British, and even the Congolese embassies, while Soviet police stood by and later had to prevent the attack from getting out of hand.[3] The OAU condemned the airdrop as an act of intervention. Indonesians stormed the U.S. cultural center in Jakarta and closed the U.S. Information Service (USIS) center in Surabaya. Meanwhile, angry students in Cairo attacked the embassy and burned the Kennedy Memorial Library. In Beijing, a huge rally of 700,000 protested the airdrop, and 300,000 marched in Shanghai. Chinese newspapers referred to Johnson as a "bloodthirsty aggressor."[4]

The Communist Bloc and radical African states determined that the Western-led intervention, masked as a "rescue," justified their own increased involvement in favor of the opposition. Algeria, Egypt, Sudan, Congo-Brazzaville, Burundi, and Tanzania increased aid to the "rightful" government

Figure 13.1. Soviet Weapons Stash Found in the Eastern Congo, February 1965

Source: William T. Close, in the William Averell Harriman Papers, Library of Congress; used with permission.

in Stanleyville. Moscow publicly announced that with the help of its Communist Bloc allies, it would provide arms and help pay for their delivery (figure 13.1). One recipient was Laurent Kabila, who directed the aid to the Congo from his base in Tanzania. By the first days of December 1964, a dozen or so planes from Ghana flew into Sudan, along with other aid from Egypt, Algeria, and the Soviet Union. Sudan was no longer ruled by Abboud, but by a provisional government that would openly help the Congolese opposition against Tshombe. In Egypt, Soumialot conferred with Nasser and the Soviet ambassador to discuss the future of the opposition movement.[5] Although Egypt and Sudan initially explored the possibility of providing aid, both eventually backed away from long-term commitments as they made efforts to improve relations with the United States, and Algeria could not have afforded much aid anyway.[6]

By the time of the Stanleyville operation, Khrushchev had been removed from power. Leonid Brezhnev was now the Communist Party's general secretary. His first deputy Alexandr Shelepin attacked Khrushchev's foreign policy for its adventurism and bringing the country dangerously close to war with the West over Suez, Berlin, and Cuba.[7] Under the influence of Mikhail Suslov and foreign policy expert Boris Ponomarev, the Politburo reasserted a more cautious ideological approach. They now emphasized the building of socialism and communism in the Soviet Union and other Communist Bloc states and tended to downgrade the national liberation movements.[8]

Despite the new ideological views, Brezhnev and the new Soviet leadership basically continued Khrushchev's policy of criticizing Western actions and supporting the rebellion. The first reference to the Congo by the new leadership was made by Brezhnev, in a speech to a Czechoslovakian delegation in Moscow on December 3, 1964. Brezhnev declared that "the armed intervention against the patriots of the Congo was undertaken under the hypocritical pretext of 'guaranteeing the safety' of white diplomats and missionaries. The pretext is not new, . . . but the Congolese patriots will not give up." And, he added, "on their side is all Africa, on their side are the forces of freedom and peace in all the world," which should meet "the collective action of the colonizers . . . with solid resistance."[9] His message kept the distance of the Soviet Union and made no extravagant promises to support the revolutionaries. The Kremlin continued its policy of quietly supplying aid via East Germany, and the fact that it did so indicated that the Soviet leadership was still interested in keeping channels open for the future. East Germany supplied or promised to supply 2,000 MP1s with ammunition, 100 tanks, grenades, and other matériel and supplies, and communication equipment, valued at more than 3 million deutsche marks. This material was to be sent via Alexandria, although it is doubtful that all or even most of it ever arrived in the Congo. If it had been delivered, it would have represented a significant escalation of support.[10]

The Reaction at the United Nations

The hostile international reaction to the hostage rescue continued at the United Nations, both in the General Assembly and the Security Council. On December 7, Gromyko lambasted the intervention and called for the immediate withdrawal of the British, French, and Belgian colonizers from the Congo. "We may be sure," he said, "that the people of the Congo has not said its final word and that it will defend its fight for freedom and independence from those who, in their death grip, are clinging to the copper, diamonds, cobalt and uranium that are the property of the Congolese people."[11] Soviet ambassador Nikolai Fedorenko followed up by lashing out at the United States for its support of Tshombe's puppet regime.[12]

Che Guevara passionately addressed the General Assembly on December 11, and protested the biased nature of the "rescue." Argentinian by birth, Guevara became an international revolutionary who fought with Fidel Castro to victory in the 1959 Cuban Revolution and served as Castro's minister of industry. In his speech, Guevara wondered "how the rights of the people can be flouted with absolute impunity and the most insolent cynicism" by the white imperialist "blood-thirsty butchers." He called "all free men throughout the world" to be "ready to avenge the crime committed in the Congo."[13] Guevara tried to use the injustice to mobilize people ideologically. His arguments resonated at a broad level and were given a mystic reverence.

Most Africans did not like the imperialist and racist nature of the intervention. In the Security Council, Ghana's foreign minister, Kojo Botsio, reckoned it "extremely ridiculous to be associated with Belgians in a so-called 'humanitarian' mission." Most African states agreed that the operation constituted military aggression and urged withdrawal of the mercenaries.[14] The debate quickly picked up on a racial component not seen in the earlier years of the crisis. Botsio charged that the United States' treatment of Congolese was similar to its treatment of African Americans who are "tortured and murdered for asserting their legitimate rights and whose lives are entrusted to the United States government."[15] The Guinean representative asked about the "thousands" of Congolese citizens "with dark skins," like those in Mississippi, who have been murdered by South Africans, Rhodesians, Belgians, and Cuban exiles.[16] Some tried to turn the question of race around. Congolese representative Theodore Idzumbuir questioned Sudan's racial policies that sent refugees into the Congo earlier that year and called the Egyptians the "whites of the North," comparing their involvement in the Congo with Tshombe's use of mercenaries.[17]

Johnson failed to preempt or respond effectively to the avalanche of criticism. Despite his dedication to civil rights at home, Johnson never adequately managed to stand behind those rights abroad, particularly in the case of the Congo. His support of Tshombe put the United States squarely on the side of the conservative reactionaries. With little help coming out of Washington, Stevenson stuck to his defense of the rescue mission as a humanitarian operation. He protested the "irrational, irresponsible, insulting and repugnant language" used in the charges against the United States.[18] He found little support except for Nigeria, which stood alone among African states in agreeing to the humanitarian basis for the operation.[19]

On December 30, 1964, the Security Council passed its final resolution on the Congo crisis. In the resolution, the secretary-general was asked to follow the situation in the Congo and report to the Security Council when appropriate.[20] It seemed to be a signing off, or a washing of hands of the whole affair. The resolution, despite being "the result of an extremely laborious compromise," meant little.[21] Botsio, supported by Fedorenko, tried to give the resolution sharper teeth by assigning more responsibility to the secretary-general.[22] Nkrumah and others now looked to the OAU to broker mediation efforts, clearly favoring the Stanleyville opposition.[23] The conservative African states that supported Tshombe generally remained silent, hoping to avoid angering their African neighbors. However, in February, Senegal, Malagasy, and others gathered in Nouakchott, Mauritania, for the inauguration of the Organization of the African and Malagasy Communities and from there moved toward aiding the Tshombe government.[24]

Just below the surface of this U.N. sign-off lingered the question of Article 19 and the very future of peacekeeping. In light of the newest "imperialist aggression" in the Congo, the Soviet Union made no move to change its public policy of nonpayment. The United States continued to insist on applying Article 19 and depriving violators of their vote in the General Assembly. As the larger implications became clear, and even the possibility of wrecking the United Nations loomed, the dispute soon faded. By late 1964 the new leadership in the Soviet Union indicated that it was willing to make some kind of payment to ease U.N. financial difficulties, as long as it was not understood to be a direct payment to the costs of ONUC. In return it expected that references to Article 19 would be dropped.[25] By mid-1965, a new U.S. representative to the United Nations, Arthur Goldberg—a lawyer and former associate justice of the U.S. Supreme Court—announced that the United States would not go against the majority and pursue application of Article 19 (figure 13.2).[26] He reserved the right for the United States to make the same exception to the principle of collective financial responsibility. Ever since, the U.S. Congress has leaped on this right to make exceptions to assessments and has opted out of financial obligations, forcing the United Nations itself to move in and out of financial crises.

An Illusory Victory

Meanwhile, the extent of rebel activity throughout the country continued to worry the Congolese government. In a New Year's Day speech on January 1, 1965, Kasavubu maintained that what the Congo needed was not national reconciliation, but reconciliation of foreign interests. Adoula agreed. From his new perch in Rome, Adoula (who no longer had any official role) urged President Johnson to talk with the rebels. Tshombe's reliance on opponents to decolonization, he warned, fueled aid to the rebels and threatened

Figure 13.2. Johnson and Goldberg, July 1965

Source: Lyndon B. Johnson Presidential Library; White House photograph.

a "Vietnamization of the Congo." Now, he said, "any solution that would exclude those called the rebels . . . would be illusory."[27]

This is not what the Kasavubu-Tshombe-Mobutu triumvirate had in mind or what Johnson wanted to hear on the verge of victory. Instead, the trio used their temporary reprieve, bought by discussion at the United Nations, to try to deal a fatal blow to the rebels. They were almost successful. Using hard-won dictatorial (not democratic) powers, the government, on January 10, executed more than 500 rebels, barring reporters from the bloodletting. They also relied on Mike Hoare and his mercenary band to clean up rebel resistance after the rescue operation had toppled the CNL in Stanleyville. Hoare's operation, called "White Giant," attracted more South African mercenaries than could be outfitted. He also relied heavily on advance strafing operations flown by the anti-Castro Cuban exiles. American diplomats turned up the pressure on Sudan and Uganda, and by mid-March, Uganda, at least, was promising to end its role in supplying the rebels, who were still strong in the Uvira area and other pockets south of Stanleyville. By April, Hoare was able to cut off supply lines from Sudan and Uganda, and Ugandan troops began withdrawing.[28]

Other areas across the country continued in a state of unrest during the first months of 1965. The ANC repulsed a rebel attack north of Leopoldville and sent a group of rebels from Congo-Brazzaville back across the Congo River. At the same time, opposition activity in Kwilu, where Mulele and his bands were still holding out, was hampered by lack of supplies but still a threat to Leopold-ville.[29] Pretty soon there was only one supply route in the east open, through Tanzania. That remaining supply line had become a "relatively blatant" conduit for arms. The aid from Tanzania supported one last major and prolonged effort by the CNL and Laurent Kabila in mid-1965 to regain territory.[30]

Still hoping to lock in a greater American commitment, Leopoldville drafted a proposal asking Washington to increase its aid to help clear the country of rebels. The cost of the U.S. assistance program for the Congo had reached $5 million in 1964, well beyond its original budget. Harriman thought that the proposal should be considered even though it seemed to involve the possibility of bombing urban areas. Ball, Bundy, and most other members of the administration were adamantly opposed to any direct U.S. involvement in the "clean-up" since it would mean a greater U.S. commitment to the Congo than the president was willing to offer. Johnson wanted to cut back the U.S. role in the Congo. He was afraid the United States would get "bogged down" in defending the rescue, especially in light of the African response, and perhaps even have to extend its commitment.[31]

U.S. relations with Africa had hit new lows after the rescue operation. Roy Wilkins, executive secretary of the NAACP, and several other civil rights figures met with Secretary Rusk in March 1965. They urged the administration to support an OAU-spearheaded solution to the crisis, while also expressing their hope that Tshombe would end his use of white mercenaries. After the meeting, they described themselves as "friendly critics" of administration policy in Africa. Although there was some suggestion they might form an informal public advisory group, Johnson discouraged that idea as fostering "a separate" African American view of foreign policy."[32]

The assistant secretary of state for African affairs, G. Mennen Williams, outlined his ideas for a new Africa policy in early March. The stated goal was to emphasize political independence and economic development in Africa. Since Johnson had denied new sources of financial support, Williams had to rely on reviving or reforming existing programs. The assistant secretary also foresaw the need to support self-determination in South Africa, Angola, and Rhodesia to address some of the issues of racial discrimination on the continent.[33] Not surprisingly, Williams's program dwindled into a halfhearted attempt to convince Africa that "America cares," but in reality the administration's focus had turned elsewhere. Administration officials found themselves having to defend Johnson's basic interest in Africa, but they had little from the president to build on. In Uganda, Soviet representative Vladimir Porshakov noticed the difference and commented that Johnson did not have the same interest in Africa as Kennedy.[34]

Che Guevara in Africa

Ever since his appearance at the United Nations in December, Che Guevara had a heightened interest in Africa. To follow up, he decided to tour the continent. Guevara had sanguine expectations and somehow became convinced that the revolution in Africa was imminent. Nasser told him flatly that an expedition to the Congo was a mistake and that he should forget about it. He could not expect to "become another Tarzan, a white man coming among black men, leading them and protecting them."[35] Guevara sloughed off the pessimism. With Moscow's approval Castro agreed to support Guevara's expedition to the Congo, planned for the spring of 1965. Preparations were kept very secret and facilitated by Pablo Rivalta, who was now the Cuban ambassador to Tanzania. Guevara, disguised by heavy-rimmed glasses and a bolero-type hat, flew to Dar es Salaam in April with Victor Dreke and twelve other Afro-Cuban soldiers. Guevara surprised Kabila, who was still in Tanzania, when he told him of 100 soldiers already on the way, with promises of another 300 to follow.

Guevara was not ready for what he was to confront in Africa. No matter how anyone looked at it, Guevara's arrival meant a significant expansion of the revolutionary effort, for which the CNL was not prepared. Kabila initially decided that it would be too dangerous to inform Nyerere of Guevara's presence, even though Tanzania had agreed to serve as a channel for aid to the revolutionary movement.[36] Kabila certainly must have feared that Nyerere would become reluctant to allow Tanzania its frontline role with such a prominent figure to attract international attention.

Guevara achieved little during his eight months in Africa. His diary reveals a deep disappointment that at times became anger. For him, the experience was miserable. The problem was not the availability of military supplies or money. Rather, Guevara believed the biggest problem from a tactical standpoint was the lack of leadership. The squabbles between Soumialot and Kabila drew further energy away from the military objectives. Guevara considered Gbenye a traitor who preferred to negotiate with Leopoldville. Despite efforts to deprive Gbenye of a central role in the opposition movement, he still managed to stir up some trouble with Kenya, Tanzania, and Uganda. Guevara also complained about Kabila, who, he said, remained shut up in his hotel in Tanzania with too much liquor and too many women. Kabila, he lamented, rarely visited the Congo, let alone build any kind of rapport with the peasants. Problems trickled down through the entire opposition movement, and the Congolese were unfamiliar with guerrilla warfare. They often fled without fighting, or were unable or unwilling to keep supply routes open to the soldiers. After a month of mercenary advances and failed rebel offensives, Tanzania began to limit Cuban, Chinese, Bulgarian, and Soviet supplies from reaching the Congo. Nyerere, whose advisers did not believe the support was worth the risks, finally may have convinced him to pull back. Hoping for help with Nyerere, Kabila asked Chinese and Soviet ambassadors to suggest talks with him. But the rebel movement was disintegrating more quickly than expected.[37]

Guevara tried not to be too critical while he was in Africa, but anyone reading his diary would wonder why, except for his commitment to the revolution, he stayed for so long in the face of such adversity. Add to this the fact that his health was suffering. He was increasingly aware that the problems facing the Congo were very different than he had at first supposed to be the case. The Congolese had no understanding of Marxist revolutionary ideology, nor did it suit their particular circumstances. They were fighting against oppression, but it was not the same tangibles that had attracted Guevara to the revolution in Latin America, especially peasant rights to the land or support against worker exploitation. The Congo had plenty of land and the few quasi-workers remained relatively isolated, except perhaps in Katanga where the revolution had not yet reached.[38]

As grim as the situation was, life was not yet over for the rebels. Continued foreign support was encouraging. The Soviet Union and China took turns courting rebel leaders and their allies. On June 9, Zhou Enlai, on another extensive visit to Africa, stopped in Tanzania to meet with Nyerere. In August 1965, Soumialot traveled to China as a guest of the Chinese People's Institute of Foreign Affairs to discuss future moves of the resistance.[39] Moscow revived the activity of the Soviet Afro-Asian Solidarity Committee. From September 13 to 25, Soumialot also visited the Soviet Union and was received by Suslov and Ponomarev.[40] The Kremlin used its post at the United Nations to try to speak out for African states in favor of decolonization. In the U.N. General Assembly, for instance, on September 22, the Soviet representative called for an end to the imperialist aggression in the Congo, trying to highlight the continued problems there.[41]

Mobutu's Second Coup

Political rivalry and personality differences hastened the implosion not only in Stanleyville, but also in Leopoldville. The growing rivalry between Kasavubu and Tshombe had consumed Leopoldville for the last several months of 1965, as Kasavubu tried to rein in Tshombe's bid for greater power. Jostling for political supporters, both began to propose constitutional changes. Kasavubu escalated the dispute by insisting that Munongo resign as interior minister. On October 14, Kasavubu dismissed Tshombe and named Evariste Kimba prime minister in his place. One month later, the parliament, in its first session since August 1963, and heavily influenced by pro-Tshombe forces, rejected Kimba's nomination. Kasavubu renominated Kimba, who continued to serve as prime minister. Tshombe protested these events, calling the whole episode "prodigiously ridiculous." He gained little sympathy or support from the international community, and even his Belgian supporters seemed to be getting tired of the whole matter.[42]

Senator Dodd reacted bitterly to Tshombe's ouster. He warned Johnson that the new political crisis was more than a personal dispute between Tshombe and Kasavubu. Rather, he said, the latter was trying to illegally usurp power. Ambassador Godley was making matters worse, Dodd complained, by allowing his air attaché to fly Bomboko around the Congo to stir up opposition to Tshombe. The danger, said Dodd, was that if Tshombe goes, so will all the white mercenaries, leaving the Western position in the Congo to hang in the balance. Johnson, however, accepted Kimba without much deliberation or agonizing. The president also quietly welcomed Kimba's appeal to anti-Tshombe African leaders, including Nkrumah, in an effort to finally quell the voices of discontent.[43]

External influences again seemed to have a hand in moving events in the Congo. At the OAU conference in Accra that October, Kasavubu tried to improve relations with African states. He promised that he would send the mercenaries home and normalize relations with African neighbors. Kasavubu also "gave the impression, at least to some, that he was willing to conciliate with the rebel leaders," according to Herbert Weiss.[44] Mobutu flatly opposed discharging the mercenaries. Their relationship cooled noticeably after Kasavubu returned from Accra.[45]

On November 24, 1965, Mobutu announced he was taking over control of the country. It was a bloodless military coup. Author Sean Kelly suggested that Godley and Devlin "were in close touch with Mobutu, urging him to intervene."[46] With his close associates, Colonel Mulamba and Major General Bobozo, he took over the offices of government, including the security forces, and ruled by fiat. Mobutu forced Kasavubu to sign letters of acceptance and escorted him and his family to a military camp where he was held in relatively good conditions. A few days later, he was released on the promise he would retire from politics. He apparently did, resettling in southern Leopoldville Province. Tshombe chose instead to flee the country. Mobutu canceled elections and installed himself as president for five years under a "regime of exception."[47]

By this time most of the American officials who had followed the crisis were tired of Kasavubu, who never seemed to be able to pull things together. They welcomed Mobutu as a decisive alternative. Devlin remembered Mobutu in the days after his second coup as "a dynamic young man who was determined to have an independent state in the Congo and [who] really seemed to believe in all the things Africa's leaders then stood for."[48] And Mobutu *was* dynamic, at first (if one overlooked his heavy-handedness). He immediately pledged a war on corruption. He asked his people to "roll up your sleeves" and work for the good of the nation. Police took the order to its literal meaning, arresting those who wore their sleeves down.[49] In less than a month after his coup, Mobutu spoke to a roaring crowd in the soccer stadium where riots had begun it all over six years ago. He said that after five years of plundering he would need five years to lead Congo to prosperity.[50] Building his public persona was a new, and for a long time an uncomfortable, role for Mobutu, who up until this point had operated largely behind the scenes.

One day after his coup d'état, Mobutu sent Mike Hoare a letter ending his contract in the Congo. Mobutu's apparent step toward dismissing mercenaries was done to disperse Tshombe's support base and create some goodwill across the Congo, Africa, and the world. In fact, his real intentions remained hidden behind this window dressing. Mercenaries continued to provide a key source of support during the next troubled year and a half while Mobutu tried to stop the unrest that continued to plague the Congo.[51] But they knew the end of their time in the Congo was near. Even Nkrumah was weary of the entire Congo affair and was willing to give Mobutu the benefit of the doubt. He believed that Mobutu would eventually fulfill his promise and dismiss the mercenaries.[52] By then, of course, Mobutu would have rejuvenated his ANC troops.

Mobutu quickly sought to consolidate his power, taking his pages right from Machiavelli. To hush his loudest domestic critics, he released Gizenga from jail, but it was more of the same window dressing. One of the first things Mobutu did was redraw the provincial administration left by Adoula. He variously installed provincial leaders or cabinets or both when necessary to establish loyalty. Once known for his ability to bridge civil and military leadership, now he found the civil leaders superfluous. Instead, he dictated harsh and often simplistic solutions that reinforced his leadership while not really solving the problems at hand. Emboldened with each step, he soon began to challenge Belgian control over the Congolese economy, which he was finding to be much more restrictive than he had realized or was willing to admit. In a similar fashion, he took control of foreign relations and worked them to increase his state's security apparatus.[53] Before his second coup, he had tried to be all things to all people; now he was fighting to get all things for himself.

The Soviet reaction to his coup was predictably negative, but muted. Khokhlov ranted at the colonialists for throwing out Kasavubu (and earlier, Tshombe) in search of someone even more subservient to their interests. The coup, Khokhlov said, was an American admission of moral defeat. He called the new "Mobutuism" a fusing of "military adventurism" and "political lack of principle."[54] Coming from the Soviet Union, the criticism was not very effective. Yet its accuracy would be proven many times over the course of the next thirty years.

The crisis in the Congo by 1965 was very different from what it had been in 1960 or even 1963. Where Eisenhower saw an unruly radical nationalist, Kennedy had seen a new challenge in Africa. Johnson knew little and cared less about the continent, but he was willing to fight the Cold War there if necessary. The U.S. public remained largely uninterested in the Congo except during the news of Lumumba's assassination and the hostage crisis much later. Unlike Vietnam, this disinterest made the search for a winning strategy easier, although in the unsavory form of mercenaries and a capitulation to Belgian imperial interests. Like Eisenhower and Kennedy, Johnson relied on the CIA in the Congo, but the CIA was allowed a much freer hand, its involvement in the training of mercenaries causing no major public scandal. Johnson did not want to lose the Congo to the communists, but he knew it would be impossible, publicly and realistically, to commit U.S. troops to defend the Congolese government, and he turned to Brussels for help. The alliance had come full circle.

By mid-1964, the two rebellions in Kwilu and Stanleyville had grown significantly. Aid from Chinese sources had contributed to this growth and encouraged the Soviet Union to renew its involvement in the crisis. The change in personalities, from Khrushchev to Brezhnev, helped diminish the likelihood of increased Soviet involvement. Conversely, the transition from the Kennedy to the Johnson administration had great implications for advancing U.S. involvement. Johnson finished the process that Kennedy had begun in abandoning a constitutional solution. He alone accepted a military solution and relied on paratrooper forces to end the hostage crisis, and then accepted Mobutu's use of mercenaries to sweep the eastern provinces of rebels.

Johnson undoubtedly faced tough decisions in the Congo, some as tough as any he faced in Vietnam. He supported a mercenary-led rescue of the hostages, timed brilliantly and with a degree of luck, to ensure the victory against the rebels. The timing of the rescue showed that he was just as concerned to defeat the communist-aided rebels as he was to save his reputation in the Congo. The "rescue" won him a favorable public reaction, as many believed in its humanitarian nature. Johnson would never fully exploit his victory with the press, and was left with a great distaste for African affairs. That bitter memory attests to the pressure that Johnson felt and his efforts to keep the situation under control—*his* control.

Khokhlov's words also verified the Soviet conclusion that the United States had finally succeeded in its quest to dominate the Congo. The seriousness and scope of the 1964 revolution have long been overlooked, in part because of the Western role and response. The paratrooper drop and Mobutu's subsequent campaign against the rebels showed that the United States was ready to offer military aid to embattled pro-Western African regimes. Johnson's reliance on the Belgians resulted in a muting of their very different economic interests. Rather, Soviet suspicion regarding the flaws within the rebel movement became self-fulfilling. Had the rebels been more unified, or even if they had won an outpost in Stanleyville, they would have had little choice but to rely on radical African nations' and Soviet aid. In this respect, the will of the Soviet Union would not be further tested. The crisis did show the failure of the Soviet ability to respond to weakly formed rebellions so far from home. So too did the Soviet campaign against U.S. domination of the United Nations linger inconclusively with the ever-growing debt crisis. The debt crisis had in fact created a divide between the United States and the Soviet Union over the nature and future of international peacekeeping. That confrontation fizzled, and so did peacekeeping during the Cold War.

Conclusion:
The Congo in Global Perspective

For the rest of his life Munongo never spoke publicly about Lumumba's assassination. Munongo, like the others involved in the sordid affair, continued to evade responsibility. Contrary to Munongo's denials, Lumumba's assassination created as many problems as it was supposed to solve. The assassination was a grave reflection of bitter imperial legacies mixed with the unbending bipolar confrontation of the Cold War. Few states made the transition from colony to independent nationhood easily. The Congo barely made it at all, and it did so only with much abuse of power and much suffering by its people. In an ironic twist of fate, after three decades of misdeeds by Mobutu (renamed Mobutu Sese Seko), who led the Congo as its president, and a tumultuous four years under the leadership of Laurent Kabila, Antoine Gizenga finally became prime minister in 2007 for about a year and a half. Regrettably, like Kabila, he had long ago sacrificed the goals of the opposition and his legacy remained marginal.

The lessons left by the crisis are many and mixed. This study highlights several. First and foremost, we can draw a clear connection between decolonization and the Cold War. The "Congo crisis" was unquestionably a Cold War crisis in the heart of Africa. It significantly increased the tension between the Western world led by the United States and the Communist Bloc states and allies, particularly in Africa but also at the United Nations. As was happening elsewhere by the 1960s, in Southeast Asia (Vietnam) and Latin America, there was also blurring at the edges of the bipolar competition. Events in the Congo thus helped bestow on Africa a legacy of Cold War ideological intervention, while sidelining economic and political development.

It is true that the Soviet Union did not commit as much material aid and weapons as the United States, but it wanted to spread its influence to the

Congo, and Khrushchev took measured risks to do so. It was not the old behemoth of orthodox history, but more nuanced and conscious of its weaknesses. The Soviets had fewer contacts and connections with Africa in general, and hoped to bandwagon onto African (and Asian) anti-imperialism to a greater extent than was ultimately possible. In many ways, the Soviet Union preferred to let the imperialists lose rather than fight their way to superiority. It is not surprising that in a region of third-tier importance, Khrushchev sought greater influence in ways that did not require an overwhelming effort. The United States, after all, did the same by working through the United Nations and relying on Belgium. But Khrushchev's optimism was also misplaced, and he overlooked or underestimated key opportunities to improve the Soviet position in the Congo. This is particularly true vis-à-vis the Soviet relationship with Lumumba. Failure to support Lumumba or try to save him must stand as Khrushchev's biggest misstep. His failure to act can be explained by the fact that he was already more involved than he wanted to be in a place more than 12,000 miles from home. As a result Soviet policy was never firmly grounded in the Congo and it lacked a loyal strongman or even a single visionary leader, which in itself was intrinsic to fighting the Cold War in Africa, as it was elsewhere in Asia and Latin America.

It has often been said that the actual Soviet threat to American interests in the Congo was needlessly exaggerated by U.S. policymakers. This might be true in a strict sense, but the seriousness of the crisis and the fact that the Congo was almost lost by the West on at least two occasions needs to be better accounted for in the literature on the Cold War. Both Lumumba's challenge to the U.S.–U.N.–Belgian triumvirate in August 1960 and the 1964 revolution significantly threatened the Western presence in the Congo. Imagining a greater role for the Soviet Union or a flip-flop in allegiances is not very far-fetched (as later events in the Horn of Africa would show). Nothing can justify U.S. actions, that is, illegally and immorally supporting the assassination of a democratically elected leader and actively working to undermine the Congolese government, as Stephen Weissman has so lucidly argued. The damaging legacy of the Cold War—its thinking, prescriptions, and excuses, all in the name of combating the single evil of communism—stands out here in its clearest form. The general failure to come to terms with this history serves as a warning that subsequent war-making against another "ism" (terrorism) could easily degenerate into another era of illegal and immoral actions.

U.S. Cold War policies in the Congo exerted strong and contradictory influences. The Cold War caused the United States to pay more attention to the Congo on the eve of its independence, for both better and worse. Although the United States initially represented democratic values and rights to self-determination, its policies tragically betrayed these values. This betrayal, based on a relentless search for dominance over the Soviet Union, became one of the basic costs of the Cold War. The Congo's liberal Constitution was repeatedly reinterpreted in a restrictive way or was ignored as heavy-handed tactics and cover action were pursued by successive U.S. presidential administrations—all in the name of battling communism. Eisenhower, Kennedy, and Johnson each had his own style, but the basic discourse did not change. Other, more equitable, options for the Congo based on trust in democratic values and equitable economic practices were overlooked. Thus, the Cold War in Africa—battleground Africa—became the focus of the crisis and for a long time delayed the progress of postcolonial Africa, in this case in the Congo.

What about the argument that the crisis was a Western one—that is, for the United States and Belgium? Many scholars have argued that the two allies were subtly competing for economic influence, while at the same time trying to jointly manage a difficult postimperial transition. The crisis, Ludo De Witte stated, was "an attempt by the West to recover a lost colony."[1] True, the allies wanted to appear united, and in this regard there were fewer differences between Eisenhower and Kennedy than has often been suggested. The jury is still out on the extent of U.S.–Belgian cooperation in the assassination of Lumumba. That remains a real possibility. Yet their competing political interests must be more directly accounted for, and available evidence suggests that their relationship was under a lot of strain. What we do know is that at many times during the crisis, the Belgians acted without considering U.S. interests and left the United States in the dark as to their real goals and intentions, in an effort to circumscribe what was becoming a heavier American hand in its former colony. The Round Table Conference, halfhearted support of the U.N. resolutions, and relations with Tshombe all represent instances where the Belgians seemed to operate in contradiction to U.S. goals and/or preferences and frustrated U.S. policymakers. Washington made little public protest, and its continued interest in at least appearing united, surprising at times, can be explained by its Cold War goals.

The personality of Lumumba will always remain an open and controversial question. Lumumba was impatient and visionary, yes, but giving his character more depth, we can see that he also acted in ways that were very rational if one considered that his goal was reunification of his country in the face of adversity. He was not all that different from such pro-Western Congolese as Justin Bomboko or Cyrille Adoula, who used his same tactics—including visiting Washington, appealing to the Soviet Union, and using the United Nations—to achieve their goals. All consistently wanted reunification first. At other times, the Congolese could be very fragmented. The differences between Kasavubu and Lumumba, and later between Tshombe and Mobutu, and even those among the numerous opposition leaders, show how internal differences could seriously affect the outcome of a crisis, even one so enmeshed in the Cold War.

The experience of U.N. peacekeeping in the Congo was certainly contro-versial and unquestionably impacted future peacekeeping. At least part of the problem was the fact that UNOC was never designed to stay out of the Congo's internal affairs, but was based on an original plan to strengthen the internal functioning of the state. Even with this in mind, the U.N. operation was made possible by the joint superpower agreement in the Security Coun-cil. It allowed the Soviet Union a degree of influence that Moscow lacked in Africa previously, and for that Khrushchev should be given credit. But the Soviet Union (and Khrushchev) could also hide behind the U.N. operation, or try to foil it, forcing important decisions aside. That left plenty of room for the United States to use the organization to achieve its own goals in the Congo, and Washington did so for at least as long as possible. Hammarskjöld was certainly pro-Western but did not always go along with the United States, particularly when he determined (or was forced to see) that its goals were not conducive to overall international security (as he saw it). Yet Hammarskjöld was also a diplomat extraordinaire, and had he lived longer the crisis might have ended sooner or more peacefully. A major problem with his legacy is that his imprint on ONUC was so subtly managed and dependent on his personal relationships that it was impossible for others to follow. He was not supposed to die, and his untimely death threw into jeopardy all he had carefully crafted and managed in the Congo.

Lumumba, conversely, was supposed to die, but his "elimination" changed very little. Khrushchev was always a fair-weather friend, not ready to inter-vene to save Lumumba, a fact perhaps reflecting the scarce resources of the Soviet Union. East German records here are particularly instructive. Khrush-chev may have lost his greatest ally in Africa when Lumumba was assassi-nated, but he was not ready to give up entirely. With Gizenga at the helm of the opposition, and located outside Leopoldville, Khrushchev could afford to continue, and even marginally increment, his aid at times. In December and January, and again in February and March 1961, Khrushchev turned down a greater commitment to Gizenga. He chose instead to continue with a lower level of aid and search for allies to do more. Like Lumumba before him, Giz-enga had a brief taste of success, only to find that the Soviet Union was not ready for him. So too with the rebels in 1964. The distancing of Moscow from ties to individual Congolese rebels themselves in fact enabled the Kremlin to continue to supply aid without attracting too much attention or escalating the crisis. By now Khrushchev had sacrificed specific goals in the Congo and looked instead to keep his international standing on decolonization.

What was the actual monetary and military U.S. role versus the Soviet presence in the Congo? The balance of activity in the Congo was definitely weighted on the Western side. Eisenhower's $5 million contingency fund established an early source of support for activity. It is unclear how much or which monies came from this source. We do know that Devlin was authorized $100,000 in pursuit of Lumumba's assassination, although he probably did not spend close to that much. Stephen Weissman found that the CIA's Project Wizard had at least $250,000 for parliamentary development in October 1960, and in February another $500,000 helped pay Mobutu's troops and buy equipment. There were also sources used to set up the "instant air force" as early as 1962. The CIA's Silver Bullets would have required a budget, but that remains classified. Richard Mahoney found that $25,000 to $30,000 were used at Lovanium (while the amount remains unverified, it does not sound unreasonable, and might have come from already earmarked sources). There were also its contributions to ONUC to consider and Belgian contributions to the United Nations–authorized payment of $1 million for Mobutu's troops. Belgium's minister of African affairs had 50 million Belgian francs ($1 million) to spend, plus all the other state resources that were dedicated to Katanga. This accounting shows that the United States (and the rest of the West) had a much stronger position to start with and had much more money to spend.

In comparison, the Soviet disbursals for the Congo were much smaller. The first Soviet offers were usually supplies and food, including the fifteen Ilyushins and other supplies in support of Lumumba's attack on Katanga in August 1960; the $500,000 offered to Gizenga's opposition (with only half reaching its destination); the £25,000 offered to Mulele by the Czechoslovakian government, but again never delivered; and the aid to the Conseil National de Libération and Mulele in 1964 and 1965. One could also include some of the African aid, especially Egyptian and Ghanaian aid offered to the Lumumbists. Aid from China was small and always very selective. What the tally here really shows is that aid and commitment were greater than previously known, but, without solid allies in the Congo, did not reap as much benefit as it might have otherwise.

Given these data, did the United States make a mountain out of a molehill regarding the Soviet role in the Congo? In many ways it did. But the Soviet Union had certain advantages. Even though there was no Soviet plan to "take over" the continent, as orthodox historians so often claimed, Khrushchev's optimism at gaining influence in Africa was well founded. He often boldly took chances to weaken Western popularity, and much of Africa, beginning with Ghana and Guinea, was ready to listen. It is doubtful that Khrushchev considered the Soviet inability to establish true influence in the Congo a complete failure. It was respectable, after all, that he kept the United States at bay for five years. In fact, like the United States, the Soviet Union did not commit a huge amount of resources to Africa, and that made events in the Congo seem less conclusive. And valuable lessons had been learned, which would be applied across the continent in the 1970s. Khrushchev did see a serious shift in African opinion, now much more ready to find its own solutions, such as via the Organization of African Unity, rather than rely on the United Nations. Africans were also becoming much more radical in their views, in part because of the failure in the Congo, and Khrushchev could take some credit for encouraging this shift in opinion. But he was frustrated time and again when it came to allying African goals with the Soviet Union. African states were not willing to transfer one imperialist system for another under the guise of Marxism-Leninism.

Khrushchev also misjudged American goals and repeatedly thought Washington had greater ambitions for the Congo, especially regarding Katanga, than was the case. This probably cooled his immediate interest, not wanting to have to commit more precious resources to a place so far from home. Only once he was sure that the United States had rejected association with Lumumba did he agree to take on this fiercely independent ally. The growing American presence can also help explain why the Soviet chairman again chose not provide more aid, this time to Gizenga. Khrushchev had already reached a level of activism that was new for the Soviet Union in Africa. When Khrushchev did act, he was also careful not to act alone, probably in light of some of his other foreign policy challenges, and so he sought proxies, notably the East Germans and Czechoslovakians. Ironically, also like the Americans, he would have trouble with his ideological counterparts, especially China. Although both were nominally "communist," the Soviet Union's and China's approaches to the crisis revealed stark differences between them. The Chinese argued for support of radical Congolese leaders, whereas Khrushchev was more willing to back horses that would win, so to speak. The Congolese were never comfortable operating in the void between the two, but they had no choice.

The crisis had a major impact on U.S.–Belgian relations. At first, Belgium wanted to keep the U.S. presence limited and by itself represent Western Cold War interests in the Congo. The internationalization of the crisis quickly put it on the defensive. Belgium could never convince Washington that saving Katanga should be an end goal in the Cold War. Looking at the crisis only from the American perspective has resulted in a view that Eisenhower was pro-Belgian while Kennedy was less so. In reality, the two administrations were never very far apart. The Belgian government's initial belligerency meant that it was much less forthright in its relations with Eisenhower than previously understood. Washington did not seem to have good information about its ally's policy, particularly about assassination plans, at least as seen in available documents. Although Johnson feared having to appear that he foisted the crisis back on the Belgians, the Belgians still had much to lose. The dissonance clearly helped prolong the crisis and made U.S. decisions in the Congo harder than they would have been otherwise.

The Belgian decision to support the secession of Katanga complicated America's long-term policy. But it did not really change it. Although Washington's original perceptions might have been colored by Brussels, the White House quickly adopted its own interpretation of events. U.S. relations with Mobutu for instance, particularly Kennedy's, were not merely transformed from the Belgian attitudes. Eventually, the two allies would come together. Though the CIA might have "discovered" Mobutu (eventually), he was more avidly supported by the Belgians, although archival evidence will certainly have more to add on this. In the matter of a few short years, by 1964, no longer was the United States concerned about maintaining appearances of cooperation; but now it believed in quid pro quos, and this meant Belgian military support for its goals.

In the context of this study, how can we understand the role of business interests? David Gibbs is right to point out the undue business influence in the Congo. The role of Union Minière du Haut Katanga in influencing and pressuring the Belgian government is crucial to understanding the duration of the crisis. But in the end, UMHK's interests did not override the concerns of the Cold War. Had politicians not been so closely connected with UMHK, its influence could have been much more quickly moderated. In January 1967, Mobutu finally nationalized UMHK. Belgium protested the seizure of company assets and imposed an embargo on copper. At the time, the United States was working hard on Mobutu to guarantee competition, that is, to finally allow other mining enterprises to move in among the Belgian monopolists. The United States now offered to help Belgium to moderate the nationalization. In a deal worked out by Kennedy aide Theodore Sorensen, full compensation for the takeover was guaranteed.[2]

What can we learn about presidential leadership during the crisis? Each president fought the Cold War differently based on his own fears of how the crisis might expand. Eisenhower equated Lumumba with the communist devil and wanted him out of power. He left it to the imperialists to manage the Katangan secession, even though this secession threatened to divide the country along Cold War lines. While Kennedy's strength may lay with his sensitivity to nationalism, he was forced to turn his attention to the creeping Cold War in the Congo and recognized the need to end the secession of Katanga. Negotiations with the irreverent and uncooperative Tshombe finally forced him to act or pull out of the Congo altogether, which he was not ready to do. Stung by the Bay of Pigs, he resisted the use of force until a near-chaotic situation had developed. Johnson wanted nothing more than to get the Congo under control so that he could turn his attention elsewhere. He micromanaged the crisis when it exploded but his solutions did not resolve much in the big picture. Juxtaposing his own belief in strong leadership, he pulled the United States into a long-term relationship with the corrupt rule of Mobutu.

What about the legacy of Lumumba and decolonization? The easiest thing to say about Lumumba was that he was not a communist but an impatient nationalist who was tragically assassinated. He was a radical visionary who wanted to lead his country to immediate and complete independence, one based on racial equality and economic justice. That was something the imperialists were not ready to accept. He refused to play by international rules. Lumumba's ultimatum to the United Nations seemed designed to challenge the limited nature of the crisis. It also changed the way the U.N. operation played out and worked against his remaining in power. But by bringing the crisis to the United Nations, he certainly changed the way decolonization, at least in Africa, was managed during the Cold War. He ensured, in the long run, that it would not be left entirely up to the imperialists.

Can the crisis teach us anything new about the influence of the United Nations? The United Nations played a key role as moderator. It was when the U.S. presence became overbearing that the organization nearly lost control. This is true after Lumumba's dismissal in September 1960, after his assassination in January 1961, and at the time of the Lovanium conference. Escalation in the end, however, was stopped, often as a result of the United Nations shift to a more neutral position. During the rounds of activity against Katanga, the crisis verged on open warfare, but was controlled by the series of negotiations that had outlined specific objectives. It is probably not too much of an exaggeration to say that the United States was saved from another "Vietnam" or perhaps even a "Cuba" (albeit a very distant one) by the role of the United Nations. The U.N. Operation in the Congo would become the largest, costliest, and most dangerous U.N. mission during the Cold War. While it did help reunite the Congo, it came at a cost in lives, including Hammarskjöld's and many Congolese, and in precedents set when considering future U.N. peacekeeping operations. Interference in the domestic affairs of the host state, the deadlock in the Security Council, and the failure to find real closure to the crisis (despite reunification) were all problems that would trouble future peacekeeping missions.

The term "peacekeeping" is problematic when applied to the Congo, since at its core, the operation was designed to end what was a military intervention. The U Thant Plan was in actuality a logical outcome of the July and August 1960 resolutions calling for an end to the undeclared Belgian occupation of Katanga. Had Washington addressed the problem of Katanga more forthrightly, and had Kennedy communicated his policy more clearly, then the use of force might have been less controversial. This shortcoming dragged out the crisis and lengthened ONUC's stay in the Congo. The international community, especially the African states, pressured U Thant to use force to end the imperialist-supported secession. U Thant was less likely than Hammarskjöld to nuance his diplomacy, but in the end his greater neutrality allowed him to distance himself from Washington and boldly use force to end the secession. As soon as the secession was formally ended, U Thant immediately pulled the United Nations out of the messy situation in the Congo. He argued that the troubles in the Congo were for the Congolese themselves to resolve.

The Congo crisis and U.N. intervention demonstrate not the folly of outside intervention (although there was some), but the need for clear goals and careful planning to achieve them. ONUC was in part a noble attempt to halt another imperialist grab at Africa. It also highlighted the need for better understanding of local conditions. The U.S. and Soviet focus on their international rivalry made agreement much more difficult than necessary and detracted significantly from the ability of ONUC to carry out its mission. Ultimately, ONUC did achieve its important objective of reunifying the Congo and ending the Belgian intervention. The costs were excessive and limited subsequent success in establishing order in the Congo. But the outcome, reunification, nonetheless was impressive.

What long-term ramifications did the crisis have on the United Nations and thus the international community more generally? Its memory probably did more to restrict peacekeeping in the Cold War than will ever be known. The budget crisis that emerged during and after the crisis reflected deeper international divisions about the role of peacekeeping in crises of decolonization. It also reflected Soviet doubts that the United Nations could act independently of the United States. And with its veto in the Security Council, this meant that U.N. activism would be curtailed. In subsequent crises in Africa, such as those in Angola and the Horn of Africa, both superpowers seemed more comfortable with simply supplying their clients with military aid. The reliance on strongmen became even more prevalent. One need only think of the Angolan triad of Joseph Savimbi, Agostino Neto, and José Eduardo dos Santos,

Siad Barre in Somalia, and Miriam Mengistu in Ethiopia. The superpowers were just as happy to leave the fractious and confusing internal politics to the leaders of those beleaguered African countries. There would be no major U.S.–Soviet approval of a peacekeeping mission until the late 1980s when the United Nations Angola Verification Mission I was established to verify the withdrawal of Cuban forces from Angola, a time when the Cold War was clearly winding down.

What insights does crisis theory give us about the Congo and the Cold War? The events in the Congo followed the stages of the crisis and were in many ways predictable. What was so different about this crisis was the disconnect between the superpowers and the Congo. These various layers are not accounted for in crisis theory. The discussions and negotiations did not connect the key issues and the major participants. The United States and the Soviet Union rarely talked directly about the crisis, or events in the Congo, but sent their messages through the United Nations. The United Nations, however, because of ONUC, had its own needs and goals. The actual negotiations in the Congo addressed the internal crisis, but the Cold War aspects were left untouched. In this scenario, a true resolution for the crisis was not likely, and indeed was never found.

Certainly the greatest ramifications were on the Congo itself. Its only truly democratically elected leader, Patrice Lumumba, was assassinated. Mobutu, of course, became legendary for taking quick retribution and for the corruption of his administration. He did as much or more to denude the Congo of its riches than any previous imperial regime. The personality cult that he swathed around himself, as shrewd as any leopard, only further obscured the deep troubles of socioeconomic development and ethnic tensions, exacerbated by the Cold War, which have raged openly, yet largely unseen by the international world, in civil war since 1998. More than 5 million have been killed so far, and the fighting continues. What more does the Congo need to suffer?

Appendix: Persons in the Book

Adoula, Cyrille. Native of Leopoldville, he joined Kalonji's MNC wing in 1959. In May 1960 represented Equateur in the Senate, where he became an ally of Kasavubu. Adoula served the Ileo government as minister of the interior until July 1961, and then became prime minister, August 1961–64.

Ball, George. Undersecretary for economic affairs, February to December 1961. Then undersecretary of state, November 1961–66, replacing Chester Bowles in a cabinet reshuffling.

Bissell, Richard. CIA deputy director for plans, 1958–February 1962. In charge of developing the U-2 spy plane and coordinating the Bay of Pigs invasion.

Boggs, Marion W. Deputy executive secretary of the National Security Council in the Eisenhower administration, 1959–60.

Bolikango, Jean. Denied a cabinet post by Lumumba in 1960 and became his implacable enemy.

Bomboko, Justin. The Congo's first foreign minister, June–September 1960. He held that same post for the College of Commissioners (until October 1960) and in the Ileo and Adoula governments, 1961–64.

Bowles, Chester B. Undersecretary of state, January–December 1961. Then served as the president's special adviser on African, Asian, and Latin American affairs, until May, when he was appointed ambassador to India.

Bunche, Ralph J. U.N. undersecretary-general for special political affairs, 1958–71; special representative of the secretary-general in the Congo, July–August 1960.

Bundy, McGeorge. National security adviser to presidents John Kennedy and Lyndon Johnson, 1961–66.

Burden, William A. M. Ambassador to Belgium, October 1959–January 1961.

Burke, Arleigh. A. U.S. chief of naval operations, as admiral, June 1961–August 1961, when he retired. He had a reputation as a strong anticommunist.

Carlucci, Frank. Foreign Service officer, 1956 to 1969. Served as second secretary in the U.S. Embassy in the Congo, 1960–63. Went on to hold a number of posts, including secretary of defense for President Ronald Reagan.

Cleveland, J. Harlan. Assistant secretary of state for international organization affairs, February 1961–September 1965.

Cordier, Andrew. Served as Dag Hammarskjöld's executive assistant, 1952–61. Served as interim U.N. representative in the Congo, from Bunche's departure to September 8, 1960.

d'Aspremont Lynden, Harold. Proposed and headed Belgium's Mistebel, a technical mission to Katanga, July 1960. Replaced de Schryver as minister for African affairs, September 1960–61.

Dayal, Rajeshwar. Indian diplomat, served as special representative of the U.N. secretary-general in the Congo from September 8, 1960 (replacing Bunche), until he was recalled by Hammarskjöld in mid-1961.

De Schryver, August. Belgian minister for the Congo; replaced Maurice van Hemmelrijck in September 1959.

Devlin, Lawrence. CIA station chief in Leopoldville, 1960–62; and again, 1965–67.

Diallo, Telli. Guinean ambassador to the United States and the United Nations, 1959–64, when he was elected secretary-general of the Organization of African Unity. Guinean negotiator in Kenya during the 1964 hostage crisis.

Dillon, C. Douglas. Served as U.S. ambassador to France and then worked for economic affairs in the State Department before becoming undersecretary of state, June 1959–January 1961. He served the Kennedy and Johnson administrations as secretary of the Treasury, January 1961–March 1965.

Dodd, Thomas. Democratic senator from Connecticut, 1959–70. He founded the Committee for Aid to Katanga.

Dulles, Allen W. CIA director, 1953–November 1961.

Eisenhower, Dwight D. President of the United States, January 1953–January 1961.

Eyskens, Gaston. A Belgian economist who served in the Belgian Chamber of Representatives, becoming prime minister of Belgium, 1949–50 and 1958–61.

Gardiner, Robert. U.N. officer in charge in the Congo, February 1962–May 1963.

Gbenye, Christophe. Elected to chamber in May 1960 and appointed minister of interior by Lumumba. Fled to Stanleyville and worked with Gizenga, representing him at the Lovanium conference. Became minister of interior in the Adoula government, 1961. Supported Soumialot's CNL in 1964, although he rivaled Soumialot for leadership of that organization.

Gizenga, Antoine. President of the Parti Solidaire Africain. Elected deputy prime minister of the Congo, June–September 1960. Led the pro-Lumumba government in Stanleyville, November 1960–August 1961; then became vice prime minister in Adoula's government until his arrest in January 1962.

Godley, McMurtie G. Counselor of the U.S. Embassy in the Congo, June 1961–August 1962; then ambassador, mid-1964–65.

Guevara, Ernesto ("Che"). Marxist revolutionary, Argentinean by birth, 1928–67. Led a contingent of Cubans to eastern Congo in 1965.

Gullion, Edmund. U.S. ambassador to the Congo, September 1961–64.

Hammarskjöld, Dag. Diplomat in Sweden's Foreign Office; U.N. secretary-general, April 1953–September 1961.

Herter, Christian A. Undersecretary of state until April 1959, whereupon he became secretary of state, April 1959–January 1961 (after John Foster Dulles resigned due to illness).

Hilsman, Roger. Director of the U.S. Bureau of Intelligence and Research, February 1961–April 1963. He then became assistant secretary of state for Far Eastern affairs.

Hoffacker, Lewis. Served as U.S. consul in Elizabethville from October 1961 to August 1962, then as first secretary in the U.S. Embassy in Leopoldville to 1963.

Hoyt, Michael P. American commercial officer in Leopoldville, 1960. In 1964, he served as consul in Stanleyville, where he was taken hostage by CNL rebels.

Ileo, Joseph. Helped Lumumba found the MNC, but broke with him in 1959. President of the Senate in June 1960, and was appointed prime minister for a brief time in September 1960, and then again in February 1961. Later served as minister of information in Adoula's government.

Janssens, Émile Gen. Belgian commander of Force Publique upon Congolese independence, but left on July 11, 1960.

Kalonji, Albert. Established his own wing of the MNC in July 1959, and became a national deputy in June 1960, and then self-declared president of the south Kasai, 1960–61. Agreed in August 1961 to participate in the Adoula government, but refused any position for himself.

Kanza, Thomas. Congolese representative to the U.N. Security Council until removed by Lumumba in September 1960; then ambassador to London during the Adoula government. By 1964 was living in exile and sympathized with the rebels.

Kasavubu, Joseph. Helped found Abako in 1956 and became its president. President of the Republic of the Congo, June 1960–65, during which time he dismissed Lumumba. Was overthrown by Mobutu.

Kashamura, Anicet. A member of Cerea elected to the chamber (for Bukavu) in May 1960. Served as minister of information, until dismissed in September 1960 when he fled to Stanleyville.

Kaysen, Carl. National Security Council staff member; then deputy special assistant to the president for National Security Affairs, 1961–63.

Kennedy, John F. President of the United States, January 1961 until his assassination in November 1963.

Khiari, Mahmoud. U.N. chief of civilian operations in the Congo, September 1961–September 1962.

Khrushchev, Nikita. Chairman of the Soviet Council of Ministers, 1956–64.

Kuznetsov, Vasili V. Soviet representative at the United Nations, 1958–September 1960. Replaced by Zorin.

Linnér, Sture. Chief of U.N. civilian operations until September 1961; then officer in charge of U.N. operations, May 1961–February 1962.

Lodge, Henry Cabot, Jr. Began his career as a senator from Massachusetts, then served as U.S. representative at the United Nations, 1953–September 1960. Was Nixon's running mate in the 1960 presidential election.

Lumumba, Patrice. Of Otetela ethnicity. Founder of the MNC in 1958. Prime minister and minister of defense, June–September 1960. Dismissed by Kasavubu in September 1960, and kept under house arrest until formally arrested in December 1960. He was imprisoned and sent to Katanga, where he was murdered on January 17, 1961.

Lundula, Victor. Commander in chief of the Congolese National Army, but was dismissed by Kasavubu in September and then commanded troops in Stanleyville for Gizenga until 1961, when he returned his loyalty back to the Adoula government.

McGhee, George. Served as a counselor in the U.S. Department of State, then became undersecretary of state for political affairs, December 1961–April 1963, after which he became ambassador to West Germany.

Miakotnikh, Yuri. Soviet representative in the Congo, 1963.

Mobutu, Colonel Joseph. Chief of staff of the Congolese National Army. He seized power in a coup d'état in September 1960 and again in 1965. Ruled the Congo (which he renamed Zaire) until 1997.

Moulin, Gaston. The only Belgian Communist Party deputy in parliament at the time of Congolese independence in 1960.

Mpolo, Maurice. President of MNC-Lumumba. Minister of sport in the Lumumba government until he was dismissed by Kasavubu in September 1960. He served as chief of staff for Lumumba and was assassinated along with him in January 1961.

Mulele, Pierre. One of the founders of the Parti Solidaire Africain; was appointed minister of education by Patrice Lumumba in July 1960, and then served him in Stanleyville as minister of defense. He organized the resistance movement in Kwilu, in Leopoldville Province, in 1963.

Munongo, Godefroid. Minister of interior for Katanga, June 1960–65.

Murphy, Robert D. Deputy undersecretary of state for political affairs until August 1959, then undersecretary of state for political affairs, August–December 1959. Led delegation to the Congolese inaugural ceremonies.

Nasser, Gamal Abdul. President of Egypt, 1956–70.

Nemchina, Sergei S. Worked in the Soviet Foreign Ministry, 1947–53, when he became ambassador to Syria and Lebanon. In August 1962, he became the Soviet ambassador to the Congo.

Nguvulu, Alphonse. Before independence, served as president of Parti du Peuple (Leopoldville). Minister of economic affairs in Lumumba's government of 1960.

O'Brien, Conor Cruise. Hammarskjöld's representative who directed U.N. operations in Katanga in the fall of 1961. He was the author of numerous works regarding the Congo.

Rakhmatov, Mirzo. Vice president of the Presidium of the Supreme Soviet and president of the Presidium of the Supreme Soviet of the Tajik Republic. He was the first Soviet ambassador to the Congo in July 1960.

Rusk, Dean. Began his career as president of the Rockefeller Foundation. U.S. secretary of state, January 1961–69.

Satterthwaite, Joseph C. U.S. assistant secretary of state for African affairs, September 1958–January 1961.

Scheyven, Raymond. Belgian minister without portfolio in charge of economic and financial affairs in the Congo and Ruanda-Urundi, 1960–61.

Soumialot, Gaston. One of the founders of the Conseil National de Libération.

Spaak, Paul-Henri. Belgian foreign minister in the Théo Lefèvre government, 1961–67.

Stans, Maurice. U.S. deputy director, then director, of the Bureau of the Budget, 1958–60.

Stearns, Monteagle. Foreign Service officer in the U.S. Embassy in Leopoldville, 1964.

Stevenson, Adlai. U.S. representative to the United Nations, January 1961–July 1965. In 1952 and 1956, he lost the election as Democratic nominee for president.

Struelens, Michel. Director of the Katanga Information Service in New York City in 1961. He later became an emissary for Tshombe to the United States.

Terve, Jean. Communist member of the Belgian Parliament in 1947. He edited the Communist newspaper *Drapeau Rouge*, 1945–54. He was a friend of Lumumba and supported the Congolese independence movement.

Thant, U. In 1953, he became Burma's representative at the United Nations. He served as U.N. acting secretary-general after Hammarskjöld's death and was elected to that post in 1962 and remained until 1972.

Timberlake, Clare H. U.S. ambassador to the Congo, July 1960–mid-1961.

Tshombe, Moise. Founder and president of Conakat. He was elected president of Katanga Province, and declared Katanga's independence in July 1960. He fled Katanga in January 1963 and returned in July 1964, to become prime minister.

Urquhart, Brian. Assistant to the U.N. secretary-general's special representative in the Congo and U.N. representative in Katanga, 1961. Thereafter, he served in the United Nations as undersecretary for special political affairs.

Vandewalle, Frederic. Belgian representative in Elizabethville in December 1960; he then returned in February 1964 to organize Mobutu's mercenary army to defeat the rebels in Orientale.

Van Hemmelrijck, Maurice. Belgian Foreign Office minister for the Congo, 1958–September 1959.

Voronin, Boris. Soviet representative in the Congo, 1963.

Wadsworth, James J. U.S. deputy representative at the United Nations, 1953–September 1960. After Lodge resigned, he served as full representative at the United Nations, September 1960–January 1961.

Wieschloff, Heinz. Hammarskjöld's adviser on African affairs; he died with Hammarskjöld in September 1961.

Williams, G. Mennon. Assistant secretary of state for African affairs, January 1961–March 1966.

Yakovlev, Mikhail D. Former foreign minister of the Russian Soviet Federated Socialist Republic. Appointed Soviet ambassador to the Congo in August 1960, and remained until expelled by Mobutu in October of that year.

Zorin, Valerian A. Served as the Soviet Union's deputy minister of foreign affairs, 1947–65 (with a brief interlude in 1955). He then represented the Soviet Union at the United Nations, 1960–62.

Notes

Introduction

1. *New York Times*, February 14, 1961; Ernest W. Lefever, *Crisis in the Congo: A U.N. Force in Action* (Washington, D.C.: Brookings Institution Press, 1965).

2. Stephen Weissman, "An Extraordinary Rendition," *Intelligence and National Security* 25, no. 2 (April 2010): 209.

3. See Larry Devlin, *Chief of Station, Congo: A Memoir of 1960–67* (New York: PublicAffairs, 2007), 127–31. See also Madeleine Kalb, *The Congo Cables: The Cold War in Africa from Eisenhower to Kennedy* (New York: Macmillan, 1982), 192.

4. Ludo De Witte, *The Assassination of Lumumba*, translated by Ann Wright and Renée Fenby (New York: Verso, 2001; orig. pub. 1999), used new documentation and extensive interviews to place primary responsibility for the assassination with Belgium, although with Katangan and U.S. complicity. For his translation of Munongo's announcement, see ibid., 144; for the assassination, see 46–124 and 140–41; and for the quote, see 121. See also a very good account by Emmanuel Gerard and Bruce Kuklick, "A Death in the Jungle: Killing Patrice Lumumba," based on their forthcoming book, http://www.history.upenn.edu/annenberg_speakers/docs/kuklick_11.pdf.

5. Odd Arne Westad, *The Global Cold War: Third World Interventions and the Making of Our Times* (Cambridge: Cambridge University Press, 2005), 110–31; H. W. Brands, *The Specter of Neutralism: The United States and the Emergence of the Third World* (New York: Columbia University Press, 1989); Cary Fraser, "Understanding American Policy toward the Decolonization of European Empires, 1945–64," *Diplomacy and Statecraft* 3, no. 1 (1992): 105–25; Ryan M. Irwin, "A Wind of Change? White Redoubt and the Postcolonial Moment, 1960–1963," *Diplomatic History* 33, no. 5 (September 2009): 897–99.

6. Jonathan E. Helmreich, *United States Relations with Belgium and the Congo, 1940–1960* (Newark: University of Delaware Press, 1998), 24.

7. Crawford Young, *Politics in the Congo: Decolonization and Independence* (Princeton, N.J.: Princeton University Press, 1964), 23–26, 48–50.

8. UMHK was owned by the Belgian holding company Société Générale de Belgique (which by the early twentieth century controlled 70 percent of the Congo's economy), and the British-owned mining company Tanganyika Concessions (Tanks) concentrated on its Northern Rhodesian investments. See *Time*, August 10, 1931.

Subsequent interest by Tanks in UMHK declined, and the company began to focus more on its northern Katangan investments. See Francis L. Coleman, *The Northern Rhodesian Copperbelt, 1899–1962* (Manchester: Manchester University Press, 1971), 7–12.

9. *New York Times*, February 14–18, 1961.

10. Arthur Gavshon, *The Mysterious Death of Dag Hammarskjöld* (New York: Walker, 1962), 47, 129–33; Conor Cruise O'Brien, *To Katanga and Back* (New York: Simon & Schuster, 1962), 285; Brian Urquhart, *Hammarskjöld* (New York: W. W. Norton, 1994; orig. pub. 1972), 577–89.

11. For these events, see Kalb, *Congo Cables*, 281–372, and Piero Gleijeses, *Conflicting Missions: Havana, Washington and Africa, 1959–1976* (Chapel Hill: University of North Carolina Press, 2001), 57–76, 125–84.

12. Some historians have argued that the crisis was not primarily a Cold War crisis. In general, they tend to focus on U.S. and Belgian policy. See, e.g., David N. Gibbs, *The Political Economy of Third World Intervention: Mines, Money, and U.S. Politics in the Congo Crisis* (Chicago: University of Chicago Press, 1991); and De Witte, *The Assassination of Lumumba*, 187. Kalb's *Congo Cables* comes the closest to focusing on the Cold War in the Congo and includes a wealth of information on Soviet policy.

13. RGANI was formerly the Tsentr Khraneniia Sovremennoi Dokumentatsii (Center for the Preservation of Contemporary Documents). Russian archives are divided into fond (collection/record group), opis (record series), dela (files of documents), papka (document), list (page), and if applicable, a rolik (microfilm reel number). Apollon B. Davidson and Sergey V. Mazov, eds., *Rossiia i Afrika: Dokumenty i Materialy, tom II, 1918–1960* (Moscow: Institut vseobshchei istorii RAN, 1999).

14. As indicative, see the Protocols in Archives of the parties and mass organizations of East Germany, DY 30 (hereafter, DY 30), Bundesarchiv, Berlin.

15. U.S. Congress, Senate, Select Committee to Study Government Operations with Respect to Intelligence Activities, *Alleged Assassination Plots Involving Foreign Leaders*, Senate report no. 94–465, 94th Congress, 1st session (Washington, D.C.: U.S. Government Printing Office, 1975) (hereafter, *Alleged Assassination Plots*), 13–70. Three important pseudonyms were used: Victor Hedgman refers to Lawrence Devlin, Michael J. Mulroney refers to Justin O'Donnell, and Joseph Scheider refers to Sidney Gottlieb.

Kalb also used extensively the State Department cables to the U.S. embassies and consulates in the Congo, which, along with other declassified U.S. documents, are given by U.S. Department of State, *The Foreign Relations of the United States, 1952–1954*, vol. 11: *Africa and South Asia*; *1955–1957*, vol. 18: *Africa*; *1958–1960*, vol. 14: *Africa*; *1961–1963*, vol. 20: *The Congo Crisis*; vol. 21: *Africa*; and microfiche supplement for vols. 20 and 21; *1964–1968*, vol. 24: *Africa* (Washington, D.C.: U.S. Government Printing Office, 1983–1999) (hereafter, *FRUS*, and cited with corresponding year and volume).Other sources that are not available include Centre des Archives Communistes en Belgique (Center for Communist Archives in Belgium), Brussels. Thanks to Luc Viaene for this information. As for the U.N. material, Brian Urquhart was granted sole access to Hammarskjöld's papers, most of which remain unpublished. See Urquhart, *Hammarskjöld*, 603.

16. Stephen Weissman, "Opening the Secret Files on Lumumba's Murder," *Washington Post*, July 21, 2002, http://www.sas.upenn.edu/AfricanStudies/Urgent_Action/

apic080102.html (August 2002); and David Gibbs, "Review: The Foreign Relations of the United States: 1961–63, vol. 20, Congo Crisis," *African Affairs* 95 (July 1996), 453(7) from Expanded Academic Index.

17. Weissman, "Extraordinary Rendition."

18. See http://www.state.gov/www/about_state/history/fruslinc.html for a list of volumes, and "Advisory Committee on Historical Diplomatic Documentation," March 1998, December 2001, and June 2010, available at http://history.state.gov/about/hac. See also Stephen Weissman's recent critique for the *Christian Science Monitor,* March 25, 2011, http://www.csmonitor.com/Commentary/Opinion/2011/0325/Why-is-US-withholding-old-documents-on-covert-ops-in-Congo-Iran.

19. For the best information on the Cold War International History Project, established by the Woodrow Wilson International Center for Scholars in Washington, D.C., see its Web site, www.wilsoncenter.org/program/cold-war-international-history-project; for its contribution to the Congo crisis, see the National Security Archive at George Washington University and its Web site, http://www.gwu.edu/~nsarchiv/.

20. See De Witte, *Assassination of Lumumba*; and Chambre des représentants de Belgique, *Enquête parlementaire visant à déterminer les circonstances exactes de l'assassinat de Patrice Lumumba et l'implication éventuelle des responsables politique belges dans celui-ci* [Parliamentary inquiry to determine the exact circumstances of the assassination of Patrice Lumumba and possible involvement of Belgian politicians] (Brussels: Chambre des représentants de Belgique, 2001–2), available at http://www1.lachambre.be (hereafter, *Belgian Parliamentary Commission Report*).

21. These comments are based on a reading of secondary sources and published document collections. See Alan James, *Britain and the Congo Crisis, 1960–1963* (New York: St. Martin's Press, 1996), 66–91; and John Kent, *America, the U.N. and Decolonisation: Cold War Conflict in the Congo* (New York: Routledge, 2010). See also Catalogue of the National Archives, and National Archives Online Documents, available at www.nationalarchives.gov.uk. For the United Nations, see Archives and Records Management System, at archives.un.org, which is currently opening some of its archives to online access. Unfortunately, I have not had the chance to visit London, Stockholm, or New York to review the full archival holdings.

22. Apollon Davidson, Sergey Mazov, and Georgiy Tsypikin, eds., *SSSR i Afrika, 1918–1960: Dokumentirovanniia isotriia vzaimootnoshenii* (Moscow: Institute of World History, Russian Academy of Sciences, 2002).

23. See Sergey Mazov, *A Distant Front in the Cold War: The USSR in West Africa and the Congo, 1956–1964* (Washington, D.C., and Stanford, Calif.: Woodrow Wilson Center Press and Stanford University Press, 2010); and Sergey Mazov, "Soviet Aid to the Gizenga Government in the Former Belgian Congo (1960–1961) as Reflected in Russian Archives," *Cold War History* 7, no. 3 (August 2007): 425–38. The new information is not interpreted unanimously. Some Russian historians have cautioned that events in Africa at end of the 1950s were a surprise to the communist establishment, which really had little interest there. See Vadim Kirpichenko, *Razvedka: Litsa i lichnosti* (Moscow: Gea, 1998), 89.

24. The historian H. W. Brands has suggested a self-reinforcing mechanism at work, where a perceived threat was met as a communist one, and decisions were justified in Cold War terms as the best way to get rid of the potential danger, whether real or not. H. W. Brands, *The Devil We Knew: Americans and the Cold War* (New

York: Oxford University Press, 1993), 62–66. See also Kent, *America, the U.N. and Decolonisation*, 4–5.

25. "Third world" is a Cold War–era term used loosely to identify the nonaligned or "southern" states in Africa and Asia, usually underdeveloped and poor. Today, the term "developing world" is instead commonly used.

26. For newer perspectives on the Cold War in other regions, see Frederic Logevall, *Choosing War: The Lost Chance for Peace and the Escalation of War in Vietnam* (Berkeley: University of California Press, 1999); Nick Cullather; *Illusions of Influence: The Political Economy of United States–Philippines Relations, 1942–1960* (Stanford, Calif.: Stanford University Press, 1994); and Chen Jian, *Mao's China and the Cold War* (Chapel Hill: University of North Carolina Press, 2001).

27. On the U.S. response to neutralism, see Brands, *Specter of Neutralism*; and Cary Fraser's two articles, "Understanding American Policy" and "An American Dilemma: Race and Realpolitik in the American Response to the Bandung Conference, 1955," in *Window on Freedom: Race, Civil Rights, and Foreign Affairs, 1945–1988*, edited by Brenda Gayle Plummer (Chapel Hill: University of North Carolina Press, 2003), 115–19.

28. See, e.g., Michael Brecher and Jonathan Wilkenfeld, *A Study of Crisis* (Ann Arbor: University of Michigan Press, 1997), 4–5; and Michael Brecher and Patrick James, *Crisis and Change in World Politics* (Boulder, Colo.: Westview Press, 1986), 22.

29. Glenn H. Snyder and Paul Diesing, *Conflict among Nations: Bargaining, Decision-Making and System Structure in International Crises* (Princeton, N.J.: Princeton University Press, 1977), 183.

30. Karl DeRouen Jr. and Christopher Sprecher, "International Crisis Reaction and Poliheuristic Theory," *Journal of Conflict Resolution* 48, no. 1 (February 2004): 57.

31. John Lewis Gaddis, *We Now Know: Rethinking Cold War History* (Oxford: Clarendon Press, 1997), and Gaddis, *The Cold War: A New History* (New York: Penguin Press, 2005).

32. Vladislav Zubok and Constantine Pleshakov, *Inside the Kremlin's Cold War: From Stalin to Khrushchev* (Cambridge, Mass.: Harvard University Press, 1996), 4–5.

33. Westad, *Global Cold War*, 3–6, 68–70, 403–5; the quote is at 405. Similarly, Melvin P. Leffler has suggested that ideologies, political pressures, history, and fear resulted in a perpetuation of hostility. See Melvin P. Leffler, *For the Soul of Mankind: The United States, the Soviet Union and the Cold War* (New York: Hill & Wang, 2007), 3–8. See also the following articles: Nigel Gould-Davis, "Rethinking the Role of Ideology in International Politics during the Cold War," *Journal of Cold War Studies* 1 (Winter 1999): 90–109; Odd Arne Westad, "The New International History of the Cold War," *Diplomatic History* 24 (Fall 2000): 551–66; and Tony Smith, "New Bottles for New Wine: A Pericentric Framework for the Study of the Cold War," *Diplomatic History* 24 (Fall 2000): 567–92.

34. Christopher Layne, *American Empire: A Debate* (New York: Routledge, 2006), Robert McMahon, *Limits of Empire: The United States and Southeast Asia since World War II* (New York: Columbia University Press, 1999). The author would like to thank David Gibbs here for his critique.

35. See Logevall, *Choosing War*; and Mark Atwood Lawrence, *Assuming the Burden: Europe and the American Commitment to War* (Berkeley: University of California Press, 2005).

36. See Thomas Noer, *Cold War and Black Liberation: The United States and White Rule in Africa, 1948–1968* (Columbia: University of Missouri Press, 1985).

37. Thomas Borstelmann, *The Cold War and the Color Line: American Race Relations in the Global Arena* (Cambridge, Mass.: Harvard University Press, 2001), 269; Robert McMahon, "Eisenhower and Third World Nationalism: A Critique of the Revisionists," *Political Science Quarterly* 101 (3): 455–57.

38. See, e.g., Arthur M. Schlesinger, *A Thousand Days: John F. Kennedy in the White House* (Boston: Houghton Mifflin, 1965); and some of the articles in *Kennedy's Quest for Victory: American Foreign Policy, 1961–1963*, edited by Thomas G. Paterson (New York: Oxford University Press, 1989), including Douglas Little, "From Even-Handed to Empty-Handed: Seeking Order in the Middle East," 156–77, who argued that Kennedy's "even-handed" policy came closer to solving the riddle of the Middle East than that of any other president. For the most recent interpretation, see Philip E. Muehlenbeck, "Kennedy and Touré: A Success in Personal Diplomacy," *Diplomacy and Statecraft* 19 (2008): 69–95; and Philip E. Muehlenbeck, *Betting on the Africans: John F. Kennedy's Courting of African Nationalist Leaders* (New York: Oxford University Press, 2012).

39. Kalb, *Congo Cables*, xxvi–xxviii; Stephen Weissman, *American Foreign Policy in the Congo* (Ithaca, N.Y.: Cornell University Press, 1974). Richard D. Mahoney agreed that U.S. officials saw the main threat in the Congo as one of preventing the rise of communism; see Richard D. Mahoney, *JFK: Ordeal in Africa* (New York: Oxford University Press, 1983), esp. 223–48.

40. Mazov, *Distant Front in the Cold War*, 10–75; Clifford A. Kiracofe Jr., "Marxist-Leninist Theory and the Third World," *Journal of Social and Political Studies* 4 (Fall 1979): 219, for quote. See also Leszek Kolakowski, *Main Currents of Marxism, Volume 2: The Golden Years* (New York: Oxford University Press, 1978), 398–404; Hamza Alavi, "Marxism and the Third World," in *A Dictionary of Marxist Thought*, 2nd ed., edited by Tom Bottomore (Cambridge, Mass.: Basil Blackwell, 1991), 350–53.

41. Mazov, *Distant Front in the Cold War*, 7, 78.

42. Bruce D. Larkin, *China and Africa, 1949–1970* (Berkeley: University of California Press, 1971), 2–14; Alaba Ogunsanwo, *China's Policy in Africa, 1958–1971* (Cambridge: Cambridge University Press, 1974), 23. For a general view of the Sino-Soviet split, see Lorenz M. Lüthi, *The Sino–Soviet Split: Cold War in the Communist World* (Princeton, N.J.: Princeton University Press, 2008).

43. Sergey Radchenko, *Two Suns in the Heavens: The Sino–Soviet Struggle for Supremacy, 1962–1967* (Washington, D.C., and Stanford, Calif.: Woodrow Wilson Center Press and Stanford University Press, 2009), 82–83.

44. For an outline of the noncapitalist path of development, see Robert Legvold, *Soviet Policy in West Africa* (Cambridge, Mass.: Harvard University Press, 1970), 50–52, 176–79. For a Soviet view, see Ivan I. Potekhin's work, especially Ivan I. Potekhin, "Problemy bor'by s perezhitkami proshlogo na afrikanskom kontinente" [Problems of the fight with the survivals of the past on the African continent], *Sovetskaia etnografiia* no. 4 (1964): 191–94; Rachik M. Avakov and Georgi Mirskii, "Sovremenniia epokha i puti razvitiia osvobodivshikhsia stran" [The contemporary epoch and the path of development in the liberated countries], *Mirovaia ekonomika i mezhdunarodnie otnosheniia*, no. 4 (1962): 68; and V. I. Pavlov and I. B. Red'ko,

"Gosudarstvo natsioinal'noi demokratii i perexod nekapitalisticheskomu razvitiu" [National democracy and the transition to noncapitalist development], *Narody Azii i Afriki* no. 1 (1963): 29–40.

45. See the comments related to Egypt by Nikita Khrushchev in his autobiography—Nikita Khrushchev, *Khrushchev Remembers* (Boston: Little, Brown, 1970), 440; see also 507.

46. Oleg Grinevsky, *Tysiacha i oden den' Nikity Sergeevicha* [A thousand and one days in the life of Nikita Serge'evich] (Moscow: Vagrius, 1998), 326–37. See also Fedor Burlatsky, *Khrushchev and the First Russian Spring: The Era of Khrushchev through the Eyes of His Advisor*, translated by Daphne Skillen (New York: Macmillan, 1991; orig. pub. 1988).

47. Alexandr Fursenko and Timothy Naftali, *Khrushchev's Cold War: The Inside Story of an American Adversary* (New York: W. W. Norton, 2006); William Taubman, *Khrushchev: The Man and His Era* (New York: W. W. Norton, 2003), xi–xv, xix–xx, 325–60.

48. Zubok and Pleshakov, *Inside the Kremlin's Cold War*, 1–8. See also John Lewis Gaddis, *We Now Know: Rethinking Cold War History* (New York: Oxford University Press, 1997), 281–95, esp. 290; William J. Tompson, *Khrushchev: A Political Life* (New York: St. Martin's Griffin, 1995), 229–56; and David Nordlander, "Khrushchev's Image in the Light of Glasnost and Perestroika," *Russian Review* 52 (April 1993): 249–64.

49. Gleijeses, *Conflicting Missions*, 60–76, 106–23.

50. Gibbs, *Political Economy of Third World Intervention*, 84–86, 196–97; for the quote, see 84. Gibbs argued that the conflict among domestic business interests explained the prosecession policy of Eisenhower and the antisecessionist policies of Kennedy. Pro-Belgian business interests, especially those which had invested in Katangan mines dominated by Belgian capital, supported the Eisenhower administration, "causing Eisenhower to favor the Belgian position" and Katanga's secession. Companies with predominantly American or British capital, such as those in the diamond, oil, and textile industries, supported Kennedy, and "Kennedy's policies were, accordingly, anti-Belgian" and opposed to Katangan secession. Thus the contrasting business interests that dominated each administration prevailed over policy formation.

51. Brian Urquhart, interview, May 30, 1984, United Nations Oral History Collection (hereafter, UNOH) at http://www.un.org/depts/dhl/dag/oralhist.htm. Actually, he said that it "damn nearly wrecked this organization," emphasizing the seriousness, but this wording is not included in the main text herein so as not to offend.

52. See, e.g., Javier Perez de Cuellar, "The Role of the U.N. Secretary-General," in *United Nations, Divided World: The U.N.'s Roles in International Relations*, edited by Adam Roberts and Benedict Kingsbury (Oxford: Clarendon, 1989), 61–78. One historian who highlights the importance of the United Nations from an international perspective is William Stueck, *The Korean War: An International History* (Princeton, N.J.: Princeton University Press, 1995), 4, who suggested that while it could often be an instrument of U.S. policy, it also served as "a setting for allied and neutral pressure" on the United States.

53. The historian (and former U.N. representative in the Congo) Brian Urquhart argued in *Hammarskjöld* (New York: W. W. Norton, 1994; orig. pub. 1972) that under the circumstances and despite U.S. pressure, Hammarskjöld did his best to remain

neutral in the internal Congolese debate, even though this might have meant several actions that appeared anti-Soviet.

54. Zachary Karabell, *Architects of Intervention: The United States, the Third World, and the Cold War, 1947–1962* (Baton Rouge: Louisiana State University Press, 1999), 225. The political scientist Fred Marte found that African leaders like Lumumba used Cold War arguments to play one superpower off against the other and enhance their own power, which in turn fueled Cold War tensions. See Fred Marte, *Political Cycles in International Relations: The Cold War in Africa, 1945–1990* (Amsterdam: VU Press, 1994), 196, 371. See also Fred Halliday, *From Kabul to Managua: Soviet-American Relations in the 1980s,* American ed. (New York: Pantheon, 1989), 29–30.

55. See Washington Okumu, *Lumumba's Congo: Roots of Conflict* (New York: Ivan Obolensky, 1963). Georges Nzongola-Ntalaja, "Crisis and Change in Zaire, 1960–1985," and Illunga Kabongo, "Myths and Realities of the Zairean Crisis," 29, discussed this tendency, in *The Crisis in Zaire: Myths and Realities,* edited by Georges Nzongola-Ntalaja (Trenton, N.J.: Africa World Press, 1986).

56. Although this topic has long been studied very little, the last few years have seen a number of excellent scholarly works. See, e.g., Borstelmann, *Cold War and the Color Line*; George White Jr., *Holding the Line: Race, Racism, and American Foreign Policy toward Africa, 1953–1961* (Lanham, Md.: Rowman & Littlefield, 2005); Plummer, *Window on Freedom*; Mary L. Dudziak, *Cold War Civil Rights: Race and the Image of American Democracy* (Princeton, N.J.: Princeton University Press, 2000); and Fraser, "Understanding American Policy."

Chapter 1

1. The chapter title derives from Basil Davidson, *Which Way Africa? The Search for a New Society* (Baltimore: Penguin Books, 1964).

2. Fraser, "American Dilemma," 115–19. For the assassination attempt, see Joseph J. Trento, *The Secret History of the CIA* (New York: Carroll & Graf, 2005), 195.

3. Chen Jian, "Bridging Revolution and Decolonization: The 'Bandung Discourse' in China's Early Cold War Experience," in *Connecting Histories: Decolonization and the Cold War in Southeast Asia, 1845–1962,* edited by Christopher E. Goscha and Christian F. Ostermann (Washington, D.C., and Stanford, Calif.: Woodrow Wilson Center Press and Stanford University Press, 2009), 159–60.

4. See the original charter of the Bandung Conference, April 1955, as given by Odette Jankowitsch and Karl P. Sauvant, *The Third World without Superpowers: The Collected Documents of the Non-Aligned Countries,* vol. 1 (Dobbs Ferry, N.Y.: Oceana Publications, 1978).

5. Jason C. Parker, "Small Victory, Missed Chance: The Eisenhower Administration, the Bandung Conference, and the Turning of the Cold War," in *The Eisenhower Administration, the Third World, and the Globalization of the Cold War,* Harvard Cold War Studies Book Series, edited by Kathryn C. Statler and Andrew L. Johns (Lanham, Md.: Rowman & Littlefield, 2006), 153–74; Fraser, "American Dilemma."

6. Borstelmann, *Cold War and the Color Line,* 110–11.

7. James Meriwether, *Proudly We Can Be Africans: Black Americans and Africa, 1935–1961* (Chapel Hill: University of North Carolina Press, 2002), 169–71.

8. Noer, *Cold War and Black Liberation,* 45–52.

9. Rupert Emerson, *From Empire to Nation: The Rise to Self-Assertion of Asian and African Peoples* (Boston: Beacon Press, 1960); Walter Goldschmidt, *The United States and Africa*, rev. ed. (New York: Frederick A. Praeger, 1963; orig. pub. 1958); McKay, *Africa in World Politics*, 425. See also Martin Staniland, *American Intellectuals and African Nationalists, 1955–1970* (New Haven, Conn.: Yale University Press, 1991), 68–69; and Steven Metz, "U.S. Attitudes toward Decolonization in Africa," *Political Science Quarterly* 99 (Fall 1984): 527–30.

10. Dulles first used these words in a speech at Iowa State College, *Department of State Bulletin* 34 (June 18, 1956), 999–1000. See also H. W. Brands, *Specter of Neutralism: The United States and the Emergence of the Third World* (New York: Columbia University Press, 1989), 305–6; Noer, *Cold War and Black Liberation*, 34–36; Memorandum (Sears, U.S. representative at the Trusteeship Council) to Lodge, January 29, 1959, *FRUS 1958–1960*, vol. 14, 40–42; Azza Salama Layton, *International Politics and Civil Rights Policies in the United States, 1941–1960* (Cambridge: Cambridge University Press, 2000); Cary Fraser, "Crossing the Color Line in Little Rock: The Eisenhower Administration and the Dilemma of Race for U.S. Foreign Policy," *Diplomatic History* 24 (Spring 2000): 233–64; Mary Dudziak, *Cold War Civil Rights: Race and the Image of American Democracy* (Princeton, N.J.: Princeton University Press, 2000), 115–51, 157–63; and Borstelmann, *The Cold War and the Color Line*, 110–25.

11. Melville Herskovits, *The Human Factor in Changing Africa* (New York: Alfred A. Knopf, 1962); George Eaton Simpson, *Melville J. Herskovits* (New York: Columbia University Press, 1973), 120–28.

12. Chester Bowles, *Africa's Challenge to America* (Berkeley: University of California Press, 1956), 103; see also editorial note, *FRUS 1955–1957*, vol. xi, 7–8.

13. Kennedy remarks at Rockhurst College, Kansas City, June 2, 1956, reprinted in *Congressional Record*, 84th Congress, 2nd session, June 6, 1956; see 9614–15 for quote. Also see Metz, "U.S. Attitudes toward Decolonization in Africa," 523.

14. Helmreich, *United States Relations with Belgium and the Congo*, 159–63; Memorandum, Office of African Affairs (Hadsel), August 4, 1955, *FRUS 1955–1957*, vol. 18, 13–14.

15. Nixon visited Morocco, Ghana, Liberia, Uganda, Ethiopia, Sudan, Libya, and Tunisia from February 28 to March 21, 1957. Memorandum of Conversation, Accra (Nixon and Nkrumah), March 4, 1957, confidential file, subseries, box 100 (Nixon and Africa), Dwight D. Eisenhower Library, Abilene, Kansas (hereafter, DDEL). See also Noer, *Cold War and Black Liberation*, 49, for the argument that Nixon "led the push for a more active African policy."

16. The public version was issued as a pamphlet: Richard Nixon, *The Emergence of Africa* (Washington, D.C.: U.S. Department of State, 1957), which contained a section on the "effect of discrimination in U.S. on African attitudes," which (curiously) was not included in the classified report. See also Noer, *Cold War and Black Liberation*, 48–49.

17. Borstelmann, *Cold War and the Color Line*, 88–91.

18. "Report to the President on the Vice President's Visit to Africa," April 5, 1957, *FRUS 1955–1957*, vol. 18, 57–66; and National Security Council (hereafter, NSC) 5719/1, "Statement of U.S. Policy toward Africa South of the Sahara Prior to the Calendar Year 1960," August 23, 1957, *FRUS 1955–1957*, vol. 18, 75–87. See White's insightful and important analysis of NSC 5719/1, in *Holding the Line*, 30–32.

19. "Report to the President on the Vice President's visit to Africa," April 5, 1957, *FRUS 1955–1957*, vol. 18, 57–66; and NSC 5719/1, "Statement of U.S. Policy toward Africa South of the Sahara prior to the Calendar Year 1960," August 23, 1957, *FRUS 1955–1957*, vol. 18, 75–87.

20. U.S. Consul James Green to State, December 20, 1958, decimal file 755A, box 3427, record group (hereafter, RG) 59, U.S. National Archives and Records Administration, College Park, Md. (hereafter, NARA); Helmreich, *United States Relations with Belgium and the Congo*, 164–167.

21. Gibbs, *Political Economy of Third World Development*, 60–69. In the 1950s, the Congo produced more than 85 percent of the cobalt produced in Africa, 65 percent of its industrial diamonds, and 35 percent of its copper. For the strategic importance of the Congo in U.S.–Belgian relations, see Memorandum of Conversation between U.S. assistant secretary of state for European affairs George Perkins and Belgian ambassador Baron Silvercruys, July 25, 1952, *FRUS 1952–1954*, vol. xi, 406–09. See also Jonathan E. Helmreich, *Gathering Rare Ores: The Diplomacy of Uranium Acquisition, 1943–1954* (Princeton, N.J.: Princeton University Press, 1986), 149–72; Jonathan E. Helmreich, "Belgium, Britain, the United States and Uranium, 1952–1959," *Studia Diplomatica* 43, no. 3 (1990); and Hampton Smith, Tim Merrill, and Sandra W. Meditz, "The Economy," in *Zaire: A Country Study* (Washington, D.C.: U.S. Government Printing Office, 1993), 135–200. For the changing nature of U.S. investment, see Gibbs, *Political Economy of Third World Intervention*, 44–52, 60–69. Gibbs noted that in 1958, the Rockefeller-associated firm Dillon, Read, and Company loaned the Belgian colonial government $15 million, and Morgan Trust led consortia that provided $40 million in loans to the colony. The Rockefeller-owned Socony Vacuum Oil Co., Texaco, and Gulf Oil owned service stations, while Rockefeller also controlled several firms, including textile, mineral processing, and automotive distribution enterprises. See also Young, *Politics in the Congo*, 17; and James, *Britain and the Congo Crisis, 1960–1963*, 31.

22. Memorandum of Conversation, Dulles and Wigny, October 8, 1958, decimal file 755a, box 3427, RG59, NARA.

23. Satterthwaite had served as deputy director and then director of the office of Near Eastern and African affairs (from 1947 to 1949) and as ambassador to Ceylon until appointed to the new Africa bureau. See Haskins to Cutler, August 20, 1957, White House Office (hereafter, WHO), NSC staff, special staff file, box 1, file "Africa South of the Sahara (3)," DDEL, for the origins of this development.

24. The Council of Foreign Economic Policy made the most comprehensive official assessments of the Congo. National Planning Association, "The Role of the United States in the Development of Tropical Africa," April 27, 1958, Council of Foreign Economic Policy paper series, box 12, DDEL; "Briefing for Mr. Clarence Randall on United States Foreign Economic Policy in Africa," March 29, 1958, by James F. Green, and another identically titled by Ruth Torrance, Council of Foreign Economic Policy paper series, special studies, box 1, DDEL.

25. Memorandum of Discussion, 365th NSC meeting, May 8, 1958, *FRUS 1958–1960*, vol. 14, 13–16.

26. Memorandum of Discussion, 375th NSC meeting, August 7, 1958, *FRUS 1958–1960*, vol. 14, 20.

27. Fred I. Greenstein, *The Hidden-Hand Presidency: Eisenhower as Leader* (New York: Basic Books, 1982); Richard Immerman, "Confessions of an Eisenhower

Revisionist: An Agonizing Reappraisal," *Diplomatic History* 14 (1990): 319–22; John Robert Greene, "Bibliographic Essay: Eisenhower Revisionism, 1952–1992: A Reappraisal," in *Reexamining the Eisenhower Presidency*, edited by Shirley Anne Warshaw (Westport, Conn.: Greenwood Press, 1993), 209–20.

28. Memorandum of Discussion at 375th NSC meeting, August 7, 1958, *FRUS 1958–1960*, vol. 14, 21.

29. This phrase was used repeatedly. See Memorandum of Discussion among Eisenhower, Ivory Coast prime minister Felix Houphouet-Boigny, and French ambassador Herve Alphand, November 12, 1959, *FRUS 1958–1960*, vol. 14, 70. For problems with Guinea, see Satterthwaite to Herter, December 4, 1959, *FRUS 1958–1960,* vol. 14, 71–73.

30. Tompson, *Khrushchev*, 149, 218.

31. For a good summary of Stalin's approach to decolonization in Asia, see Ilya Gaiduk, "Soviet Cold War Strategy and Prospects of Revolution in South and Southeast Asia," in *Connecting Histories: Decolonization and the Cold War in Southeast Asia, 1845–1962*, edited by Christopher E. Goscha and Christian F. Ostermann (Washington, D.C., and Stanford, Calif.: Woodrow Wilson Center Press and Stanford University Press, 2009), 123–36.

32. Taubman, *Khrushchev*, 348.

33. Sergei Khrushchev, *Nikita Khrushchev and the Creation of a Superpower* (University Park: Pennsylvania State University, 2000), 404.

34. Joseph L. Nogee, *Soviet Foreign Policy since World War II* (Elmsford, N.Y.: Pergamon Press, 1984), 2nd ed., 148–49.

35. Taubman, *Khrushchev*, 354.

36. Legvold, *Soviet Policy in West Africa,* 54–55; see also comments by Georgii I. Mirskii, "Khrushchev i Naser" [Khrushchev and Nasser] from *Argumenty i fakty*, 1988, in *Nikita Sergeevich Khrushchev: Materialy k biografii* [Nikita Sergeevich Khrushchev: materials for biography], edited by Iurii V. Aksiutin (Moscow: Izdatel'stvo politicheskoi literatury, 1989), 88–89.

37. Khrushchev, "Report of the Central Committee of the Communist Party of the Soviet Union to the 20th Party Congress," February 25, 1956, in *Current Soviet Policies*, vol. 2, edited by Leo Gruliow (New York: Praeger, 1957), 33.

38. 20th Party Congress of the CPSU, "On Overcoming the Cult of Personality and Its Consequences," June 30, 1956, in *Resolutions and Decisions of the Communist Party of the Soviet Union, Volume 4: The Khrushchev Years*, 1953–1964 (Toronto: University of Toronto Press, 1974), 70–71. See also "XX S'ezd Kommunisticheskoi Partii Sovetskogo Soiuza i zadachi izucheniia sovremennogo Vostoka" [The 20th Congress of the Communist Party of the Soviet Union and the problems of studying the contemporary East], *Sovetskaia Etnografiia*, no. 1 (1956), 3–12. See also Christopher Andrew, with Vasili Mitrokhin, *"The World Was Going Our Way": The KGB and the Battle for the Third World* (New York: Basic Books, 2005); Alan Hutchison, *China's African Revolution* (London: Hutchinson, 1975), 16–23; Lüthi, *Sino–Soviet Split*, 46–52; and Larkin, *China and Africa,* 21–23.

39. CIA, "Soviet Policy toward the Underdeveloped Countries," April 28, 1961, 74, http://www.foia.cia.gov/CPE/CAESAR/caesar-28.pdf.

40. Chen Jian, *Mao's China and The Cold War* (Chapel Hill: University of North Carolina Press, 2001), 211.

41. Maxim Matusevich, "Probing the Limits of Internationalism: African Students Confront Soviet Ritual," *Anthropology of East European Review* 27, no. 2 (Fall 2009): 21, http://docs.google.com/viewer?a=v&q=cache:UT8_cJwKZ7UJ:scholarworks. iu.edu/journals/index.php/aeer/article/viewPDFInterstitial/166/259+mazov+stalin+- africa&hl=en&gl=us&pid=bl&srcid=ADGEESgZ_-FdMDO6fAYJj8vtj3FFCh66 QMrjqz3S_ocaZLKhSQmRqJj1s24C0ungfN_2Vh92TDfswLeTfVE6-2bqmltBhe- sqkF3FNMHnX7pOzbBmHJ1rezNY3O_mcPwi_k5PJ4iXc3z&sig=AHIEtbQ57WL zCCWTd7oIqDGSldL3r9LAyg.

42. Mazov, *Distant Front in the Cold War*, 26.

43. See the decree of the CC CPSU, "O meropriiatiiakh po rasshireniiu kul'turnykh i obshcheskvennykh sviazei so stranami Azii i Afriki" [Regarding measures for the broadening of cultural and social ties with countries of Asia and Africa], March 24, 1958, in *Rossiia i Afrika*, ed. Davidson and Mazov, 158–60.

44. Georgii A. Zhukov to the CC CPSU, November 14, 1958, "Rekomendatsii po propagande na strany Azii i Afriki soveshchaniia sovetskikh vostokovedov po prob- lemam sovremennogo polozheiia v stranakh Vostoka" [Recommendation regarding propaganda in the countries of Asia and Africa for the conference of Soviet Oriental- ists on the contemporary situation in the Eastern countries] in *Rossia i Afrika*, ed. Davidson and Mazov, 161–65. For a good description of Zhukov's relations with Khrushchev and his attitude toward the United States, see *Current Biography 1960*, 472–74.

45. CIA, "Soviet Policy toward the Underdeveloped Countries," 69.

46. Ibid., 74–89.

47. Kirpichenko, *Razvedka*, 97.

48. Leonard Schapiro, "The International Department of the CPSU: Key to Soviet Policy," *International Journal* 32 (Winter 1996–1997): 41–44. For the type of cautious reporting, see Savinov's diaries, cited below in chapter 3, notes 7 through 18.

49. For the burst of publications about Africa, see entire issue of *Sovetskaia etno- grafiia* no. 1 (January 1960); and K. S. Kremen' and Iu. M. Ilyin, *Problems of African Studies in the USSR, 1959–1984* (Moscow: Africa Institute, USSR Academy of Sci- ences, 1985), 9–18, esp. 11–12. For the growing interest in the Congo, see Vladimir A. Martynov, *Kongo pod gnetom imperializma* (Moscow: Izdatel'stvo vostochnoi lit- eratury, 1959).

50. Davidson, Mazov, and Tsypkin, *SSSR i Afrika*, 144–45.

51. Potekhin also served as head of the Soviet Afro-Asian Solidarity Committee. See B. A. Savinov, Memorandum of Conversation with Patrice Lumumba, February 19, 1960, fond 5, opis 50, delo 257, list 22–25, Russian Government Archive of Contempo- rary History, Moscow (hereafter, RGANI); and Legvold, *Soviet Policy in West Africa*, 17–33, 56–57. For his own views, see Potekhin, "Pozemel'nie otnosheniia v strankakh afriki," *Narody Azii i Afriki* no. 3 (1962): 16–31. The formation of the Africa Institute did have some opposition; see Mazov, *Distant Front in the Cold War*, 23. In particular, the opposition came from Nuritdin Mukhitdinov, the secretary of the CC CPSU, who wanted to see African problems handled on a more ad hoc, case-by-case basis. He would also be influential in 1962 in having the institute moved from the History Depart- ment to the Economics Department, thus affecting its research and influence.

52. Khrushchev, Postavlenie CC CPSU, "O raschirenii kul'turnykh i obshchestven- nykh sviazei s negritianskimi narodami Afiki i ysilenii vlianiia Sovetskogo Couza na

eta narody" [Decree of the CC CPSU, "The expansion of cultural and public relations with the black peoples of Africa and strengthening the influence of the Soviet Union on these peoples"], January 20, 1960, Davidson and Mazov, *Rossia i Afrika*, 165–68; CIA, "Soviet Policy toward the Underdeveloped Countries," 77. See also Matusevich, "Probing the Limits of Internationalism," 22–24.

Chapter 2

1. See Smith, Merrill, and Meditz, "The Economy," 135–200; Helmreich, *Gathering Rare Ores*; and Helmreich, "Belgium, Britain, the United States and Uranium."

2. The term *bula matari* was first applied to Henry Morton Stanley, but eventually came to be applied to "the state in general and to the European agents who exercised its hegemony." See Crawford Young, "The Colonial State and Post-Colonial Crisis," in *Decolonization and African Independence: The Transfers of Power, 1960–1980*, edited by Prosser Gifford and William Roger Louis (New Haven, Conn.: Yale University Press, 1988), 11–12.

3. The history of Leopold's Congo is taken largely from *King Leopold's Ghost: A Story of Greed, Terrorism, and Heroism in Colonial Africa*, by Adam Hochschild (Boston: Houghton Mifflin, 1998), 36–42, 42–100. See also Roger Anstey, *King Leopold's Legacy: The Congo under Belgian Rule, 1908–1960* (London: Oxford University Press, 1966); Neal Ascherson, *The King Incorporated: Leopold II in the Age of Trusts* (Garden City, N.Y.: Doubleday, 1964); and Ch. Didier Gondola, *The History of the Congo* (Westport, Conn.: Greenwood Press, 2002), 45–106.

4. For the figures of the Belgian purchase, see Hochschild, *King Leopold's Ghost*, 259.

5. Anstey, *King Leopold's Legacy*, 24–25, 47–50.

6. Some of his fellow countrymen thought Van Bilsen was guilty of treason for suggesting that the Congolese would be ready for independence even after thirty years. See Réné Lemarchand, *Political Awakening in the Belgian Congo: The Politics of Fragmentation* (Berkeley: University of California Press, 1964), 153–59; Alan P. Merriam, *Congo: Background of Conflict* (Evanston, Ill.: Northwestern University Press, 1961), 68–69; Young, *Politics in the Congo*, 22–23; and Antoine A. J. Van Bilsen, "Un plan de trente ans pour l'émancipation politique de l'Afrique Belge," excerpts from *Dossiers de l'Action Sociale Catholique* (Brussels), February 1956.

7. Jean Stengers, "Precipitous Decolonization: The Case of the Belgian Congo," in *The Transfers of Power: Decolonization in Africa, 1940–1960*, edited by Prosser Gifford and William Roger Louis (New Haven, Conn.: Yale University Press, 1982), 315, 325.

8. For a useful discussion of the meaning of "*évolué*," see Roger Anstey, "Belgian Rule in the Congo and the Aspirations of the '*Évolué*' Class," in *Colonialism in Africa, 1870–1960*, vol. 2, *History and Politics of Colonialism, 1914–1960*, edited by L. H. Gann and Peter Duignan (Cambridge: Cambridge University Press, 1970), 194–225.

9. Even a year later, Lumumba praised De Gaulle for his willingness to negotiate with "nationalists-extremists." See Lumumba's speech, "Discours de clôture du

congrès du M.N.C.," October 28, 1959, reprinted in *Stanleyville 1959: Le procès de Patrice Lumumba et les émeutes d'octobre*, edited by E. Simons, R. Boghossian, and B. Verhaegen (Paris: Éditions l'Harmattan, 1996), 108. Lumumba also acknowledged British recognition of the right to independence for its colonies; see "Discours prononcé par P. Lumumba au congrès," October 29, 1959, in *Stanleyville 1959*, ed. Simons, Boghossian, and Verhaegen, 116. See Lemarchand, *Political Awakening in the Congo*, 161, for a brief account of de Gaulle's impact in the Congo.

10. Young, *Politics in the Congo*, 23–26, 48–50.

11. In *American Intellectuals and African Nationalists, 1955–1970* (New Haven, Conn.: Yale University Press, 1991), 218, Martin Staniland noted this line of thought and found that *Time* and *U.S. News & World Report* consistently praised the Belgian colonial administration, e.g., *Time*, May 16, 1955. See also James F. Green, "Briefing for Mr. Clarence Randall on United States Foreign Economic Policy in Africa," U.S. Council on Economic Foreign Policy, March 29, 1958, Special Studies, box 1, DDEL; and Stengers, "Precipitous Decolonization," 315–25.

12. Taxes might even have reached 50 percent. Merriam, *Congo: Background of Conflict*, 36–39, noted that while John Gunther suggested the UMHK paid 50 percent of all taxes, this claim was refuted by Jan Albert Goris, editor of the *Belgian Congo-American Survey*, 1956–57, published by the Belgian Chamber of Commerce. The five holding companies were Brufina, which controlled the Banque de Bruxelles and the financial life of the colony; Banque Empain, which had strong transportation interests; Unilever, which, via its subsidiary Huilever, controlled the production and export of vegetable products; Cominière and Société Générale, which established both UMHK and La Société Internationale Forestière et Minière du Congo, or Forminière (in Kasai), and dominated mining, agriculture, and other interests in those two provinces. See also Gibbs, *Political Economy of Third World Intervention*, 59–60; and entry for Paul Gillet in "Milestones," *Time*, January 8, 1965.

13. Gibbs, *Political Economy of Third World Intervention*, 44–52, 60–69. See also Young, *Politics in the Congo*, 17; and Alan James, *Britain and the Congo Crisis, 1960–1963* (New York: St. Martin's Press, 1996), 31.

14. Van Bilsen, "Un plan de trente ans"; Merriam, in *Congo: Background of Conflict*, 38–47, noted that "a great many projects were realized," but did not specify the projects, nor consider their value as either humanitarian efforts or whether they simply masked further official exploitation of the Congo. For a revised, more skeptical view of Belgian contributions to Congo development, see Jacques Depelchin, *From the Congo Free State to Zaire: How Belgium Privatized the Economy—A History of Belgian Stock Companies in Congo-Zaire from 1885 to 1974*, translated by Ayi Kwei Armah (Dakar: Codesria Books, 1992).

15. For an English translation of the *Conscience Africaine* manifesto, see Merriam, *Congo: Background of Conflict*, 321–29.

16. For an English translation of Abako's countermanifesto, see Merriam, *Congo: Background of Conflict*, 330–36. For a history of Abako, see Benoît Verhaegen and Charles Tshimanga, *L'Abako et l'indépendance du Congo belge: Dix ans de nationalisme kongo (1950–1960)* (Paris: Éditions L'Harmattan, 2003).

17. In his first political move, Kasavubu joined the missionary-sponsored society known as the Union des Intérêts Sociaux Congolais, but his first major speech to

this organization was deemed too radical and he alienated the more moderate activists. Verhaegen, *L'Abako*, esp. 272–73; and Verhaegen and Tshimanga, *L'Abako et l'indépendance du Congo belge;* Lemarchand, *Political Awakening in the Congo*, 184–93; Merriam, *Congo: Background of Conflict*, 75–80; and Young, *Politics in the Congo*, 118–21, 504–12, and the biography at http://www.bookrags.com/biography/joseph-kasavubu (accessed in June 2006).

18. U.S. Consul James Green to State, December 20, 1958, decimal file 755A, box 3427, RG59, NARA.

19. "Discours de clôture du congrès M.N.C. prononcé le 28 octobre," October 28, 1959, in *Stanleyville 1959*, ed. Simons, Boghossian, and Verhaegen, 109: "J'ai toujours dit: L'indépendance n'a jamais été donnée, il faut l'arracher." See the same speech, 107, for reference to Kamina and Kitona. For the reference to a "gift," see his speech of December 28, 1958, also quoted by Robert Edgerton, *The Troubled Heart of Africa: A History of the Congo* (New York: St. Martin's Press, 2002), 182.

20. See Thomas Turner, "'Lumumba Delivers the Congo from Slavery': Patrice Lumumba in the Minds of the Tetela," in *Patrice Lumumba entre dieu et diable*, edited by Pierre Halen and János Riesz (Paris: Harmattan, 1997), 322–25.

21. Lemarchand, *Political Awakening in the Congo*, 20, 47–49, 160–62, 198–201; Benoît Verhaegen, "L'Association des évolués de Stanleyville et les débuts politiques de Patrice Lumumba (1944–1958)," *Les Cahiers du CEDAF* 2 (May 1983). See also "Biographic information on Patrice Lumumba," April 24, 1959, decimal file, 1955–59, box 3428, RG59, NARA (for "foreign subjection quote"); John Henrik Clarke, "The Passing of Patrice Lumumba," http://www.africawithin.com/clarke/passing_of_patrice_lumumba.htm. Clarke was a U.N. correspondent on African affairs, and this is a reprint of his famous article first published in *Journal of Human Relations*, Summer 1962, 383–93. See also Edgerton, *Troubled Heart of Africa*, 182.

22. Lemarchand, *Political Awakening in the Congo*, 20, 47–49, 160–62, 198–201; Young, *Politics in the Congo*, 184–93; Verhaegen, "L'Association des évolués de Stanleyville"; and Karen Bouwer, *Gender and Decolonization in the Congo: The Legacy of Patrice Lumumba* (New York: Palgrave Macmillan, 2010), 8, 28–31. See also "Biographic information on Patrice Lumumba," April 24, 1959, decimal file, 1955–59, box 3428, RG59, NARA.

23. Catherine Hoskyns, *The Congo since Independence: January 1960–December 1961* (London: Oxford University Press, 1965), 29–30.

24. Kanza, *Conflict in the Congo*, 50. No evidence of the CIA role at Accra has yet surfaced in the available archives.

25. Lumumba's speech at the Accra conference, December 11, 1958, and Lumumba's speech at Leopoldville, December 28, 1958, in *Lumumba Speaks: The Speeches and Writings of Patrice Lumumba, 1958–1961*, edited by Jean van Lierde and translated by Helen R. Lane, with an introduction by Jean-Paul Sartre (Boston: Little, Brown, 1972; orig. pub. 1963), 220–25; for quotes, 58 and 60, respectively. See also Jean-Claude Willame, "Patrice Lumumba et les Belges," in *Patrice Lumumba entre dieu et diable*, edited by Pierre Halen and János Riesz (Paris: Harmattan, 1997), 189–91; and David Macey, *Frantz Fanon: A Biography* (New York: Picador, 2000), 414–15, 433–35.

26. Georges Nzongola-Ntalaja, *The Congo from Leopold to Kabila: A People's History* (London: Zed Books, 2002), 84–86.

27. Mazov, *Distant Front in the Cold War*, 82–83.

28. Verhaegen, *L'Abako*, 301–23; Hoskyns, *Congo since Independence*, 10–11; Lemarchand, *Political Awakening in the Congo*, 43, 46–51; Weiss, *Political Protest in the Congo*, 18–22. Weiss challenged Rupert Emerson, who followed "accepted" stages in the development of nationalism, based on protonationalism (the rise of cultural associations), and the subsequent rise of a new intellectual leadership as nationalist ideas extended to the masses. In the Congo, Weiss found a different situation, where the masses were actually ahead of the elite in their demands for an independent nation. See also Nzongola-Ntalaja, *Congo from Leopold to Kabila*, 86–87.

29. *Pravda*, January 8–18, 1959.

30. *Soviet News* (Soviet Embassy in London), February 6, 1959.

31. Martynov, *Kongo pod gnetom*, 215–30. Martynov's argument is similar to Potekhin's, who wrote favorably about the trade unions in Ghana and Guinea as they moved toward independence. See Potekhin, "Kharakternye cherty raspada kolonial'noi sistemy imperializma v Afrike," 19. In "The Soviet Union and the Congo" (PhD diss., Columbia University, 1971), 144–63, Madeleine Kalb found that Martynov exaggerated the strength of the socialist-oriented workers' movement. But Lemarchand, in *Political Awakening*, 265, stated that the Christian Democrats and Socialists had preempted the communist workers' unions. However, there is some agreement among Western scholars on the radical nature of the peasants. Herbert Weiss concluded that "the rural masses tended to be radical and the leaders frequently tried to dampen these predilections." See his *Political Protest in the Congo*, 185. Lumumba also recognized this phenomenon; see his speech, October 29, 1959, in *Stanleyville 1959*, ed. Simons, Boghossian, and Verhaegen, 116–25. Often young people, such as the youth group of the MNC-L, were given the right to serve as "party whips." This led to independent, often quasi-terrorist activity, and eventually the youth groups served as a center of opposition. See Lemarchand, *Political Awakening*, 266–67.

32. Notes from "The Congo Crisis, 1960–1961: A Critical Oral History Conference," September 23–24, 2004, Cold War International History Project, Woodrow Wilson Center for International Scholars.

33. Rakhmaninov, "Ob Ianvarskikh sobytiiakh v Bel'giiskom Kongo" [About the January events in the Belgian Congo], January 25, 1959, Archiv vneshnei politiki Rossiskoi Federatsii (Archive of the Foreign Policy of the Russian Federation) (hereafter, AVPRF), fond 72, opis 40, delo 26, papka 31, 7; for quote, see 13.

34. Ambassador I. Gerasimov, "Zapis' besedy s predsedatelem Natsional'nogo dvizheniia Kongo Patrisom Lumumoi o perspektivakh sovetsko-kongolezskikh otnoshenii, 18 aprelia 1959g." [Notes on conversation with Mouvement National Congolais president Patrice Lumumba about prospective Soviet–Congolese relations], April 28, 1959, in *Rossia i Afrika*, ed. Davidson and Mazov, 232–33. See also Mazov, *Distant Front in the Cold War*, 83.

35. B. A. Savinov, memo of conversation with Patrice Lumumba, February 19, 1960, fond 5, opis 50, delo 257, list 22–25, RGANI. For Potekhin's trip to Accra, see Legvold, *Soviet Policy in West Africa*, 56–57. Lumumba was angry that his visit to

the Soviet Embassy fueled rumors that he was a communist. Lumumba pointed out that a Belgian parliamentary delegation visited the Soviet Union every year, and that trip was not taken to mean that they were selling out to the communists, nor should his trip be understood in this way. See Jules Raskin to Lumumba, January 6, 1960, in *Stanleyville 1959*, ed. Simons, Boghossian, and Verhaegen, 155–56.

36. Nzongola-Ntalaja, *Congo from Leopold to Kabila*, 86–87.

37. I. I. Marchuk, "Iz besedy s kogolezckimi politikami o soveskoi pomoshchi natsional'no-osvoboditel'nomu dvizheniiu Kongo, 28 December 1959g.," January 15, 1960, in *Rossia i Afrika*, ed. Davidson and Mazov, 236–39. The feminist revolutionary Andrée Blouin maintained that Touré met with the PSA leaders Pierre Mulele and Antoine Gizenga with advice on how to conduct their election campaign in the Congo. Andrée Blouin, *My Country, Africa: Autobiography of the Black Pasionaria* (New York: Praeger, 1983), 201–4. The journalist Pierre Davister gave Blouin the name "black pasionaria," which was picked up by the European press, and later in defiance by Blouin herself; see 236. For a typical Western assessment of Blouin, see Bartlett, *Communist Penetration and Subversion*, 23. See also Ludo Martens, *Pierre Mulele ou la seconde vie de Patrice Lumumba* (Antwerp: Éditions EPO, 1985), 59–61.

38. Davidson, Mazov, and Tsypkin, *SSSR i Afrika*, 260–61.

39. Leopoldville consulate (James R. Lavallee) to State, summary of Sattherthwaite and Kasavubu meeting, June 23, 1959, *FRUS 1958–1960*, vol. 14, 255–57.

40. For the first quote, see Meriwether, *Proudly We Can Be Africans*, 170; for the second one, see Memorandum of Discussion, 432nd NSC meeting, January 14, 1960, *FRUS 1958–1960*, vol. 14, 74.

41. Memorandum of Discussion (Boggs), November 5, 1959, quoted in editorial note in *FRUS 1958–1960*, vol. 14, 257–58.

42. Memorandum of Discussion, 432nd NSC meeting, January 14, 1960, *FRUS 1958–1960*, vol. 14, 77. At this meeting, Stans, who was also present, agreed with Merchant and lamented that "many Africans still belonged in the trees."

43. Helmreich, *United States Relations with Belgium and the Congo*, 213.

44. See Brussels (Stanley Cleveland) to State, November 25, 1959, decimal file, 1955–59, box 3428, RG59, NARA.

45. Ruth Slade, *The Belgian Congo*, 2nd ed. (London: Institute of Race Relations, Oxford University Press, 1961), 60; Merriam, *Background of Conflict*, 96–97, 152–54, 196–97.

46. Verhaegen, *L'Abako*, 333–85; Young, *Politics in the Congo*, 125–26, 164–66; Merriam, *Congo: Background of Conflict*; Lemarchand, *Political Awakening in the Congo*, 173, 230–32; Thomas Kanza, *The Rise and Fall of Patrice Lumumba: Conflict in the Congo* (Rochester, Vt.: Schenkman, 1994; orig. pub. 1972), 85–87; Weiss, *Political Protest in the Congo*, 26–40.

47. Gibbs, *Political Economy of Third World Intervention*, 84–86.

48. Matthew Hughes, "Fighting for White Rule in Africa: The Central African Federation, Katanga, and the Congo Crisis, 1958–1965," *International History Review* 25, no. 3 (September 2003): 599, 603.

49. Lemarchand, *Political Awakening in the Congo*, 299.

50. For the Belgian political situation, see Catherine Hoskyns, *The Congo: A Chronology of Events, January 1950–December 1961* (London: Oxford University Press,

1962), 36–37; Merriam, *Congo: Background of Conflict*, 100–104; Weiss, *Political Protest in the Congo*, 122; and Lemarchand, *Political Awakening in the Congo*, 48–50. See also Brussels to State, April 16, 1959, and "Further Comment on the Ousting of Petillon," Leopoldville to State, December 13, 1958, in decimal file, 1955–59, box 3428, RG59, NARA.

51. See D. A. Low, "The Asian Mirror to Tropical Africa's Independence," in *Transfer of Power in Africa*, ed. Gifford and Louis, 1–19.

52. *Time*, February 22 and March 21, 1960.

53. Hoskyns, *Congo: A Chronology*, 36–37.

54. For a photograph of Lumumba with bandaged wrists, see *Time*, February 22, 1960.

55. Hoskyns, *Congo since Independence*, 33–41; Anstey, *King Leopold's Legacy*, 238; Paule Bouvier, *L'accession du Congo belge à l'indépendance: Essai d'analyse sociologique* (Brussels: Éditions de l'Institut de Sociologie, 1965), 236–43; Young, *Politics in the Congo*, 171–83.

56. During the conference, Tshombe insisted that the provincial government be based on elected assemblies, another measure that would have favored Belgian interests. The result was a politicization of provincial politics, as Crawford Young has pointed out, that did much to help destabilize the country by increasing the significance of the dominant ethnic majority. See Young, *Politics in the Congo*, 514–15.

57. Merriam, *Congo: Background of Conflict*, 100–104.

58. Chambre des représentants de Belgique, *Enquête parlementaire visant à déterminer les circonstances exactes de l'assassinat de Patrice Lumumba et l'implication éventuelle des responsables politique belges dans celui-ci* [Parliamentary inquiry to determine the exact circumstances of the assassination of Patrice Lumumba and possible involvement of Belgian politicians] (Brussels, 2001–2002) (hereafter, *Belgian Parliamentary Commission*), 454–55.

Chapter 3

1. Decree of the CC CPSU, "O raschirenii kul'turnykh i obshchestvennykh sviazei s negritianskimi narodami Afriki i usilenii vlianiia Sovetskovo Soiuza na eti narody" [The expansion of cultural and public relations with the black peoples of Africa and strengthening the influence of the Soviet Union on these peoples], January 20, 1960, in *Rossiia i Afrika*, ed. Davidson and Mazov, 165–68.

2. Albert de Coninck, "Kongo v bor'be za nezavisimost'" [The Congo and the fight for independence], *Mirovaia ekonomika i mezhdunarodnie otnosheniia* no. 1 (1960): 72–78. No French version of this article has been found. See also Bartlett, *Communist Penetration and Subversion*, 14.

3. See Gruliow, ed., *Current Soviet Policies,* vol. 2, 28, and vol. 3, 38–39, for references to Burnelle. There is virtually no published information available about the Belgian Communist Party. See Rik Hemmerijckx, "The Belgian Communist Party and the Socialist Trade Unions, 1940–1960," *Journal of Communist Studies* (1990): 124–42. Also see "History of the Belgian Communist Party, Colonial Section, 1945–1952," in decimal file, 1955–59, box 3428, RG59, NARA (and sent to State by Leopoldville, February 6, 1956).

4. Savinov's role also freed the Soviet ambassador to Belgium, S. A. Afanas'iev, from direct contact with the Congolese, which would have sparked great alarm in Brussels and Washington. Afanas'iev served as ambassador to Belgium from October 1958 through August 1962. As a measure of the importance of the Congo, I. Gerasimov, the former ambassador to Guinea, became Soviet ambassador to Brussels until March 1967. See Edward L. Crowly, *The Soviet Diplomatic Corps, 1917–1967* (Metuchen, N.J.: Scarecrow Press, 1970), 26.

5. Symbolic of the Sino-Soviet struggle to represent the Afro-Asian community, the exchange of invitations was conducted through the Chinese and Soviet Afro-Asian Solidarity Committees. Savinov, Notes of Conversation with representatives of Congolese political parties, February 11, 1960, fond 5, opis 50, delo 257, list 8–11, RGANI; and Savinov, Memorandum of Conversation with de Coninck, February 10, 1960, fond 5, opis 50, delo 257, list 30–32, RGANI.

6. Savinov, Memorandum of Conversation with A. Nguvulu, February 16, 1960, fond 5, opis 50, delo 257, list 22–25, RGANI.

7. Savinov, Memorandum of Conversation with representatives of Congolese political parties, February 11, 1960, fond 5, opis 50, delo 257, list 8–11, RGANI. Despite his prominence at the Round Table, Kasongo seems to have faded from the political limelight, and after independence there are few references to him.

8. Savinov, Notes of Conversation with representatives of Congolese political parties, February 11, 1960, fond 5, opis 50, delo 257, list 8–11, RGANI. In *Communist Penetration and Subversion*, 19, Bartlett wrote that on June 22, 1960, the *Katanga* weekly reported that Kasongo had traveled with the Parti du Peuple to China. Little else of his activities is known.

9. See Savinov, Memorandum of Conversation with Lumumba, February 19, 1960, fond 5, opis 50, delo 257, list 22–25, RGANI.

10. Savinov, Memorandum of Conversation with Nguvulu, February 22, 1960, fond 5, opis 50, delo 257, list 37–38, RGANI. See also *Courrier Africain*, no. 9, April 26, 1960, 14–17.

11. Savinov, Memorandum of Conversation with Nguvulu, February 22, 1960.

12. Ibid., fond 5, opis 50, delo 257, list 37–38, RGANI; Bartlett, *Communist Penetration and Subversion of the Belgian Congo*, 21 (based on Lang), reported that Terfve advised Nguvulu during the election campaign.

13. Savinov, Notes of Conversation with Terfve, February 17, 1960, fond 5, opis 50, delo 257, list 30–32, RGANI.

14. The preparations for the meeting are found in Savinov, Notes of Conversation with Terfve, February 15, 1960, fond 5, opis 50, delo 257, list 30–32, RGANI, and Memorandum of Conversation with representatives of Congolese political parties, February 11, 1960, fond 5, opis 50, delo 257, list 8–11, RGANI.

15. Savinov, Memorandum of Conversation with Lumumba, February 19, 1960, fond 5, opis 50, delo 257, list 22–25, RGANI. See also *Courrier Africain*, no. 6, March 25, 1960, 6–8, and for an outline of opinions, 18; and Mazov, *Distant Front in the Cold War*, 84.

16. See Bartlett, *Communist Penetration and Subversion*, 4, quoting *Drapeau Rouge*, July 11, 1956, which explained the BCP attitude toward Lumumba; see also Savinov, Notes of Conversation with representatives of Congolese political parties, February 11, 1960, fond 5, opis 50, delo 257, list 8–11, RGANI.

17. Savinov, Memorandum of Conversation with Lumumba, February 19, 1960, fond 5, opis 50, delo 257, list 22–25, RGANI. Writing ten years after the events, Nikolai Khokhlov still supported the interpretation found in these documents and chided Kasavubu's politically unwise decision to withdraw from the Round Table Conference, but then states that Lumumba was not strong enough politically to warrant serious support. See his *Patris Lumumba* (Moscow: Molodaia gvardiia, 1971), 119–36.

18. Hoskyns, *Congo since Independence*, 48–53.

19. For a good discussion of the Congo Portfolio, see Kent, *America, the U.N. and Decolonisation*, 11, and Depelchin, *From the Congo Free State to Zaire*, 166–69; Colin Legum, *Congo Disaster* (Baltimore: Penguin Books, 1961), 92; Hoskyns, *Congo since Independence*, 48–53; Livier Boehme, "The Involvement of the Belgian Central Bank in the Katangan Secession, 1960–1963," *African Economic History* 33 (2005): 2. Depelchin, based on information from Pierre Joye and Rosine Lewin, *Les Trusts au Congo* (Brussels: Societé Populaire d'Éditions, 1961), found the following distribution of portfolio stock before June 27: Comité Spécial du Katanga, 662,768; Tanganyika Concessions, 375,160; Société Générale, 128,792; and Compagnie du Katanga, 18,500. And it found the following distribution of portfolio stock after June 27: Congolese government, 478,292; Tanganyika Concessions, 375,160; Société Générale, 128,792; and Compagnie du Katanga, 202,976.

20. Savinov, Notes of Conversation with de Coninck, May 2, 1960, fond 5, opis 50, delo 257, list 44–46, RGANI; Savinov, Notes of Conversation with Terfve, February 15, 1960, fond 5, opis 50, delo 257, list 30–32, RGANI.

21. From the Diary of A. Ustinov and G. Uranov, Memorandum of Conversation with Philippe and Thomas Kanza, May 7, 1960, fond 5, opis 50, delo 257, list 47–50, RGANI; and G. Uranov, "O predstoiashei belgiisko-kongolezskoi economicheskoi konferentsii "kryglogo stola" (spravka), March 16, 1960, fond 590, delo 20, opis 3, papka 3, 117, AVPRF.

22. Burden was at the Commerce Department from 1943 to 1947 and in the Air Force from 1950 to 1952. See the entry for William Armistead Burden, *The Scribner Encyclopedia of American Lives*, vol. 1, 1981–1985 (Charles Scribner's Sons, 1998), available at www.galenet.com.

23. State (Dillon) to Brussels, January 8, 1960, *FRUS 1958–1960*, vol. 14, 260 n. 4, referring to dispatch 817 from Brussels, February 2, 1960.

24. State (Dillon) to Brussels, January 8, 1960, *FRUS 1958–1960*, vol. 14, 260. See also Weissman, *American Foreign Policy in the Congo*, 3–36.

25. Memorandum of Conversation, Burden and Lumumba, February 25, 1960, *FRUS 1958–1960*, vol. 14, 263. Burden wrote that Lumumba's ideas on foreign investment were "considerably more clear and developed" than other aspects of his economic ideas. Lumumba conveyed to Burden that he was willing to protect larger foreign investment, but had not given as much thought to more specific investment projects, except perhaps for the INGA hydroelectric power project.

26. Memorandum of Conversation, Nendaka, McKinnon, and Devlin, March 25, 1960, decimal file, RG 59, 1960–1963, box 1831, RG 59, NARA.

27. Devlin, *Chief of Station*, 72.

28. Brussels (Burden) to Dillon, April 7, 1960, *FRUS 1958–1960*, vol. 14, 266–70.

29. *New York Times*, March 16, 1960.

30. U.S. Department of State, "Educational and Cultural Exchange with Africa: The Program of the Department of State," *African Studies Bulletin* (May 1961): 1–8; Michael Krenn, "The Unwelcome Mat: African Diplomats in Washington, D.C., during the Kennedy Years," in *Window on Freedom: Race, Civil Rights, and Foreign Affairs, 1945–1988*, edited by Brenda Gayle Plummer (Chapel Hill: University of North Carolina Press, 2003), 165, whose experiences were no different from that of other Africans. See also Borstelmann, *Cold War and the Color Line*, 164–68.

31. G. McMurtrie Godley, interview, April 20, 1990, UNOH, 12–13.

32. State (Satterthwaite) to Accra, April 28, 1960, *FRUS 1958–1960*, vol. 14, 271. Flake subsequently reported that he shared Satterthwaite's interest in recruiting Nkrumah, and after having approached the *osagyefo* (leader), received a positive response.

33. Brussels (Tony Freeman) to State, May 1, 1960, *FRUS 1958–1960*, vol. 14, 272–74.

34. For quotes by Eisenhower and Anderson, see Memorandum of Discussion, 438th NSC meeting, March 24, 1960, *FRUS 1958–1960*, vol. 14, 97. For support of Eisenhower's position, see Memorandum of Discussion, 432nd NSC meeting, January 14, 1960, *FRUS 1958–1960*, vol. 14, 74. The discussion was mainly about West Africa but could be applicable to the entire continent.

35. Memorandum of Discussion, 438th NSC meeting, March 24, 1960, *FRUS 1958–1960*, vol. 14, 97; Satterthwaite to Dillon, March 30, 1960, *FRUS 1958–1960*, vol. 14, 99–106; and Memorandum of Conversation, Dillon and Satterthwaite, et al., April 7, 1960, *FRUS, 1958–1960*, vol. 14, 109–16; and Satterthwaite to Deputy Coordinator for Mutual Security John O. Bell, June 30, 1960, *FRUS, 1958–1960*, vol. 14, 143–46.

36. Memorandum of Conversation, meeting with Under Secretary Dillon, April 7, 1960, *FRUS 1958–1960*, vol. 14, 109–16; Dillon to Brussels, January 8, 1960, *FRUS 1958–1960*, vol. 14, 258–60. See also Arthur H. House, *The U.N. and the Congo: The Political and Civilian Efforts* (Washington, D.C.: University Press of America, 1978), 41, who interviewed Robert L. West on June 11, 1970.

37. Data from Michael Hoyt, "Republic of the Congo (Leopoldville)," *International Commerce*, Special Report on Africa, March 1963, 29.

38. See note in *Time*, October 17, 1960.

39. See quote in Memorandum of Discussion, 423rd NSC meeting, November 5, 1960, in editorial note, *FRUS 1958–1960*, vol. 14, 257.

40. Hoskyns, *Congo since Independence*, 64–68.

41. See D'Lynn Waldron's Web site, http://www.dlwaldron.com/Lumumba.html. She also stated that these references were all removed by the Scripps-Howard newspaper chain, for which she worked.

42. Bouwer, *Gender and Decolonisation in the Congo*, 90–93. Bouwer interviewed Kamitatu and his wife in 2008.

43. The timing of the break between Lumumba and the Belgians has generated a debate. Lemarchand, *Political Awakening in the Congo*, 218–32, and Merriam, *Congo: Background of Conflict*, 195–203, find the break occurring with the events surrounding Lumumba's arrest in Stanleyville. Legum, *Congo Disaster*, 107, argued that the break came after the Belgians tried to deny Lumumba leadership when parliament met on June 17, 1960. Others—such Urquhart, *Hammarskjöld*, 391—argued that the break

happened at Congolese independence. Others still have suggested that the break came as early as 1959. In *Stanleyville 1959*, Simons, Boghossian, and Verhaegen presented the argument that the break came during the third quarter of the tumultuous year 1959. Martens, *Pierre Mulele*, 72–77, argued that by early 1959, Lumumba's desire to be spokesperson for the masses, who were much more radical than the *évolués*, led him to anti-imperialist revolutionary activity.

44. *New York Times*, April 22 and May 14, 1960.

45. *Courrier Africain*, April 26, 1960, 16–17.

46. Gizenga statement, *Pravda*, July 1, 1960; Kalb, "Soviet Union and the Congo," 227–28.

47. From the Diary of A. Ustinov and G. Uranov, Memorandum of Conversation with Philippe and Thomas Kanza, May 7, 1960, fond 5, opis 50, delo 257, lost 47–50, RGANI.

48. Savinov, Memorandum of Conversation with Lumumba, February 19, 1960, fond 5, opis 50, delo 257, list 22–25, RGANI.

49. Savinov, Memorandum of Conversation with de Coninck, May 2, 1960, fond 5, opis 50, delo 257, list 44–46, RGANI.

50. W. A. C. Adie, "China, Russia and the Third World," *China Quarterly* 11 (July–September 1962): 211.

51. Kalb, "Soviet Union and the Congo," 166–67. See Bartlett, *Communist Penetration and Subversion*, 26–27, for an account of the funds that Lumumba allegedly received from communists. Pierre Houart estimated that the communists together donated about $140 million Belgian francs to Lumumba. See Houart, *La Pénétration communiste au Congo: Commentaires et documents sur les événements juin–novembre 1960* (Brussels: Centre de Documentation Internationale, 1960). Jules Chomé questioned Houart's evidence; Jules Chomé, *M. Lumumba et le Communisme: Variations à partir du livre de M. Houart* (Brussels: Editions de Remarques Congolaises, 1961). In 1959, the Soviet Union provided the Belgian Communist Party with $60,000 in aid, which was comparable with other small European communist parties (Netherlands, Norway, Denmark, and Luxembourg). See Andrew Campbell, "Moscow's Gold," *National Observer*, Autumn 1999, available at www.britannica.com/bcom/magazine.

52. Fritz Schatten, *Communism in Africa* (New York: Praeger, 1966), 210.

53. See, e.g., Hoskyns, *Congo since Independence*, 73, who referred to the surprising results, and Young, *Politics in the Congo*, 302–306, who mentioned the fragmentation it revealed; but neither suggested that the results were tampered with or flawed in principle. Young again noted that the trend toward fragmentation was visible at the provincial level, where only in Orientale did a single party (MNC-L) win a majority of votes.

54. Young, *Politics in the Congo*, 303–305; Centre de Recherche et d'Information Socio-Politiques (hereafter, CRISP), *Congo 1960*, edited by Jules Gerard-Libois and Benoît Verhaegen (Brussels: CRISP, 1960), 206–66. See also House, *U.N. in the Congo*, for the following tally: MNC-L party, 703,407 total votes, 41 deputies and 19 senators; PSA, 278,971, 13 deputies and 4 senators; PNP, 234,333, 15 deputies and 3 senators; Abako, 210,542, 12 deputies and 4 senators; MNC-K, 161,942, 8 deputies and 3 senators; PUNA and NGWEKA, 118,661, 7 deputies and 7 senators; Union Katangaise, 110,091, 7 deputies and 3 senators; Conakat, 104,871, 8 deputies and 6 senators; CEREA, 95,721, 10 deputies and 6 senators; other parties, 7 deputies and 4

senators; individuals, 4 deputies and 2 senators; and traditional authorities, 5 deputies and 23 senators.

55. Young, *Politics in the Congo*, 302; Jules Gerard-Libois, *Katanga Secession*, translated by Rebecca Young (Madison: University of Wisconsin Press, 1966), 63–83; Hoskyns, *Congo since Independence*, 64–77.

56. *Time*, July 4, 1960; Hoskyns, *The Congo since Independence*, 64–77; Legum, *Congo Disaster*, 107; and Nzongola-Ntalaja, *The Congo from Leopold to Kabila*, 97.

57. Lumumba, "A Morning in the Heart of Africa," originally published in *Kulturny Zivot*, August 1960, and reproduced by Frank Uhlir, "Red Sky Over Africa," *Est Europe* 9 (October 1960): 36.

58. Lumumba created a government made up of himself as prime minister and minister of national defense; Antoine Gizenga, vice prime minister; Justin Bomboko (Unimo), minister of foreign affairs; Marcel Bisukiro (Cerea), minister of foreign trade; Albert Delvaux (PNP), resident minister in Belgium; Thomas Kanza (Abako), delegate to the United Nations; Remy Mwamba, minister of justice; Christophe Gbenye (MNC), minister of the interior; Pascal Nkayi (Abako), minister of finance; Joseph Yav (Conakat), minister of economic affairs; Alois Kabangi (MNC), minister of economic coordination; Alphonse Ilunga (UNC), minister of public works; Alphonse Songolo (MNC), minister of communications; Joseph Lutula (MNC), minister of agriculture; Joachim Massena (PSA), minister of labor; Joseph M'Buyi (MNC), minister of middle classes; Gregoire Kamanga (Coaka), minister of public health; Edmond Rudahindwa (Reco), minister of mines; Alexandre Mahamba (MNC), minister of property; Antoine Ngwenza (Puna), minister of social affairs; Pierre Mulele (PSA), minister of national education; Anicet Kashamura (Cerea), minister of information and cultural affairs; and Maurice Mpolo (MNC), minister of youth and sports.

The proposed provincial commissioners included Sylvain Kama for Leopoldville, Tamusu Fumu for Equateur, Isaac Kalonji for Kasai, Jason Sendwe for Katanga, Hubert Sangara for Kivu, and Christophe Musungu for Orientale. Ministry heads follow: two presidents, Joseph Mobutu (MNC) and Jacques Lumbala (PNP); foreign affairs, Andre Mandi (none); commerce, Antoine Kiwena (MNC); finance, Andre Tshibangu (none); justice, Maximilien Liongo (MNC); interior, R. Batshikama (Abako); economic planning, Alphonse Nguvulu (PP); national defense, Albert Nyembo (Conakat); information, Antoine Bolanba (MNC); and two ministers of state, Paul Boya (PNP) and Georges Grenfell (MNC).

All the MNC members listed here are from the Lumumba wing. See René Lemarchand, "How Lumumba Came to Power," in *Footnotes to the Congo Story,* edited by Helen Kitchen (New York: Walker, 1967), 9–17; Hoskyns, *Congo since Independence*, 481–82; Hoskyns, *Congo: A Chronology*, May 1962, 24; Kanza, *Rise and Fall of Patrice Lumumba*, 94–99, 100–16 (for biographical sketches); and Weiss, *Political Protest in the Congo*, 288.

59. Azarov, "Politika SWA v otnoshenii stran Afriki, poluchaiushchikh status nezavisimykh stran" [The policy of the USA in relations with newly independent countries of Africa], June 23, 1960, Referentura po SWA, fond 129, opis 47, por. 55, papka 135, AVPRF. Soon after the crisis began, the Soviet argument switched from emphasizing tensions within the NATO alliance to NATO collusion.

60. Omajuwa Igho Natufe, "The Cold War and the Congo Crisis, 1960–1961," *Africa* (Rome) 39 (1984): 362, which refers to the *Daily Telegraph*, June 28, 1960. To

jump ahead a bit, Secretary-General Hammarskjöld made a trip to the Congo around this time to study the question of a technical aid package for the Congo (discussed in the next chapter).

61. *Pravda*, June 26 and July 12, 1960; *Izvestia*, July 10, 1960. See also Kalb, "Soviet Union and the Congo," 78–79, 202–4. For a different interpretation of Khrushchev's belated support, see Kalb, *Congo Cables*, 10.

62. Brussels (Freeman) to State, May 1, 1960, *FRUS 1958–1960*, vol. 14, 272.

63. Devlin, *Chief of Station*, 35.

64. Ann Whitman file, June 30, 1960, NSC series, box 12, no. 449, DDEL. The president here was in one of his reflective moods, during which he tended to make very general statements like this one. Castro in Cuba, of course, was troubling him. But here he also made mention of events in Turkey, where in May 1960 a military coup d'état had overthrown the democratically elected government, and in Japan where political protests brought down the government of Nobusuke Kishi after he signed the renewed Treaty of Mutual Security and Cooperation in January 1960.

Chapter 4

1. Varying accounts of the celebrations are given by Jack Mendelson, "'Uhuru' Comes to the Congo," *Africa Today* 7 (September 1960); *Newsweek*, July 4, 1960; *Time*, July 11, 1960; and *New York Times,* July 1, 1960. For a discussion of the different versions, see *Belgian Parliamentary Commission Report*, 455–56.

2. For the text of Lumumba's address, see van Lierde, ed., *Lumumba Speaks*, 220–25. Many accounts have cited Lumumba's famous line, "We are no longer your monkeys," or macaques, as part of this speech. Whether he actually said this has been called into question. See Michela Wrong, "The Mystery of a Famous Quotation," September 4, 2008, http://www.newstatesman.com/africa/2008/09/famous-quotation-wrong-lumumba.

3. Robert Murphy, *Diplomat among Warriors* (Garden City, N.Y.: Doubleday, 1964), 334.

4. Handwritten notes, June 30, 1960, Congo file, box 178, Bunche Papers, University of California, Los Angeles.

5. Murphy was accompanied by the chargé d'affaires, John D. Tomlinson. See Leopoldville (Tomlinson) to State, July 4, 1960, *FRUS 1958–1960*, vol. 14, 280–81.

6. Devlin, *Chief of Station*, 23–24; Mazov, *Distant Front in the Cold War*, 88–89.

7. Devlin, *Chief of Station*, 1–10; Kalb, *Congo Cables*, 26.

8. Oleg Orestov, *Pravda*'s correspondent on the scene, charged that General Janssens intentionally provoked the unrest in the ANC to justify an invasion, not suspecting that the mutineers would turn against the Belgians. There might be some truth to Orestov's charges. General Janssens was unhappy with the new government and contested Lumumba's decision, made after the onset of the mutiny, to Africanize the army. A few days after independence, Janssens ordered aerial maneuvers and sent commandos to Leopoldville to intimidate the government. In the wake of this activity, Lumumba reported an attack on his life and charged that it was a Belgian assassination plot. Lumumba, "Report to the Chamber," July 15, 1960, in *Lumumba Speaks*, ed. van Lierde, 251; Jean-Claude Willame, *Patrice Lumumba: La crise congolaise revisitée* (Paris: Éditions Karthala, 1990), 131–51. See Orestov's report in *Pravda*, July 12,

1960. See also the similar story in *Izvestia*, July 14, 1960. Nikolai Khokhlov's first report, in which he interviewed Gizenga, was published in *Izvestia*, July 23, 1960. Gizenga suspected that the Belgians intended to use the soldiers to overthrow the government, but that instead the soldiers remained loyal.

9. For Lumumba's speeches, see his two statements on July 6, 1960, in *Lumumba Speaks*, ed. van Lierde, 229–31.

10. Bouwer, *Gender and Decolonization in the Congo*, 1–6.

11. *Belgian Parliamentary Commission Report*, 40–42, 63–65, 81, 456–58, 903.

12. Willame, *Patrice Lumumba*, 120–52; Hoskyns, *Congo since Independence*, 87–104.

13. See the correspondence between Lumumba and the Belgian officers, July 11, 1960, in *Lumumba Speaks*, ed. van Lierde, 232–34.

14. *Belgian Parliamentary Commission Report*, 40, 46, 456–458.

15. Devlin, *Chief of Station*, 35; Urquhart, *Hammarskjöld*, 392–93; see also Memorandum of Conversation, Herter and Hammarskjöld, July 12, 1960, 12:50 p.m., Herter Telephone Conversation Series (hereafter, HTCS), microfilm no. 11, 865, DDEL.

16. Belgium (Burden) to State, quoting Timberlake, July 10, 1960, *FRUS 1958–1960*, vol. 14, 287.

17. Tshombe would make his declaration on July 11, although Kasavubu and Lumumba learned about it a few days earlier. Gerard-Libois, *Katanga Secession*, 75; see 328–29 for the "Katangan Proclamation of Independence." A few days later (July 17), Tshombe began advocating the reconstitution of "a confederation" and Belgium tried to rally other provinces to consider this alternative. See Young, *Politics in the Congo*, 512.

18. *Belgian Parliamentary Commission Report*, 41.

19. Elizabeth Schmidt, *The Cold War and Decolonization in Guinea* (Athens: Ohio University Press, 2007), 167–69. See also *Belgian Parliamentary Commission Report*, 41; and Urquhart, October 19, 1984, UNOH, interview 5, 10.

20. Gibbs, *Political Economy of Third World Intervention*, 84–86.

21. See "Milestones" in *Time*, January 8, 1965.

22. Lemarchand, *Political Awakening in the Congo*, 237–43.

23. Gibbs, *Political Economy of Third World Intervention*, 84–86; *Belgian Parliamentary Commission Report*, 86.

24. Gerard-Libois, *Katanga Secession*, 75; see 328–29 for the text of the "Katangan Proclamation of Independence."

25. Ibid., 110.

26. Lumumba, "Report to the Chamber," in *Lumumba Speaks*, ed. van Lierde, 237–57; Gerard-Libois, *Katanga Secession*, 94; Hoskyns, *Congo since Independence*, 113–14. Anicet Kashamura, *De Lumumba aux colonels* (Paris: Buchet/Chastel, 1966), 114–15, maintained that Lumumba and Kasavubu remained divided over whom to ask for aid, with Lumumba favoring Nasser and Kasavubu favoring the Soviet Union.

27. Bomboko returned later that night, possibly on orders from Lumumba, to state that the troops were requested within the context of the U.N. operation. Kalb argued that Lumumba's decision to reverse the request for U.S. troops came as an effort to blunt Soviet criticism. However, she also found evidence that led her to believe the initial request for U.S. intervention was inspired by Timberlake. See Kalb, *Congo Cables*, 7–9; and Devlin, *Chief of Station*, 36. See also commentary on these events by

Andrew Cordier and Wilder Foote, eds., *Public Papers of the Secretaries-General of the United Nations, Volume 5: Dag Hammarskjöld* (New York: Columbia University Press, 1975) (hereafter, *Public Papers of Dag Hammarskjöld*), 18–20; and "Analytical chronology," box 27, Congo, National Security Files (hereafter, NSF), John F. Kennedy Presidential Library (hereafter, JFKL), quoting Leopoldville telegram 59.

28. Kasavubu and Lumumba Joint Telegram to the Secretary-General, July 12, 1960, United Nations, Security Council, *Official Records* (hereafter, *SCOR*), 15th year, suppl. for July, August, and September, document S/4382. This second appeal is the only one that appears in the Security Council records.

29. Assistant Staff Secretary (Eisenhower) to Staff Secretary (Goodpaster), July 12, 1960, *FRUS, 1958–1960*, vol. xiv, 194.

30. *New York Times*, July 13, 1960.

31. *New York Times*, July 12, 1960; Herter news conference, July 21, 1960, reprinted in *Department of State Bulletin*, August 8, 1960, 205–206. For Herter's follow-up on these concerns, see State (Herter) to U.S. Mission to the United Nations (hereafter, USUN), July 13, 1960, *FRUS 1958–1960*, vol. 14, 303.

32. *Pravda*, July 12, 1960; *Izvestia*, July 13, 1960. See also V. Kaboshkin and I. Kuznetsov, "Kongo perestaet byt' 'bel'giiskim,'" *Sovremennyi Vostok* 6 (June 1960): 20–23.

33. Soviet statement, July 13, 1960, *SSSR i strany Afrika*, vol. 1, 557.

34. Kasavubu and Lumumba joint telegram to the Secretary-General, July 13, 1960, *SCOR*, 15th year, suppl. for July, August, and September 1960, document S/4382. For these telegrams, see also Cordier and Foote, *Public Papers of Dag Hammarskjöld*, 18–20.

35. *New York Times*, July 16, 1960; Kalb, *Congo Cables*, 15; Devlin, *Chief of Station*, 41–45.

36. For Khrushchev's letter to the Congo, see *Izvestia*, July 16, 1960, from which these quotes are taken. *Pravda*, July 14, 1960, reproduced the letter as excerpts of Khrushchev's press conference, in *SSSR i strany Afriki: 1946–1962 gg: Dokumenty i materialy*, 2 vols. [USSR and the countries of Africa, 1946–1960: documents and materials] (Moscow: Gosudarstvennoe Izdatel'stvo Politicheskoi Literatury, 1963), vol. 1, 553. See also Mazov, *Distant Front in the Cold War*, 90–96.

37. *Belgian Parliamentary Commission Report*, 592.

38. Ibid., 708–13.

39. For an interesting eyewitness account, see D'Lynn Waldron, journalist and scholar, available at www.dlwaldron.com.

40. Urquhart, *Hammarskjöld*, 9–23.

41. See the difference between memoranda of telephone conversations, Herter and Hammarskjöld, July 12, 1960, 12:50 p.m., HTCS, microfilm no. 11, 865–66, DDEL and Lodge and Hammarskjöld, July 12, 1960, 11:10 a.m., HTCS, microfilm no. 11, 863–64, DDEL. For Hammarskjöld's comments to his special representative Piero Spinelli, see Urquhart, *Hammarskjöld*, 394.

42. Urquhart, *Hammarskjöld*, 378–79, 389–92.

43. For the quote, see interview with Brian Urquhart, January 6, 2000, 4, in *The Complete Oral History Transcripts from U.N. Voices*, edited by United Nations Intellectual History Project (New York: United Nations, 2007). See also similar statements by Urquhart, June 1, 1984, UNOH, interview 2, 27; and Urquhart, *Hammarskjöld*,

369–388, esp. 385. For a good reflection on Hammarskjöld, see *New Routes* 16 (2011), "Special Issue: Dag Hammarskjöld and the United Nations: Vision and Legacy, 50 Years Later," www.life-peace.org/sajt/filer/pdf/New_Routes/NR112.pdf, esp. Thomas Weiss, "Global Leadership of the Secretaries and Generals," 21–24.

44. See Caroline Pruden, "Conditional Partners: Eisenhower, the United Nations, and the Search for a Permanent Peace" (PhD diss., Vanderbilt University, 1993); and Gary Ostrower, *The United Nations and the United States* (New York: Twayne, 1998).

45. Edmund Gullion, May 8, 1990, UNOH, 5–6.

46. *New York Times*, July 11 and 12, 1960; telephone conversation, Douglas and Burke, July 14, 1960, HTCS, microfilm no. 11, 830, DDEL.

47. State (Herter) to Leopoldville, July 12, 1960, *FRUS 1958–1960*, vol. 14, 298. Even Ralph Bunche, a light-skinned African American, sent alarming reports about the antiwhite sentiment in Leopoldville that put him in fear of his life. See Brian Urquhart, *Ralph Bunche: An American Life* (New York: W. W. Norton, 1993), 307–8.

48. *Belgian Parliamentary Commission Report*, 53–58.

49. Brussels (Burden) to State, July 9, 1960, *FRUS 1958–1960*, vol. 14, 284–86.

50. Belgium (Burden) to State, quoting Timberlake, July 10, 1960, *FRUS 1958–1960*, vol. 14, 287.

51. For a history of Soviet–U.N. relations, see Alexander Dallin, *The Soviet Union at the United Nations* (New York: Praeger, 1962), 36–41; and Khrushchev, *Memoirs*, 284–90. For a development of this idea, see M. Baturin, "The 11th Session of the U.N. General Assembly," *International Affairs* (Moscow), 1957, no. 1, 98. Svetlana Krasil'chikova, *O.O.N. i natsional'no-osvoboditel'noe dvizhenie* [The U.N. and the national liberation movement] (Moscow: Mezhdunarodnye Otnosheniia, 1964).

52. See Mark Kramer, "Declassified Materials from CPSU Central Committee Plenums," *Cahiers du Monde Russe* 40 (January–June 1999): 287–90; and Michael Tatu, *Power in the Kremlin: From Khrushchev to Kosygin* (New York: Viking Press, 1968), 109–14.

53. Statement of July 19, 1960, in *Survey of China Mainland Press* (U.S. Consulate, Hong Kong), July 25, 1960. See also *Renmin Ribao*, July 20, 1960; and editorial in *Survey of China Mainland Press*, July 26, 1960, which explicitly criticized the U.S.–U.N. role in the Congo.

54. Urquhart, *Hammarskjöld*, 394–95; telephone conversation, Eisenhower and Herter, July 13, 1960, *FRUS 1958–1960*, vol. 14, 300. This memorandum suggests that Hammarskjöld intended to go to the Security Council even upon receiving the first (oral) request.

55. In a gesture that might have been intended to placate the Congolese and emphasize the importance of his action, Hammarskjöld invoked Article 99 and called for a Security Council session to discuss the crisis as a "threat to international peace and security." See July 13, 1960, *SCOR*, 15th year, 873rd meeting, para. 23.

56. State (Herter) to USUN, July 13, 1960, *FRUS 1958–1960*, vol. 14, 303.

57. Security Council Resolution, July 14, 1960, document S/4387, reproduced by Higgins, *United Nations Peacekeeping*, 15; Hoskyns, *Congo: A Chronology*, 27.

58. Phrase used by Hammarskjöld in "Opening Statement to the Security Council," July 13, 1960, *SCOR*, 873rd meeting, para. 27. He said, "I personally wish to see the request of military assistance, which has been addressed to me by the Government of the Congo. Although I am fully aware of all the problems, difficulties and even

risks involved, I find that the stopgap arrangement envisaged by the Government of the Congo is preferable to any other formula. It is therefore my conclusion that the United Nations should accede to the request of the Government of the Congo and, in consequence, I strongly recommend the Council to Authorize the Secretary-General to take the necessary steps, in consultation with the Government of the Congo, to provide the Government with military assistance. . . . It would be understood that were the United Nations to act as proposed, the Belgian Government would see its way to a withdrawal."

59. See *Belgian Parliamentary Commission Report*, 82, 86; and www.africawithin. com/lumumba/conclusions.htm.

60. James, *Britain and the Congo Crisis*, 29–39; British Cabinet Meeting Minutes, July 14, 1960, available at www.nationalarchives.gov.uk.

61. Kalb, *Congo Cables*, 13.

62. Kevin Spooner, *Canada, the Congo Crisis and U.N. Peacekeeping* (Vancouver: University of British Columbia Press, 2009).

63. Note reproduced in *Pravda*, July 14, 1960; for an English version, see *Soviet News*, July 14, 1960.

64. For this rationale, see commentary by Cordier and Foote, *Public Papers of Dag Hammarskjöld*, 26. Hammarskjöld would try to delay the arrival of Guinean troops, but he realized this was politically impossible, and they soon arrived in the Congo.

65. Telephone conversation, Herter and Lodge, July 14, 1960, 9:05 a.m., HTCS, microfilm no. 11, 855, DDEL; July 13, 1960, *SCOR*, 15th year, 873rd meeting. See para. 241–42 for quote on Soviet reference to an absence of conditions; para. 103 for Soviet government statement; para. 95 for Lodge quote; and para. 222–25 for vote on the Soviet amendments.

66. Memorandum of Conversation with Canada's Undersecretary of External Affairs, Norman Robertson, August 6, 1960, Ot'del mezhdunarodniia otnosheniia (hereafter, OMO), delo 194, opis 6, por. 30, papka 78, AVPRF. For evidence that the Soviet Union believed the United States wanted to divide the Congo, see also I. Azarov, October 2, 1960, "K voprosu SWA v otnoshenii Kongo," opis 46, por. 65, papka 123, AVPRF; E. Primakov, "Ten' NATO nad Kongo," *Novoe Vremia* no. 6 1961, 15; Iu. Bochkarev, "Aktsiia O.O.N. v Kongo," *Novoe Vremia* no. 11 (March 10, 1961), 7; *Pravda*, July 6, 1960.

67. Khrushchev's telegram of July 15, 1960, in *SSSR i strany Afriki*, 560–63.

68. Kalb, *Congo Cables*, 14–16.

69. Memorandum of Discussion, 451st NSC meeting, July 15, 1960, *FRUS 1958– 1960*, vol. 14, 309–10.

70. Memorandum of Conversation, Herter and Scheyven, July 15, 1960, *FRUS 1958–1960*, vol. 14, 314–17.

71. Leopoldville (Timberlake) to State, July 18, 1960, *FRUS 1958–1960*, vol. 14, 322–23, including fn. 4, providing a translation of the Kasavubu and Lumumba letter. It is at this point, two weeks into the crisis and after the Congolese decision to turn to the Soviet Union, that Kalb argues the Eisenhower administration finally put events in the Congo high on the list of priorities. See Kalb, *Congo Cables*, 14–15. See also Urquhart, *Bunche*, 313.

72. Lumumba, "Leopoldville Radio Address," July 22, 1960, 279–85, in *Lumumba Speaks* ed. van Lierde. Lumumba's carrot-and-stick approach, also used in Stanleyville

in 1959, first led him to refer to the "brutal attack" of the Belgians backed by "financial groups and the enemies of our freedom." Later he reassured those who were willing to accept Congolese independence that "we have no bitterness toward the Belgians" and those of "good will" will be welcomed.

73. Memorandum of conference, Eisenhower and Herter, July 19, 1960, *FRUS 1958–1960*, vol. 14, 328–30. Eisenhower also commented that if the Soviets tried to send in combat forces, "we should try to get Hammarskjöld to say that no troops other than those requested by the United Nations will be allowed to come in."

74. Bomboko and Kanza later told Timberlake that they would try to persuade the Congolese Cabinet to oppose the ultimatum. Leopoldville (Timberlake) to State, July 18, 1960, *FRUS 1958–1960*, vol. 14, 322–23.

75. Quoted in situation report, July 19, 1960, Congo, box 3, DDEL.

76. Urquhart, *Hammarskjöld*, 399–401; *New York Times*, July 15, 1960.

77. For Gromyko's statement, see *Pravda*, July 20, 1960. The Soviet permanent representative at the United Nations, Vasili Kuznetsov, repeated his government's demand that the American military group be withdrawn; see July 20, 1960, *SCOR*, 15th year, 877th meeting, para. 171–73.

78. One such report was submitted to the Central Committee by M. I. Ibragimov, secretary of the Uzbekistan Komsomol, and V. B. Iordanskii correspondent for *Komsomolskaya Pravda*, who led a youth group to the Congo. The Soviet envoys had talked with the head of the MNC's executive branch, Dominic Tshiteya, and the leader of the MNC's youth group, Emanuel Nzuzi. Nzuzi, with Tshiteya's corroboration, told the Soviet delegation that "the position of Lumumba in the MNC is extremely unstable," that "party discipline does not exist,"and Lumumba's "parliamentary majority is unstable." M. Ibragimov and V. Iordanskii, "Report of the Soviet Youth Delegation to the Congo," July 19, 1960, 3–5, fond 5, opis 50, dela 257, RGANI. See Lemarchand, *Political Awakening*, 205, for Tshiteya's background.

79. USUN (Lodge) to State, August 7, 1960, *FRUS 1958–1960*, vol. 14, 397.

80. Dallin, *Soviet Union and the United Nations*, 140.

81. For coverage of the humanitarian aid, see *Pravda*, July 17–20, 1960. Khrushchev's telegram offering this aid went directly to Lumumba. Devlin, *Chief of Station*, 25–26; Mazov, *Distant Front in the Cold War*, 107–108.

82. Urquhart, *Hammarskjöld*, 405.

83. Security Council Resolution, July 22, 1960, document S/4405, reproduced by Higgins, *United Nations Peacekeeping*, 17.

84. Kuznetsov said that "the restoration of law and order" will undoubtedly "be effected by the Central Government . . . and by no one else," implying that it was for the central government to decide how best to restore order. See July 21, 1960, *SCOR*, 15th year, 879th meeting, para. 116, for Kuznetsov's statement; and Higgins, *United Nations Peacekeeping*, 18. See the commentary by Cordier and Foote, *Public Papers of Dag Hammarskjöld*, 43–45; they noted that personality might have played a role because Kuznetsov "was a man who used moderate language in representing the Soviet position," and thus his statements did not attract as much attention as they deserved.

85. *Izvestia*, July 21, 1960.

86. July 21, 1960, *SCOR*, 15th year, 877th meeting, para. 193.

87. The major battle was between Wigny and Gilson. See *Belgian Parliamentary Commission Report*, 52, 63–64, 458; and Gerard-Libois, *Katanga Secession*, 102–5.

88. Higgins, *United Nations Peacekeeping*, 88.

Chapter 5

1. See State (Herter) to USUN, July 20, 1960, *FRUS 1958–1960*, vol. 14, 334–35, and Memorandum of Discussion, 452ndnd NSC meeting, July 21, 1960, *FRUS 1958–1960*, vol. 14, 338–41. For characterizations of Allen Dulles, see *Time*, August 3, 1953; and James Srodes, *Allen Dulles: Master of Spies* (Washington, D.C: Regnery, 1999), 3.

2. Alexandr Fursenko and Timothy Naftali, *"One Hell of A Gamble": Khrushchev, Castro and Kennedy, 1958–1964* (New York: W. W. Norton, 1997), 39–55.

3. Anonymous, "Since the breakdown of the Summit Conference," n.d., WHO, staff secretary, subject series, State Department subseries, box 4, June–July 1960 (4) folder, DDEL. Notations suggest that this document was circulated on or after July 19, 1960 (declassified June 1997). See also Paris (Wolf) to State, August 10, 1960, telegram, WHO staff secretary, international series, Belgium, DDEL.

4. Circular from State to Certain Diplomatic Missions, July 21, 1960, *FRUS 1958–1960*, vol. 14, 344–45; State (Herter) to Leopoldville, August 12, 1960, *FRUS 1958–1960*, 410. Historians have overwhelmingly portrayed Eisenhower as pro-Belgian (especially in comparison with Kennedy), but have differed over the reasons underlying this strategy. Gibbs argued that Eisenhower did little to secure U.N. presence in Katanga; Gibbs, *Political Economy of Third World Intervention*, 90–94. Kalb, *Congo Cables*, 31–32, and Weissman, *American Foreign Policy in the Congo*, 66–67, characterized Eisenhower as strongly pro-Belgian and suggested that the president left open the option to recognize Katanga in the disastrous case of the communists ensconcing themselves in Leopoldville.

5. *Belgian Parliamentary Commission Report*, 458.

6. Urquhart, *Hammarskjöld*, 407; telephone conversation, Lodge and Herter, July 26, 1960, Herter Papers, box 13, DDEL; Kalb, *Congo Cables*, 34.

7. See O'Brien, *To Katanga and Back*, 50–54. The other members of the Congo Club, obviously less influential, included C.V. Narasimhan (India), Sir Alexander MacFarquhar (United Kingdom), General Rikhye (India), and Francis Nwokedi (Nigeria). For another discussion of the Congo Club, see James O. C. Jonah, "Then and Now: Ralph Bunche and the Integrity of the International Civil Service," transcript of remarks by Jonah at the final Ralph Bunche Lecture series at the Dag Hammarskjöld Auditorium, February 5, 2004, http://web.gc.cuny.edu/ralphbunchecentenary/then_now_trans.pdf. Jonah also includes Henry Labouisse. See also Princeton Lyman, "Ralph Bunche's International Legacy: The Middle East, Congo and International Peacekeeping," *Journal of Negro Education* 73, no. 2 (April 2004): 162–65. For Cordier, see also Carole J. L. Collins, "The Cold War Comes to Africa: Cordier and the 1960 Congo Crisis," *Journal of International Affairs* 47, no. 1 (Summer 1993): 243–69.

8. Richard Welch, *Response to Revolution: The United States and the Cuban Revolution, 1959–1961* (Chapel Hill: University of North Carolina Press, 1985), 34–36.

9. It was at this meeting that Lumumba brought up the Detwiler affair. Lumumba had signed a bogus agreement with Edgar Detwiler, based on the latter's false representation that he was working with the support of the State Department. Lumumba apparently believed Detwiler, but quickly disavowed the contract once he learned of Detwiler's past. *Pravda* expressed surprise at the deal, and perhaps the affair still suggested to Moscow Lumumba's willingness to deal with the West. For a biography of Detwiler, see *Time*, August 1, 1960. This report also suggests that rumors were circulating that communists agreed to this to try to discredit all Western businesses.

10. Memorandum of Conversation, Lumumba and Herter, July 27, 1960, *FRUS 1958–1960*, vol. 14, 359–66.

11. *New York Times*, July 29, 1960.

12. Telephone conversation, Herter and Burden, 9:00 a.m. and 1:35 p.m., August 2, 1960, Herter Papers, box 13, DDEL, restated less directly in Burden to Herter, August 4, 1960, *FRUS 1958–1960*, vol. 14, 384.

13. Memorandum of Conversation, July 15, 1960, among Belgian ambassador Louis Scheyven, Satterthwaite, and McBride, *FRUS 1958–1960*, vol. 14, 314–16; Helmreich, *United States Relations with Belgium and the Congo*, 222–31.

14. Gerard-Libois, *Katanga Secession*, 127, 302. The telegram was from the minister of justice and leader of the Balubakat cartel (of northern Katanga), Prosper Mwamba-Ilunga. Mwamba walked out of the provincial assembly and threatened to set up his own government in Katanga in support of a unified central government. In September, he set up his own government with Lumumba's help, known as the Lualuba government, then in 1962 would form the government of North Katanga.

15. See *New York Times*, July 29, 1960; and Edgerton, *Troubled Heart of Africa*, 192, quoting "An Analytical Chronology of the Congo Crisis," January 25, 1961, box 27, Congo, NSF, JFKL; now also available at http://www.jfklibrary.org/Asset-Viewer/Archives/JFKPOF-114-015.aspx.

16. Borstelmann, *Cold War and the Color Line*, 129–31.

17. *Current Biography 1961*, 453–55.

18. Memorandum of Discussion, 454th meeting, NSC, August 1, 1960, *FRUS 1958–1960*, vol. 14, 372–75.

19. Kalb, *Congo Cables*, 38.

20. Telephone conversation, Herter and Labouisse, August 4, 1960, Herter Papers, box 13, DDEL. Eisenhower mused over "the psychological importance of recommending to the coming session of the Congress some additional Defense expenditures." See memorandum (Herter) to Gates, July 20, 1960, WHO staff secretary, subject series, State Department subseries, box 4, DDEL.

21. Telephone conversation, Herter and Burden, August 2, 1960, Herter Papers, box 13, DDEL; and Urquhart, *Hammarskjöld*, 415–16.

22. "Statement to the Press," August 10, 1960, *SCOR*, 15th year, suppl. for July, August, and September 1960, 58; and Telegram to the President of the Security Council, August 7, 1960, *SCOR*, document S/4421, 90. See also Lumumba, "Support for Attempts at Secession," August 9, 1960, in *Lumumba Speaks*, ed. van Lierde, 326–27.

23. *Courrier Africain*, September 30, 1960; *New York Times*, August 14 and 21, 1960. For Belgian support, see *Belgian Parliamentary Commission Report*, 97–112.

24. *Belgian Parliamentary Commission Report*, 113.

25. Days after this meeting on July 29, the king (on August 5) demanded the resignation of Eyskens, but it was agreed that Eyskens would reformulate his cabinet. *Belgian Parliamentary Commission Report*, 64–68, 93.

26. Urquhart, *Bunche*, 321–25.

27. *New York Times*, August 4, 1960.

28. Second Report of the Secretary-General, August 6, 1960, *SCOR*, 15th year, suppl. for July, August, and September 1960, document S/4417, 53.

29. Letter from Representative of the USSR to President of Security Council, August 6, 1960, official statement of the Soviet government, August 6, 1960, enclosed,

SCOR, 15th year, suppl. July, August, September 1960, document S/4418, 82–83. See also *Soviet News*, August 8, 1960. The Soviet press had already begun to talk about the U.N. trusteeship being established over the Congo; see *Pravda*, July 31, 1960.

30. Bomboko claimed that the opposition party Cartel Katangaise received 70 percent of the vote, when in fact the figure was closer to 50 percent. See Gerard-Libois, *Katanga Secession*, 65.

31. August 8, 1960, *SCOR*, 15th year, 885th meeting, paras. 8–15.

32. For Security Council Resolution, August 9, 1960, document S/4426, see Higgins, *United Nations Peacekeeping*, 19–20.

33. *Pravda*, August 11, 1960.

34. Grinevsky, *Tysiacha i odin den' Nikity Sergeevicha*, 334–35.

35. For the Soviet government statement, see *Pravda*, August 1, 1960; see also Soviet Representative Platon Morozov to President of Security Council, August 4, 1960, *SCOR*, 15th year, suppl. July, August, September 1960, document S/4419, 44. See also Mazov, *Distant Front in the Cold War*, 103.

36. Kirpichenko, *Razvedka*, 97–98.

37. Shelepin to CC, August 13, 1960, fond 5, opis 30, delo 336, RGANI.

38. Rajeshwar Dayal, *Mission for Hammarskjöld: The Congo Crisis* (Princeton, N.J.: Princeton University Press, 1976).

39. Shelepin to CC, August 13, 1960, fond 5, opis 30, delo 336, RGANI; A. I. Pozharov, "KGB i Partiia (1954–1964)" [The KGB and the Party (1954–1964)], *Otechestvenaia Istoriia* no. 4 (1999): 172.

40. Zhukov to CC, April 29, 1959, fond 5, opis 33, delo 94, rolik 7792, 190, AVPRF; "Georgy Zhukov," *Current Biography 1960*, 472.

41. Kalb, *Congo Cables*, 61.

42. Protokoll Nr. 34/60, "Der Sitzungdes Politbüros des Zentralkomitees am Dienstage, dem 9.8.60 im Sitzungssaal des Politbüros," DY 30, J IV 2/2/715, Bundesarchiv. I have been unable to find further information on representative Thun, but did come across a note to an F. Thun and had reason to suspect it was the same person.

43. Protokoll Nr. 35/60, "Der Sitzung des Politbüros des Zentralkomitees am Dienstage, dem 16.8.[60] im Sitzungssaal des Politbüros," DY 30, J IV 2/2/716, Bundesarchiv.

44. *New York Times*, August 2, 5, and 7, 1960; Nkrumah, *Challenge*, 28–34; Thompson, *Ghana's Foreign Policy*, 125–26, 135–37.

45. Hammarskjöld, "Memorandum on Implementation of the Security Council Resolution of August 9, 1960, Operative Paragraph 4," *SCOR*, 15th year, suppl. for July, August, and September 1960, document S/4417/add 6, 64–71.

46. Urquhart, *Hammarskjöld*, 426–27.

47. Hammarskjöld insisted that he did consult with the Congolese delegation in New York, including the vice prime minister, the foreign minister, and the minister to the United Nations. He further maintained that "consultation with responsible, constitutionally responsible members of the Cabinet concerning a certain question covers the whole need for consultation with the government." See September 18, 1960, *SCOR*, 4th emergency special session, 859th meeting, para. 158.

48. See the exchange between Lumumba and Hammarskjöld, August 14–15, 1960, *SCOR*, 15th year, suppl. for July, August, and September 1960, document S/4417, add. 7, 71–77.

49. August 18, 1960, *SCOR*, 15th year, suppl. for July, August, September 1960, document S/4417, add. 8 plus annexes i, ii, and iii, 77–79.

50. Synopsis, August 16, 1960, WHO, staff secretary subject series, alphabetical series, box 14, DDEL.

51. State (Dillon) to USUN, August 16, 1960, *FRUS 1958–1960*, vol. 14, 413–14.

52. Synopsis, August 30, 1960, WHO staff secretary, subject series, alphabetical subseries, box 14, DDEL.

53. USUN (Lodge) to State, August 26, 1960, *FRUS 1958–1960*, vol. 14, 445.

54. Memorandum of Discussion (Johnson), 456th NSC meeting, August 18, 1960, *FRUS 1958–1960*, vol. 14, 423.

55. See Hammarskjöld's Presentation to the Security Council, August 21, 1960, *SCOR*, 887th meeting, esp. para. 18, 29, 33, 36.

56. Memorandum by the Secretary-General on the Organization of the U.N. Civilian [ONUC] Operation in the Republic of the Congo, August 21, 1960, *SCOR*, 15th year, suppl. for July, August, and September, document S/4417, add. 5, 60–64.

57. Letter from Kuznetsov to Hammarskjöld, August 21, 1960, *SCOR*, 15th year, suppl. for July, August, and September, document S/4450, para. 13, 19; Higgins, *United Nations Peacekeeping*, 248. Letter from Kuznetsov to Hammarskjöld enclosing official statement of the Soviet government, August 20, 1960, *SCOR*, 15th year, suppl. for July, August, and September, document S/4446, 102–104.

58. August 12, 1960, *SCOR*, 15th year, 887th meeting, para. 70, 90–95. According to Urquhart the Soviets now opposed such a committee, despite the fact that Hammarskjöld professed to be following their advice in setting one up in the first place. Hammarskjöld's shift to talking about an "advisory" committee (as opposed to a supervisory one) is probably a key to Soviet opposition. For a Soviet interpretation suggesting disappointment that Lumumba did not carry through with his demand for entry into Katanga, see Vladimir Brykin, "Operatsiia OON v Kongo" [The UN Operation in the Congo], *Narody Azii i Afriki*, no. 6 (1966), 39–40.

59. Kalb, *Congo Cables*, 26, 64–65.

60. Leopoldville to Director, August 18, 1960, partially reproduced in U.S. Congress, *Alleged Assassination Plots*, 14–15. For more extensive quote here, see Richard Bissell, *Reflections of a Cold Warrior: From Yalta to the Bay of Pigs* (New Haven, Conn.: Yale University Press, 1996), 143.

61. Hellström, quote from his interview with Devlin, in "Instant Air Force," 18–19.

62. Kalb, *Congo Cables*, 53.

63. Edgerton, *Troubled Heart of Africa*, 193.

64. NSC minutes, August 18, 1960, in U.S. Congress, *Alleged Assassination Plots*, 58; and Memorandum of Discussion at 456th meeting of NSC, August 18, 1960, *FRUS 1958–1960*, vol. 14, 421–24.

65. For quotes, see U.S. Congress, *Alleged Assassination Plots*, 15, and see also 54–59; Memorandum of Discussion at 456th meeting of NSC, August 18, 1960, *FRUS 1958–1960*, vol. 14, 421–24; Richard Bissell, *Reflections of a Cold Warrior*, 142–44.

66. U.S. Congress, *Alleged Assassination Plots*, 15.

67. Cable is reproduced in ibid.; brackets found in original. The report noted that it was a rarity for Allen Dulles to sign cables and this in itself illustrated the importance of the policy.

68. Kalb, *Congo Cables*, 65; U.S. Congress, *Alleged Assassination Plots*, 16; Devlin, *Chief of Station*, 63.

69. Eyskens's threat came just after a reportedly bitter cabinet meeting in Brussels. See *New York Times*, August 10 and 11, 1960. The Belgian threat turned out to be a bluff, and by January 1961 Brussels had recanted and was even talking about strengthening the alliance. In "The United States, Belgium and the Congo crisis of 1960," *Review of Politics* 29, no. 2 (1967), 242–43, Lawrence Kaplan discussed the Belgian reaction to Lumumba's visit and U.S. policy during the Congo crisis in general. For the "NATO reflex" among members of the Eisenhower administration, see Weissman, *American Foreign Policy in the Congo*, 74, 76.

70. See David Gibbs, "The United Nations, International Peacekeeping and the Question of 'Impartiality': Revisiting the Congo Operation of 1960," *Journal of Modern African Studies* 38 (2000): 359–82; and Gibbs, *Political Economy of Third World Intervention*, 86, 238 n. 43, who cites an untitled U.N. report of October 18, 1960. See also the discussion of Belgian influence in Leopoldville in the *Hansard Debates*, December 21, 1960, volume 632, cc 1336–65, http://hansard.millbanksystems.com/commons/1960/dec/21/united-nations-and-congo.

71. *Belgian Parliamentary Commission Report*, 128–29, 138, 437–41; De Witte, *Assassination of Lumumba*, 25, 37.

72. Ibid., 39, and esp. Weber to Lefebure, October 19, 1960, 473.

73. The meeting included Cameroon, Congo-Brazzaville, Ghana, Guinea, Liberia, Mali, Morocco, Somali Republic, Sudan, Togoland, Tunisia, and the UAR.

74. Khrushchev to Conference of Independent African Nations, August 25, 1960. For the English version, see *Soviet News*, August 26, 1960, and for the Russian version, see *SSSR i strany Afrimki*, vol. 1, 612–14.

75. *New York Times*, August 29, 1960. August 27 was the same day that Zhukov arrived in the Congo.

76. "Summary" by African Department, sent from Ia. Malik to Gromyko, August 31, 1960, and from Gromyko to Suslov, September 1, 1960, fond 5, opis 30, delo 337, list 124–26, RGANI; reprinted in Davidson and Mazov, *Rossiia i Afrika*, 246–47. For the quote, see Mazov, "Soviet Aid to the Gizenga Government," 427, and Mazov, *Distant Front in the Cold War*, 97–98. See also *Izvestia*, August 14 and September 3, 1960; *Pravda*, September 11, 1960; and Kalb, *Congo Cables*, 56. The AN-2, or Antonov Colt, was a small biplane used for transport. The AN-12, or Antonov Cub, was a four-engine transport plane slightly larger than the C-130, which the United States used in the Congo. By comparison, the Ilyushin-14 was a twin-engine transport. For aircraft details, see http://www.topedge.com/panels/aircraft/sites/gustin/sov/AN2ANTON.html, AN12ANTO.html, IL14ILYU.html (October 2004), and http://www.kiwiaircraftimages.simplenet.com/an12.htm.

77. Mazov, *Distant Front in the Cold War*, 105.

78. See the proposed "Accord entre l'Union soviétique et la République du Congo," n.d., given by CRISP, *Congo 1960: Annexes et biographies* (Brussels: CRISP, 1961), 56. The accord includes terms that are remarkably similar to what was actually given, but seems to have been written after the fact since it was with Gizenga acting as a representative, and therefore may have been drafted after Lumumba's dismissal.

79. G. Raiskii, "Ghana's Position on the Congolese Question," November 18, 1960, Referentura po Ghana, opis 6, por. 28, papka 6, AVPRF.

80. Kanza, *Rise and Fall of Patrice Lumumba*, 273; Van Lierde comments in *Lumumba Speaks*, 354.

81. Hoskyns, *Congo since Independence*, 186–94.

82. See Hammarskjöld, "Third Report to the Security Council: Belgium Delays Withdrawal," August 30, 1960, *Public Papers of Dag Hammarskjöld*, 143–47.

83. State (Herter) to USUN, September 2, 1960, *FRUS 1958–1960*, vol. 14, 456–57. Herter expressed apprehension that Lumumba with increased Soviet aid might be able to take over Katanga.

84. For evidence of the growing concern about Soviet shipments to the Congo, see State (Dillon) to USUN, August 27, 1960, *FRUS 1958–1960*, vol. 14, 446–47, Johnson, Memorandum of Discussion at 458th meeting of NSC, September 7, 1960, *FRUS 1958–1960*, vol. 14, 460–62; Boggs, 459th NSC meeting, September 15, 1960, *FRUS 1958–1960*, vol. 14, 489–90; and USUN (Cook) to State, September 7, 1960, *FRUS 1958–1960*, vol. 14, 464–65, describing conversation with Wieschhoff, U.S. member of the U.N. Secretariat.

85. Deputy undersecretary of state (Hare) to Herter, August 30, 1960, *FRUS 1958–1960*, vol. 14, and esp. fn. 3 therein, Satterthwaite to Hare, September 9, 1960, outlines contingency plans, 449–50. After maintaining the U.N. assistance, the working group proposed, second, encouraging the African states to create a new international framework for assistance, and third, U.S. economic bilateral aid to the Congo. Only fourth did it suggest direct U.S. military aid.

86. Joint Chiefs of Staff (Burke) to Gates, September 2, 1960, *FRUS 1958–1960*, vol. 14, 453–55.

87. Fursenko and Naftali, *"One Hell of a Gamble,"* 39–40. See also August 27, 1990 interview with E. B. Potter, author of a biography of Burke, http://www.c-span-video.org/program/13701-1.

88. State (Herter) to USUN, September 3, 1960, *FRUS 1958–1960*, vol. 14, 455–56.

89. De Witte, *Assassination of Lumumba*, 18, for Eyskens's quote, and *Belgian Parliamentary Commission Report*, 118, 123–26. The two agents were Etienne Davignon and Jacques Westhof. The Parliamentary Commission argued nevertheless that the dismissal "fell from the sky"; 125. argued that he was primarily interested in finding grounds for reconciliation among Kasavubu, Lumumba, and Tshombe; see Jef van Bilsen, *Congo 1945–65: La fin d'un colonie* (Brussels: CRISP, 1993), 255–74. He also gave no indication that he knew until moments before Kasavubu's intention regarding the dismissal of Lumumba. He does suggest, however, that Kasavubu's plans, especially regarding the reformulation of his government, were not well thought out. For reasons of safety, van Bilsen left the Congo shortly after Kasavubu's announcement, fleeing first to Brazzaville, and then returning to Belgium.

90. Weissman, "Opening the Secret Files"; Weissman, "Extraordinary Rendition," 203.

91. Devlin, *Chief of Station*, 64.

92. Collins, "The Cold War Comes to Africa: Cordier and the 1960 Congo Crisis," 260–61; Lise Namikas, "History through Documents and Memory: Report on a Critical Oral History Conference of the Congo Crisis, 1960–1961," Cold War International History Project, Woodrow Wilson International Center for Scholars, Washington, 2004, http://www.wilsoncenter.org/article/history-through-documents-and-memory-report-cwihp-critical-oral-history-conference-the-congo.

93. See Dayal, *Mission for Hammarskjöld*, 283–84, 296–97. For the characterization, see also *Time*, June 2, 1961.

Chapter 6

1. In his nervousness, Kasavubu referred to Lumumba as first burgomaster. The slip arose because Kasavubu had used the tactic of dismissal previously in February 1960 when he ousted rival Daniel Kanza as first burgomaster of Leopoldville.

2. The ministers included Antoine Gizenga, Remy Mwamba, Christophe Gbenye, Anicet Kashamura, Antoine Bolamba, and Jacques Lumbala.

3. For the text of the speech, see Charles-André Gilis, *Kasavubu au coeur du drame congolaise* (Brussels: Europe-Afrique, 1964), 276–77. The extent to which Kasavubu was willing to negotiate with Lumumba after September 5 remains a mystery. Catherine Hoskyns, a careful student of Congolese politics, suspected that Kasavubu did not intend to exclude Lumumba "permanently from power" but only to discipline him for his "authoritarian methods." See Hoskyns, *United Nations Peacekeeping*, 199. For the influences on Kasavubu, see the account by Justine M'Poya Kasa-Vubu, *Kasa-vubu et le Congo indépendant* (Brussels: Le Cri Éditions, 1997), 49–51. Although only eleven years of age at the time of the crisis, Justine Kasa-Vubu provided an insightful account in part based on access to private archives.

4. Kanza, *Rise and Fall of Patrice Lumumba*, 286.

5. For quotes from Lumumba's speech, see *Lumumba Speaks*, ed. van Lierde, 353–57. For particularly good eyewitness accounts, see Kanza, *Rise and Fall of Patrice Lumumba*, 288; and Serge Michel, *Uhuru Lumumba* (Paris: René Julliard, 1962), 206–8.

6. *Lumumba Speaks*, ed. van Lierde, 399–400; Kanza, *Rise and Fall of Patrice Lumumba*, 300.

7. See commentary by Cordier and Foote, *Public Papers of Dag Hammarskjöld*, 176. In the Chamber of Representatives, Hoskyns records, in *Congo since Independence*, 203, that there were "about" 90 members out of 137 present for the gathering. Conakat had not attended the parliament, since Katanga's declaration of independence and MNC-K also regularly boycotted the proceedings. They accounted for a total of 16 absences. Other members were caught away from Leopoldville and unable to return speedily enough. In the Senate between 50 and 60 were present out of a total of 84, with 11 Conakat and MNC-K regularly boycotting the proceedings. A question remains whether a quorum was met at the joint session of parliament. Congolese parliamentary records list a total of 113 present, but journalists present suggested 90 or 95 to be a more accurate number (which coincides with the initial reporting of the vote). The official records, apparently, were later changed to reflect 88 in favor and 25 against.

8. Devlin, *Chief of Station*, 70.

9. Urquhart, *Hammarskjöld*, 441. "People on the spot," Hammarskjöld wrote his temporary representative a few days before September 5, 1960, "might commit themselves to what the Secretary-General could not justify doing himself—taking the risk of being disowned when it no longer mattered." See commentary by Cordier and Foote, *Public Papers of Dag Hammarskjöld*, 160, for quote.

10. Collins, "Cold War Comes to Africa," 261. Years later, Cordier defended his action by saying that the closures were designed to thwart Lumumba's "communist" ambitions of defeating Kasai and then moving his troops to Leopoldville to battle for power.

11. For Cordier's own account, see Andrew W. Cordier, "Challenge in the Congo," *Think* 31 (July–August 1965): 27. Kalb, *Congo Cables*, 73–75, suggested that Cordier tried to find guidance from Hammarskjöld but was told to use his own judgment. See also Collins, "The Cold War Comes to Africa: Cordier and the 1960 Congo Crisis," 260–64; Urquhart, *Hammarskjöld*, 110, on the contrary, argued that Hammarskjöld sent the message as a farsighted attempt to prevent violence. Also see Dayal, *Mission for Hammarskjöld*, 31–47, 172; and Kwame Nkrumah, *Challenge of the Congo* (New York: International Publishers, 1967), 39–44.

12. USUN (Cook) to State, September 7, 1960, *FRUS 1958–1960*, vol. 14, 464.

13. See the proposed "Accord entre l'Union soviétique et la République du Congo," n.d., in CRISP, *Congo 1960, annexes et biographies* (Brussels: CRISP, 1961), 56.

14. Mohamed Hassanein Heikal, *The Cairo Documents: The Inside Story of Nasser and his Relationship with World Leaders, Rebels and Statesmen* (Garden City, N.Y.: Doubleday, 1973), 176; Memorandum of Discussion (Johnson), September 7, 1960, *FRUS 1958–1960*, vol. 14, 461.

15. Leopoldville (Timberlake) to State, October 19, 1960, *FRUS 1958–1960*, vol. 14, 534–36; Dayal reproduced the telegram sent to him by Hammarskjöld at the end of the Security Council discussion on September 16, 1960, in *Mission for Hammarskjöld*, 83; State (Herter) to USUN, September 12, 1960, *FRUS 1958–1960*, vol. 14, 481–82.

16. [Notes by Jan Terfve], n.d., "Note sur le contact réalisée à Leopoldville en septembre 1960 avec l'Ambassadeur de Chine au Caire en mission au Congo," Centre des archives communistes en Belgique (hereafter, CarCob), Congo (hereafter, CO-5). I am grateful to Erik Kennes for providing these documents.

17. Larkin, *China and Africa*, 54–55.

18. Situation report, October 3, 1960, October 5, 1960, Congo, box 3, DDEL. Mobutu released a letter from Lumumba and Gizenga to the Chinese, found during a brief arrest of Lumumba on September 12. Twenty-nine members of the MNC, including several members of parliament and the minister of communication, Songolo, took the occasion to break with Lumumba, thus fueling the misperception in Washington that they were primarily opposed to Lumumba's communist ambitions. In reality, Lumumba's differences with the parliament were far greater than those stemming from relations with communists, as they stemmed from the growing separatist movements. News published in the *New York Times*, October 1, 1960, makes the connection between the minister's break with Lumumba and his appeal to the communists. However, in the Second Progress Report, November 2, 1960, *SCOR*, 15th session, suppl. for October, November, and December 1960, document S/4557, para. 20, Dayal cites estrangement with Songolo as resulting from growing separatist movements at this time. Lumumba and Gizenga would later deal harshly with Songolo, arresting him during a trip to Orientale. The Congolese representative at the United Nations, Cardoso, cited the harsh treatment of Lumumba in December as payment in kind for the treatment of Songolo. December 8–9, 1960, *SCOR*, 915th meeting, para. 22, 35, 43. See also Kasavubu's letter to Hammarskjöld, December 7, 1960, *SCOR*, suppl. for October, November, December 1960, document S/4572, annex 3, 73–74.

19. Gizenga's letter was dated October 8, 1960. Quoted by Schatten, *Communism in Africa*, 211, from *Die Weltwoche*, November 11, 1960. The letter and sum of £1 million in aid to Gizenga was also quoted and given credence by Larkin in *China and*

Africa, 58, fn. 61, possibly explaining why the Chinese did not contribute to the Afro-Asian People's Solidarity Organization in early 1961; see also 54–55. Western sources reported that China had agreed to supply £1 million. That amount was wildly exaggerated, and Stanleyville would have to wait to see any traces of aid from China.

20. USUN (Cook) to State, September 7, 1960, *FRUS 1958–1960*, vol. 14, 464–65.

21. *New York Times*, September 12 and 13, 1960.

22. NSC, 458th meeting, September 7, 1960, *FRUS 1958–1960*, vol. 14, 460.

23. Memorandum (Boggs) of Discussion, September 21, reprinted in editorial note, *FRUS 1958–1960*, vol. 14, 496–97; Leopoldville (Timberlake) to State, September 26, 1960, *FRUS 1958–1960*, vol. 14, 503– 506.

24. See USUN (Wadsworth) to State, September 10, 1960, *FRUS 1958–1960*, vol. 14, 475; and State (Herter) to USUN, September 12, 1960, *FRUS 1958–1960*, vol. 14, 479–80, where the State Department argued that parliament cannot overrule the chief of state; USUN (Barco) to State, October 22, 1960, *FRUS 1958–1960*, vol. 14, 543. On Ileo and Belgium, see *Belgian Parliamentary Commission Report*, 136–39.

25. Memorandum, 458th meeting, NSC, September 7, 1960, *FRUS 1958–1960*, vol. 14, 462.

26. USUN (Cook) to State, September 7, 1960, *FRUS 1958–1960*, vol. 14, 466. For Herter's follow-up, see memorandum, September 9, 1960, *FRUS 1958–1960*, vol. 14, 470.

27. Hammarskjöld sent a draft statement for Eisenhower's possible use at the press conference, but the administration preferred a tougher statement prepared by the State Department. See USUN (Cook) to State, September 7, 1960, *FRUS 1958–1960*, vol. 14, 465–68. See also U.S. Congress, *Alleged Assassination Plots*, 62.

28. Eisenhower press conference, September 7, 1960, *Public Papers of the President*, 284. Eisenhower reiterated this justification in his memoirs: Dwight D. Eisenhower, *Waging Peace, 1956–1961: The White House Years* (Garden City, N.Y.: Doubleday, 1965), 575. The closing of the airports was necessary, he wrote in his memoirs, because Soviet pilots in the Congo "might be military personnel prepared to engage in military activities in support of Lumumba." The president continued, "The Soviet invasion received a setback the first week of September when President Kasavubu dismissed Prime Minister Lumumba. . . . The move was engineered awkwardly, according to reports reaching me." Lumumba "seized" the radio station "to issue an impassioned plea to the Congolese population." See also the account in *Christian Science Monitor,* August 31, 1960, quoting the State Department as saying that the Congo would have to be "pacified" in order to prevent certain communist domination.

29. Memorandum, September 9, 1960, *FRUS 1958–1960*, vol. 14, 468–71. Later in September, Twinning would be replaced by General Lyman Lemnitzer.

30. *Pravda*, September 8–11, 1960; Legvold, *Soviet Policy in West Africa*, 78–79.

31. Burlatsky, *Khrushchev and the First Russian Spring*, 158.

32. Statement of September 14, 1960, in *Survey of China Mainland Press*, September 21, 1960, 18–19.

33. Report from September 15, 1960, ibid.; and report of Mandungo visit, October 15, 1960, in *Survey of China Mainland Press*, October 21, 1960, 25–27.

34. *Pravda*, September 11, 1960.

35. September 12, 1960, *SCOR*, 15th year, suppl. for July, August, and September, document S/4506, 160–61; Dallin, *The Soviet Union and the United Nations*, 143.

36. Khrushchev, *Memoirs*, 260–265.

37. September 9, 1960, *SCOR*, 15th year, 896th meeting, para. 91.

38. Ibid., paras. 91–92, 101–102.

39. Several days in advance of the opening session he released a proposed plan for financial and technical aid to the central government, including reorganization of the ANC, in fulfillment of the July 14 resolution. See esp. September 9, 1960, *SCOR*, 15th year, 896th meeting, para. 83–111; for quotes, see para. 110. See also September 10, 1960, *SCOR*, 15th year, 897th meeting, para. 62–63. For the report itself, see September 7, 1960, *SCOR*, 15th year, suppl. for July, August, and September, document S/4482, 135–40; and Urquhart, *Hammarskjöld*, 448–50.

40. USUN (Cook) to State, September 5, 1960, *FRUS 1958–1960*, vol. 14, 458.

41. Zorin statement, September 14, 1960, *SCOR*, 15th year, 901st meeting, para. 2–70, esp. 33, 38, and 67; a Russian version is available in *SSSR i strany Afriki*, 639–55.

42. For U.S. support of Hammarskjöld's actions, see September 15, 1960, *SCOR*, 15th year, 902nd meeting, para. 24, 39–44.

43. See discussion about this phrase in September 15, 1960, *SCOR*, 903rd meeting, para. 86–87. See also Satterthwaite's comments in Memorandum of Discussion at the Department of State–Joint Chiefs of Staff meeting, September 9, 1960, *FRUS 1958–1960*, vol. 14, 469. For a biography of Wadsworth, see *Time*, August 22, 1960.

44. Kalb, *Congo Cables*, 88–89; Higgins, *United Nations Peacekeeping*, 21–22; commentary by Cordier and Foote, *Public Papers of Dag Hammarskjöld*, 185; Dayal, *Mission for Hammarskjöld*, 98–100.

45 Hoskyns, *United Nations Peacekeeping*, 217; *Izvestia*, September 16, 1960, reported Mobutu's call to end the operation in Kasai and Katanga, illustrating his quick decision to pull his support from the operation. See also *New York Times*, September 6, 1960.

46. Michela Wrong, *In the Footsteps of Mr. Kurtz : Living on the Brink of Disaster in Mobutu's Congo* (New York: HarperPerennial, 2002), 72–77.

47. Namikas, "History through Documents and Memory"; Devlin, *Chief of Station*, 72–86.

48. Weissman, "Extraordinary Rendition," 203, 209.

49. Andrew Tully, *CIA: The Inside Story* (New York: Morrow, 1962), 178–86. In State (Herter) to USUN, October 26, 1960, *FRUS 1958–1960*, vol. 14, 555, Herter stated that "Mobutu, who in our judgement still retains good deal of strength with CNA [i.e., ANC], must be, for lack of anyone with comparable strength, force which maintains caretaker government. We believe he can be brought around to cooperating." Leopoldville (Timberlake) to State, September 26, 1960, *FRUS 1958–1960*, vol. 14, 503–506.

50. Leopoldville (Timberlake) to State, September 16, 1960, *FRUS 1958–1960*, vol. 14, 491. Kashamura, in *De Lumumba aux colonels*, 145–46, claimed that on September 9, Timberlake dropped by Lumumba's home and proposed that if he gave his assurances that the Soviets would be expelled and if he broke relations with the socialist countries (Ghana, Guinea, UAR), then the United States would provide assistance to his government.

51. See editorial notes regarding Boggs, 459th NSC meeting, September 15, 1960, and Boggs, 460th NSC meeting, *FRUS 1958–1960*, September 21, 1960, vol. 14, 489–90 and 496–97.

52. Editorial note regarding Boggs, 462nd NSC meeting, October 6, 1960, *FRUS 1958–1960*, vol. 14, 516. For Devlin's recounting of the assassination attempt, see Devlin, *Chief of Station*, 89–90.

53. State to Leopoldville, November 12, 1960, *FRUS 1958–1960*, vol. 14, 584.

54. For an account, see Dayal, *Mission for Hammarskjöld*, 63, and Dayal, Second Progress Report, November 2, 1960, *SCOR*, 15th session, suppl. for October, November, and December 1960, document S/4557, para. 39–55, for a detailed description of the role of returning Belgians. See also Hoskyns, *Congo since Independence*, 237–41.

55. Weissman, "Opening the Secret Files."

56. Kalb, *Congo Cables*, 96–99, 133–34.

57. Mazov, *Distant Front in the Cold War*, 116–19.

58. September 9, 1960, *SCOR*, 896th meeting, para. 83–89; Hoskyns, *United Nations Peacekeeping*, 217; Urquhart, *Hammarskjöld*, 447. Commentary, Cordier and Foote, *Public Papers of Dag Hammarskjöld*, 161, states that Hammarskjöld would justify the payment as designed to prevent an attack on U.N. troops guarding the airport; see also *New York Times,* September 11 and 14, 1960.

59. DeWitte, *Assassination of Lumumba*, 28.

60. Leopoldville (Timberlake) to State, September 29, 1960, *FRUS 1958–1960*, vol. 14, 510–11. Problems with the ANC were endemic. See Leopoldville (Timberlake) to State, November 2, 1960, *FRUS 1958–1960*, vol. 14, 565.

61. Kalb, *Congo Cables*, 137; quote from Dayal, *Mission for Hammarskjöld*, 134.

62. Kalb, *Congo Cables*, 133–39. See also Leopoldville (Timberlake) to State, September 26, 1960, *FRUS 1958–1960*, vol. 14, 503–506; Leopoldville (Timberlake) to State, October 19, 1960, *FRUS 1958–1960*, vol. 14, 534–36; and Leopoldville (Timberlake) to State, November 2, 1960, *FRUS 1958–1960*, vol. 14, 562–66.

63. Timberlake to State, October 11, 1960, *FRUS 1958–1960*, vol. 14, 518; Elizabethville (Canup) to State, September 29, 1960, *FRUS 1958–1960*, vol. 14, 512–13; Higgins, *United Nations Peacekeeping*, 318.

64. *Pravda* solemnly announced the recall of the embassy, explaining that its operation had become impossible under the puppet regime set up by the colonizers and their stooges; see *Pravda*, September 19, 1960.

65. Dayal, *Mission for Hammarskjöld*, 75–76; *Izvestia,* September 25, 1960.

66. Grinevsky, *Tysiacha i odin den' Nikity Sergeevicha*, 330–31.

67. Ibid., 336. He does not specify exactly when Khrushchev made this outburst, only that it occurred after Hammarskjöld's protest.

68. Shevchenko, *Breaking with Moscow*, 102–106. There is some question of Shevchenko's bias. See Edward Jay Epstein, "The Spy Who Came In to Be Sold: The Invention of Arkady Shevchenko, Supermole," *New Republic*, July 15, 1985. Many commentators, including Leslie Gelb, believe that he adds insight, if complex and contradictory. See Leslie Gelb, review of *Breaking with Moscow* in the *New York Times*, February 17, 1985. Also see the use of Shevchenko's memoirs by Taubman in *Khrushchev*, 473.

69. Grinevsky, *Tysiacha i odin den' Nikity Sergeevicha*, 337.

70. Khrushchev, *Vremia, Liudi, Vlast*, vol. 2, 466; or see the English version, *Memoirs*, 281–283. Khrushchev reported on the plan in a Politburo meeting, October 15, 1960, see A. A. Fursenko, *Prezidium TsK KPSS, 1954–1964* (Moscow: Rosspen, 2003), vol. 1, 444.

71. Shevchenko, *Breaking with Moscow*, 102–106, explained that the Soviet representatives had asked that their port be nothing fancy, but had failed to follow up on the request to verify that it met Soviet needs. The result was a rather dilapidated pier.

72. State (Herter) to USUN, September 17, 1960, *FRUS 1958–1960*, vol. 14, 493–94.

73. See speech by Kwame Nkrumah, September 23, 1960, http://www.nkrumah. net/un-1960/index-nkun-1960.htm; and Nkrumah, *Challenge of the Congo*, 70. See also Mazov, *Distant Front in the Cold War*, 142–43.

74. An advisory committee had been proposed by the secretary-general on August 21 to operate as had the United Nations Emergency Force advisory committee. See August 21, 1960, *SCOR*, 15th year, 888th meeting; and Hoskyns, *United Nations Peacekeeping*, 232–34.

75. General Assembly Official Records, United Nations, New York (hereafter, *GAOR*), 4th Emergency Special Session, September 19, 1960, 863rd meeting, para. 263–66; Higgins, *United Nations Peacekeeping*, 24, 222–25. See also *Izvestia*, September 21, 1960.

76. Commentary, Cordier and Foote, *Public Papers of Dag Hammarskjöld*, 193–94.

77. NSC Memorandum of Discussion (Boggs), reprinted as editorial note no. 223, *FRUS 1958–1960*, vol. 14, 497; Taubman, *Khrushchev*, 472; Ebere Nwaubani, "Eisenhower, Nkrumah, and the Congo Crisis," *Journal of Contemporary History* 36 (2001): 613–14.

78. Eisenhower, Address before 15th General Assembly of the United Nations, September 22, 1960, *Public Papers of the Presidents, 1960–1961,* 708–14.

79. *New York Times*, September 24, 1960.

80. Khrushchev's last day would end with the shoe-banging incident, when a Philippine delegate questioned Khrushchev's dedication to decolonization, given that the Soviet Union had deprived Eastern Europe of civil rights. Taubman, *Khrushchev*, 475–76. For Khrushchev's words, see his *Memoirs*, 279; and Khrushchev, September 23, 1960, *GAOR*, 15th session, reprinted in *Khrushchev in New York*, 20–23. The Afro-Asians would submit their own declaration that would be accepted by the General Assembly.

81. Khrushchev, October 3, 1960, *GAOR*, 882nd plenary meeting, para. 2-66, esp. 30 (for quote), and 39. For Macmillan, see BBC, http://news.bbc.co.uk/onthisday/hi/dates/stories/september/29/newsid_3087000/3087171.stm; and UniversalNewsReels, October 3, 1960, available at http://www.youtube.com/watch?v=-F_V2fQCKe4&playnext=1&list=PL9C7EB9F53498E741.

82. October 3, 1960, *GAOR*, 15th session, 883rd plenary meeting, para. 9–12; Cordier and Foote, *Public Papers of Dag Hammarskjöld*, 187–92. See also Urquhart, *Hammarskjöld*, 462–72.

83. USUN (Wadsworth) to State, October 15, 1960, *FRUS 1958–1960*, vol. 14, 529–32. For a similar view of events from an eyewitness, see Bartlett, *Communist Penetration in the Congo*, 30–33.

84. The United States expected this shift and was not happy about it. See USUN (Wadsworth) to State, October 15, 1960, *FRUS 1958–1960*, vol. 14, 529–32; see also USUN (Barco) to State, October 22, 1960, duplicating letter to Hammarskjöld, *FRUS 1958–1950*, vol. 14, 545, which threatened a revision if Hammarskjöld changed course.

85. Heikal, *Cairo Documents*, 184.

Chapter 7

1. John S. Eisenhower, Memorandum of Conversation between President and British Foreign Secretary Lord Home, September 19, 1960, *FRUS 1958–1960*, vol. 14, 495. Home responded that "regretfully we have lost many of the techniques of old-fashioned diplomacy."

2. Memorandum of Conversation between Herter and Hammarskjöld, September 26, 1960, *FRUS 1958–1960*, vol. 14, 506–507.

3. U.S. Congress, *Alleged Assassination Plots*, 23.

4. Dulles to Leopoldville, September 24, 1960, reproduced in U.S. Congress, *Alleged Assassination Plots*, 24.

5. Kalb, *Congo Cables*, 63–67, provides a very good account of the development of the assassination plot based on U.S. Congress, *Alleged Assassination Plots*.

6. Devlin, *Chief of Station*, 95.

7. See Devlin's memoirs, *Chief of Station*. Devlin, of course, has become a very controversial figure. He is often accused of hiding his true intentions, trying to exculpate himself from the assassination. Or he is accused of defending the CIA. His memoirs suggest that he is not apologizing for the CIA but rather explaining why the assassination affected his rise in the organization. U.S. Congress, *Alleged Assassination Plots*, 27–28.

8. Weissman, "Extraordinary Rendition," 203, 213.

9. Devlin, *Chief of Station*, 97; Director (Dulles) to Leopoldville, October 15, 1960, reproduced in U.S. Congress, *Alleged Assassination Plots*, 31. Brackets in original.

10. U.S. Congress, *Alleged Assassination Plots*, 31.

11. *Belgian Parliamentary Commission Report*, 393; De Witte, *Assassination of Lumumba*, 50–51.

12. In addition to the scholar René Clemens, it would encompass "a large number of military men," including the commander in chief of the gendarmerie, Jean Marie Crèvecoeur, Lieutenant Colonel André Grandjean, and Major Guy Weber. See De Witte, *Assassination of Lumumba*, 46–50, 64; and Weissman, "Extraordinary Rendition," 10.

13. U.S. Congress, *Alleged Assassination Plots*, 30, 41.

14. Ibid., 39–42.

15. See Devlin, *Chief of Station*, 94–99; Kalb, *Congo Cables*, 46–71, 128–56, U.S. Congress, *Alleged Assassination Plots*, 42–48; Joseph J. Trento, *The Secret History of the CIA* (Roseville, Calif.: Prima Lifestyles, 2001), 196–97.

16. For the U.S. analysis of Hammarskjöld's views, see USUN (Wadsworth) to State, October 15, 1960, *FRUS 1958–1960*, vol. 14, 529–30; Memorandum of Discussion (Johnson), 464th NSC meeting, October 20, 1960, *FRUS 1958–1960*, vol. 14, 539–40; USUN (Barco) to State, October 22, 1960, *FRUS 1958–1960*, vol. 14, 547.

17. Kalb, *Congo Cables*, 145–46.

18. Weissman, "Opening the Secret Files."

19. Dayal, Second Progress Report, November 2, 1960, *SCOR*, 15th session, suppl. for October, November, and December 1960, document S/4557, para. 4–5, 75. Dayal sent his first report a few days after taking over responsibility in the Congo.

20. Higgins, *United Nations Peacekeeping*, 152, quoting resolution 1474 of the U.N. General Assembly special session.

21. In its entirety, Ethiopia, Ghana, Guinea, Liberia, Mali, Morocco, Nigeria, Senegal, Sudan, Tunisia, UAR, India, Indonesia, Malaya, and Pakistan formed the

Conciliation Commission. The appointment of its chairman Jaja Wachuku, a Nigerian who had supported much of U.S. policy, would hopelessly divide the commission, although this was not known at the time.

22. Unsigned attachment to Herter, Memorandum of Conversation between Herter and Hammarskjold, September 26, 1960, *FRUS 1958–1960*, vol. 14, 507.

23. See State (Herter) to USUN, November 4, 1960, *FRUS 1958–1960*, vol. 14, 566–67; and State (Herter) to USUN, November 23, 1960, *FRUS 1958–1960*, vol. 14, 594; Hoskyns, *Congo since Independence*, 298, describes the difficulties finding French-speaking volunteers.

24. State (Herter) to USUN, November 23, 1960, *FRUS 1958–1960*, vol. 14, 593; Leopoldville (Timberlake) to State, September 18, 1960, *FRUS 1958–1960*, vol. 14, 494–95.

25. For General Cabell's warning, see editorial note on 465 NSC meeting, October 31, 1960, *FRUS 1958–1960*, vol. 14, 560; and for estimates on Lumumba forces, see USUN (Wadsworth) to State, December 2, 1960, *FRUS 1958–1960*, vol. 14, 608. See also USUN (Wadsworth) to State, November 25, 1960, *FRUS 1958–1960*, vol. 14, 595–98. According to De Witte, neither did Dayal want to see Lumumba escape to Stanleyville. See *The Assassination of Lumumba*, 53–54.

26. Kalb, *Congo Cables*, 152–56; Higgins, *United Nations Peacekeeping*, 24–25. Those voting against the resolution included the Soviet Bloc and the most staunchly pro-Lumumba states, including Ceylon, Cuba, Ghana, Guinea, India, Indonesia, Mali, Morocco, and Togo. If just three more states would have abstained, the resolution would have failed.

27. Ibid., 146–49; Weissman, "Opening the Secret Files."

28. *New York Times*, September 29, 1960. Metz is quoted in "U.S. Attitudes toward Decolonization in Africa," 515; Kalb, *Congo Cables*, 125; and Pruden, "Conditional Partners," 651.

29. Luce posed the question of America's national purpose. The scholar John Jeffries made the latter comment on history running out. See John Jeffries, "The Quest for 'National Purpose' of 1960," *American Quarterly* 30, no. 4 (Autumn 1978): 451–53.

30. Protected by the U.N. troops, Lumumba could be reasonably assured of his safety. But it was questionable whether Hammarskjöld would still agree to guard him after the General Assembly had recognized Kasavubu as the legitimate head of state. While Kasavubu was still in New York, a skirmish between ANC and U.N. troops (of Tunisian nationality) broke out for the first time on November 22 in Leopoldville, suggesting that the U.N. role in guarding Lumumba was becoming increasingly difficult. The skirmish occurred while the Tunisian troops were trying to protect a Ghanaian diplomat, Nathaniel Welbeck, after he was accused of aiding Lumumba, and resulted in the death of one Tunisian and the commander of the Congolese troops, Colonel Kokolo. Tensions remained high between the two groups, and on December 12, Mobutu's soldiers again fired on the Tunisians. See Thompson, *Ghana's Foreign Policy*, 142. See also *New York Times*, November 22, 23, and 29, 1960. Lumumba wrote about his fears regarding this affair to van Lierde, *Lumumba Speaks*, 418–21.

31. Weissman, "Extraordinary Rendition," 205–206.

32. Devlin to Tweedy PROP cable, November 14, 1960, in *Assassination Plots*, 48.

33. *Belgian Parliamentary Commission Report*, 222.

34. De Witte, *Assassination of Lumumba*, 53–57; U.S. Congress, *Alleged Assassination Plots*, 48. See also the interesting account by Lev Volodin, *Patrice Lumumba: Fighter for Africa's Freedom* (Moscow: Progress Publishers, 1961), 104–10, transcribed by Thomas Schmidt, http://www.marxists.org/subject/africa/lumumba/reminiscences/volodin/last.htm.

35. Report by the Special Representative Regarding Actions Taken Against Patrice Lumumba, December 5, 1960, *SCOR*, 15th year, suppl. for October, November, December 1960, document S/4571, 67–74.

36. For instance, see photos in *New York Times,* December 7, 1960; Kasavubu to Hammarskjold, December 7, 1960, *SCOR*, suppl. for October, November, and December 1960, document S/4571, annex 3, 73–74.

37. December 7, 1960, *SCOR*, 15th year, 913th meeting, para. 39.

38. Heikal, *Cairo Documents*, 177–78; in "Operatsiia O.O.N. v Kongo" [The U.N. Operation in the Congo], Brykin cites the Egyptian newspaper *Al'-Akhbar*, December 8, 1960, as the source.

39. For the December 6, 1960, statement, see *Pravda* or *SSSR i Strany Afriki*, December 7, 1960, 95–101; and for an English translation, see *SCOR*, suppl. for October, November, and December 1960, document S/4573, 75–80. For commentary on Lumumba's arrest, see *Izvestia*, December 4, 1960.

40. December 10, 1960, *SCOR*, 15th year, 917th meeting, para. 34, 68ff, 133; *Pravda*, December 14, 1960.

41. Higgins, *United Nations Peacekeeping*, 27–29. A General Assembly resolution calling for the full and immediate implementation of the U.N. resolutions, including the withdrawal of Belgian paratroopers and the restoration of law and order, failed by 42 votes to 28 with 27 abstentions.

42. For the immediate reaction, see *New York Times*, October 3 and 4, 1960.

43. *New York Times,* October 18 and 22, November 30, and December 1, 1960; Higgins, *United Nations Peacekeeping*, 274–76.

44. *Courrier Africain*, April 18, 1961. Lumumba's old ally, Remy Mwamba, became minister of justice; Andre Mandi, secretary of state for foreign affairs; Edmond Rudahinda, minister of mines; Joachim Massena, minister of labor; and Joseph Lutula, minister of agriculture. All had served in the Lumumba government in the same positions.

45. Gizenga to CC, December 15, 1960, OMO, opis 9, delo 40, papka 105, 70, AVPRF.

46. Protokoll Nr. 7/61, "Der Sitzung des Politbüros des Zentralkomitees am Dienstag, dem 14, Februar 1961 im Sitzungssaal des Politbüros," and "Anlage Nr. 1," DY 30, J IV 2/2/749.

47. Khrushchev to Gizenga, December 24, 1960, in *SSSR i strany Afriki*, 140–41; and Mazov, "Soviet Aid to the Gizenga Government," 429.

48. February 7, 1961, *SCOR*, 932nd meeting, para. 6; and Kanza, *The Rise and Fall of Patrice Lumumba*, 316.

49. Kanza, *Rise and Fall of Patrice Lumumba*, 317; *Izvestia*, December 28, 1960.

50. *Izvestia*, December 16, 1960.

51. See Mazov, *Distant Front in the Cold War*, 129.

52. Deputy Minister of Foreign Affairs V. S. Semenov to the MID, December 15, 1960. From a conversation with UAR ambassador to the USSR (Muhammed El-Kuni)

about the problems of creating a joint command of the armed forces of African countries in connection with the situation in the Congo, December 13, 1960, in unofficial translation. Congo briefing book prepared for Cold War International History Project (hereafter, CWIHP) Oral History Conference on the Congo, September 2004.

53. See comments in Kirpichenko, *Razvedka*, 96.

54. Khrushchev to Gizenga, December 24, 1960, in *SSSR i strany Afriki*, 140–41; and Mazov, "Soviet Aid to the Gizenga Government," 429. In December, the Soviet Union also dusted off the Soviet committee of solidarity with the Afro-Asian countries, the voice through which it usually fought against Chinese and Western influence in the days before Congolese independence. The committee issued a statement in support of the Congolese; see *Pravda*, December 11, 1960. For protests from factory meetings, see *Pravda*, December 13, 1960.

55. December 10, 1960, *SCOR*, 917th meeting, para. 126–27.

56. See *Courrier Africain*, March 12, 1961, 12. Mobutu eventually reoccupied Kivu by using Belgian help, and the trust territory of Ruanda-Urundi was his staging ground. But before he could do this, 400 of his soldiers were taken prisoner by a Stanleyville brigade, an unprecedented setback for Mobutu.

57. Synopsis, December 28, 1960, WHO staff secretary, subject series, alphabet subseries, box 14, DDEL; "Analytical chronology," 29, 73, NSF, box 27, JFKL.

58. Gizenga to CC, January 4, 1961, opis 4, delo 11, papka 5, 130, AVPRF. See also Gizenga to CC, December 15, 1960, OMO, opis 9, delo 40, papka 105, 70, AVPRF. Kuznetsov's notes on this copy verify that the CC and Foreign Ministry sent information.

59. Ghana to Hammarskjöld, Transmitting Declaration of Conference of Independent African States, January 12, 1961, *SCOR,* suppl. for January, February, and March 1961, document S/4626, 31–32; The Casablanca conference included the heads of states from Morocco (King Mohammed V), UAR (Nasser), Ghana (Nkrumah), Guinea (Touré), Mali (Keita), provisional government of Algeria (Ferhat Abbas), and the foreign ministers from Libya (Abdelkader al Alam) and Ceylon (Alwin Perera).

60. Kalb, *Congo Cables*, 181–82. See *Pravda*, January 12, 1960, for statement. For a reflection of the importance placed on the Casablanca conference as a turning point for African support of Lumumba, see *Novoe Vremia* no. 4 (1961); and A. M. Sivolobov, *The National Liberation Movement in Africa* (Moscow: Znanie Publishing House, 1961), 47–51. See also A. Mikhailov, "A New Phase of the People's Struggle," *International Affairs* [Moscow], (March 1961), 86–88.

61. Statement by Evariste Lokiki, Congolese representative at the United Nations, February 7, 1961, *SCOR*, 932nd meeting, para. 22. For reference to gifts, see exchange between Dayal and Kasavubu in January 7 and 14, 1961, *SCOR*, 16th year, suppl. for January, February, and March, document S/4360, 40–48.

62. "Nachtrag" attached to Protokoll Nr. 7/61, February 1961, "Der Sitzung des Politbüros des Zentralkomitees am Dienstag, dem 14, Februar 1961 im Sitzungssaal des Politbüros" and "Anlage Nr. 1," DY 30, J IV 2/2/749; and Department of State to Certain Diplomatic Missions, December 15, 1960, *FRUS 1958–1960*, vol. 14, 630.

63. Protokoll Nr. 7/61, February 1961, "Der Sitzung des Politbüros des Zentralkomitees am Dienstag, dem 14, Februar 1961 im Sitzungssaal des Politbüros" and "Anlage Nr. 1," DY 30, J IV 2/2/749. Brykin's conversation is with a Representative Thun.

64. *Pravda*, January 30, 1960.

65. Zorin to the President of the Security Council, January 12, 1961, *SCOR*, 16th year, suppl. for January, February, and March 1961, document S/4622, 24–29. See also Higgins, *United Nations Peacekeeping*, 29, 257–58.

66. *Izvestia*, February 9, 1961. See *Mizan Newsletter*, March 3, 1961, 30, for suggestion that Soviet newspapers charged Belgian, French, South African, and NATO sources with sending equipment to Katanga.

67. Hoskyns, *Congo: A Chronology*, 9; Weissman, "Extraordinary Rendition," 208.

68. *Belgian Parliamentary Commission Report*, 216–17, 393.

69. Kalb, *Congo Cables*, 184–85, 190–96; U.S. Congress, *Alleged Assassination Plots*, 49–50; Editorial note, *FRUS 1961–1963*, vol. 20, 17.

70. Weissman, "Extraordinary Rendition," 213–14.

71. De Witte, *Assassination of Lumumba*, 107–40, 174–83, "Summary of the Activities, Expert's Report and Full Conclusions," in *Belgian Parliamentary Commission Report*; and Urquhart, UNOH, interview 5, 23–24.

72. De Witte, *Assassination of Lumumba*, 104–33.

73. "Summary of the Activities, Expert's Report."

74. There is not a lot written on morality and foreign policy. See George F. Kennan, "Morality and Foreign Policy," *Foreign Affairs* (Winter 1985–86): 205–33; and Kenneth Thompson, *Morality and Foreign Policy* (Baton Rouge: Louisiana State University Press, 1982).

75. Lumumba's last message was given to a journalist sometime after January 5, 1961. See *Lumumba Speaks*, 426–31, and Van Lierde's comments, 431–33; and Nkrumah, *Challenge of the Congo*, 121–33.

Chapter 8

1. Khrushchev, "Za novye pobedy mirovogo kommunisticheskogo dvizheniia," *Kommunist* no.1 (January 1961), 16–20. For an English version of speech, see Khrushchev, "For New Victories for the World Communist Movement," *World Marxist Review* 4 (January 1961): 2–27. See also Light, *Soviet Theory of International Relations*, 217. In his speech, Khrushchev specifically mentions Vietnam, Algeria, and Cuba.

2. Frederick Kempe, *Berlin 1961: Kennedy, Khrushchev, and the Most Dangerous Place on Earth* (New York: Putnam, 2011), 73–80, argued that Kennedy's interpretation of the speech as the clue to understanding Khrushchev was his first mistake and led to his assumption of the need to respond. Deborah Welch Larson, *Anatomy of Mistrust: U.S.–Soviet Relations during the Cold War* (Ithaca, N.Y.: Cornell University Press, 1997), 110. For the original telegram, see Thompson to State, 19 January 1961, JFK Digital, http://www.jfklibrary.org/asset-viewer/archives/JFKPOF-125-018.aspx.

3. John F. Kennedy, "Inaugural Address," January 20, 1961; and John F. Kennedy, "A Message to Congress on the State of the Union," January 30, 1961, in *Public Papers of the President, John F. Kennedy, 1961* (Washington, D.C.: U.S. Government Printing Office, 1962), 19–28; see 22–23 for quote.

4. Madeleine Kalb has argued that Kennedy's heart "was with the activists" as he worked to end the crisis, while Richard Mahoney concluded that the president exhibited a thoughtful restraint of power. Only Stephen Weissman, author of the first comprehensive account of the crisis, concluded that Kennedy's "incapacity as a statesman"

led him to mismanage the crisis. Weissman, *American Foreign Policy in the Congo*, 53, 194; Kalb, *Congo Cables*, 239, 353–60; Mahoney, *JFK: Ordeal in Africa*, 153–56. See also Gibbs, *Political Economy of Third World Intervention*, 196–97; and Borstelmann, *Cold War and the Color Line*, 149.

5. Fursenko and Naftali, *"One Hell of a Gamble,"* 54, 90–100.

6. Freedman, *Kennedy's Wars*, 293–303.

7. Ibid., 340. Freedman did not include the case of the Congo, where the preference for negotiation would not serve him well. A briefing paper prepared by the Department of State for a January 19 meeting between President Eisenhower and president-elect Kennedy, which was at least read by Kennedy's adviser Clark Clifford and secretary of defense–designate Robert McNamara and summarized for Kennedy, contained virtually no information on the Congo situation that was not already public knowledge. "The Congo and the African Situation," n.d., *FRUS 1961–1963*, vol. 20, 19–20.

8. Quoted by William Minter, "The Limits of a Liberal Africa Policy: Lessons from the Congo Crisis," *TransAfrica Forum* 2 (Fall 1984): 34; Harriman Report to Kennedy, September 20, 1960, box 404, William Averell Harriman Papers, Library of Congress (hereafter, WAHP). Kennedy posed the question to Harriman during a briefing in November 1960.

9. *New York Times*, December 6 and 23, 1960, and January 18, 1961; Minter, "Limits of a Liberal Africa Policy," 34.

10. See Namikas, "History through Documents and Memory"; and De Witte, *Assassination of Lumumba*, 130.

11. Borstelmann, *Cold War and the Color Line*, 149.

12. "Suggested New United States Policy on the Congo," n.a., n.d., *FRUS 1961–1963*, vol. 20, 42–45, but probably drafted by the deputy assistant secretary of international organizations, Woodruff Wallner, and approved by the Department of Defense and the CIA.

13. Schlesinger, *Thousand Days*, 553–54; Robert Dallek, *An Unfinished Life: John F. Kennedy, 1917–1963* (Boston: Little, Brown, 2004), 313–21; *Time*, December 26, 1960; Chester Bowles, *Africa's Challenge to America* (Berkeley: University of California Press, 1956); Roger Hilsman, *To Move a Nation: The Politics of Foreign Policy in the Administration of John F. Kennedy* (Garden City, N.Y.: Delta Books, 1964), 246. Freedman, *Kennedy's Wars*, 28–41; Noer, *Cold War and Black Liberation*, 61–67. Compare with Weissman's interpretation of Kennedy as overly cautious. Weissman portrayed Ball and McGhee as Europeanists who criticized the soft-line Africanists in the administration but who also brought a "schizophrenia" into the decisionmaking process. See *American Foreign Policy in the Congo*, 192–93. See also Kalb, *Congo Cables*, 199–239. For Williams's views, see also handwritten notes, February 2, 1961, Lot files, Bureau of African Affairs, box 8, RG59, NARA. For characterization on Bowles, see *Time*, December 26, 1960, available at www.time.com.

In *Political Economy of Third World Intervention*, 105–14, Gibbs pointed out that virtually all those who favored an anti-Katangan position had close connections to three business interests who had a strong desire to diminish the Belgian presence in the Congo: LAMCO (Liberian-American Swedish Minerals Company), diamond investor Maurice Tempelsman, and the Rockefellers. He argued that their financial connections would have led them to prefer a policy of unification and the weakening of Katanga in a Congo union. LAMCO and its subsidiaries, one of which was headed by Bo Gustav

Hammarskjöld (Dag's brother), helped staff the Congo aid program. One prominent employee included Sture Linnér, a managing director of LAMCO. Maurice Tempelsman showed some interest from 1957 onward in establishing a greater role in the Congo, and he often hired Stevenson to conduct his legal business. Rockefeller interests, although complicated, essentially sought to reduce the Belgian presence and gave important support to the Africa Bureau of the State Department. Rusk and Bowles both had been involved in the Rockefeller Foundation, although Gibbs argued that Rusk failed to play a decisive role in foreign policymaking with regard to the Congo. Fredericks would later serve as vice president of Chase Manhattan, a Rockefeller-controlled bank.

14. Dallek, *Unfinished Life*, 316.

15. Memorandum (Rusk) to Kennedy, February 1, 1961, *FRUS 1961–1963*, vol. 20, 40–41.

16. Assistant Secretary of Defense for International Security Affairs (Nitze) to Assistant Secretary of State–Designate for International Organization Affairs (Cleveland), January 31, 1961; and Rusk, Memorandum to President Kennedy, February 1, 1961, with enclosure, "Suggested New United States Policy on the Congo," *FRUS 1961–1963*, vol. 20, 38–45.

17. State (Rusk) to Leopoldville, February 2, 1961, Cables, box 29, JFKL. Rusk also wrote that regarding Lumumba, "our view is that the [secretary-general] would be able to obtain the release of and insure the protection of political prisoners when the military neutralization of the Congolese forces is at least well under way and it is clear that a civil war has been averted." See State (Rusk) to New Delhi, February 2, 1961, *FRUS 1961–1963*, vol. 20, 48.

18. Schlesinger, *Thousand Days*, 555–76; Roger Hilsman, director of the Bureau of Intelligence and Research (1961–63), in his memoirs, *To Move a Nation*, 246, categorized Ball with the "New Africa" group in the State Department; Noer, *Cold War and Black Liberation*, 63–66.

19. Rusk worked in Truman's State Department, first in the Office of United Nations Affairs and then as assistant secretary of state for Far Eastern Affairs. Rusk's sentiments, which were expressed to the Belgian ambassador in Washington, Louis Scheyven, are summarized in State (Rusk) to Brussels, January 28, 1961, *FRUS 1961–1963*, vol. 20, 31–32.

20. See Mahoney, *JFK: Ordeal in Africa*, 107–25, for a good discussion of Ball's role.

21. Memorandum (Rostow) of Conversation with Kennedy, February 2, 1961, cited in editorial note, *FRUS 1961–1963,* vol. 20, 46.

22. See editorial note on Kennedy's meeting with the Joint Chiefs of Staff, January 25, 1961, *FRUS 1961–1963*, vol. 20, 24.

23. Chairman of the Joint Chiefs of Staff Lemnitzer, Memorandum to the Secretary of Defense, January 30, 1961, with enclosure, "Evaluation of Courses of Action," and Lemnitzer to Secretary of Defense, January 31, 1961, *FRUS 1961–1963*, vol. 20, microfiche suppl., documents 329 and 331.

24. Editorial note reproduced portions of Dulles memorandum to Bundy, February 5, 1961, *FRUS 1961–1963*, vol. 20, 46.

25. Handwritten notes, February 2, 1961, Lot files, Bureau of African Affairs, box 8, RG59, NARA.

26. Editorial note quoting memorandum from McGhee (a Department of State adviser) to Rusk, March 3, 1961, *FRUS 1961–1963*, vol. 20, 89.

27. Weissman, July 21, 2002, *Washington Post*; see also his "Extraordinary Rendition," 209.

28. Schlesinger, *Thousand Days*, 554, 557.

29. Rusk circular, February 2, 1961, Cables, box 29, JFKL.

30. Kennedy to Nkrumah, February 2, 1961 letter reproduced in telegram from State Department to embassy in Accra, February 2, 1961, *FRUS 1961–1963*, vol. 20, microfiche suppl., document 332; Rusk to Leopoldville, February 2, 1961, cables, box 29, JFKL; Kennedy to Nehru, February 18, 1961, *FRUS 1961–1963*, vol. 20, microfiche suppl., document 336. For concerns that Nigeria was the only one to respond positively, see Williams to Rusk, "Current Situation in the Congo," February 7, 1961, *FRUS 1961–1963*, vol. 20, microfiche suppl., document 334.

31. See Memorandum of Conversation, Rusk and British Ambassador Harold Caccia, February 4, 1961, *FRUS 1961–1963*, vol. 20, 51.

32. U.S. representatives insisted that Kasavubu hurt his position by continuing to send enemies to their execution in Kasai. Britain at least agreed to use suggestions as a basis for discussion, while France and Belgium continued to resist the U.S. plan. See Kennedy to de Gaulle, February 2, 1961 letter reproduced in telegram from State Department to embassy in Paris, February 2, 1961, document 333, *FRUS 1961–1963*, vol. 20, microfiche suppl., document 333; USUN to State summarizing Memorandum (Stevenson) regarding conversation with Hammarskjöld, February 6, 1961, *FRUS 1961–1963*, vol. 20, 57; Stevenson to State, February 22, 1961, *FRUS 1961–1963*, vol. 20, 76; Williams to Rusk, "Current Situation in the Congo," February 7, 1961, *FRUS 1961–1963*, vol. 20, microfiche suppl., document 334.

33. Hoskyns, *Congo: A Chronology*, 10.

34. Kennedy, February 15, 1961, *Current Documents 1961*, 774; *New York Times*, February 16, 1961.

35. *New York Times*, February 20, 1961; Weissman, *American Foreign Policy in the Congo*, 142. Mahoney, *JFK: Ordeal in Africa*, 73, refers to these plans. No documentary evidence has yet been released confirming the plans. On February 15, 1961, Rusk wrote to the embassy in the United Kingdom that he was considering what response the United States would take if Hammarskjöld asked for assistance, and Rusk wanted to know what military forces Britain had in the area. See *FRUS 1961–1963*, vol. 20, 65.

36. Bernard Kalb, author of the editorial, believed that this silence was made at Soviet insistence. See *New York Times*, February 19, 1961. See *Pravda*, February 19, 1961, for a description of the Chinese protest.

37. For the best account of the protests, see Meriwether, *Proudly We Can Be Africans*, 233–40. See also John Henrik Clarke, "The New Afro-American Nationalism," http://www.nbufront.org/html/MastersMuseums/JHClarke/ArticlesEssays/NewAfroAmNationalism.html.

38. The chair of the Communist Party, B. A. Davis, and a member, Paul Robeson Jr., were also present at the protests. See *New York Times*, February 16, 1961; and Maya Angelou, *Heart of a Woman* (New York: Bantam Books, 1997; orig. pub. 1981), 144–70, quote on 158. Angelou was married to a South African civil rights activist. By 1964, Malcolm X would regularly criticize U.S. policy in the Congo.

39. *Izvestia*, January 21, 1961; *Pravda*, January 20, 1961.

40. See his letter to Nehru, dated February 22, 1961, in *Pravda*, February 26, 1961; and see charges in *Pravda*, February 15, 1961.

41. "Zaiavlenie Sovetskogo pravitel'sctva v sviazi s ubiistvom Patrisa Lumumby" [Declaration of the Soviet government in connection with the murder of Patrice Lumumba], February 14, 1961, *SSSR i Strany Afriki*, 194–97. For an English version, see the Declaration of the Soviet Government in Connection with the Murder of Patrice Lumumba, February 14, 1961, *SCOR*, 15th year, suppl. for January, February, and March, document S/4704, 112–15.

42. Transcript of the talk between Deputy Foreign Minister of the USSR V.S. Semenov and President of the United Arab Republic Gamal Abdel Nasser, January 31, 1961, unofficial translation, Congo briefing book prepared for CWIHP Oral History Conference on the Congo, September 2004. See also Mazov, "Soviet Aid to the Gizenga Government," 430.

43. See Thomas Ofcansky, "The Abboud Military Government, 1958–1964," in *A Country Study: Sudan* (Washington, D.C.: Library of Congress, 1991), http://lcweb2.loc.gov/frd/cs/sdtoc.html.

44. Protokoll Nr. 7/61, "Der Sitzung des Politbüros des Zentralkomitees am Dienstag, dem 14, Februar 1961 im Sitzungssaal des Politbüros" and "Anlage Nr. 1," DY 30, J IV 2/2/749.

45. Protokoll Nr. 10/61, "Der Sitzung des Politbüros des Zentralkomitees am Dienstag, dem 28, Februar 1961 im Sitzungssaal des Politbüros" and "Anlage Nr. 12," DY 30, J IV 2/2/752.

46. Khrushchev to Gizenga, March 3, 1961, opis 4, delo 11, papka 5, 130, AVPRF.

47. Transcript of the talk between Deputy Foreign Minister of the USSR A. A. Sobolev and Ambassador of Czechoslovakia in Moscow G. R. Dvorzhak, February 9, 1961, unofficial translation, Congo briefing book prepared for CWIHP Oral History Conference on the Congo, September 2004.

48. Transcript of the talk between Deputy Foreign Minister of the USSR N. P. Firubin and Ambassador of Czechoslovakia in Moscow G. R. Dvorzhak, March 9, 1961," unofficial translation, Congo briefing book prepared for CWIHP Oral History Conference on the Congo, September 2004.

49. Stevenson Speech, February 15, 1961, *SCOR*, 934th meeting, para. 58–62. In para. 61, Stevenson mentioned that the "during the past week we advocated the release of all political prisoners and their participation in the political process." There is no evidence whatsoever that this was the case. For Stevenson's role during this session, see John Bartlow Martin, *Adlai Stevenson and the World: The Life of Adlai E. Stevenson* (Garden City, N.Y.: Doubleday, 1977), 60–73.

50. See February 15, 1961, *SCOR*, 16th year, 935th meeting, para. 32–35.

51. Zorin, February 7, 1961, *SCOR*, 16th year, 934th meeting, para. 71.

52. Resolution of February 21, 1961. See *SCOR*, 16th year, suppl. for January, February, and March 1961, document S/4741, 147; or Higgins, *United Nations Peacekeeping*, 30–31. Hoskyns, *The Congo since Independence*, 328–36; and *Pravda*, February 17, 1961, reported Nasser's efforts to seek consultations with Ghana, Guinea, India, and Mali.

53. Mahoney, *JFK: Ordeal in Africa*, Harlan Cleveland interview, 76; and Hoskyns, *Congo since Independence*, 332–33.

54. Lokiki had charged that known rebels had approached the Sudanese government asking it to facilitate deliveries of arms to Gizenga and Kashamura. February 7, 1961, *SCOR*, 16th year, 932nd meeting, para. 32. Just hours before the resolution

was passed, there were rumors that Sudan was reconsidering its ban on Soviet shipments. See *New York Times,* February 20, 1961. The commitment of Sudan to this position was immediately thrown into question when, on February 22, 1961, Stevenson reported in a telegram to State that Sudan sent a public cable to Hammarskjöld, warning that it could not continue indefinitely to cooperate with the United Nations. See also *FRUS 1961–1963*, vol. 20, 76; and *New York Times*, February 8, 1961.

55. Even though the commission recommended support for dissident groups, the support for Ileo was a huge step forward. See Hoskyns, *Congo since Independence*, 318–37.

56. Notes outlining the positive and negative aspects of S/4722, fond 047, opis 77, papka 130, delo 39, 29–31, AVPRF.

57. The Soviet amendments included the withdrawal of all Belgian citizens working in a military or enforcement capacity in the Congo, all territory being restored to the legal government, only troops friendly to the legal government allowed to remain in the Congo, the creation of a commission subordinate to the Security Council (not the secretary-general) to implement Council decisions and control ONUC, and the immediate disarmament of all troops under Belgian control. See discussion of amendments in February [9,] 1960, Gromyko to CC, fond 047, opis 7, papka 130, delo 39, 1–8, AVPRF.

58. "O rabote predstavitel'stva SSSR pri OON v 1961 godu" [About the work of the Soviet government regarding the United Nations in the year 1961], fond 89, opis 28, delo 8, list 1–18, RGANI.

59. Hoskyns, *Congo since Independence*, 332–35. After the adoption of the February 21 resolution, the Security Council continued its debate over whether to grant ONUC the right to use force to reunify the state. A UAR-Ceylon resolution cited "persons in high places" as responsible for the assassination of Lumumba and others, and called on ONUC to use force to prevent such outrages. Stevenson introduced an amendment that not only condemned the political violence of Kasavubu, Tshombe, and Kalonji (as did the original resolution), but also the violence of the Lumumbists. Stevenson found little support among the radicals, although perhaps they would have changed their minds had they known that fifteen political prisoners had been shot that morning in Stanleyville. The Soviet Union voted for the UAR-Ceylon resolution, but five abstentions guaranteed that it would not achieve the required seven votes in its favor.

60. *New York Times*, February 26 and 27, and March 1, 1961; Kalb, *Congo Cables*, 236–39.

61. *New York Times*, February 19 and 24, 1961.

62. Mulele to CC, February 22, 1961, 144; Mulele to CC, February 14, 1961, 91, in opis 4, delo 11, papka 5, AVPRF.

63. February 22 and 27, 1961, Gizenga to CC, opis 4, delo 11, papka 5, 131–33, AVPRF.

64. *New York Times*, March 1, 1961.

65. Protokoll Nr. 10/61, "Der Sitzung des Politbüros des Zentralkomitees am Dienstag, dem 28, Februar 1961 im Sitzungssaal des Politbüros" and "Anlage Nr. 12," DY 30, J IV 2/2/752.

66. Gizenga to CC, March 1, 1961, opis 4, delo 11, papka 5, 137, AVPRF.

67. Transcript of the talk between deputy foreign minister of the USSR V. V. Kuznetsov and minister of education and arts in the Gizenga government Pierre

Mulele, March 8, 1961, unofficial translation, Congo briefing book prepared for CWIHP Oral History Conference on the Congo, September 2004; Mazov, "Soviet Aid to the Gizenga Government," 432–33.

68. Namikas, "History through Documents and Memory"; Mazov, "Soviet Aid to the Gizenga Government," 430–32; Devlin, *Chief of Station*, 140–41. Devlin has suggested that the entire sum was snatched by the CIA officer, but Mazov found claims that only the second installment was seized.

69. Transcript of the talk between Deputy Foreign Minister of the USSR V. V. Kuznetsov and Minister of Education and Arts in the Gizenga government Pierre Mulele, March 8, 1961, unofficial translation, Congo briefing book prepared for CWIHP Oral History Conference on the Congo, September 2004; and Mazov, "Soviet Aid to the Gizenga Government," 432–33.

70. See "Entretiens avec les représentants du Gouvernement Tchécoslovaque," March 14–15, 1961, "Aide Mémoire sur les conversations et négotiations à Moscou," and "Action Diplomatique a entreprendre immédiatement," March 16, 1961, "Propositions pour aide militaire," March 16, 1961, and "Entretiens avec les autorités soviétiques," in Papers of Jan Terfve, C05-3, CarCob.

71. Mazov, *Distant Front in the Cold War*, 167.

72. Quoted by Hutchison, *China's African Revolution*, 30, from *Renmin Ribao*, November 25, 1960.

73. *Bulletin of Activities*, no. 6, January 27, 1961, reproduced in People's Liberation Army, *The Politics of the Chinese Red Army*, edited by J. Chester Cheng (Stanford, Calif.: Hoover Institution on War, Revolution, and Peace, 1966; orig. pub. in Chinese in late 1960 or early 1961), 180–81.

74. Legvold, *Soviet Policy in West Africa*, 148–49; Schatten, *Communism in Africa*, 211.

Chapter 9

1. Khrushchev rebuffed Thompson by making a trip to Novosibirsk timed for the ambassador's return to Moscow. Thompson and his aide Boris Klosson followed Khrushchev around the Soviet Union in an effort to give him Kennedy's letter. Thompson was aware that Khrushchev had been planning to confront Kennedy on the recent aggressive acts of the United States that had begun with the U-2 affair in May 1960, the shootdown of an RB-47 in Siberia several months later, and continuous U.S. support for reactionary figures in Laos, Cuba, and the Congo. See Beschloss, *Kennedy vs. Khrushchev*, 55, 79–82.

2. Draft telegram State to Moscow, n.d., JFKL, POF, USSR Security, box 125a; for original telegram State to Moscow, February 28, 1961, *FRUS 1961–1963*, vol. 20, microfiche suppl., document 337.

3. Moscow (Thompson) to State, March 10, 1961, POF, CO, USSR Security, box 125a, JFK, and *FRUS 1961–1963*, vol. 20, 99–101.

4. *Time,* May 10, 1948; CIA Daily Brief, February 18, 1961, RG59, NARA; Gibbs, *Political Economy of Third World Intervention*, 114–15, and Minter, *King Solomon's Mines Revisited*, 146–48.

5. For Congolese complaints against the United Nations, see February 7, 1961, *SCOR*, 932nd meeting, para. 12, 55–56. Lokiki also charged India with using the

Congo for its own internal political reasons, including resolution of problems such as mass emigration to the Congo. Kasavubu to Hammarskjöld, January 14, 1961, and Hammarskjöld's reply, January 15, 1961, *SCOR*, 15th year, suppl. for January, February, and March, document S/4629, 34–37.

6. Hammarskjöld report to Security Council, March 6, 1961, *SCOR*, 16th year, suppl. for January, February, and March 1961, document S/4758, add. 3, 219–20. See also the report of the special representative to Hammarskjöld, March 8, 1961, document S/4761, reprinted in Higgins, *United Nations Peacekeeping*, 342–46; and *New York Times*, February 28 and March 2 and 7, 1961. It also put in doubt the viability of Hammarskjöld's two-day-old request for a total of 25,000 troops and an additional $135 million to support the U.N. operation.

7. Timberlake to State, March 2, 1961, *FRUS 1961–1963*, vol. 20, 87–88.

8. Timberlake would stay in the Congo for another five months. Kalb, *Congo Cables*, 240–41. Penfield to Rusk, March 7, 1961, *FRUS 1961–1963*, vol. 20, microfiche suppl., document 338. For the public accounting of the incident, see Rusk news conference, March 9, 1961, *Current Documents 1961*, 433. Leopoldville (Timberlake) to State, March 4, 1961, *FRUS 1961–1963*, vol. 20, 89–91. Kalb, *Congo Cables*, 240–42.

9. Quoted in Kalb, *Congo Cables*, 231.

10. The ANC was the first to express its dissatisfaction over the alliance with Tshombe, and it was reported that "hundreds" of Mobutu's troops defected to Gizenga. See *New York Times*, March 2 and April 20, 1961.

11. Congo press release, April 6, 1961, reprinted in *Congo 1961*; Hoskyns, *Congo since Independence*, 334–37. Historians have generally followed Bomboko's analysis in suggesting that Kasavubu was seeking to destroy his rivals in turn, but this is an overstatement of his strength. See State (Ball) to Leopoldville, *FRUS 1961–1963*, vol. 20, 248–49 for Bomboko's analysis.

12. State (Rusk) to Leopoldville, March 16, 1961, *FRUS 1961–1963*, vol. 20, 106–8.

13. After his trip to Stanleyville, Carlucci suggested to Washington that his treatment stemmed from Gizenga's desire to end the economic blockade that had been imposed on Stanleyville since December. Rusk then approved a shipment of non-strategic supplies of food and medicine to Stanleyville, hoping this would encourage Gizenga's "better attitude." See State (Rusk) to Leopoldville, March 16, 1961, *FRUS 1961–1963*, vol. 20, 106–107. But the timing of Gizenga's overture so soon after the Tananarive conference was indicative that he wanted something more. Gizenga in fact seemed insulted by the shipment and tried to refocus attention on diplomatic recognition. He ordered five Western consuls to leave Stanleyville (Britain, France, West Germany, Netherlands, and Denmark) as a protest against their refusal to recognize his government. Shortly after the consuls left, Williams made his statement in support of Gizenga's representation in a new government. On these events, see Leopoldville (Timberlake report on Carlucci trip) to State, March 12, 1961, *FRUS 1961–1963*, vol. 20, 102–103. This new treatment of Carlucci was also noted in the *New York Times*, March 12, 1961. By May, Gizenga was again charging Carlucci with subversion. See *New York Times*, May 9, 1961. Kalb, *Congo Cables*, 26, 249–51, 259–60, 266–67, is a good source for Carlucci's experiences in the Congo. See also Leopoldville (Timberlake) to State, April 6, 1961, *FRUS 1961–1963*, vol. 20, 121. For Williams's announcement, see *New York Times*, March 25 and April 1, 1961.

14. For a good outline of the Coquilhatville conference, see Hoskyns, *Congo since Independence*, 358–66. Tshombe refused to begin discussions unless the U.N.–Kasavubu agreement of April 17 be abrogated and the conference delegates be limited to those who had participated at Tananarive (specifically excluding Jason Sendwe of Balubakat, who had proposed a state of Luluaba in northern Katanga). Two U.N. representatives, Robert K. Gardiner of Ghana and Francis Nwokedi of Nigeria, facilitated the negotiations. When the talks showed the Gizengists to be more marginalized than on previous occasions, the Afro-Asian states in New York clamored for Dayal's return to the Congo. As soon as he heard of these rumors, Kasavubu threatened to break the April 17 agreement. Hammarskjöld had little choice but to formally and permanently remove Dayal as his special representative.

14. USUN (Stevenson) to State, transmitting message verbatim from Hammarskjöld, March 13, 1961, *FRUS 1961–1963*, vol. 20, 104–106.

15. See, e.g., Memorandum of Conversation, Rusk and Nehru, March 30, 1961, *FRUS 1961–1963*, vol. 20, 114–15; and State (Rusk) to USUN, April 6, 1961, *FRUS 1961–1963*, vol. 20, 121–22.

16. Hoskyns, *Congo since Independence*, 349–50.

17. The agreement (document S/4741, annex I), often referred to as the April 17 agreement, is reprinted in Higgins, *United Nations Peacekeeping*, 191–92.

18. *New York Times*, April 27, 1961; Urquhart, UNOH, interview 5, 22–23.

19. Hoskyns, *Congo since Independence*, 363–65. See USUN (Plimpton) to State, May 22, 1961, *FRUS 1961–1963*, vol. 20, 139–40, for Dayal's removal. There have been suggestions that Dayal's withdrawal was also accompanied by Kennedy's withdrawal of Timberlake so as to appease Nehru.

20. *Courrier Africain*, June 12, 1961, 2–17; also reprinted in *Pravda*, May 23, 1961. There might also be some truth to Hammarskjöld's suspicion that Nasser was looking ahead to Angola's struggle with the Portuguese and wanted to see the situation in the Congo resolved. USUN (Yost) to State, June 13, 1961, *FRUS 1961–1963*, vol. 20, 144–46.

21. Mazov, *Distant Front in the Cold War*, 170–71; O. I. Nazhestkin, "Gody kongolezkogo krizisa (1960–1963 gg.): Zapiski razvedchika" [The years of the Congo crisis, 1960–1963: Notes from a secret service agent], *Novaia i noveishaia istoriya*, 6 (2003): 159.

22. Kalb, *Congo Cables*, 272; Chi-ping Tung with Humphrey Evans, *The Thought Revolution* (New York: Coward-McCann, 1966), 222–23, 239–49.

23. Ogunsanwo, *China's Policy in Africa*, 104, quoting a *Red Flag* editorial and *People's Daily* (*Renmin Ribao*), dated October 22, 1963.

24. Communist Party of China, "Apologists of Neo-Colonialism: Fourth Comment on the Open Letter of the Central Committee of the CPSU," October 22, 1963, in *The Polemic on the General Line of the International Communist Movement* (Peking: Foreign Languages Press, 1965), 199–200, www.marx2mao.org/other/ANC63.html.

25. *New York Times*, July 18, 1961, 1.

26. Chester Cheng, ed., *The Politics of the Chinese Red Army: A Translation of the Bulletin of Activities of the People's Liberation Army* (Stanford, Calif.: Hoover Institution on War, Revolution, and Peace, 1966), 399.

27. See State (Bowles) to Leopoldville, June 5, 1961, *FRUS 1961–1963*, vol. 20, 143; Kalb, *Congo Cables*, 263; Schlesinger, *Thousand Days*, 577. In *American*

Foreign Policy in the Congo, 235–36, Weissman characterized Godley as "a capable career officer of a more conventional type" than Gullion.

28. Leopoldville (Timberlake) to State, April 28, 1961, *FRUS 1961–1963*, vol. 20, 130.

29. *Belgian Parliamentary Commission Report*, 954–62; Gibbs, *Political Economy of Third World Intervention*, 128. As Gibbs also noted, the AFL-CIO also had a record of cooperating with the CIA. See also Mahoney, *JFK: Ordeal in Africa*, 79.

30. Rusk's speech to the NATO Council of Ministers on May 8 reaffirmed Western aid to help newly independent countries avoid communism and communist subversion. Rusk, Speech at NATO Council of Ministers meeting, May 8, 1961, *Department of State Bulletin* (May 29, 1961), 800–802; *New York Times*, May 9, 1961.

31. Memorandum (Rusk) for President, August 3, 1961, *FRUS 1961–1963*, vol. 20, 184–85; and Mahoney, *JFK: Ordeal in Africa*, 77. See also Memorandum (Williams) for Rusk, July 15, 1961, *FRUS 1961–1963*, vol. 20, 160.

32. Kalb, *Congo Cables*, 268–76. See also Gerard-Libois, *Katanga Secession*, 151–55; State (Rusk) to Leopoldville, June 27, 1961, *FRUS 1961–1963*, vol. 20, 154; State (Rusk) to Brussels, July 8, 1961, *FRUS 1961–1963*, vol. 20, 156; Memorandum of Conversation, Vance and Struelens, July 28, 1961, *FRUS 1961–1963*, vol. 20, microfiche suppl., document 342; State (Rusk) to Leopoldville, July 8, 1961, *FRUS 1961–1963*, vol. 20, microfiche suppl., document 340, which also cites *New York Times*, July 4, 1961, as evidence that opinion was forming against Leopoldville moderates if they opposed parliamentary negotiations.

33. In the Senate, Victor Kourmoriko won 37 votes, resulting in a narrow victory over Justin Matiti, who ran as a PSA rather than a bloc nationaliste candidate and who won 31 votes. CIA efforts appear to have had some success, and his margin was reduced from 74 to 61 in favor and 57 against. In the Chamber vote, 120 of 137 delegates were present. Hoskyns, *Congo since Independence*, 375; Devlin, *Chief of Station*, 156.

34. On the growing support for Adoula within the administration, see Stevenson to State, April 22, 1961, *FRUS 1961–1963*, vol. 20, 126–27. See also State (Bowles) to Congo, June 5, 1961, *FRUS 1961–1963*, vol. 20, 143.

35. Information based on recollections of Cleophas Kamitatu at the CWIHP's Oral History Conference on the Congo Crisis, 1960–61. See Namikas, "History through Documents and Memory."

36. Hoskyns, *Congo since Independence*, 376–77.

37. For the United States, see Memorandum (Rostow) for the President, as Supplement to Rusk Memorandum of Day Before, August 4, 1961, *FRUS 1961–1963*, vol. 20, microfiche suppl., document 343.

38. See editorial note, *FRUS 1961–1963*, vol. 20, 144, quoting Bundy Memorandum to the President, June 10, 1961. As David Gibbs noted in his review of the *FRUS* volume in *African Affairs* 95 (July 1996), 453–54, this is virtually the only mention of CIA activities in this *FRUS* volume, even when evidence publicly available at the time of the crisis suggested a much more intimate role for the CIA in the Congo.

39. Mahoney, *JFK: Ordeal in Africa*, 85–88; Kalb, *Congo Cables*, 273.

40. Devlin, *Chief of Station*, 187.

41. See Rusk to Kennedy, August 3, 1961, and footnote quoting Rostow to Kennedy, August 4, 1961, *FRUS 1961–1963*, vol. 20, 184–85.

42. In *China and Africa*, 57 n. 59, Larkin speculated that China wanted to keep its mission in the Congo but Adoula would not agree.

43. See Protokoll Nr. 48/61 "Der Sitzung des Politbüros des Zentralkomitees am Dienstag, dem 12, September 1961 im Sitzungssaal des Politbüros," DY 30, J IV 2/2 730, Bundesarchiv.

44. Devlin, *Chief of Station*, 194–95.

45. On the issue of recognition, see Memorandum of Conversation, Rusk and Bomboko, October 10, 1961, *FRUS 1961–1963*, vol. 20, microfiche suppl., document 348; Memorandum of Conversation, Fredericks and Bomboko, October 10, 1961, *FRUS 1961–1963,* vol. 20, microfiche suppl., document 349; Memorandum of Conversation, Bomboko and Fredericks, October 10, 1960, *FRUS 1961–1963*, vol. 20, microfiche suppl., document 349. See also Kalb, *Congo Cables*, 304–308; Hoskyns, *Congo since Independence*, 399–400; Mahoney, *JFK: Ordeal in Africa*, 132–34; Mazov, *Distant Front in the Cold War*, 170–71; and Nazhestkin, "Gody kongolezkogo krizisa," 159.

46. See Vladislav Zubok, "Spy vs. Spy: The KGB vs. the CIA," *CWIHP Bulletin*, no. 4 (Fall 1994): 28–29, quoting Shelepin to Khrushchev, July 29, 1961, fond 4, opis 13, delo 81, ll. 130–34, RGANI. Zubok concluded that "the KGB documents" show "even at that time of escalating covert superpower rivalry in their Third World, the Kremlin leadership retained clear Realpolitik priorities . . . as pawns in a geostrategic game centered firmly on Berlin," 31. See also Christopher Andrew and Vasili Mitrokhin, *The Sword and the Shield: The Mitrokhin Archive and the Secret History of the KGB* (New York: Basic Books, 1999), 181.

47. Rudolf Schlesinger, "The CPSU Programme: Historical and International Aspects," *Soviet Studies* 8 (January 1962): 312–17.

48. Gizenga was threatening to send ANC forces against Katanga, in an effort to push Adoula to act. Adoula tried to dominate by confusion, redrawing provincial boundaries into 21 smaller entities. See Leopoldville (Gullion) to State, August 22, 1962, JFKL cables, box 31. See reference to Embassy Telegram 589 in Leopoldville (Gullion) to State, September 11, 1961, *FRUS 1961–1963*, vol. 20, 207. See also Leopoldville (Gullion) to State, September 15, 1961, *FRUS 1961–1963*, vol. 20, 214–16; State (Rusk) to Brussels, September 16, 1961, *FRUS 1961–1963*, vol. 20, 222; Eric Packham, *Success or Failure: The U.N. Intervention in the Congo after Independence* (Commack, N.Y.: Nova Science Publishers, 1998), esp. 187–88; and *New York Times*, February 19 and April 21, 1962.

49. See, e.g., Memorandum of Conversation, Rusk, Home, and Murville, August 7, 1961, and Rusk to State, August 8, 1961, *FRUS 1961–1963*, vol. 20, 186–89.

50. O'Brien, *To Katanga and Back*, 208–13. See also Hoskyns, *Congo since Independence*, 400–401; and Devlin, *Chief of Station*, 187.

51. Hammarskjöld authorized ONUC to set up a refugee camp outside Elizabethville to house the Baluba fleeing from Tshombe. The director of U.N. operations in Katanga, O'Brien, recalled how the camp had adopted slogans of communism as a way of protest against Tshombe or "anyone who supported a party not sponsored by the Union Minière." In the camp, there was an "avenue" named after Lumumba, and one named after Khrushchev. Although the Baluba knew little about communism, they did know that Khrushchev had supported Lumumba, while Belgium and the United States had wanted him executed. O'Brien, *To Katanga and Back*, 294. For U.N. documentation on the camp, see Report, August 20, 1962, *SCOR*, 17th year, suppl. for

July, August, and September 1962, document S/5053, add. 11, 8–10. See also USUN (Stevenson) to State, September 6, 1961, *FRUS 1961–1963*, vol. 20, 203.

52. For figures, see USUN (Stevenson) to State, September 6, 1961, *FRUS 1961–1963*, vol. 20, 202–203; O'Brien, *To Katanga and Back*, 129–33; and Gerard-Libois, *Katanga Secession*, 212.

53. A. Walter Dorn and David J. H. Bell, "Intelligence and Peacekeeping: The U.N. Operation in the Congo, 1960–1964," *International Peacekeeping* 2 (Spring 1995): 11–33, The Military Information Branch, according to Dorn and Bell, "was established as part of ONUC to enhance the security of U.N. personnel, to support specific operations, [and] to warn of outbreaks of conflict and to estimate outside interference." Also available at https://docs.google.com/viewer?a=v&q=cache:yQ6rwfY_D6wJ:www. oss.net/dynamaster/file_archive/090906/c53f590a896ebff9aac17b9881efd316/028 %2520CH15%2520Dorn%2520Bell%2520Intel%2520PK%2520UK%2520OK.doc +&hl=en&gl=us&pid=bl&srcid=ADGEESgNlxMABSQrHC-zyetfWHvYHVPJP pIZP25-D9Xw2MOLqnioZH16ja4dbLZHNDDWYmgFqMDOLS0ZbWAmM-YLW 8eS9Yjms9yTvAzgjKC2SkQAi5tBWPSZnUlTKxL85J6x4qhgHcY6&sig=AHIEtbR SVyraJ492bgjKS58zwUrLTnBQEw&pli=1.

54. For the asylum charges against the Belgian government, see O'Brien, *To Katanga and Back*, 221; and Urquhart, *Hammarskjöld*, 556.

55. State (Ball) to Rusk at Paris, December 12, 1961, *FRUS 1961–1963*, vol. 20, 306. It has been estimated that UMHK paid Tshombe $44 million in tax revenues in 1961. See Special National Intelligence Estimate 65-2-61, December 7, 1961, *FRUS 1961–1963*, vol. 20, 295.

56. O'Brien, *To Katanga and Back*, 197–98; *New York Times*, December 13, 1961.

57. O. Schachter, "Observations on the Legal Aspects of the Present Katanga Situation," September 7, 1961; Khiari to Secretary-General, September 10, 1961; and Secretary-General to Linnér, September 10, 1961, in *The Guardian*, August 17, 2011.

58. The others included the minister of finance, Jean-Baptiste Kibwe, and the president of the Katanga Assembly, Charles Mutaka. Vladimir Fabry was also involved in formulating the plans for Morthor, giving testimony to Hammarskjöld's concern for its legality. O'Brien, *To Katanga and Back,* 247–53; Hoskyns, *Congo since Independence*, 404–20; Urquhart, *Hammarskjöld*, 555–71; Kalb, *Congo Cables*, 287–96.

59. See CRISP, *Congo 1960: Annexes,* 80. O'Brien himself would resign after Morthor's failure. Elizabethville (Canup) to State, September 14, 1961, *FRUS 1961–1963*, vol. 20, 212; *New York Times*, September 15, 1961; Villafana, *Cold War in the Congo*, 59. See also Keith Kyle, *The U.N. in the Congo*, Incore Occasional Paper (Coleraine: University of Ulster, 1995), http://www.incore.ulst.ac.uk/home/publication/ occasional/kyle.html; Kyle covered the operation as a reporter for the BBC.

60. Bunche to Secretary-General, September 14, 1961, in *The Guardian*, August 17, 2011.

61. Leopoldville (Gullion) to State, September 17, 1961, *FRUS 1961–1963*, vol. 20, 226.

62. Bunche to Secretary-General, September 14, 1961, posted online by *The Guardian*, August 17, 2011.

63. State (Rusk) to Brussels, September 16, 1961, *FRUS 1961–1963*, vol. 20, 221. In fact, the day after Hammarskjöld's plane crash, three C-130s and one C-124 were

authorized for use in the emergency. See reference to Joint Chiefs of Staff telegram in editorial note, *FRUS 1961–1963*, vol. 20, 226–27 n. 1.

64. Madeleine Kalb has argued quite plausibly that Hammarskjöld's authorization to Linnér provided a deliberate opening for ONUC field leaders to take a Cordier-like, preemptive action without his full knowledge. Brian Urquhart, who later replaced O'Brien, maintained that the secretary-general expected no violence before he arrived in Leopoldville. Kalb, *Congo Cables*, 292–93. See also Urquhart, *Hammarskjöld*, 564.

65. Leopoldville (Gullion) to State, September 17, 1961, *FRUS 1961–1963*, vol. 20, 226.

66. Rusk to Cleveland, September 16, 1961, *FRUS 1961–1963*, vol. 20, microfiche suppl., document 344. State (Rusk) to Brussels, September 15, 1961, *FRUS 1961–1963*, vol. 20, 218; O'Brien, *To Katanga and Back*; *New York Times*, September 16, 1961.

67. See copy of Secretary-General to Bunche, September 15, 1961, in *The Guardian*, August 17, 2011.

68. Ibid.

69. Hammarskjöld, who tried to shroud the nature of the operation, let it continue. After Tshombe's lone Fouga Magister aircraft assaulted U.N. troops making their way to Jadotville to replace the exhausted Irish battalion, Hammarskjöld sensed that with every U.N. loss he risked U.S. support. The Fouga Magister attack hit a sore spot with Hammarskjöld, since it highlighted U.N. air vulnerability. Urquhart, *Hammarskjöld*, 578.

70. There was one survivor who died several days later from his injuries and was never able to provide any information about the crash. Gavshon, *Mysterious Death of Dag Hammarskjöld*, 47, 129–33; O'Brien, *To Katanga and Back*, 285; Urquhart, *Hammarskjöld*, 577–89.

71. See Bengt Rosio, "The Ndola Crash and the Death of Dag Hammarskjöld," *Journal of Modern African Studies* 31, no. 4 (December 1993): 661–71. The fact that the crash had occurred in British colonial territory aroused suspicion of a British connection. But since Hammarskjöld was negotiating a cease-fire, the British would have little reason to become involved in his death. Alternatively, Soviet defector Arkady Shevchenko raised the unlikely possibility of Soviet complicity. "Friends working on African affairs once told me they had seen a top-secret KGB report indicating that the aircraft [carrying Hammarskjöld] had been shot down by pro-Soviet Congolese forces penetrated and guided by operatives from the USSR," he wrote. Shevchenko, *Breaking with Moscow*, 102–03. Khrushchev himself said the KGB implicated forces loyal to Lumumba, see *Vremia, Liudi, Vlast*, v. 2, 467. Although unreviewed and indiscriminate in her use of evidence, Lisa Pease raised the question of the role of the British intelligence; see Lisa Pease, "Midnight in the Congo: The Assassination of Lumumba and the Mysterious Death of Dag Hammarskjöld," *Probe* 6 (March–April 1999), www.webcom.com/~stka/pr399-congo.html. The British journalist Arthur Gavshon researched the accident and subsequent investigations; see Gavshon, *Mysterious Death of Dag Hammarskjöld*. He found two pieces of evidence that suggested foul play: a dozen or so sightings of a second plane in the vicinity just before Hammarskjöld's plane went down; and the fact that the bodies and the plane were riddled with bullets and bullet fragments at angles that allegedly indicated they were fired directly and were not the result of an explosion. For a good

review article of the literature on this topic, see David Gibbs, "Dag Hammarskjöld, the United Nations, and the Congo Crisis of 1960–1: A Reinterpretation," *Journal of Modern African Studies* 31 (March 1993): 163–74. Again, more recent evidence has pointed to the Katangan gendarmerie. As a result of some investigative reporting by Goran Bjorkdahl and reports by *The Guardian*, Hammarskjöld's nephew is calling for an investigation into the death of the secretary-general. See *The Guardian*, August 17, 2011, August 24, 2011 (response by Brian Unwin), and September 16, 2011, available at, respectively, http://www.guardian.co.uk/world/2011/aug/17/dag-hammarskjold-un-secretary-general-crash?INTCMP=ILCNETTXT3487, http://www.guardian.co.uk/commentisfree/2011/aug/24/worng-suggestion-hammarskjold-murdered?INTCMP=ILCNETTXT3487, and http://www.guardian.co.uk/world/2011/sep/16/dag-hammarskjold-call-for-new-inquiry. See also the newest work by Susan Williams, *Who Killed Hammarskjöld? The U.N., the Cold War and White Supremacy in Africa* (London: C. Hurst & Co., 2011). She again returns to the question of a subsequent and conscious third-party action, based on claims made by Major General Bjorn Egge, a Norwegian in charge of U.N. military intelligence who claimed that he saw a bullet hole in Hammarskjöld's forehead, but that this hole had been removed from subsequent photographs. See Williams, *Who Killed Hammarskjöld*, 5.

72. *New York Times*, September 19, 1961.

73. In October 1961, Kennedy supporters senators Albert Gore Sr. (D-Tennessee), chairman of the African Affairs Sub-committee of the Foreign Relations Committee, Maurine Neuberger (D-Oregon), and Philip Hart (D-Michigan) visited the Congo to reassure the American public and Adoula of U.S. support for a solution in the Congo. See also *New York Times*, October 13, 1961.

74. Hoskyns, *Congo since Independence*, 436–37; *Pravda*, September 10, 1961; *Izvestia*, September 22 and October 5, 1961.

75. See U Thant statements, September 20 and November 3, 1961, in *Public Papers of the Secretaries General of the United Nations, Volume 6: U Thant, 1961–1964*, edited by Andrew W. Cordier and Max Harrelson (New York: Columbia University Press, 1976) (hereafter, *Public Papers of U Thant*), 22–25.

76. Ball to Kennedy, September 23, 1961, *FRUS 1961–1963*, vol. 20, 234–37.

77. State (Bowles) to Leopoldville, September 18, 1961, *FRUS 1961–1963*, vol. 20, 227–28; National Security Action Memorandum No. 97, Bundy to Rusk, September 19, 1961, *FRUS 1961–1963*, vol. 20, 231–32.

78. See statements by Bomboko and Ethiopian Representative Gebre-Egzy, November 13, 1961, *SCOR*, 16th year, 973rd meeting, para. 109–21 and 44–51, respectively. Villafana, *Cold War in the Congo*, 59. For UMHK support of Tshombe, see Special National Intelligence Estimate (hereafter, SNIE) 65-2-61, in *FRUS 1961–1963*, December 7, 1961, vol. 20, 295.

79. November 13, 1961, *SCOR*, 16th year, 973rd meeting, para. 51–52; and State (Rusk) to MacArthur, October 21, 1961, *FRUS 1961–1963*, vol. 20, 255. For Rusk's earlier views on the United Nations, see State (Rusk) to Brussels, January 28, 1961, *FRUS 1961–1963*, vol. 20, 32; Memorandum (Rusk) to Kennedy, November 11, 1961, *FRUS 1961–1963*, vol. 20, 268–70; Memorandum (Rusk) to Kennedy, November 11, 1961, *FRUS 1961–1963*, vol. 20, 270–74. See also Harriman to State, November 4, 1961, *FRUS 1961–1963*, vol. 20, microfiche suppl., document 351. As if to underline his fear, Mobutu led his forces against Katanga on November 16, 1961; see *New York*

Times, November 17, 1961. Any CIA involvement is unclear. For an alternative view of Rusk than the one presented here, see Thomas Zeiler, *Dean Rusk: Defending the American Mission Abroad* (Wilmington, Del.: Scholarly Resources, 2000), esp. 88–90.

80. Resolution S/5002 and U.S. amendments S/4985 and S/4989 (in part) are found in Higgins, *United Nations Peacekeeping*, 37–39.

81. USUN (Stevenson) to State, November 25, 1961, *FRUS 1961–1963*, vol. 20, 280.

82. State (Rusk) to Leopoldville, November 7, 1961, *FRUS 1961–1963*, vol. 20, 265–66; Memorandum of Conversation, Kennedy and Spaak, November 20, 1961, *FRUS 1961–1963*, vol. 20, 275–77.

83. November 24, 1961, *SCOR*, 16th year, 982nd meeting, para. 118; and Macmillan, *Pointing the Way*, 448–49.

84. November 15, 1961, *SCOR*, 16th year, 974th meeting, para. 56–74.

85. See Conclusions of Cabinet Meeting, November 14, 1961, CAB 125/36 at www.nationalarchives.gov.uk.

86. Dodd apparently was paid $50,000 a year by Armas. See Gibbs, *Political Economy of Third World Intervention*, 121–24, for a good outline of the Katanga lobby. See also Borstelmann, *Cold War and the Color Line*, 148–49; Weissman, *American Foreign Policy in the Congo*, 168–72; and Staniland, *American Intellectuals and African Nationalists*, 236–43.

87. Urquhart, UNOH, interview 5, 40.

88. See William F. Buckley Jr., "Why the South Must Prevail," *National Review*, August 24, 1957.

89. Hilsman, *To Move a Nation*, 263; for an outline of Dodd's argument, see Thomas Dodd, "Congo: The Untold Story," *National Review*, August 28, 1962, 136–42. For a glimpse at Krock's editorials, see *New York Times*, December 24, 1961, and January 7, 1962.

90. *Time*, December 22, 1961.

91. Elizabethville (Hoffacker) to State, November 30, 1961, *FRUS 1961–1963*, vol. 20, 283–84. See Brian Urquhart, *A Life in Peace and War* (New York: W. W. Norton, 1991), 179–84; O'Brien, *To Katanga and Back*, 320–26; State to Luanda, transmitting message from Kennedy, December 1, 1961, *FRUS 1961–1963*, microfiche suppl., document 354.

92. See, e.g., Memorandum of Telephone Conversation, Kennedy and Macmillan, December 13, 1961, *FRUS 1961–1963*, vol. 20, 311, and Rusk to Kennedy, December 9, 1961, *FRUS 1961–1963*, vol. 20, 299–300. Hammarskjöld had asked for and received this support in the case of emergencies in September 1961. See State (Bowles) to Leopoldville, September 18, 1961, *FRUS 1961–1963*, vol. 20, 227, fn, 1.

93. U.N. bombs also inadvertently hit the Leopoldville hospital and the hospital at Shikolobwe, near which Katangan mercenaries tended to locate military camps. After these accidents, anti–United Nations sentiment appeared in newspapers worldwide. Leopoldville (Godley) to State, December 5, 1961, *FRUS 1961–1963*, vol. 20, 291; Elizabethville (Hoffacker) to State, December 6, 1961, *FRUS 1961–1963*, vol. 20, 292; Leopoldville (Gullion) to State, December 15, 1961, *FRUS 1961–1963*, vol. 20, 319; *New York Times*, December 15 and 16, 1961.

94. Lincoln White, press spokesperson for the State Department, publicly endorsed the Adoula-Tshombe negotiations and stated that "the cessation of hostilities is up to the United Nations," but as long as Tshombe was serious, then "the fighting could

be suspended." White statement, December 15, 1961, 10–11; and Ball statements, December 10 and 13, 1961; *Department of State Bulletin*, January 1, 1962, 12.

95. See documents reproduced in Higgins, *United Nations Peacekeeping*, 432–33.

96. See Leopoldville (Gullion) to State, December 21, 1961, *FRUS 1961–1963*, vol. 20, 335–36; Leopoldville (Gullion) to State, December 22, 1961, *FRUS 1961–1963*, vol. 20, microfiche suppl., document 357.

97. U Thant report on negotiations at Kitona, December 21, 1961, *SCOR*, 16th year, supplements for October, November, and December. For a good discussion of the U.S. efforts to see the Kitona Accords signed, see Kalb, *Congo Cables*, 320–22.

98. State (Rusk) to West Palm Beach, to President, December 23, 1961, *FRUS 1961–1963*, vol. 20, 344–45, *New York Times*, January 5, 1962.

99. T. Kolesnichenko, *Pravda,* December 20, 1961. See also *Izvestia*, November 24, 1961.

100. See USUN (Stevenson) to State, December 20, 1961, *FRUS 1961–1963*, vol. 20, 332–33; Leopoldville (Gullion) to State, January 25, 1962, *FRUS 1961–1963*, vol. 20, 369, for quote.

101. The Chamber called on Gizenga to return to Leopoldville. Gizenga promised to return only once the Katangan secession was ended. The announcement brought fighting between his forces and those now loyal to Lundula, who advocated cooperation with Leopoldville. State (Rusk) to Leopoldville, January 13, 1962, *FRUS 1961–1963*, vol. 20, 359–60; and State (Rusk) to Leopoldville, January 16, 1962, *FRUS 1961–1963*, vol. 20, 360–61; Hoskyns, *Congo since Independence*, 459.

102. Telephone conversation, McGhee and Dungan, January 12, 1962, Office Files of U.S. Political Affairs, 1961–1963, box 4, RG59, NARA.

103. See *New York Times*, January 13, 14, and 21, 1962; Kalb, *Congo Cables*, 326–30; Nzongola-Ntalaja, *Congo from Leopold to Kabila*, 131; Devlin, *Chief of Station*, 159.

104. See Memorandum from the deputy chief of the CC CPSU International Department, V. Korionov, to the CC CPSU on the necessity of launching a solidarity campaign with Antoine Gizenga, May 16, 1962, including a copy of "Plan of action to defend Antoine Gizenga approved by the CC CPSU Secretariat on May 24, 1962," translated by Sergey Mazov, unofficial translation, Congo briefing book prepared for CWIHP Oral History Conference on the Congo, September 2004.

105. "Daily Congo digest," country files, Bureau of African Affairs, box 5, RG59, NARA; *Pravda*, January 26–28, 1962.

106. *Pravda*, January 18 and 25, and February 1, 1962. Volodin did point a finger at Mobutu's role since he was in charge of the "Binza" camp where Gizenga was being held. See also summary of Soviet newspaper articles in *Mizan Newsletter*, January 1962, 30–33.

107. *Pravda*, April 23, 1962; Kalb, *Congo Cables*, 343.

108. Mazov, *Distant Front in the Cold War*, 176–77. Mazov transcribed the name as Boshele, but given the pronunciation, the name certainly refers to Egide Bocheley-Davidson (also referred to as simply Bocheley in the literature). See CRISP, *Congo 1960: Annexes*, for biographies.

109. Legvold, *Soviet Policy in West Africa*, 124–28, 139–41.

110. Heikal, *Cairo Documents,* 202–205.

111. Higgins, *United Nations Peacekeeping*, 275–98.

112. *New York Times*, March 29 and 30, October 17, and December 6, 1961.

Chapter 10

1. Leopoldville (Gullion) to State, April 18, 1962, *FRUS 1961–1963,* vol. 20, 420; and State (Rusk) to Leopoldville, April 20, 1962, *FRUS 1961–1963*, vol. 20, 421–23; Leopoldville (Gullion) to State, May 30, 1962, *FRUS 1961–1963*, vol. 20, 469–70; S/5053, add. 10, annex 46.

2. Memorandum (Brubeck, Department of State Executive Secretary) to Bundy, May 21, 1962, *FRUS 1961–1963*, vol. 20, 462–64, for quote; State (Rusk) to Leopoldville, May 19, 1962, *FRUS 1961–1963*, vol. 20, 460; State (Ball) to London, May 11, 1962, JFKL, cables, box 30; London (Bruce) to State, May 16, 1962, 8 p.m., JFKL, cables, London talks, box 30. Kennedy sent a family friend and president of the Belgo-American Development Corporation, Admiral Alan Kirk, to hold talks with Herman Robliart, UMHK's representative in Brussels. Brussels (MacArthur) to State, July 19, 1962, JFKL, cables, box 31. While Kirk was in Brussels, McGhee conferred with representatives from Mobil, and the U.S. ambassador in London held talks with officials from Tanganyika Concessions. Gibbs argued that these U.S. efforts began to chisel away at Belgian and British interests and the coherence in their business communities. One success was the election of Max Nokin as president of Société Générale in December 1962. Nokin preferred a cooperative approach with the United States and NATO, even though the community as a whole still sympathized with Tshombe; see Gibbs, *Political Economy of Third World Development*, 133–35. For negotiation efforts, see also Brussels (MacArthur) to State, March 4, 1962, *FRUS 1961–1963*, vol. 20, 401–e405.

3. Macmillan Notebook, January 3, 1962, CAB 195/20, National Archives Documents Online, United Kingdom, available at www.nationalarchives.gov.uk.

4. London (Bruce) to State, May 16, 1962, 7:00 p.m., *FRUS 1961–1963*, vol. 20, 452–55. See also letter from Macmillan to Kennedy, May 25, 1962, *FRUS 1961–1963*, vol. 20, 467–68. See also James, *Britain and the Congo Crisis*, 172–81.

5. See two Memoranda of Conversation, February 5, 1962, *FRUS 1961–1963*, vol. 20, 374–80, and February 5, 1962, Adoula and Ball et al., *FRUS 1961–1963*, vol. 20, microfiche suppl., documents 359 and 360; USUN (Stevenson) to State, June 5, 1962, JFKL, cables, box 30 for Bunche's comments regarding Adoula-Mobutu differences.

6. *New York Times*, February 13, 1962.

7. *New York Times*, July 21, 1962.

8. Leopoldville (Godley) to State, July 27, 1962, JFKL, NSF, box 31.

9. U Thant made no secret of this. See *New York Times*, July 21, 1962.

10. *New York Times*, July 20, 1962; Leopoldville (Godley) to State, July 27, 1962, JFKL, cables, box 31.

11. U Thant Plan, November 29, 1962, *SCOR*, 17th year, suppl. for October, November, and December, document S/5053, add. 13, annex 1, excerpted in Higgins, *United Nations Peacekeeping*, vol. 3, *Africa*, 435–39, and for the British view opposing sanctions, see Conclusions of Cabinet Meeting, July 10, 1962, CAB 128/36, available at www.nationalarchives.gov.uk.

12. Rusk to State, July 23, 1962, *FRUS 1961–1963,* vol. 20, 514–15. For an alternative view of Rusk, see Thomas Zeiler, *Dean Rusk: Defending the American Mission Abroad* (Wilmington, Del.: Scholarly Resources, 2000), esp. 88–90.

13. Record of Understanding (of meeting with the President, July 25, on the Congo), n.d., *FRUS 1961–1963,* vol. 20, 525–27; and Ball to Kennedy, August 3, 1962, *FRUS 1961–1963,* vol. 20, 527–32. See also Kalb, *Congo Cables*, 345–55.

14. State (Ball) to USUN, June 27, 1962, *FRUS 1961–1963*, vol. 20, 488–92, for Ball quote. See also Leopoldville (Gullion) to State, July 16, 1962, JFKL, cables, box 31; and Leopoldville (Gullion) to State, May 30, 1962, *FRUS 1961–1963*, vol. 20, 469–70.

15. State (Ball) to USUN, July 21, 1962, *FRUS 1961–1963*, vol. 20, 512–14.

16. USUN (Yost) to State, July 26, 1962, *FRUS 1961–1963*, vol. 20, 522–23; Record of Understanding of Meeting with the President, July 25, 1962, *FRUS 1961–1963*, vol. 20, 525–26; Ball to Kennedy, August 3, 1962, *FRUS 1961–1963*, vol. 20, 530. See U Thant Plan in November 29, 1962, *SCOR*, 17th year, document S/5053, add. 13, annex 1, suppl. for October, November, and December, excerpted in Higgins, *United Nations Peacekeeping*, 435–39. For an excellent outline of this complex plan, see Gérard-Libois, *Katanga Secession*, 255–58. See also Kalb, *Congo Cables*, 345–50.

17. State (Ball) to USUN, July 21, 1962, *FRUS 1961–1963*, vol. 20, 512–14.

18. Record of understanding of meeting with the President, July 25, 1962, *FRUS 1961–1963*, vol. 20, 526.

19. Report in Brubeck files, *FRUS 1961–1963*, vol. 20, microfiche suppl., document 368; Memorandum from Ball to Kennedy, August 3, 1960, *FRUS 1961–1963*, vol. 20, 527–32. Frank Carlucci at the Africa desk in Washington reinforced Gullion's reports from Leopoldville with what Ball called weekly "horror stories." For good discussions of these differences and Ball's contribution to Congo policy, see Mahoney, *JFK: Ordeal in Africa*, 145; James A. Bill, *George Ball: Behind the Scenes in U.S. Foreign Policy* (New Haven, Conn.: Yale University Press, 1997), 145–50; and Schlesinger, *Thousand Days*, 578.

20. Colonel E. R. Frédéric Vandewalle, *Mille et Quatre jours: Contes du Zaire et du Shaba* (Brussels: F. Vandewalle, 1974), vol. 10, 140–56. For a good overall analysis of Tshombe's motives in agreeing to the U Thant Plan, see Herbert Weiss, "The Tshombe Riddle," *The New Leader*, September 17, 1962, 3–6.

21. See editorial note, quoted from Memorandum of Telephone Conversation, Ball, Bundy, and Dungan, August 14, 1962; and Memorandum of Conversation, Ball and Dungan, August 15, 1962, *FRUS 1961–1963*, vol. 20, 551–52. Ball later called the plan "not very sensible." See Memorandum of Conversation, Rusk, Ball, Williams, Godley, et al., November 5, 1962, *FRUS 1961–1963*, vol. 20, 649.

22. State (Rusk) to Leopoldville, August 19, 1962, *FRUS 1961–1963*, vol. 20, 556–57; and Leopoldville (Gullion) to State, August 28, 1962, *FRUS 1961–1963*, vol. 20, 563–66.

23. *New York Times*, September 14, 1962.

24. State (Ball) to Leopoldville reproduced Kennedy to Dodd, August 24, 1962, *FRUS 1961–1963*, vol. 20, 558–59; and Leopoldville (Gullion) to State, August 30, 1962, *FRUS 1961–1963*, vol. 20, 565–67. See also Kennedy to Dodd, August 17, 1962, and November 19, 1962, President's Office files, http://www.jfklibrary.org/Asset-Viewer/Archives/JFKPOF-029-014.aspx.

25. Hilsman, *To Move a Nation*, 253–54.

26. See, for instance, L. Volodin, *Pravda*, August 2, 1962.

27. *New York Times*, August 31, 1961.

28. Soviet government statement on the Congolese question, September 5, 1962, *SSSR i strany Afriki*, vol. 2, 638–40; *Pravda*, September 7, 1962.

29. *New York Times*, August 10, 1962.

30. The General Assembly requested the Court's advisory ruling. *New York Times*, July 21, 1962.

31. *New York Times*, September 22, 1962.

32. In *Success or Failure*, 71–255, Parkham recounted the troubles in Kasai that he experienced as U.N. representative. See also Leopoldville (Gullion) to State, September 13, 1962, *FRUS 1961–1963*, vol. 20, 574–77.

33. *New York Times*, October 11 and November 27, 1961.

34. Paper prepared by Ball, [September 29, 1962], *FRUS 1961–1963*, vol. 20, 594–97; and Memorandum of Conversation, Rusk, Ball, Williams, and Godley, November 5, 1962, *FRUS 1961–1963*, vol. 20, 647–51.

35. Leopoldville (Gullion) to State, September 28, 1962, *FRUS 1961–1963*, vol. 20, 587–89; Leopoldville (Gullion) to State, transmitting letter from McGhee, September 29, 1962, *FRUS 1961–1963*, vol. 20, 591–92; Leopoldville (Gullion) to State, October 4, 1962, *FRUS 1961–1963*, vol. 20, 600–601; Elizabethville (Dean) to State, October 4, 1962, *FRUS 1961–1963*, vol. 20, 603–605; two memoranda of telephone conversations, Ball and Kennedy, September 21, 1962, *FRUS 1961–1963*, vol. 20, microfiche suppl., documents 373 and 374.

36. *New York Times*, October 10 and 21, 1962.

37. Memorandum (Kaysen) to Kennedy, November 7, 1962, *FRUS 1961–1963*, vol. 20, 652. For Carl Kaysen and Ralph Dungan's opposition to deeper involvement, see Schlesinger, *Thousand Days*, 577.

38. Memorandum (Kaysen) for the record, November 8, 1962, *FRUS 1961–1963*, vol. 20, 656, which recorded that "the President summed up by saying that the issue was the relative staying power of Adoula and Tshombe, and their relative virtue"; and Memorandum of Conversation, Kennedy, McGhee, Williams, Godley, Sloan (Defense), et al., October 31, 1962, *FRUS 1961–1963*, vol. 20, 641–43.

39. Memorandum of Conversation, Kennedy, Rusk, Ball, et al., November 7, 1962, *FRUS 1961–1963*, vol. 20, microfiche suppl., document 386.

40. USUN (Stevenson) to State, November 26, 1962, *FRUS 1961–1963*, vol. 20, 685–86.

41. Hellström, "The Instant Air Force," 30–31; Frank Villafana, *Cold War in the Congo: The Confrontation of Cuban Military Forces, 1960–1967* (New Brunswick, N.J.: Transaction, 2000), 37. See also *New York Times*, April 26, 1966. An earlier reference to Cuban involvement appeared on June 26, 1961 when the *New York Times* reported that the Congolese central government arrested five Cuban pilots. However, the background or involvement of these pilots is not clear.

42. Leopoldville (Gullion) to State, December 5, 1962, JFKL, NSF, box 33.

43. Leopoldville (Gullion) to State, November 25, 1962, JFKL, NSF, box 33; Leopoldville (Gullion) to State, December 6, 1962, JFKL, NSF, box 33. Mobutu expressed the belief that the ANC would not follow him if he attempted a coup at this time.

44. Hellström, "Instant Air Force," 34.

45. Leopoldville (O'Sullivan) to State, November 23, 1962, JFKL, NSF, box 33; Leopoldville (Gullion) to State, November 26, 1962, JFKL, NSF, box 33, declassified in 1997.

46. USUN (Stevenson) to State, November 26, 1962, JFKL, NSF, box 33, declassified in 1997.

47. *New York Times*, November 28, 1962.

48. January 30, 1963, *SCOR*, suppl. for January, February, and March 1963, document S/5053, add. 15, 60–65; for quote, see para. 6.

49. James, *Britain and the Congo Crisis*, 180–81.

50. Leopoldville to State, December 6, 1962, *FRUS 1961–1963*, vol. 20, 708–709; Hellström, "Instant Air Force," 34.

51. USUN (Stevenson) to State, December 13, 1962, JFKL, NSF, box 33.

52. For U.S. recognition of this fact, see USUN (Stevenson) to State, November 26, 1962, *FRUS 1961–1963*, vol. 20, 685–86.

53. Memorandum for Kennedy, December 13, 1962, and Memorandum for the Record, December 14, 1962, *FRUS 1961–1963*, vol. 20, 729–37. The suggestion to supply U.S. fighter planes had been made as early as November 7, 1961, and now the Pentagon was recommending a step further in supply forces to tip the balance toward the United Nations, if necessary. See Kalb, *Congo Cables*, 359–64.

54. Memorandum for the Record, December 14, 1962, *FRUS 1961–1963*, vol. 20, 735; handwritten notes from Brubeck series, December 14, 1962, *FRUS 1961–1963*, vol. 20, microfiche suppl., document 396. See also Cleveland to Acting Secretary (Ball) and McGhee, December 15, 1962, *FRUS 1961–1963*, vol. 20, microfiche suppl., document 399; Memorandum of Telephone Conversation, Kennedy and Ball, December 15, 1962, *FRUS 1961–1963*, vol. 20, microfiche suppl., document 400. Regarding Kennedy's concerns that the issue did not appear as anticommunist containment, see Memorandum for the Record, December 14, 1962, *FRUS 1961–1963*, vol. 20, 734–37; "Operating Plan for the Congo," December 17, 1962, *FRUS 1961–1963*, vol. 20, microfiche suppl., document 404.

55. Rusk's comments are in an editorial note quoting notes by Kaysen, *FRUS 1961–1963*, vol. 20, 747.

56. Memorandum (Kaysen) to Kennedy, December 17, 1962, *FRUS 1961–1963*, vol. 20, 748–49.

57. Editorial notes in *FRUS 1961–1963*, vol. 20, 751.

58. Hellström, "Instant Air Force," 34–37.

59. Editorial notes in *FRUS 1961–1963*, vol. 20, 751, for quote. Provisions of material began in late November, see McGhee to Cleveland, November 30, 1962, *FRUS 1961–1963*, vol. 20, microfiche suppl., document 392. See also Spaak's reaction in Brussels (MacArthur) to State, December 19, 1962, *FRUS 1961–1963*, vol. 20, 757–60. See attempt to get U Thant to go along with an air squadron. Ball to Stevenson, December 15, 1962, *FRUS 1961–1963*, vol. 20, microfiche suppl., document 401; and Stevenson notes, December 15, 1962, in *FRUS 1961–1963*, vol. 20, microfiche suppl., document 402; handwritten notes from Brubeck series, meeting by Kennedy, Rusk, Ball, McGhee, and Stevenson, [after December 17, 1962,] *FRUS 1961–1963*, vol. 20, microfiche suppl., document 405.

60. State (Rusk) to USUN, December 21, 1962, *FRUS 1961–1963*, vol. 20, 777–78.

61. Memorandum of Telephone Conversation, Yost and Ball, December 15, 1962, *FRUS 1961–1963*, vol. 20, microfiche suppl., document 398.

62. Villafana, *Cold War in the Congo*, 60; Conclusions of cabinet meeting, November 14, 1961, CAB 125/35, and July 10, 1962, CAB 128/36, available at www.national archives.gov.uk.

63. Kalb, *Congo Cables*, 365.

64. Memorandum (Brubeck) for Kaysen, December 28, 1962, JFKL general file, box 28A; Brubeck to Kaysen, December 28, 1962, *FRUS 1961–1963*, vol. 20, 788–89. See also USUN (Stevenson) to State, December 19, 1962, JFKL cables, box 33. See also Jonathan Dean interview, February 21, 1990, UNOH, 8–9.

65. State (Ball) to USUN, January 6, 1963, *FRUS 1961–1963*, vol. 20, 815–16; State (Rusk) to Leopoldville, January 8, 1963, *FRUS 1961–1963*, vol. 20, 817. See also Hellström, "Instant Air Force," 36–37.

66. Stanley Meisler, *The United Nations: The First Fifty Years* (New York: Atlantic Monthly Press, 1995), 132. For the Gardiner quote, see *New York Times*, December 31, 1961.

67. State (Rusk) to USUN, December 29, 1962; and editorial note in *FRUS 1961–1963*, vol. 20, 793–95.

68. Memorandum of Conversation, McGhee, Kaysen, Godley, et al., December 28, 1962, *FRUS 1961–1963*, vol. 20, 791.

69. *New York Times*, January 1, 1963; Thomas Hughes (Bureau of Intelligence and Research, or INR), to Williams, January 2, 1963, JFKL general box 29; State (Ball) to London, January 3, 1963, JFKL cables, box 34; Kalb, *Congo Cables*, 367.

70. National Security Affairs (Kaysen) to Kennedy, January 1, 1963, *FRUS 1961–1963*, vol. 20, 801.

71. See Villafana, *Cold War in the Congo*, 62.

72. Thant, *View from the U.N.*, 145.

73. Memorandum of Conversation, Rusk and U Thant, January 9, 1963, *FRUS 1961–1963*, vol. 20, 820–23. See also Leopoldville (Gullion) to State, January 9, 1963, *FRUS 1961–1963*, vol. 20, 822–25.

74. Gerard-Libois, *Katanga Secession*, 273–76.

75. *New York Times*, May 20, 1963; "Report to the Secretary-General," January 30, 1963, *SCOR*, suppl. for January, February, March 1963, document S/5053, add. 13, 65–77.

76. Report on the Congo situation, March 21, 1963, JFKL, general files, box 29; *New York Times*, March 4, 1963.

77. *New York Times*, March 4 and 5 and June 2, 1963.

78. Report on the Congo situation, March 21, 1963, JFKL, general files, box 29; and *New York Times*, February 8, 9, and 14, March 4, and May 4, 1963.

79. USUN (Stevenson) to State, January 29, 1963, JFKL cables, box 34.

80. Memorandum of Conversation, Kennedy, Bundy, Rusk, Ball, Stevenson, et al., September 9, 1963, *FRUS 1961–1963*, vol. 20, 870–71; USUN (Stevenson) to State, September 20, 1963, *FRUS 1961–1963*, vol. 20, 872–74. The *FRUS* volume contains about 50 pages on 1963, seriously downplaying the importance of events that year. See also State (Harriman/Rusk) to Leopoldville, August 14, 1963, Congo cables, box 35, JFKL.

81. U Thant, February 4, 1963, *SCOR*, suppl. for January, February, and March 1963, document S/5240, 104; and U Thant Report, September 17, 1963, *SCOR*, suppl. for July, August, and September 1963, 174, para. 31.

82. USUN (Stevenson) to State, January 30, 1963, cables, box 34, JFKL. For Adoula's request, see his Letter to Secretary-General, August 22, 1963, *SCOR*, suppl. for July, August, and September 1963, document S/5428/annex 1, 176–77. For U.S.

attempts to pressure the United Nations into a retraining program, see Memorandum (Kaysen) for the Record, March 27, 1963, *FRUS 1961–1963*, vol. 20, 485–87.

83. Harlan Cleveland's report to Kennedy, February 21, 1963, *American Foreign Policy, Current Documents*, 1963, 653–57. I am grateful to Marcia Wright and Glenn Adler for sending me their paper, "'To Keep It Going Our Way': Designs and Policy by the United States toward the Congo, 1963," Columbia University, Department of History, New York, 1985.

84. For a summary of the various Western contributions, see Memorandum for the President, June 7, 1963, *FRUS 1961–1963*, vol. 20, microfiche suppl., document 425; Williams to Rusk, May 13, 1963, *FRUS 1961–1963*, vol. 20, 852–54. See also Thomas P. Odom, "Dragon Operations: Hostage Rescues in the Congo, 1964–1965," U.S. Army Command and General Staff College, Combat Studies Institute, *Leavenworth Papers*, 14 (1988): 7.

85. Memorandum (Kaysen) to Kennedy, March 25, 1963, *FRUS 1961–1963*, vol. 20, microfiche suppl., document 422; Memorandum of Conversation, Spaak and Williams, May 28, 1963, *FRUS 1961–1963*, vol. 20, microfiche suppl., document 424; Memorandum (Rusk) for Kennedy, June 7, 1963, *FRUS 1961–1963*, vol. 20, microfiche suppl., document 425.

86. See Kalb, *Congo Cables*, 371; and Kelley, *America's Tyrant*, 89.

87. Memorandum of Conversation, Kennedy, Williams, and Mobutu, May 31, 1963, *FRUS 1961–1963*, vol. 20, 858–62.

88. Memorandum (Benjamin Read, executive secretary) for Bundy, October 9, 1963, *FRUS 1961–1963*, vol. 20, microfiche suppl., document 428; State (Ball) to Leopoldville, October 28, 1963, *FRUS 1961–1963*, vol. 20, 881–83; Memorandum of Conversation, Kennedy and Adoula, October 10, 1963, *FRUS 1961–1963*, vol. 20, 876–79.

89. Congress cut the original projection of the military aid package from $6 million to $4 million. Memorandum, [September] 1963, Congo general file, box 383; "Administrative History of the Department of State," vol. I, chap. 5, "Problem Areas," 5–6, box 2, Lyndon B. Johnson Library, Austin (hereafter, LBJL).

90. George C. Herring, *America's Longest War: The United States and Vietnam, 1950–1975*, 2nd ed. (New York: Alfred A. Knopf, 1979), 20, 86.

91. Leopoldville (Gullion) to State, January 19, 1963, JFKL cables, box 34. See also Ovinnokov, third secretary at UN, "Kongolezskii vopros v okt–dek 1962 g" [The Congolese question in Oct.–Dec. 1962], OMO, opis 8, delo 30, p35, AVPRF; and *New York Times*, December 22, 1962. See also V. Maevskii, *Pravda*, January 6, 1963.

92. *Pravda*, February 2, 1963.

93. M. Petrov, 2nd adviser to the Africa department, "K Polozhenie v Kongo (kr. spravka)," [The situation in the Congo], January 18, 1963, fond 047, opis 6, delo 15, papka 10, AVPRF.

94. N. Fedorenko to the Secretary-General, March 2, 1963, *SCOR*, suppl. for January, February, March 1963, document S/5249, 107–10.

95. Leopoldville (Gullion) to State, January 19, 1963, JFKL cables, box 34. Gullion assessed the Soviet lost opportunity: "We probably have Soviet Bureaucratic inflexibility and lack of foresight to thank for our escape from this debacle; that and U.S. and [the government of the Congo] support for U.N. solution in Congo. Soviet Union could not bring itself to offer aid through [the United Nations], and confident that

Adoula would soon fall, it withheld formal offer of direct miliary assistance to his government while dangling possibilities before dazzled eyes of individual soldiers and ambitious Ministers." The successful operation also ended Nasser's flirtation with the rebels. In January, the UAR returned $1.6 million to the central government sent by the Stanleyville government for arms.

96. V. Suvorov, May 28, 1964, "Vizit komanduiushchego kongolzskoi natsional'noi armiei generala Mobutu v Bel'giiu 30 aprelia–14 maia 1964 g." [The visit of Congolese national army commander General Mobutu to Belgium], fond 72, delo 11, papka 45, listi 25–32, AVPRF.

97. *New York Times,* July 14, 1963; *Pravda*, July 14, 1963.

98. *New York Times*, June 6 and 13, 1963.

99. V. Suvorov, attaché in Brussels, April 30–May 14, 1964, "Visit komanduiushchego kongolezskoi natsional'noi armiei generala Mobutu v Bel'giiu 30 april-14 maia 1964g.," fond 72, por, 11, opis 45, papka 45, AVPRF.

100. Leopoldville (Gullion) to State, March 4, 1963, JFKL cables, box 34.

101. *Izvestia*, June 14 and 15, 1963; *Pravda*, June 29 and July 26, 1963; Leopoldville (Gullion) to State, February 3, 1963, JFKL, cables, box 34.

102. *Izvestia*, March 26, 1963.

103. *Izvestia,* August 11, 1963.

104. The Conseil National de Libération (CNL) included major representatives from the MNC-L, PSA-Gizenga, the African Democratic Union (UDA), and the Convention People's Party (PNCP). Nkrumah, *Challenge of the Congo*, 240.

105. *Izvestia*, July 16, 1963.

106. See L. Stepanov's article on world revolution in *Pravda*, July 18, 1963.

107. "Material k obsuzhdeniia voprosa o sovetskoi propagande na Afriku" [Material for discussion of the Soviet propaganda question in Africa], March 1, 1963, Otdel pechati, fond 5, opis 57, rolik 7727, RGANI. See *Pravda*, February 5, 1961, about the new university.

Chapter 11

1. Leopoldville (Gullion) to State, October 18, 1963, Congo cables, box 35, JFKL.

2. For background on the Congo, see esp. Crawford Young, "Rebellion and the Congo," in *Protest and Power in Black Africa*, edited by Robert I. Rothberg and Ali Mazrui (New York: Oxford University Press, 1970), 969–90; Administrative History of the Department of State, vol. I, chap. 5, "Problem Areas," 5–6, box 2, LBJL.

3. Martens, *Pierre Mulele*, 170–71, 251–52; Ogunsanwo, *China's Policy in Africa*, 175, fn. 2, quoted *African Mail*, January 10, 1964, of Lusaka, which published the documents seized from Soviet diplomats returning to Leopoldville in 1963: "We have done everything to get our Russian comrades [i.e., Moscow] to help us, but they have never comprehended our difficulties. That is the reason Comrade Mulele left for China. China gave him a course to enter a Military School. . . . We do not wish to offend our Russian friends, but we judge it best to address ourselves to China. . . . China has aided Mulele." See also Benoît Verhaegen, "La rebellion mulélist au Kwilu: Chronologie des événements et essai d'interprétation (janvier 1962–juillet 1964), in *Rebellions-Révolution au Zaire*, edited by Catharine Coquery-Vidrovitch, Alain Forest, and Herbert Weiss (Paris: l'Harmattan, 1987), 127–29; Young, "Rebellion and the

Congo," 971–75; Renée C. Fox, Willy de Craemer, and Jean-Marie Ribeaucourt, "The Second Independence: A Case Study of the Kwilu Rebellion in the Congo," *Comparative Studies in Society and History* 8 (October 1965): 78–109.

4. Moise Tshombe, *My Fifteen Months in Government*, translated by Lewis Barnays (Plano, Tex.: University of Plano, 1967), 36; Nzongola-Ntalaja, *Congo from Leopold to Kabila*, 131.

5. Verhaegen, "La rebellion," 142; *New York Times*, June 2, 1964; Villafana, *Cold War in the Congo*, 69.

6. David Reed, *111 Days in Stanleyville* (New York: Harper & Row, 1965), 9, 54–64; Fox, de Craemer, and Ribeaucourt, "Second Independence," 78–109; Young, "Rebellion and the Congo," 969–1011; Nzongola-Ntalaja, *Congo from Leopold to Kabila*, 132.

7. See esp. *Le Martyr* (Stanleyville), August–November 1964.

8. Nzongola-Ntalaja, *Congo from Leopold to Kabila*, 129; Bouwer, *Gender and Decolonization in the Congo*, 103.

9. Mazov, *Distant Front in the Cold War*, 178–80; Nazhestkin, "Gody kongolez-kogo krizisa," 160.

10. Interior Ministry official Damien Kandolo was also allied with the Binza group; see Weissman, *American Foreign Policy in the Congo*, 109, 230–32.

11. Benjamin Read (Department of State, executive secretary) to Bundy, October 25, 1963, *FRUS 1961–1963*, vol. 20, 880–81; Leopoldville (Gullion) to State, November 4, 1963, *FRUS 1961–1963*, vol. 20, 883–84; CIA, Current Intelligence Memorandum, October 29, 1963, *FRUS 1961–1963*, vol. 20, microfiche suppl., document no. 432.

12. Leopoldville (Gullion) to State, October 18, 1963, Congo cables, box 35, JFKL.

13. Leopoldville (Gullion) to State, October 25, 1963, Congo cables, box 35, JFKL.

14. State (Ball) to Leopoldville, October 28, 1963, Congo cables, box 35, JFKL.

15. Leopoldville (Stearns) to State, November 19, 1963, Congo cables, box 35, JFKL. The Congolese eventually explained that the seized documents indicated "Soviet connivance with Congolese ex-patriots in Brazzaville" to overthrow the Adoula regime. See State (Rusk) to Moscow, November 19, 1963, Congo cables, box 35, JFKL. For a very interesting account of what became a sensationalized version of the Voronin and Miakotnikh affair, see the account by B. G. Beknazar-Iubashev in *Izvestia*, November 26, 1963. For confirmation of his connection to the KGB, see Kirpichenko, *Razvedka*, 98; and for Nazhestkin's account, see "Gody kongolezkogo krizisa," 160–64.

16. Leopoldville (Stearns) to State, November 20, 1963, Congo cables, box 35, JFKL; 22 November 1963, *Pravda*.

17. Leopoldville (Stearns) to State, November 20, 1963, Congo cables, box 35, JFKL.

18. The article was noted in *Pravda*, November 1, 1963; the article was analyzed by Stoessel in Moscow to State, November 2, 1963, Congo cables, box 35, JFKL.

19. *Pravda* or *Izvestia*, November 24, 1963, for Gromyko statement to Kini.

20. Adlai Stevenson urged that the U.S. Embassy in Leopoldville should be allowed to do what they could to obtain release of the diplomats. Soviet representatives, however, never approached the Leopoldville diplomatic community for help. Instead, Mikhail Suslov, who oversaw ideology and foreign policy for the Central Committee

Secretariat, turned to the United Nations for help in freeing Voronin and Miakotnykh. Nemchina asked the chief of civilian operations for ONUC, Max Dorsinville, to help secure release of detained Soviet diplomats. When Adoula avoided a meeting with Dorsinville, U Thant threatened to make a public démarche, and Adoula finally granted him a meeting. USUN (Stevenson) to State, November 20, 1963, Congo cables, box 35, JFKL; Leopoldville (Stearns) to State, November 20, 1963, Congo cables box 35, JFKL; and Leopoldville (Stearns) to State, November 20, 1963, Congo cables, box 35, JFKL. For an indirect mention of this affair, see Kirpichenko, *Razvedka*, 97–98.

21. Leopoldville (Stearns) to State, November 20, 1963, Congo cables, box 35, JFKL; Weissman, *American Foreign Policy in the Congo*, stated that Godley "felt that Gullion's attitude was too anti-Belgian. Godley was also more skeptical of the virtues of African nationalism," 235–36.

22. Weissman, *American Foreign Policy in the Congo*, 235. His assessment, written more than three decades ago, remains true. Weissman found that Godley reflected a more conservative view of Africa than had Gullion.

23. Leopoldville (Stearns) to State, November 20, 1963, Congo cables, box 35, JFKL; Leopoldville (Stearns) to State, November 21, 1963 (received 10:12 a.m.), Congo cables, box 35, JFKL.

24. Leopoldville (Stearns) to State, November 21, 1963 (received 12:30 p.m.), Congo cables, box 35, JFKL.

25. See Memorandum of Working Luncheon with Senators on Topic of the Congo, February 13, 1962, *FRUS 1961–1963*, vol. 20, microfiche suppl., document no. 362.

26. Johnson apparently so disliked the subject of the Congo that several years later Rostow said to him: "I know the Congo is not one of our favorite subjects; I think we could all survive very nicely if we were never forced to deal with it again." See Rostow to Johnson, December 1, 1967, White House Central Files (hereafter, WHCF), CO52, box 24, LBJL.

27. See Fred E. Wagoner, *Dragon Rouge: The Rescue of Hostages in the Congo* (Washington, D.C.: U.S. Government Printing Office, 1981), 61.

28. Rowan Memorandum to Johnson, June 19, 1964, Confidential File CO 52, box 8, LBJL. See also Terrence Lyons, "Keeping Africa Off the Agenda," in *Lyndon Johnson Confronts the World: American Foreign Policy, 1963–1968*, edited by Warren I. Cohen and Nancy Bernkopf Tucker (New York: Cambridge University Press, 1994), 245–78.

29. Administrative History of the Department of State, vol. I, chap. 5, "Africa," 4, 23, box 2, LBJL.

30. E.g., Robert Dallek does not mention Africa in his book; Robert Dallek, *Flawed Giant: Lyndon Johnson and His Times, 1961–1973* (New York: Oxford University Press, 1988). For Lyons's quote, see "Keeping Africa Off the Agenda," 245–78.

31. Dallek, *Flawed Giant*, 86–106.

32. Draft National Security Action Memorandum, [April 9, 1964], *FRUS 1964–1968*, vol. 24, 279–80.

33. Administrative History of the Department of State, vol. I, chap. 5, "Special Problem Areas," 8, box 2, LBJL. Harriman visited the Congo in March 1964.

34. See Thomas Noer, "Phone Rage: LBJ, Averell Harriman, and G. Mennen Williams," in *Society for Historians of American Foreign Relations Newsletter*, December 2004, http://www.shafr.org/passport/2004/december/noer.htm.

35. For a full discussion of the budget crisis, see Lise Namikas, "A Silver Lining: President Johnson and the U.N. Peacekeeping Budget Crisis of 1964–1965," *Diplomacy & Statecraft* (September 2004): 593–612.

36. State (Rusk) to USUN, February 14, 1964, NSF, U.N. file, box 289, LBJL; Cleveland Memorandum to Rusk, January 31, 1964, NSF country file, memos and misc. file, box 287, LBJL.

37. See Eisenhower, *Waging Peace*, 576 n. 16; Namikas, "Silver Lining."

38. *New York Times*, March 18, 1964.

39. *Pravda*, March 22, 1964.

40. U Thant, "From Report on the Withdrawal of the United Nations Forces from the Congo," June 29, 1964, in *Public Papers of U Thant*, 597–603. For the full report, see *SCOR*, 19th year, supplement for April, May, and June 1964, 259–97, document S/5784, esp. para. 141–95 on 291–93; and U Thant, *View from the U.N.*, 145–47.

41. See Moyers's conversation with LBJ, February 8, 1964, in *Taking Charge: The Johnson White House Tapes, 1963–1965*, edited by Michael Beschloss (New York: Simon & Schuster, 1997), 234.

42. Gleijeses, *Conflicting Missions*, 85.

43. *New York Times*, January 17 and February 12, 1964. Sean Kelly, *America's Tyrant: The CIA and Mobutu and Zaire* (Washington, DC: American University Press, 1993), 96–97, gives a particularly good description of the events in Kwilu, based on Vandewalle, *L'Ommegang*, 63–64.

44. Kelly, *America's Tyrant*, 102.

45. Ibid., 98–99. News of the rapid CNL advance encouraged the provincial assembly in Stanleyville to replace its progovernment representative Isombuma with pro-Lumumba François Aradjabu, further upsetting the control of the central government. See *New York Times*, July 19 and 27, 1964.

46. Villafana, *Cold War in the Congo*, 68.

47. Ibid., 70.

48. Reed, in *111 Days in Stanleyville*, gives a good description of the mounting anti-Americanism and its impact in targeting the Americans as the first hostages. Kelly, *America's Tyrant*, 101, quoted *New York Times*, June 13, 1964, reference to a Congolese who shouted, in response to the bombing campaign: "Look, we are a people who fight for liberty with spears and clubs. You, the powerful Americans, are crushing us with bombs and planes. God will judge you! God will punish you!" See also Villafana, *Cold War in the Congo*, 70.

49. *New York Times*, June 16 and 17, 1964. For the role of Cuban exiles in the Congo, see Piero Gleijeses, "Havana's Policy in Africa, 1956–76: New Evidence from Cuban Archives," *CWIHP Bulletin*, nos. 8–9 (Winter 1996–97); and Gleijeses, *Conflicting Missions*.

50. "The Legality of the Tshombe Regime," *The World Today*, February 1965, reprinted by Catherine Hoskyns, *The Organization of African Unity and the Congo Crisis: Documents* (London: Oxford University Press, 1969), 8.

51. For a view of the Kennedy administration's favorable attitude on Mobutu's return, see Leopoldville (Stearns) to State, November 19, 1963, Congo cables, box 35, JFKL; Kelly, *America's Tyrant*, 102.

52. Tshombe, *My Fifteen Months in Government*, 8–9.

53. *New York Times*, June 30 and July 11, 1964.

54. The rest of Tshombe's government included G. Munongo as minister of interior (the position in which he served in Katanga) and minister of establishments; D. Ndinga of Leopoldville as finance minister; L. Mamboleo from Kivu as minister of justice; J. Ebosiri from Stanleyville as minister of national economy, Albert Kalonji as agricultural minister; J. L. Kidicho from Stanleyville and a former Lumumbist as minister of public works; F. Baloji from Kasai as minister of national education; A. Lubaya, former secretary of the CNL as minister of public health; J. Ndamu from Equateur as minister of youth and sports; and A. Kshwe from Kwilu as minister of mines and energy. Tshombe himself said that he initially appointed Thomas Kanza, who represented a group of "rebels," as minister of foreign affairs, but rescinded the offer after Mobutu found incriminating evidence linking him to the rebel group in Brazzaville. See Tshombe, *My Fifteen Months in Government*, 21–22; and 34 for quote.

55. Administrative History of the Department of State, vol. I, Chapter 5, "Special Problem Areas," 9, box 2, LBJL.

56. Gibbs, *Political Economy of Third World Intervention*, 154–55.

57. Ibid., 152–55.

58. Ibid., 154.

59. Ibid., 156; *Time*, December 17, 1965.

60. *Life*, July 17, 1964.

61. *Public Papers of the Presidents: Lyndon Baines Johnson, 1964*, vol. 2, July 24, 1964, 890. See "Administrative History of the Department of State," vol. I, chap. 5, "Special Problem Areas," 9, box 2, LBJL.

62. Dodd to Johnson, August 24, 1965, confidential file, Congo, box 8, LBJL.

63. Malcolm X, "The Oppressed Are Shaking Off the Shackles," December 3, 1964, http://www.hartford-hwp.com/archives/45a/645.html; Malcolm X, "After the Bombing," February 14, 1965, 131–32, http://www.malcolm-x.org/speeches/spc_021465.htm; and Gleijeses, *Conflicting Missions*.

Chapter 12

1. Memorandum (Brubeck) for the Files, NSC meeting on the Congo, August 11, 1964, NSF files, memos, box 1, LBJL.

2. Ibid.

3. Memorandum of Telephone Conversation, President and Ball, November 25, 1964, Ball Papers, Congo III file, box 2, LBJL.

4. Radchenko, *Two Suns in the Heavens*, 81–119; for quotes, see 83, 92, and 95–96. See also Lüthi, *Sino-Soviet Split*, 279–84.

5. Ogunsanwo, *China's African Policy*, 176–79.

6. Quoted by Larkin, *China and Africa*, 71, citing *Africa Report*, May 1, 1964.

7. Martens, *Pierre Mulele*, 253–55.

8. *New York Times*, August 5 and September 29, 1964; Larkin, *China and Africa*, 72; Tung, *Thought Revolution*, 223.

9. Compare *Izvestia*, May 11, 1963, which makes note of the ethnic, isolated nature of the Jadotville protests with Khokhlov's analysis at the end of his article in *Izvestia*, September 11, 1964.

10. *Pravda*, February 11, 1964.

11. N. Khokhlov, *Izvestia*, March 22, 1964.

12. Statement by Fedorenko to the United Nations, July 4, 1964, *SCOR*, 19th year, supplement for July, August, and September 1964, document S/5798, 24–26. For a similar earlier sentiment, see *Pravda*, July 12, 1963.

13. Gleijeses, *Conflicting Missions*, 75–76.

14. Nzongola-Ntalaja, *Congo from Leopold to Kabila*, 132.

15. Odom, "Dragon Operations," 8.

16. Kelly, *America's Tyrant*, 109–11.

17. CRISP, *Congo 1964*, 381–82; Odom, "Dragon Operations," 8. See also the accounts by Reed, *111 Days in Stanleyville*; Wagoner, *Dragon Rouge*, 19–31; and Michael Hoyt, *Captive in the Congo: A Consul's Return to the Heart of Darkness* (Annapolis, Md.: Naval Institute Press, 2000).

18. *Izvestia*, August 2, 1964; see *Mizan Newsletter*, September 1964, 26, for reference to Khokhlov's radio broadcast.

19. Primakov, *Pravda*, August 12, 1964. When in Africa a year later, Guevara still believed that the two movements were designed to meet. He referred to Mulele as the "great unknown" and gently questioned his (Mulele's) lack of cooperation with the eastern provinces. See Galvez, *Che in Africa*, 282.

20. *New York Times*, August 17, 1964.

21. *Pravda*, August 26, 1964; *Izvestia*, August 26, 1964. For an account of this statement, see also *New York Times*, August 26, 1964.

22. For Goldwater's speech at the Republican convention accepting the presidential nomination, see "Barry Goldwater's 1964 Acceptance Speech," http://www.national center.org/Goldwater.html.

23. *New York Times*, August 15, 1964.

24. Harriman to Rusk, August 7, 1964, box 448, WAHP; Gleijeses, "Flee! The White Giants Are Coming!" 213–14; Wagoner, *Dragon Rouge*, 24–25; Administrative History of the Department of State, vol. I, chap. 5, "Special Problem Areas," 10, box 2, LBJL.

25. Gleijeses, "Flee! The White Giants Are Coming!" 219; Alain Rouvez, *Disconsolate Empires: French, British and Belgian Military Involvement in Post-Colonial Sub-Saharan Africa* (Washington, D.C.: University Press of America, 1994), 328–30; Kelly, *America's Tyrant*, 118–19; *New York Times*, August 18, 1964.

26. Tshombe, *My Fifteen Months in Government*, 33–38; see 38 for quote.

27. See *Courrier Africain*, December 4, 1964. Extracts are reprinted by Hoskyns, *Organization of African Unity and the Congo Crisis*, 10–11; and Vandewalle, *L'Ommegang*, 145–47. For the best study of U.S. use of mercenaries, see Gleijeses, "Flee! The White Giants Are Coming!" 216.

28. *New York Times*, August 8, 1964; Odom, "Dragon Operations," 16; Villafana, *Cold War in the Congo*, 78–81.

29. Memorandum of Conversation, Spaak and Harriman, November 8, 1964, box 509, WAHP; *New York Times*, August 26, 1964; Gleijeses, "Flee! The White Giants Are Coming!" 219; Wagoner, *Dragon Rouge*, 34–35; Kelly, *America's Tyrant*, 114–15; Villafana, *Cold War in the Congo*, 43.

30. Odom, "Dragon Operations," 16–18.

31. Gleijeses, "Flee! The White Giants Are Coming!" 213–14. On December 11, 1964, in *SCOR*, 19th year, 1173rd meeting, para. 94, Spaak revealed his "daring" meeting with Gbenye for the first time.

32. For a recent account of Hoyt's adventure, see Hoyt, *Captive in the Congo*, esp. 37–38, for Godley's order to stay. Michael Hoyt and David Grinwis, *A Journal of the Experiences of the Staff of the American Consulate in Stanleyville from 1 August through 24 November 1964* (n.p., 1966), 45. In *111 Days in Stanleyville*, 87, 213, 229–31, Reed reproduced Hoyt's messages, sent under duress, relaying Gbenye's request for negotiations.

33. Hoyt, *Captive in the Congo*, 159.

34. Nzongola-Ntalaja, *Congo from Leopold to Kabila*, 132–33.

35. William Attwood, *The Reds and the Blacks: A Personal Adventure* (New York: Harper & Row, 1967), 198–205. Tshombe's worsening relations with the rest of Africa were revealed during the Summit of Non-Aligned States in Cairo in the first week of October. Upon his arrival in Cairo, Nasser put Tshombe under house arrest and two days later allowed him to leave. Nasser subsequently pulled Egypt's embassy personnel out of the Congo. The Cairo conference condemned continued foreign involvement in the Congo, directing criticism at the mercenaries. See *New York Times*, September 6, 1964. See also Hoskyns, *Organization of African Unity and the Congo Crisis*; and Odom, "Dragon Operations," 17.

36. Odom, "Dragon Operations," 16–18.

37. Telephone Conversation, Bundy and Ball, October [?], 1964, Ball Papers Congo III, LBJL (conversation about Leopoldville to State no. 2004); Reed, *111 Days in Stanleyville*, 136.

38. NSC memorandum for Bundy, October 5, 1964, NSF, files of McGeorge Bundy, box 15, LBJL; for views of Ball, Vance, and McNamara, see untitled telephone conversation, October [22], 1964, Congo II file, Ball Papers, LBJL. See also Odom, "Dragon Operations," 24.

39. Wagoner, *Dragon Rouge*, 69–131. As Wagoner notes, there is no written evidence of the offer of the battalion, but Harriman insisted that he must have talked about it with Spaak. See also Odom, "Dragon Operations," 37–54.

40. Memoranda (Bundy) to the President, November 16 and 20, 1964, vol. 7, October 1–December 31, 1964, LBJL; Rouvez, *Disconsolate Empires*, 329.

41. Hoyt, *Captive in the Congo*, 191–98; and Hoyt and Grinwis, *Journal*, 60–61.

42. Telephone Conversation, President and Ball, November 25, 1965, Ball Papers, Congo III file; LBJL. The paratroopers began to assemble on Ascension Island on November 20.

43. Memorandum for the Record, Meeting with the President, November 19, 1964, NSF, Bundy Papers, box 18; Greenfield and Palmer Telephone Conversation, November [19], 1964, Ball Papers Congo III, LBJL.

44. The Attwood-Kanza meeting took place on November 23, 1964. Hoyt and Grinwis, *Journal*, 64; Attwood, *The Reds and the Blacks*, 213; Administrative History of the Department of State, vol. I, chap. 5, "Special Problem Areas," 12, box 2, LBJL.

45. Hoyt and Grinwis, *Journal*, 54.

46. Thompson, *Ghana's Foreign Policy*, 359–60.

47. Wagoner, *Dragon Rouge*, 148.

48. Edgerton, *Troubled Heart of Africa*, 205.

49. Rusk, *As I Saw It*, 279, also quoted by Lyons, "Keeping Africa Off the Agenda," 249.

50. See series of telephone calls, President and Ball no. 15, Secretary and Ball no. 13, Stevenson and Ball no. 16, November 21, 1964, Ball Papers, Congo III, LBJL; Wagoner, *Dragon Rouge*, 150–51.

51. Telephone Conversation, President and Ball, November 22, 1964, Ball Papers, Congo III, no. 26, LBJL.

52. Kelly, *America's Tyrant*, 142; Wagoner, *Dragon Rouge*, 123.

53. See Paul Semonin, "An Evaluation of the Humanitarian Aspect," excerpt from an unpublished article reproduced by Hoskyns, *Organization of African Unity and the Congo Crisis*, 42–44; Vandewalle, *L'Ommegang*, 350–57. See also Reed, *111 Days in Stanleyville*, 111.

54. Wagoner, *Dragon Rouge*, 167–68.

55. Telephone Conversation, President and Ball, November 25, 1965, Ball Papers, Congo III file, LBJL; Wagoner, *Dragon Rouge*, 182, 197; Odom, "Dragon Operation," 37–54; Villafana, *Cold War in the Congo*, 98–103.

56. Villafana, *Cold War in the Congo*, 105.

57. U.S. government statement reproduced in *SCOR*, 19th year, supplement for October, November and December 1964, document S/6055, annex 2, 188–89.

58. Johnson press conference, November 28, 1964, *Department of State Bulletin* (December 14, 1964), 845–46.

59. Rattan manuscript quoted by Kelly, *America's Tyrant*, 149.

60. For the higher figure, see *New York Times*, December 15, 1964.

61. Wagoner, *Dragon Rouge*, 166.

62. *American Journal of International Law* (1864), 614–19. In legal terms, as noted by Gerhard von Glahn, the founders of modern legal theory consider humanitarian intervention legally valid when a state treats its people "in such a way as to deny their fundamental human rights and to shock the conscience of mankind." Gerhard von Glahn, *Law among Nations: An Introduction to Public International Law*, 5th ed. (New York: Macmillan, 1986), 159.

63. Memoranda (Bundy) to the President, vol. 7, October 1–December 31, 1964, LBJL.

64. Borstelmann, *Cold War and the Color Line*, 185–86; *Time*, December 11, 1964, 4.

65. Praeger to Johnson, December 1, 1964, WHCF, Executive CO, box 24, LBJL.

66. Telephone Conversation, President and Ball, November 25, 1965, Ball Papers, Congo III file; LBJL.

67. Malcolm X, "The Oppressed Are Shaking Off Their Shackles," December 3, 1964, http://www.hartford-hwp.com/archives/45a/645.html. See also Malcolm X's entire speech at "Oxford Union Debate," http://www.brothermalcolm.net/2003/mx_oxford/index.html.

Chapter 13

1. Memorandum of Telephone Conversation, Harriman, Rusk, and Palmer, November 23, 1960, WAHP; Fedorenko to President of the Security Council, November 25, 1964, *SCOR*, 19th year, supplements for October, November, and December 1964, document S/6066, 192–94. For Radio Moscow attack, see CIA Research and Reference Service, "Foreign Media Reaction to the Congo Rescue Mission," November 27, 1964, WHCF, CO52, box 24, LBJL, 24–26. See also *Pravda*, November 22, 25, 26, and 27, 1964.

2. *Pravda*, November 26, 1964; *Izvestia,* November 27, 1964.

3. CIA Research and Reference Service, "Foreign Media Reaction to the Congo Rescue Mission," November 27, 1964, WHCF, CO52, box 24, LBJL, 24–26.

4. *New York Times*, November 29 and December 4, 9, and 13, 1964; Rusk Statement, December 9, 1964; *Department of State Bulletin*, December 28, 1964, 805; New China News Agency, English-language reports reprinted in *Survey of China Mainland Press*, 3349 (December 1964), 24–34, and 3350 (December 1964), 30, for reference to Johnson.

5. *New York Times*, December 5, 7, and 13, 1964. Tshombe accused Congo-Brazzaville of hosting three training camps for the rebels in July 1964 and broke relations with them, as well as with his Burundian neighbor on the eastern side. He accused both of allowing the Chinese Embassy to foment revolutionary activity.

6. Gleijeses, "Flee! The White Giants Are Coming!" 227–29.

7. Zubok and Pleshakov, *Inside the Kremlin's Cold War*, 272–73.

8. Legvold, *Soviet Policy in West Africa*, 228–34.

9. Brezhnev, December 3, 1964, "Ha rechi Pervogo sekretaria TsK KPSS L. I. Brezhnev na mitinge sovetsko-chekhoslovatskoi druzhby v Moskve," in *SSSR i Strany Afriki, 1963–1970, dokumenty i materialy, chast I*, edited by L. F. Il'ichev (Moscow: Ministerstvo inostranykh del, 1982), 181–82.

10. See Protokoll Nr. 1/65, "Der Sitzung des Politbüros des Zentralkomitees am Dienstag, dem 5, January 1964 im Sitzungssaal des Politbüros," and "Anlage Nr. 4," DY 30 J IV 2/2 969, Bundesarchiv.

11. Gromyko, December 7, 1964, *GAOR*, 19th year, 1292nd meeting, para. 94–96.

12. December 9, 1961, *SCOR*, 19th year, 1170th meeting, para. 67–73. For his main statement, see December 17, 1964, *SCOR*, 1178th meeting, 19th year, para. 59–125.

13. Galvez, *Che in Africa*, 28; Guevara, December 11, 1964, *GAOR*, 19th year, 1299th meeting, para. 94–100. A recording of Guevara's speech (with translator voiceover) is also available at http://www.youtube.com/watch?v=a8po84osCl8&feature=related.

14. Botsio, December 9, 1964, *SCOR*, 19th year, 1170th meeting, para. 126. See, for example, the statement of Sudan representative Mahgoub in the opening session, December 9, 1964, *SCOR*, 19th year, 1170th meeting, para. 148–77.

15. Botsio, December 9, 1964, *SCOR*, 19th year, 1170th meeting, para. 131.

16. Beovogui, December 10, 1964, *SCOR*, 19th year, 1171st session, para. 13.

17. December 11, 1964, *SCOR*, 19th year, 1173rd session, para. 126, 131, 162.

18. Stevenson, December 14, 1964, *SCOR*, 1174th session, 19th year, para. 49.

19. Juju Wachuku, December 15, 1964, *SCOR*, 19th year, 1176th meeting, para. 2–57.

20. December 30, 1964, *SCOR*, 19th year, 1189th meeting, para. 6. For complete resolution, see *SCOR*, 19th year, suppl. for October, November, and December, S/6129, 328.

21. December 29, 1964, *SCOR*, 19th year, 1187th meeting, para. 17.

22. See statement by Achkar of Guinea, December 29, 1964, *SCOR*, 19th year, 1187th meeting, para. 31; and Fedorenko, December 30, 1964, *SCOR*, 19th year, 1188th meeting, para. 10–11.

23. See his letter to Nasser, dated December 3, 1964, in Nkrumah, *Challenge of the Congo*, 265–67.

24. *New York Times*, February 13, 1965.

25. Fedorenko Statement, October 9, 1964, SC, S/PV.1160, excerpted in *Current Documents 1964*, 131; and Soviet Statement, November 7, 1964, *GAOR*, 19th session, A/5777, annex 21, 19–21. For the quid pro quo, see *New York Times*, December 20 and 22, 1964.

26. Bundy Memorandum to Johnson, May 4, 1965, NSF, UN file, box 289, LBJL; Goldberg Statement, August 16, 1965, *GAOR*, 15th meeting of the Special Committee on Peacekeeping Operations, A/5916, add. 1, annexes, 19th session, annex 21, 86–87. See also Richard Stebbins, *The United States in World Affairs* (New York: Harper & Row, 1966–67), *1965*, 264–81, and *1966*, 321–29; and Russell, *United Nations and United States Security Policy*, 198–209, 333–54.

27. Adoula to Johnson, January 7, 1965, WHCF, Executive, yellow file, CO52, box 24, LBJL. Underlining in original.

28. Kelly, *America's Tyrant*, 158–59; CIA Intelligence Memorandum, March 17, 1965, CREST database, NARA.

29. CIA Intelligence Memoranda, January 27 and March 17, 1965, CREST database, NARA.

30. Kelly, *America's Tyrant*, 158–59; CIA Intelligence Memorandum, March 17, 1965, CREST database, NARA.

31. Telephone Conversation, Fredericks and Ball, January 12, 1965, Ball Papers, Congo III file, LBJL; Bundy and Ball, December 11, 1964, Ball Papers, Congo III, no. 47, LBJL; Gleijeses, "Flee! The White Giants Are Coming!" 230, and for costs of operation, see Kelly, *America's Tyrant*, 163.

32. Memorandum (Haynes) to Bundy, March 4, 1965; and Memorandum (Komer and Haynes) to Bundy, March 30, 1965, *FRUS 1964–1968*, documents 193 and 194, vol. xxiv, http://history.state.gov/historicaldocuments/frus1964-68v24/ch6. In this, they were not so far off from recommendations of the State Department. See Komer's "Action Program" for the Congo sent to Harriman, March 30, 1960, WAHP, box 481.

33. Lyons, "Keeping Africa Off the Agenda," 261; for quotes, see State (Rusk) Circular drafted by Williams, May 6, 1965. See also Memorandum (Bundy) for the President, March 8, 1965, NSF, Africa country file, box 76, LBJL; and Memorandum (Williams) to Ambassadors, May 10, 1965, with attached "Bench marks for New Africa program (uncleared draft)," NSF, Africa country file, box 76, LBJL.

34. Memorandum of Conversation, April 27, 1965, with Second Secretary V. Porshakov and U.S. Desk Officer Beauveau Nalle, NSF, African Country file, box 76, LBJL.

35. Heikal, *Cairo Documents*, 348–52.

36. Galvez, *Che in Africa*, 47, 55, 69–71, 137–38. In ibid., 141, Galvez noted that neither the Soviets nor the Egyptians knew of Guevara's participation in the Congo, at least as late as September. By November 1965, it was assumed that Nyerere guessed that Guevara was in the Congo, although no mention was ever made of his name; see ibid., 237. See also Gleijeses, "Havana's Policy in Africa," 6.

37. Galvez, *Che in Africa*, 142–49. see also ibid., Che to Fidel, October 5, 1965, 182–85, and ibid., 238–39, 261, 265. For a good account of Che's trip to the Congo, see Jon Lee Anderson, *Che Guevara: A Revolutionary Life* (New York: Grove Press, 2010; orig. pub. 1997), 589, 596–636.

38. See Che's conclusions, given by Galvez, *Che in Africa*, 279–98.

39. Ogunsanwo, *China's Africa Policy*, 177, quoting New China News Agency, August 19, 1965; also see Larkin, *China and Africa*, 74–75.

40. *Pravda*, September 25, 1965.

41. U.N. General Assemby, September 22, 1965, *GAOR*, 20th session, 1375th plenary meeting, pt. IV, 1589.

42. Rusk to Brussels, August 11, 1965 (quotes Harriman to Spaak), box 509, WAHP; *New York Times*, July 7 and 19, October 14, 1965; Tshombe, *My Fifteen Months in Government*, 110. In 1967 amid continuing upheaval in the Congo, rumors spread that Tshombe planned to return to his native land from exile in Spain. He was kidnapped and ended up in Algeria, where government officials refused his extradition so that he could stand trial for treason. He died of a heart attack shortly thereafter.

43. Dodd to Johnson, August 24, 1965, confidential file, Congo, box 8, LBJL; Dodd to Johnson, October 27, 1965, confidential file, Congo, box 8, LBJL.

44. Weiss, "Introduction," *Congo 1965*, xiii-xiv.

45. Tshombe, *My Fifteen Months in Government*, 109.

46. Kelly, *America's Tyrant*, 167.

47. See *New York Times*, November 24 and 25, and December 5, 1965; and Gondola, *History of the Congo*, 132–34.

48. Wrong, *In the Footsteps of Mr. Kurtz*, 65. Devlin's memoirs are decidedly less enthusiastic; see *Chief of Station*, 234–36.

49. *New York Times*, December 15, 1965.

50. Mobutu statement of December 17, 1965. See Edgerton, *Troubled Heart of Africa*, 206.

51. Kelly, *America's Tyrant*, 78–79.

52. Nkrumah, *Challenge in the Congo*, 288–93.

53. *New York Times*, November 26, 1965, and June 6, 1966; "The Congo's Joseph Mobutu: Past, Present, Future," Intelligence Memorandum, Directorate of Intelligence, CREST database, NARA.

54. *Izvestia*, November 26, 1965. For attitudes toward Tshombe, see V. Fomichev, embassy officer, in fond 72, opis 46, por 15, papka 45, AVPRF. Fomichev argued that the United States preferred a change from Tshombe because of his poor performance, while Belgium preferred to keep him in power.

Conclusion

1. De Witte, *Assassination of Lumumba*, 187.

2. Nzongola-Ntalaja, *Congo from Leopold to Kabila*, 147–48.

Selected Bibliography

Note: In the interest of conserving space, this book includes only a selected bibliography. See chapter notes for additional references.

Unpublished Sources

Archiv vneshnei politiki Rossiskoi Federatsii (AVPRF; Archive of the Foreign Policy of the Russian Federation), Moscow.

Ralph Bunche Papers, University of California at Los Angeles.

Centre des Archives communistes en Belgique, Brussels. Correspondence and documents sent to the author.

CIA Records Search Tool (CREST). National Archives and Records Administration (NARA), College Park, Maryland.

Dwight D. Eisenhower Papers, Eisenhower Presidential Library, Abilene, Kansas. Collections: National Security File, Department of State File, White House Central Files, Ann Whitman Papers, Dulles/Herter Telephone Conversation Series.

Lyndon B. Johnson Papers, Johnson Presidential Library, Austin, Texas. Collections: National Security File, Department of State File, White House File.

John F. Kennedy Papers, Kennedy Presidential Library, Boston. Collections: Pre-presidential Papers, National Security Files, Department of State Files, White House Files.

Rossiiskii gosudarstvennyi arkhiv noveishei istorii (RGANI; Russian State Archive of Recent History), formerly Tsentr Khraneniia Sovremennoi Dokumentatsii (Center for the Preservation of Contemporary Documents), Moscow.

Stiftung Archiv der Parteien und Massenorganisationen der DDR im Bundesarchiv (Archive of Political Parties and Mass Organization of the German Democratic Republic), Berlin. Protocols as sent to the author.

Published Sources

Aksiutin, Iurii V. *Nikita Sergeevich Khrushchev: Materialy k biografii* [Nikita Sergeevich Khrushchev: Biographical Materials]. Moscow: Isdatel'stvo politicheskoi literatury, 1989.

Borger, Julian, and Georgina Smith. "Dag Hammarskjöld: Evidence Suggests U.N. Chief's Plane Was Shot Down." *The Guardian*, August 17, 2011. www.guardian.co.uk/world/2011/aug/17/dag-hammarskjold-un-secretary-general-crash?INTCMP=ILCNETTXT3487.

Centre de recherche et d'information socio-politiques (CRISP). *Abako 1950–1960: documents, Congo 1959: Documents belges et africains*, 2nd ed., rev. and add., *Congo 1960, Congo 1960: Annexes et biographies, Congo 1961, Congo 1962, Congo 1963, Congo 1964: Political Documents of a Developing Nation*, with an introduction by Herbert Weiss, *Congo 1965: Political Documents of a Developing Nation*, with an introduction by Herbert Weiss, *Parti Solidaire Africain (PSA): Documents 1959–1960*. Brussels and Princeton, N.J.: CRISP, 1959–67.

Chambre des représentants de Belgique. *Enquête parlementaire visant à déterminer les circonstances exactes de l'assassinat de Patrice Lumumba et l'implication éventuelle des responsables politique belges dans celui-ci*. Brussels, 2001–2.

Cheng, J. Chester, ed. *The Politics of the Chinese Red Army: A Translation of the Bulletin of Activities of the People's Liberation Army*. Stanford, Calif.: Hoover Institution on War, Revolution, and Peace, 1966.

Cordier, Andrew W., and Wilder Foote, eds. *Public Papers of the Secretaries General of the United Nations, Volume 4: Dag Hammarskjöld, 1958–1960*; and *Volume 5: Dag Hammarskjöld, 1960–1961*. New York: Columbia University Press, 1975.

Cordier, Andrew W., and Max Harrelson, eds. *Public Papers of the Secretaries General of the United Nations, Volume 6: U Thant, 1961–1964*. New York: Columbia University Press, 1976.

Davidson, Apollon B., and Sergei V. Mazov, eds. *Rossiia i Afrika: Dokumenty i Materialy, tom II, 1918–1960* [Russia and Africa: Documents and Materials, vol. 2, 1918–1960]. Moscow: Institut vseobshchei istorii RAN, 1999.

Davidson, Apollon, B., Sergey Mazov, and Georgiy Tsypkin, eds. *SSSR i Afrika, 1918–1960: Dokumentirovanniia isotriia vzaimootnoshenii* [USSR and Africa, 1918–1960: A historical documentation of relations]. Moscow: Institute of World History, Russian Academy of Sciences, 2002.

Davister, Pierre. *Katanga, Enjeu du Monde: Récits et documents*. Brussels: Éditions Europe-Afrique, 1960.

Declassified Documents Reference System. "Records of the Department of State, Relating to Internal Affairs, Congo, 1963–1966." Woodbridge, Conn.: Research Publications, 1975–2000. Microfilm original available at www.ddrs.psmedia.com.

Gruliow, Leo, ed. *Current Soviet Policies*. Vol. 2: *The Documentary Record of the Twentieth Party Congress and Its Aftermath*; Vol. 3: *The Documentary Record of the Extraordinary Twenty-First Party Congress*; and Vol. 4: *The Documentary Record of the Twenty-Second Congress of the CPSU*. New York: Praeger, 1957–62.

Higgins, Rosalyn. *United Nations Peacekeeping, 1946–1967, Documents and Commentary, Volume 3: Africa*. New York: Oxford University Press, 1980.

Hoskyns, Catherine. *The Organization of African Unity and the Congo Crisis: Documents*. London: Oxford University Press, 1969.

John F. Kennedy Digital Collection. Available at www.jfklibrary.org.

Khrushchev, Nikita S. *For Victory in Peaceful Competition with Capitalism*. New York: E. P. Dutton, 1960.

———. *Vremia, Liudi, Vlast: Vospominania v 4-x kh*. Moscow: Moskovskie Novosti, 1999. Also published in English as *Memoirs of Nikita Khrushchev*, 3 vols. University Park: Pennsylvania State University Press, 2005–7.

Namikas, Lise, and Sergey Mazov. *The Congo Crisis, 1960–1961*. Washington, D.C.: Woodrow Wilson International Center for Scholars, 2004. http://www.wilsoncenter.org/publication/the-congo-crisis-1960-1961.

Nixon, Richard. *The Emergence of Africa*. Washington, D.C.: U.S. Department of State, 1957.

Nothomb, Baron Patrick. "Stanleyville août-novembre 1964." *Chronique de Politique Etrangère*, September–November 1965.

Rouch, Jane. *En Cage avec Lumumba: Les documents du temps*. Paris: Les Éditions du Temps, 1961.

Simons, E., R. Boghossian, and Benoît Verhaegen, eds. *Stanleyville 1959: Le procès de Patrice Lumumba et les émeutes d'octobre*. Paris: Éditions l'Harmattan, 1996.

SSSR i strany Afriki, 1946–1962 gg: Dokumenty i materialy [The USSR and the countries of Africa, 1946–1962: Documents and materials]. 2 vols. Moscow: Gosudarstvennoe Izdatel'stvo Politicheskoi Literatury, 1963.

Tshombe, Moise. *My Fifteen Months in Government*, translated by Lewis Barnays. Plano, Tex.: University of Plano, 1967.

United Kingdom. National Archives Documents Online. Available at www.nationalarchives.gov.uk/ documentsonline.

United Nations, General Assembly. *Official Records*. New York: United Nations, 1960–65.

United Nations, Security Council. *Official Records.* New York: United Nations, 1960–65.

――――. *Official Records*: *Supplements.* September 1960–December 1965. New York: United Nations, 1960–66.

United Nations Intellectual History Project, ed. *The Complete Oral History Transcripts from U.N. Voices.* New York: United Nations, 2007.

United Nations Oral History Collection. http://www.un.org/depts/dhl/dag/oralhist.htm.

U.S. Congress, House of Representatives, Committee on Foreign Affairs. *United Nations Operation in the Congo. Hearings before the Subcommittee on International Organization and Movements of the Committee on Foreign Affairs.* House of Representatives, 87th Congress, 1st sess., April 13, 1961.

U.S. Congress, Senate, Select Committee to Study Government Operations with Respect to Intelligence Activities, *Alleged Assassination Plots Involving Foreign Leaders.* Senate Report no. 94-465, 94th Congress, 1st sess. Washington, D.C.: U.S. Government Printing Office, 1975.

U.S. Consulate, Hong Kong. *Survey of China Mainland Press*, July 1960–July 1965.

U.S. Department of State. *Foreign Relations of the United States, 1952–1954.* Vol. 11: *Africa and South Asia*; *1955–1957*; Vol. 18: *Africa*; *1958–1960*; Vol. 14: *Africa*; *1961–1963*; Vol. 20: *The Congo Crisis*; Vol. 21: *Africa* and microfiche supplement for vols. 20 and 21, *1964–1968*; Vol. 24: *Africa.* Washington, D.C.: U.S. Government Printing Office, 1983–99.

U.S. National Intelligence Council. Central Intelligence Agency. Library. Freedom of Information Act Electronic Reading Room. Available at www.dni.gov/nic/NIC_home.html.

U.S. Office of the Federal Register. *Public Papers of the Presidents of the United States: Dwight D. Eisenhower, 1958–1961*; *John Fitzgerald Kennedy, 1961–1963*; *Lyndon Baines Johnson, 1964–1965.* Washington, D.C.: U.S. Government Printing Office, 1959–66.

van Bilsen, A. A. J. "Un plan de trente ans pour l'émancipation politique de l'Afrique Belge." *Dossiers de l'Action Sociale Catholique*, Brussels, February 1956.

Van der Meersch, Hans Ganshof. *Fin de la Souveraineté Belge au Congo: Documents et Réflexions.* Brussels: Martinus Nijhoff, 1963.

van Lierde, Jean, ed. *Lumumba Speaks: The Speeches and Writings of Patrice Lumumba, 1958–1961.* Boston: Little, Brown, 1963.

Waldron, D'Lynn. Historic Documents and Photos. Available at http://www.dlwaldron.com/authorcontents.html.

Serials, Newspapers, and the Like

Belgian Congo Today
Christian Science Monitor
Courrier Africain du CRISP (Brussels)
Current Digest of the Soviet Press
Drapeau Rouge
International Affairs (Moscow)
Izvestia
Le Martyr (Stanleyville)
Mizan Newsletter (London)
Neizvestnaiia Rossiia
New York Times
Novoe Vremia
Pravda
Présence Africaine
Remarques Congolaises
Soviet News (London Embassy of the USSR)
Time
World Marxist Review

Secondary Works: Monographs and Series

Abi-Saab, Georges. *The United Nations Operation in the Congo, 1960–1964.* London: Oxford University Press, 1978.

Alexander, Major General H. T. *African Tightrope: My Two Years as Nkrumah's Chief of Staff.* New York: Praeger, 1965.

Allison, Roy. *The Soviet Union and the Strategy of Nonalignment in the Third World.* New York: Cambridge University Press, 1989.

Andrew, Christopher, with Vasili Mitrokhin. *The World Was Going Our Way: The KGB and the Battle for the Third World.* New York: Basic Books, 2005.

Anstey, Roger. *King Leopold's Legacy: The Congo under Belgian Rule, 1908–1960.* London: Oxford University Press, 1966.

Ascherson, Neil. *The King Incorporated: Leopold II in the Age of Trusts.* London: George Allen & Unwin, 1963.

Attwood, William. *The Reds and the Blacks: A Personal Adventure.* New York: Harper & Row, 1967.

Ball, George W. *The Past Has Another Pattern.* New York: W. W. Norton, 1982.

Bartlett, Robert E. *Communist Penetration and Subversion in the Congo.* Berkeley, Calif.: Acarn, 1962.

Beschloss, Michael, ed. *Taking Charge: The Johnson White House Tapes, 1963–1965*. New York: Simon & Schuster, 1997.

Bill, James A. *George Ball: Behind the Scenes of U.S. Foreign Policy*. New Haven, Conn.: Yale University Press, 1997.

Bissell, Richard. *Reflections of a Cold Warrior: From Yalta to the Bay of Pigs*. New Haven, Conn.: Yale University Press, 1996.

Black, Cyril E., and Thomas P. Thornton. *Communism and Revolution: The Strategic Uses of Political Violence*. Princeton, N.J.: Princeton University Press, 1964.

Bloomfield, Lincoln P. *The United Nations and U.S. Foreign Policy: A New Look at the National Interest*, rev. ed. Boston: Little, Brown, 1967. Orig. pub. 1960.

Blouin, Andrée. *My Country, Africa: Autobiography of the Black Pasionaria*. New York: Praeger, 1983.

Bohlen, Charles E. *Witness to History, 1929–1969*. New York: W. W. Norton, 1973.

Borstelmann, Thomas. *Apartheid's Reluctant Uncle: The United States and Southern Africa in the Early Cold War*. New York: Oxford University Press, 1993.

———. *The Cold War and the Color Line: American Race Relations in the Global Arena*. Cambridge, Mass.: Harvard University Press, 2001.

Bouwer, Karen. *Gender and Decolonization in the Congo: The Legacy of Patrice Lumumba*. New York: Palgrave Macmillan, 2010.

Bowles, Chester. *Africa's Challenge to America*. Berkeley: University of California Press, 1956.

Brands, H. W. *The Specter of Neutralism: The United States and the Emergence of the Third World*. New York: Columbia University Press, 1989.

Brassine, Justine, and Jean Kestergat. *Qui a tué Patrice Lumumba?* Paris: Duculot, 1991.

Briscoe, Neil. *Britain and U.N. Peacekeeping, 1947–1967*. London: Palgrave Macmillan, 2004.

Brutents, Karen N. *Protiv ideologii sovremennogo koloializma* [Against the ideology of contemporary colonialism]. Moscow: Izdatel'stvo sotsial'no-ekonomichesko literatury, 1961.

———. *Tridtsat' let na staroi ploshchadi* [Thirty years on the old square]. Moscow: Mezhdunarodnye Otnosheniia, 1996.

Brzezinski, Zbigniew, ed. *Africa and the Communist World*. Stanford, Calif.: Stanford University Press, 1963.

Burlatsky, Fedor. *Khrushchev and the First Russian Spring: The Era of Khrushchev through the Eyes of His Advisor*, translated by Daphne Skillen. 1988. New York: Macmillan, 1991.

Ceulemans, Jacques. *A. Gizenga, hier, aujourd'hui, demain*. Brussels: Éditions de Remarques Congolaises, 1964.

Chomé, Jules. *M. Lumumba et le Communisme: Variations à partir du livre de M. P. Houart*. Brussels: Éditions de Remarques Congolaises, 1961.

Colvin, Ian. *The Rise and Fall of Moise Tshombe*. London: Leslie Frewin, 1968.

Cooley, John K. *East Wind over Africa: Red China's African Offensive*. New York: Walker, 1965.

Coquery-Vidrovitch, Catharine, Alain Forest, and Herbert Weiss, eds. *Rebellions-Révolution au Zaire*. Paris: L'Harmattan, 1987.

Dallek, Robert. *Flawed Giant: Lyndon Johnson and His Times, 1961–1973*. New York: Oxford University Press, 1988.

———. *An Unfinished Life: John F. Kennedy, 1917–1963*. Boston: Little, Brown, 2004.

Dallin, Alexander. *The Soviet Union at the United Nations*. New York: Praeger, 1962.

Datlin, Sergei. *Afrika sbrasyvaet tsepi* [Africa throws off its chains]. Moscow: Gospolitizdat, 1960.

Davidson, Apollon B., Dmitri A. Olderogge, and Vasilii B. Solodovnikov. *Russia and Africa: Conference on the Historical Relations of the Peoples of the Soviet Union and Africa*. Moscow: Nauka, Central Department of Oriental Literature, 1966.

Davidson, Basil. *Which Way Africa? The Search for a New Society*. Baltimore: Penguin Books, 1964.

Davis, Kenneth S. *The Politics of Honor: A Biography of Adlai E. Stevenson*. New York: Putnam's Sons, 1967.

Dayal, Rajeshwar. *Mission for Hammarskjöld: The Congo Crisis*. Princeton, N.J.: Princeton University Press, 1976.

Depelchin, Jacques. *From the Congo Free State to Zaire: How Belgium Privatized the Economy—A History of Belgian Stock Companies in Congo-Zaire from 1885 to 1974*, translated by Ayi Kwei Armah. Dakar, Senegal: Codesria Books, 1992.

Desfosses, Helen Conn. *Soviet Policy toward Black Africa: The Focus on National Integration*. New York: Praeger, 1972.

Desiat' let Universiteta druzhby narodov [Ten years of the People's Friendship University]. Moscow: 1975.

De Witte, Ludo. *The Assassination of Lumumba*, translated by Ann Wright and Renée Fenby. 1999. New York: Verso Press, 2001.

Divine, Robert A. *Eisenhower and the Cold War*. New York: Oxford University Press, 1981.

Dobrynin, Anatoly. *In Confidence: Moscow's Ambassador to America's Six Cold War Presidents, 1962–1986.* New York: Times Books, 1995.

Dudziak, Mary L. *Cold War Civil Rights: Race and the Image of American Democracy.* Princeton, N.J.: Princeton University Press, 2000.

Duignan, P., and L. H. Gann, *The United States and Africa: A History.* Cambridge, Mass.: Cambridge University Press, 1984.

Dumont, Georges-H. *La table ronde belgo-congolaise (janvier-février 1960).* Paris: Éditions Universitaires, 1961.

Edgerton, Robert. *The Troubled Heart of Africa: A History of the Congo.* New York: St. Martin's Press, 2002.

Eisenhower, Dwight D. *Waging Peace, 1956–1961: The White House Years.* Garden City, N.Y.: Doubleday, 1965.

Ekepebu, Lawrence Baraebibai. *Zaire and the African Revolution.* Ibadan, Nigeria: Ibadan University Press, 1989.

Ekwe-Ekwe, Herbert. *Conflict and Intervention in Africa: Nigeria, Angola, Zaire.* New York: Macmillan, 1990.

El-Ayouty, Yassin. *The United Nations and Decolonization: The Role of Afro-Asia.* The Hague: Martinus Nijhoff, 1971.

Emerson, Barbara. *Leopold II of the Belgians: King of Colonialism.* New York: St. Martin's Press, 1979.

Etinger, Iakov Ia., Ovanes Melikian. *Neitralizm i mir: Neitralistskaya politika stran Azii i Afriki* [Neutralism and peace: The neutralist policies of the countries of Asia and Africa]. Moscow: Mysl', 1964.

Freedman, Lawrence. *Kennedy's Wars: Berlin, Cuba, Laos, and Vietnam.* New York: Oxford University Press, 2000.

Fursenko, Alexandr, and Timothy Naftali. *Khrushchev's Cold War: The Inside Story of an American Adversary.* New York: W.W. Norton, 2006.

Gaddis, John Lewis. *The Cold War: A New History.* New York: Penguin Press, 2005.

———. *We Now Know: Rethinking Cold War History.* Oxford: Clarendon Press, 1997.

Gálvez, William. *Che in Africa: Che Guevara's Congo Diary,* translated by Mary Todd. New York: Ocean Press, 1999.

Gavshon, Arthur L. *The Mysterious Death of Dag Hammarskjöld.* New York: Walker, 1962.

Gérard-Libois, Jules. *Katanga Secession,* translated by Rebecca Young. Madison: University of Wisconsin Press, 1966.

Gibbs, David N. *The Political Economy of Third World Intervention: Mines, Money, and U.S. Politics in the Congo Crisis.* Chicago: University of Chicago Press, 1991.

Gifford, Prosser, and William Roger Louis, eds. *The Transfer of Power in Africa: Decolonization, 1940–1960.* New Haven, Conn.: Yale University Press, 1982.

Gleijeses, Piero. *Conflicting Missions: Havana, Washington and Africa, 1959–1976.* Chapel Hill: University of North Carolina Press, 2001.

Gondola, Ch. Didier. *The History of the Congo.* Westport, Conn.: Greenwood Press, 2002.

Griffith, William E. *Sino–Soviet Relations, 1964–1965.* Cambridge, Mass.: MIT Press, 1967.

Grinevsky, Oleg. *Tysiacha i odin den' Nikity Sergeevicha* [A thousand and one days in the life of Nikita Sergeevich]. Moscow: Vagrius, 1998.

Gromyko, Anatoly A, ed. *African Countries' Foreign Policy.* Moscow: Progress Publishers, 1981.

Grose, Peter. *Gentleman Spy: The Life of Allen Dulles.* Boston: Houghton Mifflin, 1994.

Gurtov, Melvin. *The United States against the Third World: Antinationalism and Intervention.* New York: Praeger, 1974.

Halen, Pierre, and János Riesz, eds. *Patrice Lumumba entre dieu et diable.* Paris: Harmattan, 1997.

Haskin, Jeanne M. *The Tragic State of the Congo: From Decolonization to Dictatorship.* New York: Algora, 2005.

Heikal, Mohamed Hassanein. *The Cairo Documents: The Inside Story of Nasser and His Relationship with World Leaders, Rebels and Statesmen.* Garden City, N.Y.: Doubleday, 1973.

Heinz, G., and H. Donnay [pseudonym for Jules Gerard-Libois and Jacques Brassinne]. *Lumumba: The Last Fifty Days*, translated by Jane Clark Seitz. New York: Grove Press, 1970.

Heldman, Dan C. *The USSR and Africa: Foreign Policy under Khrushchev.* New York: Praeger, 1981.

Heller, Peter B. *The United Nations under Dag Hammarskjöld, 1953–1961.* New York: Scarecrow Press, 2001.

Helmreich, Jonathan E. *Gathering Rare Ores: The Diplomacy of Uranium Acquisition, 1943–1954.* Princeton, N.J.: Princeton University Press, 1986.

———. *United States Relations with Belgium and the Congo, 1940–1960.* Newark: University of Delaware Press, 1998.

Hempstone, Smith. *Katanga Report.* London: Faber & Faber, 1962.

Hilsman, Roger. *To Move a Nation: The Politics of Foreign Policy in the Administration of John F. Kennedy.* Garden City, N.Y.: Delta Books, 1964.

Hochschild, Adam. *King Leopold's Ghost*. Boston: Houghton Mifflin, 1998.

Hoskyns, Catherine. *The Congo since Independence: January 1960–December 1961*. London: Oxford University Press, 1965.

Hosmer, Stephen T., and Thomas W. Wolfe. *Soviet Policy toward Third World Conflicts*. Lexington, Mass.: Lexington Books, 1983.

Houart, Pierre. *La pénétration communiste au Congo: Commentaires et documents sur les événementes juin–novembre 1960*. Brussels: Centre de Documentation Internationale, 1960.

House, Arthur H. *The U.N. in the Congo: The Political and Civilian Efforts*. Washington, D.C.: University Press of America, 1978.

Hoyt, Michael P. E. *Captive in the Congo: A Consul's Return to the Heart of Darkness*. Annapolis, Md.: Naval Institute Press, 2000.

Hoyt, Michael P. E., and David K. Grinwis. *A Journal of the Experiences of the Staff of the American Consulate in Stanleyville from 1 August through 24 November 1964*. N.p., 1966.

Hutchison, Alan. *China's African Revolution*. London: Hutchinson, 1975.

Iur'ev, N. *Expansiia SShA v Kongo* [U.S. Expansion in the Congo]. Moscow: Mezhdunarodnye Otnosheniia, 1966.

James, Alan. *Britain and the Congo Crisis, 1960–1963*. New York: St. Martin's Press, 1996.

Janssens, Émile. *J'étais le général Janssens*. Brussels: Dessaart, 1961.

Jian, Chen. *Mao's China and the Cold War*. Chapel Hill: University of North Carolina Press, 2001.

Kalb, Madeleine. *The Congo Cables: The Cold War in Africa from Eisenhower to Kennedy*. New York: Macmillan, 1982.

Kamitatu, Cleophas. *La Grande Mystification du Congo-Kinshasa*. Brussels: Complexe, 1971.

Kanet, Roger E. *The Soviet Union and the Developing Nations*. Baltimore: Johns Hopkins University Press, 1974.

Kanza, Thomas. *The Rise and Fall of Patrice Lumumba: Conflict in the Congo*. Rochester, Vt.: Schenkman, 1994. Orig. pub. 1972.

Kashamura, Anicet. *De Lumumba aux colonels*. Paris: Buchet/Chastel, 1966.

Kelly, Sean. *America's Tyrant: The CIA and Mobutu and Zaire*. Washington, D.C.: American University Press, 1993.

Kent, John. *America, the U.N. and Decolonisation: Cold War Conflict in the Congo*. New York: Routledge, 2010.

Khokhlov, Nikolai A. *Patris Lumumba*. Moscow: Molodaia gvardiia, 1971.

———. *Tragediia Kongo* [Congo Tragedy]. Moscow: Gospolitizdat, 1961.

Khrushchev, N. S. *Khrushchev Remembers: The Last Testament*. Introduction by Jerrold Schecter. Boston: Little, Brown, 1974.

Khrushchev, Sergei. *Nikita Khrushchev and the Creation of a Superpower*, translated by Shirley Benson. University Park: Pennsylvania State University Press, 2000.

Kirpichenko, Vadim. *Razvedka: Litsa i lichnosti* [An intelligence memoir: People and personalities]. Moscow: Geiia, 1998.

Kitchen, Helen, ed. *Footnotes to the Congo Story*. New York: Walker, 1967.

Kletskii, L. R. *Chernaia Afrika obretaet svobodu* [Black Africa gains freedom]. Saint Petersburg: Obshchestvo po Rasprostraneniiu Politicheskikh i Nauchnykh Znanii RSFSR, 1961.

Kornienko, Georgi. *Kholodnaia voina: Svidetelstvo ee uchastnika* [Cold War: Testimony of a participant]. Moscow: International Affairs, 1994.

Krasil'shchikova, Svetlana A. *O.O.N. i natsional'no-osvoboditel'noe dvizhenie* [The United Nations and the national liberation movement]. Moscow: Mezhdunarodnye Otnosheniia, 1964.

Kremen' K. S., and Iu.M. Ilyin. *Problems of African Studies in the USSR, 1959–1984*. Moscow: USSR Academy of Sciences, Africa Institute, 1985.

Kunz, Diane B, ed. *The Diplomacy of the Crucial Decade: American Foreign Relations during the 1960s*. New York: Columbia University, 1994.

Larkin, Bruce D. *China and Africa, 1948–1970*. Berkeley: University of California Press,1971.

Lash, Joseph P. *Dag Hammarskjöld: Custodian of the Brush Fire Peace*. Garden City, N.Y.: Doubleday, 1961.

Lefever, Ernest W. *Crisis in the Congo: A U.N. Force in Action*. Washington, D.C.: Brookings Institution Press, 1965.

———. *Uncertain Mandate*. Baltimore: Johns Hopkins University Press, 1967.

Legvold, Robert. *Soviet Policy in West Africa*. Cambridge, Mass.: Harvard University Press, 1970.

Lemarchand, René. *Political Awakening in the Belgian Congo: The Politics of Fragmentation*. Berkeley: University of California Press, 1964.

———. "How Lumumba Came to Power." In *Footnotes to the Congo Story*, edited by Helen Kitchen. New York: Walker, 1967.

London, Kurt, ed. *New Nations in a Divided World: The International Relations of the Afro-Asian States*. New York: Praeger, 1963.

Lumumba, Patrice. *Congo, My Country*. New York: Praeger, 1962.

Lüthi, Lorenz M. *The Sino–Soviet Split: Cold War in the Communist World*. Princeton, N.J.: Princeton University Press, 2008.

Macmillan, Harold. *Pointing the Way, 1959–1961*. New York: Harper & Row, 1972.

Mahoney, Richard D. *JFK: Ordeal in Africa*. New York: Oxford University Press, 1983.

Martelli, George. *Experiment in World Government: An Account of the United Nations Operation in the Congo, 1960–1964.* London: Johnson, 1966.

Martens, Ludo. *The Way of Patrice Lumumba and Pierre Mulele: The People's Uprising in the Congo (Kinshasa), 1964–1968.* Brussels: Belgian Labour Party, 1968.

———. *Pierre Mulele ou la seconde vie de Patrice Lumumba.* Antwerp: Éditions EPO, 1985.

Martin, John Bartlow. *Adlai Stevenson and the World: The Life of Adlai E. Stevenson.* New York: Doubleday, 1977.

Martynov, Vladimir A. *Kongo pod gnetom imperializma: Sotsial'no-ekonoicheskie problemy bel'giiskoi kolonii* [The Congo under the yoke of imperialism: Socioeconomic problems of the Belgian colony]. Moscow: Isdatel'stvo vostochnoj literatury, 1959.

———. *Zagovor protiv Kongo* [Conspiracy against the Congo]. Moscow: Izdatel'stvo Vostochnoi Literatury, Akad. Nauk SSSR, Institut Afriki, 1960.

Mazov, Sergey. *A Distant Front in the Cold War: The USSR in West Africa and the Congo, 1956–1964.* Washington, D.C., and Stanford, Calif.: Woodrow Wilson Center Press and Stanford University Press, 2010.

Melanson, Richard A., and David Mayers, eds. *Reevaluating Eisenhower: American Foreign Policy in the 1950s.* Urbana: University of Illinois Press, 1987.

Mendiaux, Edouard. *Moscou, Accra, et le Congo.* Brussels: Charles Dessart, 1960.

Meriwether, James. *Proudly We Can Be Africans: Black Americans and Africa, 1935–1961.* Chapel Hill: University of North Carolina Press, 2002.

Merlier, Michel. *Le Congo de la colonisation belge à l'indépendance.* Paris: François Maspero, 1962.

Merriam, Alan P. *Congo: Background of Conflict.* Evanston, Ill.: Northwestern University Press, 1961.

Michel, Serge. *Uhuru Lumumba.* Paris: René Julliard, 1962.

Minter, William. *King Solomon's Mines Revisited: Western Interests and the Burdened History of Southern Africa.* New York: Basic Books, 1986.

Morison, David. *The USSR and Africa.* London: Oxford University Press, for the Institute of Race Relations and the Central Asian Research Centre, 1964.

M'poyo Kasa-Vubu, Z. Justine. *Kasa-Vubu et le Congo indépendant.* Brussels: Le Cri Éditions, 1997.

Murphy, Robert. *Diplomat among Warriors.* Garden City, N.Y.: Doubleday, 1964.

Nkrumah, Kwame. *Challenge of the Congo*. New York: International Publishers, 1967.

Noer, Thomas J. *Cold War and Black Liberation: The United States and White Rule in Africa, 1948–1968*. Columbia: University of Missouri Press, 1985.

Nzongola-Ntalaja, Georges. *The Congo from Leopold to Kabila: A People's History*. New York: Zed Books, 2002.

O'Brien, Conor Cruise. *To Katanga and Back*. New York: Simon & Schuster, 1962.

Ogunsanwo, Alaba. *China's Policy in Africa, 1958–1971*. Cambridge: Cambridge University Press, 1974.

Orestov, Oleg L., and Lev D. Volodin. *Trudnie Dni Kongo* [Troubled Days in the Congo]. Moscow: Gospolitizdat, 1961.

Ostrower, Gary B. *The United Nations and the United States*. New York: Twayne, 1998.

Packham, Eric. *Success or Failure: The U.N. Intervention in the Congo After Independence*. Commack, N.Y.: Nova Science, 1998.

Paterson, Thomas G, ed. *Kennedy's Quest for Victory: American Foreign Policy, 1961–1963*. New York: Oxford University Press, 1989.

Plummer, Brenda Gayle, ed. *Window on Freedom: Race, Civil Rights, and Foreign Affairs, 1945–1988*. Chapel Hill: University of North Carolina Press, 2003.

Potekhin, Ivan I. *Afrika smotrit v budushchee* [Africa looks to the future]. Moscow: Izdatel'stvo Vostochnoi Literatury, 1960.

———, ed. *Afrika 1956–1961*. Moscow: Izdatel'stvo Vostochnoi Literatury, Akad. Nauk SSSR, Institute Afriki, 1961.

Quaison-Sackey, Alex. *Africa Unbound: Reflections of an African Statesman*. New York: Praeger, 1963.

Ra'anan, Uri. *The USSR Arms the Third World: Case Studies in Soviet Foreign Policy*. Cambridge, Mass.: MIT Press, 1969.

Radchenko, Sergey. *Two Suns in the Heaven: The Sino–Soviet Struggle for Supremacy, 1962–1967*. Washington, D.C., and Stanford, Calif.: Woodrow Wilson Center Press and Stanford University Press, 2009.

Rakhmatov, Mirzo. *Afrika idet k svobode*. Moscow: Gospolitizdat, 1961.

Reed, David. *111 Days in Stanleyville*. New York: Harper & Row, 1965.

Richter, James G. *Khrushchev's Double Bind: International Pressures and Domestic Coalition Politics*. Baltimore: Johns Hopkins University Press, 1994.

Rikhye, Indar Jit. *Military Adviser to the Secretary-General: U.N. Peacekeeping and the Congo Crisis*. London: C. Hurst, 1990.

Rothberg, Robert I., and Ali Mazrui, eds. *Protest and Power in Black Africa.* New York: Oxford University Press, 1970.

Russell, Ruth. *The United Nations and United States Security Policy.* Washington, D.C.: Brookings Institution Press, 1968.

Ryan, David, and Victor Pungong, eds. *The United States and Decolonization: Power and Freedom.* New York: St. Martin's Press, 2000.

Schatten, Fritz. *Communism in Africa.* New York: Praeger, 1966.

Scott, Ian. *Tumbled House: The Congo at Independence.* London: Oxford University Press, 1969.

Sheng, Michael M. *Battling Western Imperialism: Mao, Stalin, and the United States.* Princeton, N.J.: Princeton University Press, 1997.

Shevchenko, Arkady N. *Breaking with Moscow.* New York: Alfred A. Knopf, 1985.

Singham, A.W., and Shirley Hune. *Non-Alignment in an Age of Alignments.* Westport, Conn.: Lawrence Hill, 1986.

Slade, Ruth. *The Belgian Congo,* 2nd ed. London: Institute of Race Relations and Oxford University Press, 1961.

Spaak, Paul-Henri. *Combats inachevés, II.* Paris: Fayard, 1969.

Staniland, Martin. *American Intellectuals and African Nationalists, 1955–1970.* New Haven, Conn.: Yale University Press, 1991.

Statler, Kathryn C., and Andrew L. Johns, eds. *The Eisenhower Administration, the Third World and the Globalization of the Cold War.* Lanham, Md.: Rowman & Littlefield, 2006.

Stoessinger, John G. *The United Nations and the Superpowers: China, Russia, and America,* 4th ed. New York: Random House, 1977.

Stueck, William. *The Korean War: An International History.* Princeton, N.J.: Princeton University Press, 1995.

Tarabrin, Evgenii A., ed. *SSSR i strany Afriki: Druzhba, sotrudnichestvo, podderzhka antiimperialisticheskoi borby* [The USSR and the countries of Africa: Friendship, cooperation and support of the anti-imperialist struggle]. Moscow: Mysl', 1977.

Taubman, William, and Khrushchev, Sergei, eds. *Nikita Khrushchev.* New Haven, Conn.: Yale University Press, 2000.

Thant, U. *View from the U.N..* Garden City, N.Y.: Doubleday, 1978.

Thompson, Scott W. *Ghana's Foreign Policy, 1957–1966: Diplomacy, Ideology, and the New State.* Princeton, N.J.: Princeton University Press, 1969.

Thornton, Thomas Perry, ed. *The Third World in Soviet Perspective: Studies by Soviet Writers on the Developing Areas.* Princeton, N.J.: Princeton University Press, 1964.

Tompson, William J. *Khrushchev: A Political Life*. New York: St. Martin's Griffin, 1995.

Trento, Joseph, J. *The Secret History of the CIA*. New York: Carroll & Graf, 2005.

Tully, Andrew. *CIA: The Inside Story*. New York: Morrow, 1962.

Tung, Chi-ping with Humphrey Evans. *The Thought Revolution*. New York: Coward-McCann, 1966.

Turner, Thomas. *The Congo Wars: Conflict, Myth, Reality*. London: Zed Books, 2007.

Ulam, Adam. *Expansion and Coexistence: Soviet Foreign Policy, 1917–1973*, 2nd ed. New York: Praeger, 1974.

Urquhart, Brian. *A Life in Peace and War*. New York: W. W. Norton, 1991.

———. *Ralph Bunche: An American Life*. New York: W. W. Norton, 1993.

———. *Hammarskjöld*. New York: W. W. Norton, 1994. Orig. pub. 1972.

Ushakov, Vladimir G. *Sovetskii Soiuz i O.O.N.* [The Soviet Union and the U.N.]. Moscow: Gosudarstvennoe isdatel'stvo opliticheskoi literaury, 1962.

Valkenier, Elizabeth K. *Revolutionary Change in the Third World: An Economic Bind*. New York: Praeger, 1983.

van Bilsen, Jef. *Congo, 1945–1965: La fin d'une colonie*. Brussels: CRISP, 1993.

van den Bosch, Jean. *Pré-Zaire: le cordon mal coupé: Document*. Brussels: Le Cri, 1986.

Vanderlinden, Jacques. *Du Congo au Zaire*. Brussels: CRISP, 1980.

Vandewalle, Frédéric. *L'Ommegang: Odysée et reconquête de Stanleyville 1964*. Brussels: F. Vandewalle–Le Livre Africain, 1970.

———. *Mille et Quatre jours: Contes du Zaire et du Shaba*. Brussels: F. Vandewalle, 1974.

van Lierde, Jean. *La Pensée politique de Patrice Lumumba*. Paris: Présence Africaine, 1963.

Verhaegen, Benoît, and Charles Tshimanga, *L'Abako et l'indépendance du Congo belge: Dix ans de nationalisme kongo (1950–1960)*. Paris: Éditions L'Harmattan, 2003.

Volodin, Lev. *Patrice Lumumba: Fighter for Africa's Freedom*. Moscow: Progress Publishers, 1961.

Vol'skii, Dmitrii A. *Patris Lumumba: Geroi Afriki*. Moscow: Gospolitizdat, 1961.

von Horn, Carl. *Soldiering for Peace*. New York: David McKay, 1966.

Vos, Pierre de. *Vie et mort de Lumumba*. Paris: Calmann-Lévy, 1961.

Wagoner, Fred E. *Dragon Rouge: The Rescue of Hostages in the Congo.* Washington, D.C.: U.S. Government Printing Office, 1981.

Wallerstein, Immanuel. *Africa: The Politics of Independence: An Interpretation of Modern African History.* New York: Random House, 1961.

Warshaw, Shirley Anne, ed. *Reexamining the Eisenhower Presidency.* Westport, Conn.: Greenwood Press, 1993.

Wauters, Arthur, ed. *Le Monde Communiste et la Crise de Congo Belge.* Brussels: Éditions de l'Institut de Sociologie Solvay, 1961.

Weiss, Herbert F. *Political Protest in the Congo: The Parti Solidaire Africain during the Independence Struggle.* Princeton, N.J.: Princeton University Press, 1967.

Weissman, Stephen. *American Foreign Policy in the Congo, 1960–1964.* Ithaca, N.Y.: Cornell University Press, 1974.

White, George, Jr. *Holding the Line: Race, Racism, and American Foreign Policy toward Africa, 1953–1961.* Lanham, Md.: Rowman & Littlefield, 2005.

Wilcox, Francis O., and H. Field Haviland Jr., eds. *The United States and the United Nations.* Baltimore: Johns Hopkins University Press, 1961.

Willame, Jean-Claude. *Patrice Lumumba: La crise congolaise revisitée.* Paris: Éditions Karthala, 1990.

Williams, Susan. *Who Killed Hammarskjöld? The U.N., the Cold War and White Supremacy in Africa.* London: C. Hurst & Co., 2011.

Wilson, Henry S. *The Imperial Experience in Sub-Saharan Africa since 1870.* Minneapolis: University of Minnesota Press, 1977.

Wiseman, Henry. *Peacekeeping: Appraisals and Proposals.* New York: Pergamon Press, 1983.

Wrong, Michela. *In the Footsteps of Mr. Kurtz: Living on the Brink of Disaster in Mobutu's Congo.* New York: HarperPerennial, 2002.

Young, Crawford. *Politics in the Congo: Decolonization and Independence.* Princeton, N.J.: Princeton University Press, 1965.

Zeiler, Thomas. *Dean Rusk: Defending the American Mission Abroad.* Wilmington, Del.: Scholarly Resources, 2000.

Zhai, Qiang. *China and the Vietnam Wars, 1950–1975.* Chapel Hill: University of North Carolina Press, 2000.

Zubok, Vladislav M. *A Failed Empire: The Soviet Union in the Cold War from Stalin to Gorbachev.* Chapel Hill: University of North Carolina Press, 2007.

Zubok, Vladislav, and Constantine Pleshakov. *Inside the Kremlin's Cold War: From Stalin to Khrushchev.* Cambridge, Mass.: Harvard University Press, 1996.

Secondary Sources: Articles in Periodicals and Edited Collections

Antsey, Roger. "Belgian Rule in the Congo and the Aspirations of the 'Evolué' Class." In *Colonialism in Africa, 1870–1960, Volume 2: History and Politics of Colonialism, 1914–1960*, edited by L. H. Gann and Peter Duignan. Cambridge: Cambridge University Press, 1970.

Avakov, Rachik M., and Georgi Mirskii. "Sovremenniia epokha i puti razvitiia osvobodivshikhsia stran" [The contemporary epoch and the path of development of the liberated countries]. *Mirovaia ekonomika i mezhdunarodnie otnosheniia* no. 4 (1962): 68–82.

Bloomfield, Lincoln. "The United Nations in Crisis: The Role of the United Nations in United States Foreign Policy." *Daedalus* 3 (1962): 749–65.

Borstelmann, Thomas. "'Hedging Our Bets and Buying Time': John Kennedy and Racial Revolutions in the American South and Southern Africa." *Diplomatic History* 24 (Summer 2000): 435–64.

Brykin, Vladimir A. "Operatsiia O.O.N. v Kongo" [The U.N. operation in the Congo]. *Narody Azii i Afriki* no. 1 (1966): 35–44.

Campbell, Andrew. "Moscow's Gold: Soviet Financing of Global Subversion." *National Observer* (Autumn 1999). Available at www.britannica.com/bcom/magazine.

Collins, Carole J. L. "The Cold War Comes to Africa: Cordier and the 1960 Congo Crisis." *Journal of International Affairs* 47, no. 1 (Summer 1993): 243–69.

Combs, James Joseph. "France and United Nations Peacekeeping." *International Organization* 21 (1967): 306–25.

De Coninck, Albert. "Kongo v bor'be za nezavisimost'" [The Congo and the fight for independence]. *Mirovaia ekonomika i mezhdunarodnie otnosheniia* no. 1 (1960): 72–78.

DiEugenio, Jim. "Dodd and Dulles vs. Kennedy in Africa." *Probe* 6 (January–February 1999). Available at www.webcom.com/~ctka.

Dodd, Thomas J. "Congo: The Untold Story." *National Review*, August 28, 1962, 136–42.

Dorn, A. Walter, and David J. H. Bell. "Intelligence and Peacekeeping: The U.N. Operation in the Congo, 1960–1964." *International Peace-Keeping* 2 (Spring 1995): 11–33.

Durch, William J. "The U.N. Operation in the Congo: 1960–1964." In *The Evolution of U.N. Peacekeeping: Case Studies and Comparative Analysis*. New York: St. Martin's Press, 1993.

Fox, Renée C., Willy de Craemer, and Jean-Marie Ribeaucourt. "The Second Independence: A Case Study of the Kwilu Rebellion in the Congo." *Comparative Studies in Society and History* 8 (October 1965): 78–109.

Fraser, Cary. "Understanding American Policy toward the Decolonization of European Empires, 1945–64." *Diplomacy and Statecraft* 3, no. 1 (1992): 105–25.

Gibbs, David. "Let Us Forget Unpleasant Memories: The U.S. State Department's Analysis of the Congo Crisis." *Journal of Modern African Studies* 33 (1995): 175–80.

———. "Misrepresenting the Congo Crisis (Review Article): *The Foreign Relations of the United States: 1961–63, Vol. 20, Congo Crisis.*" *African Affairs* 95 (July 1996): 453–59.

———. "Secrecy and International Relations." *Journal of Peace Research* 32 (1995): 213–28.

———. "The United Nations, International Peacekeeping and the Question of 'Impartiality': Revisiting the Congo Operation of 1960." *Journal of Modern African Studies* 38 (2000): 359–82.

Gleijeses, Piero. "Havana's Policy in Africa, 1959–1976: New Evidence from Cuban Archives." *Cold War International History Project Bulletin*, nos. 8–9 (Winter 1996–97): 5–18.

Heathcote, Nina. "American Policy towards the United Nations Operation in the Congo." *Australian Outlook* 18, no. 1 (April 1964): 77–97.

Helmreich, Jonathan E. "Belgium, Britain, the United States and Uranium, 1952–1959." *Studia Diplomatica* 43, no. 3 (1990): 27–81.

———. "U.S. Foreign Policy and the Belgian Congo in the 1950s." *The Historian* 58 (Winter 1996): 315–28.

Hemmerijckx, Rik. "The Belgian Communist Party and Socialist Trade Unions, 1940–1960." *Journal of Communist Studies* 6, no. 4 (1990): 124–42.

Hoyt, Michael P. "Republic of the Congo (Leopoldville)." *International Commerce*, "Supplement: Special Report on Africa," March 1963.

Ismagilova, Roza N. "Zasedanie uchenogo soveta instituta Afriki AN SSSR posviashchennoe problemam Kongo" [Meeting of the Council of the Soviet Institute of Africa, RAN, USSR, regarding the problem of the Congo]. *Sovetskaia etnografia* 3 (1961).

Iur'ev, N. "Uzel imperialisticheskogo sopernichestva v Kongo" [The knot of imperialist rivalry in the Congo]. *Mirovaia ekonomika i mezhdunarodnie otnosheniia* no. 1 (1963): 24–35.

Johnson, Robert Craig. "Heart of Darkness: The Tragedy of the Congo, 1960–1967." *Chandelle: Journal of Aviation History* 2, no. 3 (October 1997). http://worldatwar.net/chandelle/v2/v2n3/index.shtml.

Kanet, Roger E. "African Youth: The Target of Soviet African Policy." *Russian Review* 27 (April 1968): 161–75.

Kaplan, Lawrence S. "The United States, Belgium, and the Congo Crisis of 1960." *Review of Politics* 29, no. 2 (1967): 239–56.

Kramer, Mark. "Declassified Materials from CPSU Central Committee Plenums." *Cahiers du Monde Russe* 40 (January–June 1999): 271–306.

Kyle, Keith. *The U.N. in the Congo.* INCORE Occasional Paper. Coleraine: University of Ulster, 1995. http://www.incore.ulst.ac.uk/home/publication/occasional/kyle.html.

Lyons, Terrence. "Keeping Africa Off the Agenda." In *Lyndon Johnson Confronts the World: American Foreign Policy, 1963–1968*, edited by Warren I. Cohen and Nancy Bernkopf Tucker. New York: Cambridge University Press, 1994.

Mazov, Sergei. "Soviet Aid to the Gizenga Government in the Former Belgian Congo (1960–1961) as Reflected in Russian Archives." *Cold War History* 7, no. 3 (August 2007): 425–38.

Mazrui, Ali. "Socialism as a Mode of International Protest: The Case of Tanzania." In *Protest and Power in Black Africa*, edited by Robert I. Rothberg and Ali Mazrui. New York: Oxford University Press, 1970.

McMahon, Robert J. "Eisenhower and Third World Nationalism: A Critique of the Revisionists." *Political Science Quarterly* 101, no. 3 (1986): 453–73.

Meriwether, James H. "'A Torrent Overrunning Everything': Africa and the Eisenhower Administration." In *The Eisenhower Administration, the Third World, and the Globalization of the Cold War*, edited by Kathryn C. Statler and Andrew L. Johns. Harvard Cold War Studies Book Series. Lanham, Md.: Rowman & Ltitlefield, 2006.

Metz, Steven. "American Attitudes Toward Decolonization in Africa." *Political Science Quarterly* 99 (Fall 1984): 515–33.

Minter, William. "Limits of Liberal Africa Policy: Lessons from the Congo Crisis." *TransAfrica Forum* 2 (Fall 1984): 27–47.

Mohan, Jitendra. "Ghana, the Congo and the United Nations." *Journal of Modern African Studies* 7, no. 3 (October 1969): 369–406.

Muehlenbeck, Philip E. *Betting on the Africans: John F. Kennedy's Courting of African Nationalist Leaders.* New York: Oxford University Press, 2012.

———. "Kennedy and Touré: A Success in Personal Diplomacy." *Diplomacy and Statecraft* 19 (2008): 69–95.

Namikas, Lise. "History through Documents and Memory: Report on a Critical Oral History Conference on the Congo Crisis, 1960–1961." Cold War International History Project, Woodrow Wilson International Center for Scholars, Washington, 2004. http://www.wilsoncenter.org/article/history-through-documents-and-memory-report-cwihp-critical-oral-history-conference-the-congo.

———. "A Silver Lining: President Johnson and the U.N. Peacekeeping Budget Crisis of 1964–1965." *Diplomacy & Statecraft*, September 2004, 593–612.

Natufe, Omajuwa Igho. "The Cold War and the Congo Crisis, 1960–1961." *Africa* (Rome) 39 (1984): 353–74.

Nazhestkin, O. I. "Gody kongolezkogo krizisa (1960–1963 gg.): Zapiski razvedchika" [The years of the Congo crisis (1960–1963): Notes from a secret service agent]. *Novaia i noveishaia istoriya* 6 (2003): 154–64.

Noer, Thomas J. "'Non-Benign Neglect': The United States and Black Africa in the Twentieth Century." In *American Foreign Relations: A Historiographical Review*, edited by Gerald K. Haines and J. Samuel Walker, 271–92. Westport, Conn.: Greenwood, 1981.

———. "New Frontiers and Old Priorities in Africa." In *Kennedy's Quest for Victory: American Foreign Policy, 1961–1963*, edited by Thomas G. Paterson. New York: Oxford University Press, 1989.

Nordlander, David. "Khrushchev's Image in the Light of Glasnost and Perestroika." *Russian Review* 52, no. 2 (April 1993): 248–64.

Nwaubani, Ebere. "Eisenhower, Nkrumah, and the Congo Crisis." *Journal of Contemporary History* 36 (2001): 599–622.

Parker, Jason C. "Small Victory, Missed Chance: The Eisenhower Administration, the Bandung Conference, and the Turning of the Cold War." In *The Eisenhower Administration, the Third World, and the Globalization of the Cold War*, edited by Kathryn C. Statler and Andrew L. Johns. Harvard Cold War Studies Book Series. Lanham, Md.: Rowman & Littlefield, 2006.

Pavlov, V. I., and I. B. Red'ko. "Gosudarstvo natsioinal'noi demokratii i perexod nekapitalisticheskomu razvitiu" [National democracy and the transition to noncapitalist development]. *Narody Azii i Afriki* no. 1 (1963): 29–40.

Pistrak, Lazar. "Soviet Views on Africa." *Problems in Communism*, 1962, 24–31.

Pleshakov, Constantine. "Nikita Khrushchev and Sino-Soviet Relations." In *Brothers in Arms: The Rise and Fall of the Sino–Soviet Alliance, 1945–1963*, edited by Odd Arne Westad. Stanford, Calif.: Stanford University Press, 1998.

Potekhin, Ivan I. "Pozemel'nye otnosheniia v strankakh afriki" [Land relations in African countries]. *Narody Azii i Afriki* no. 3 (1962): 16–31.

———. "Problemy bor'by s perezhitkami proshlogo na afrikanskom kontinente" [The problem of the fight against the survivals of the past on the African continent]. *Sovetskaia etnografiia* no. 4 (1964): 186–95.

Pozharov, Alexandr I. "KGB i Partiia (1954–1960g.)" [The KGB and the Party (1954–1960)]. *Otechestvennaia Istoriia* no. 4 (1999): 169–74.

Prybyla, Jan. "Communist China's Economic Relations with Africa, 1960–1964." *Asian Survey* 4, no. 11 (1964): 1135–43.

Rubenstein, Alvin Z. "Lumumba University: An Assessment." *Problems of Communism* 20 (November–December 1971): 64–69.

Semonin, Paul F. "Killing Them Definitively." *The Nation*, January 31, 1966, 129–32.

Sivolobov, A. M. *The National Liberation Movement in Africa*. Moscow: Znanie, 1961.

Thomas, Darryl C. "The Impact of the Sino–Soviet Conflict on the Afro-Asian People's Solidarity Organization: Afro-Asianism versus Non-Alignment, 1955–1966." *Journal of Asian and African Affairs* 1992 3, no. 2: 167–91.

Turner, Thomas. "L'Ethnie tetela et le MNC-Lumumba." *Etudes Congolaises* 12 (October–December 1969): 36–57.

Uhlub, Frank. "Red Sky over Africa: Czechoslovak Relations with New Countries." *Eastern Europe* 9 (October 1960): 32–40.

Ul'ianovsky, Rostislav A. "Nekotorie voprosy nekapitalisticheskogo razvetiia" [Several questions of noncapitalist development]. *Kommunist* 1 (1966): 109–19.

Urqhart, Brian. "'The Tragedy of Lumumba': Review of Ludo De Witte, *The Assassination of Lumumba*, translated from the Dutch by Ann Wright and Reneé Fenby, Verso, 2001." *New York Times Book Review* 48, no. 15 (October 2001).

Valkenier, Elizabeth Kridl. "Great Power Economic Competition in Africa: Soviet Progress and Problems." *Journal of International Affairs* 34, no. 2 (1980–81): 259–68.

Verhaegen, Benoît. "L'Armeé Nationale congolaise." *Etudes Congolaise* 10 (July–August 1967): 1–29.

Vinokurov, Iurii N. "Formirovanie politicheskikh vzgliadov Patrica Lumumbi" [The formation of the political views of Patrice Lumumba]. *Narody Azii i Afriki* no. 5 (1965): 23–33.

Volskii, Dmitrii A. *Patris Lumumba: Geroi Afriki* [Patrice Lumumba: Hero of Africa]. Moscow: Gospolizdat, 1961.

Wallerstein, Immanuel. "What Next in the Congo?" *The New Leader*, March 6, 1961, 3–5.

Weiss, Herbert. "The Tshombe Riddle." *The New Leader*, September 17, 1962, 3–6.

Weissman, Stephen R. "CIA Covert Action in Zaire and Angola: Patterns and Consequences." *Political Science Quarterly* 94, no. 2 (1979): 263–86.

———. "The CIA and U.S. Policy in Zaire and Angola." In *American Policy in Southern Africa: The Stakes and the Stance*, edited by René Lemarchand. Washington, D.C.: University Press of America, 1981.

———. "Opening the Secret Files on Lumumba's Murder." *Washington Post*, July 21, 2002. http://www.sas.upenn.edu/African_Studies/Urgent_ Action/apic080102.html.

Westad, Odd Arne. "The New International History of the Cold War: Three (Possible) Paradigms." *Diplomatic History* 24 (Fall 2000): 551–66.

Young, Crawford. "The Congo Rebellion." *Africa Report* 10, no. 4 (1965): 6–11.

———. "Rebellion and the Congo." In *Protest and Power in Black Africa*, edited by Robert I. Rothberg and Ali Mazrui. New York: Oxford University Press, 1970.

Yu, George T. "China's Failure in Africa." *Asian Survey* 6, no. 8 (August 1966): 461–68.

Unpublished Papers and Theses

Cogan, Charles. "Avoiding the Breakup: The U.S.–U.N. Intervention in the Congo, 1960–1965." Case Program CR14-99-1549.0. John F. Kennedy School of Government, Harvard University, Cambridge, Mass., November 1999. Available at http://www.ksgcase.harvard.edu.

Gerard, Emmanuel, and Bruce Kuklick. "A Death in the Jungle: Killing Patrice Lumumba." Annenberg Seminar in History, University of Pennsylvania, January 2011.

Kalb, Madeleine. "The Soviet Union and the Congo." PhD diss., Columbia University, 1971.

Pruden, Caroline. "Conditional Partners: Eisenhower, the United Nations, and the Search for a Permanent Peace." PhD diss., Vanderbilt University, 1993.

Williams, Michael Wayne. "America and the First Congo Crisis, 1960–1963." PhD diss., University of California, Irvine, 1992.

Wright, Marcia, and Glenn Adler. "'To Keep It Going Our Way': Designs and Policy by the United States toward the Congo, 1963." Columbia University, New York, 1985.

Index

Abako. *See* Alliance des Bakongo
Academy of Sciences (Soviet Union),
  and Africa, 30–31
Accra, 28–29, 58, 86, 107, 139; and
  OAU conference, 219
Adoula, Cyrille, 214, 220, 225; background, 39, 115–16; and Binza
  group, 183–86; government crisis
  of, 166–70, 175–76, 180–81, 189; at
  Lovanium, 146–48; and Kasavubu
  "coup," 191; as prime minister, 149,
  152–58, 160–61; and Soviet Union,
  166–69, 178–79; and U Thant Plan,
  164–65, 167, 173–74
Africa, and Cold War, 3–9, 11–12,
  14–15, 18, 47; and Eisenhower,
  25–27; and Kennedy, 132; and
  Johnson, 186–87; and Soviet Union,
  27–31
African Americans' views, of Congo,
  133–34, 155, 193, 209, 216. *See also*
  Angelou, Maya; Bunche, Ralph;
  Malcolm X
Africans, views on Cold War of, 21, 39,
  119, 202, 213; in United States, 54,
  82; in Soviet Union, 31, 48, 158
Afro-Asian conference of 1955 (Bandung Conference), 21–22, 32, 68
Afro-Asian People's Solidarity Organi-
  zation: Chinese branch of, 58, 194;
  Soviet branch of, 29, 218
Afro-Asian states (at United Nations),
  7, 8, 94, 108, 123, 136–37, 143, 157;

and Hammarskjöld, 96, 104, 111; and
  Kennedy, 129, 131–32, 146; pressure
  to end secession, 149, 154; relations
  with Khrushchev, 27–28, 30, 93–93,
  101, 120, 137, 158
All-African People's Conference, 28–29,
  39, 41, 99
ANC. *See* Armée National Congolaise
Anderson, Robert B., 55
Angelou, Maya, 134
Angola, 5, 36, 216, 231–32, 291n20; and
  mercenaries, 192, 199
anti-Castro Cuban exiles, 190, 206, 215
anticolonialism, 54; and Soviet Union,
  14–15, 149; and United States,
  22–23
Armée National Congolaise (ANC), 64,
  85, 111, 118, 144, 184, 220; against
  Katanga and Kasai, 103, 153–54,
  156, 180; against Lumumbists, 118,
  122; and 1964 rebellions, 189–92,
  196–201, 204, 208, 215–16; and
  retraining of, 97, 136–37, 160, 162,
  167, 176–78, 181, 189; and unruliness of, 106, 181. *See also* Force
  Publique; Mobutu, Joseph
Article 19 (U.N.), 166, 178, 188, 214.
  See also U.N. financial crisis
Arutyunyan, Suren, 86
assassination, of Lumumba. *See*
  Lumumba, Patrice, assassination of
Athos (Belgian agent), 73
Attwood, William, 202, 204

Katanga Information Services, 156. *See also* Struelens, Michel

Katanga Province, 1–2, 125; Belgian support for independence of, 73–74, 76–77, 91–92; and business interests, 17, 25, 36, 51–52; Kennedy's policy on, 129, 143–44, 153–56, 160–61, 170–74 (*see also* Operation Grand Slam; U Thant Plan); gendarmerie, role in 1964 rebellions, 218; and Lumumba's offensive, 92–94, 98, 104; secession of, 7–9, 58–59, 65–69; and United Nations, 83–85, 87, 89, 149–52 (*see also* United Nations, and ONUC military activity); and United States, 70–71, 79–80, 90, 95, 229–30. *See also* Conakat; Tshombe, Moise; UMHK

Kaysen, Carl, 167, 171

Keita, Mobido, 121, 134

Kennedy, Edward, 128

Kennedy, John F., 14, 141, 167, 181, 185; and Afro-Asian states, 8, 23, 118; Congo policy of, 127–33, 136–37, 157; after intervention, 175–77; and new policy, 142–45, 146–47; and United Nations, 160–61, 163–65, 166–75; and U.N. military interventions, 151–52, 153–56. *See also* Lovanium conference; Spaak, Paul-Henri; United States; U Thant Plan

Kettani, General Ben Hammon, 106

KGB (Komitet Gostudarstvennoy bezopastnosti), 63, 85–86, 145, 148, 183–84

Khokhlov, Nikolai, 67, 124, 179, 195, 197, 221–22

Khrushchev, Nikita, 5, 8, 15–16, 224, 226–27; and aid to Gizenga, 121–24, 134–36, 138–41, 157–58; appeals to Afro-Asian states by, 92–93; Brezhnev continues policy of, 212; and China, in Congo, 72, 195; and Lumumba, 67–68, 82, 85–87, 120; and Kennedy, 127, 142–43; and military aid to Congo, 93; and relations with Hammarskjöld, 101–4, 107–11;

and Soviet foreign policy for Congo, 27–31, 41–42, 59–60, 112, 148–49; and United Nations, 72, 75–76, 84, 165–66. *See also* U.N. financial crisis; United Nations; United States; USSR

King, Martin Luther, 209

Kirpichenko, Vadim, 86

Kitona meeting and accords, 156, 160–61

Kivu Province, 83, 94, 122, 124; and 1964 rebellions, 138–39, 156, 166, 182, 188–91

Kozlov, Frol, 72

Krock, Alfred, 155, 165

Kuznetsov, Vasili, 76, 85, 86, 89, 102, 139

Kwilu Province, 41, 57; and 1964 rebellions, 182–83, 189, 195, 216, 221

LeHaye, Andre, 114

Lemnitzer, Lyman, 131, 162

Leopold II (king of Belgium), 6–7, 13, 34–36, 63

Leopoldville Province, 37–38, 41, 182, 190, 219

Lodge, Henry Cabot, 73–74, 76, 82, 88, 90, 120

Loi Fundamentale, 46, 97, 156

Loos, Major, 92, 114

Lovanium conference of 1961, 18, 143, 185, 227, 230; aftermath of, 149, 178; overturned, 191; proceedings of, 145–48

Lulua peoples, 39, 57, 69

Lumumba, Patrice: arrest of, 106, 118–19; assassination of, 1–3, 112–16, 118–19, 124–26, 133; background and views of, 5, 39–40, 45–46; and Congo's independence, 56, 58–59, 63–69; and Katanga, 80; and relations with Belgians, 43–45; and September crisis, 97–101; and Soviet Union, 41, 50–51, 60, 85–87, 92–93, 141–433; and United Nations, 73–75, 83–84, 87–89; and United States, 53–54, 78–83, 89–95, 128–30

NSC meeting (July 31, 1960), 83; and U.N. operation, 65, 67; and U.S. Navy task force, 144
Touré, Sekou, 3, 5, 8, 23, 35, 41, 101; pro-Lumumba policy of, 87, 109, 121; and Soviet Union, 30–31, 41, 101, 158
trade unions, 41, 48, 68–69, 115–16
troika proposal (for U.N. secretary-generalship): Hammarskjöld opposes, 110–11; Khrushchev and, 108–9, 110
Truman, General Louis W. (Mission to Congo), 172
trusteeship, Congo as, 89, 178
Trusteeship Council (U.N.), 29, 40
Tshimanga, Antoine, 40, 58
Tshombe, Moise, 8, 44, 151, 213, 225–26, 230; African American criticism of, 209; Belgian relations with, 45, 92; Kennedy and, 8–9, 129, 149, 160, 171; and Lumumba's assassination, 1, 3, 114, 125; and 1962 conference, 144–45, 147; as prime minister, 200–202, 213–16, 218–20; and relations with Congolese, 57, 58–59, 93–94; return to Congo by, 185, 189, 191–93; and secession, 65–67; Soviet criticism of, 134, 137, 178, 210, 212, 221; and United Nations, 83–84, 87, 149, 150–56, 161–62, 172–74; and U Thant Plan, 162, 164–65, 167, 169. *See also* Conakat; Katanga Province
Tunisia, 72, 77, 102, 104, 108; Mahmoud Khiary and, 149
Tweedy, Bronson, 90, 113, 114, 115, 170
Twining, Nathan, 101

UAR (United Arab Republic). *See* Egypt
Uganda, 21, 182, 198, 215, 216–17
Ulbricht, Walter (East Germany), 121
ultimatum to U.N., by Lumumba, 74–75, 78, 87; to Tshombe, 169
UMHK (Union Minière du Haut Katanga), 6, 8, 36, 44–45, 229; and support of Tshombe, 66, 150, 154–56, 192; and U Thant plan, 164, 169, 174, 179

United Kingdom (Great Britain), 36, 60, 181, 210; and U.N. operation, 73, 75, 117, 133, 147, 151, 154; and U Thant plan, 160, 164, 169, 173
United Nations, 1, 18, 161; and Afro-Asian position, 93, 99, 129; and China, 140, 143; and creation of ONUC, 65–77; General Assembly of, 101–4 (September 1960 meeting), 108–11, 107–9 (September 19, 1960, resolution), 116–18 (credentials debate); and Lumumba, 80–82, 87–89, 118–19; and Mobutu, 106–7; and ONUC military activity (1962), 153–56, 172–74; and ONUC phaseout, 175–78, 181, 187–90; and question of Katanga, 83–85; Security Council of, debates and resolutions on Congo, 72 (July 14, 1960, resolution), 76 (July 22, 1960, resolution), 85 (August 9, 1960, resolution), 136–40 (February 21, 1961, resolution); and Soviet Union, 67–69, 71, 177–79; sponsors' negotiations (1962), 143–48; and U.S. position toward, 67, 95, 99–100, 133, 166–70. *See also* Dayal, Rajeshwar; Hammarskjöld, Dag; ONUC; Operation Grand Slam, Operation Morthor; Round Two; U.N. financial crisis
U Thant Plan
U.N. Conciliation Commission, 116, 137, 279–80n21
U.N. financial crisis, 120–21, 158–59, 187–88, 214
United States: and assassination plans, 112–16, 118–19, 124–26; foreign policy of (before Congo's independence), 22–27, 42–44, 55–56, 61; and Congo's independence crisis, 62–64, 67, 70; and Hammarskjöld and U.N. policy, 70, 109, 116–18, 133–34, 136–38, 151–52 (*see also* United Nations); historiography and, 5–8, 13–14, 16; and hostages and Dragon Rouge, 198–203, 203–9;